Hauke Lehmann
Affect Poetics of the New Hollywood

Cinepoetics

———

Edited by
Hermann Kappelhoff and Michael Wedel

Volume 7

Hauke Lehmann

Affect Poetics of the New Hollywood

Suspense, Paranoia, and Melancholy

DE GRUYTER

ISBN 978-3-11-077681-2
e-ISBN (PDF) 978-3-11-058076-1
e-ISBN (EPUB) 978-3-11-057972-7
ISSN 2569-4294

Library of Congress Control Number: 2019949155

Bibliographic information published by the Deutsche Nationalbibliothek
The Deutsche Nationalbibliothek lists this publication in the Deutsche Nationalbibliografie;
detailed bibliographic data are available on the Internet at http://dnb.dnb.de.

Contents

Acknowledgments

Writing a book is a solitary and collaborative matter at the same time. At this point I would like to thank all those who made it easier and possible for me to write and complete this work. My first thanks go to my doctoral supervisor, Prof. Hermann Kappelhoff, who helped me to find a topic, who over the years has repeatedly given me conceptual and theoretical orientation and has supported me in many ways and in many respects. In particular, the translation of this work into English would never have been possible without the generous support of the *Cinepoetics* research group, which he heads. Furthermore, I would like to thank my second supervisor, Prof. Gertrud Koch, who has provided me with numerous valuable advice and tips, both on a thematic and methodological level.

In general I would like to express my thanks to the colloquia of Prof. Kappelhoff, Prof. Koch, and the Graduate School of the Cluster *Languages of Emotion* for a whole series of stimulating, motivating and fruitful discussions about my work. In particular, I would like to thank Sarah Greifenstein (for proofreading and for many helpful suggestions, especially on suspense), Sarah-Mai Dang (for proofreading), David Gaertner (for his generous help in getting me started with the corpus), as well as Jan-Hendrik Bakels and Hye-Jeung Chung for thoughts that have helped this work forward. James Lattimer has translated this book from German into English in an empathetic way and has been an attentive conversation partner for me. Naomi Vaughan has revised the translation dedicatedly and carefully. I would like to thank Alena Horbelt for the final corrections and the entire formal revision of the English version. Finally, I would like to thank the Cluster *Languages of Emotion* – on the one hand for the financial support, without which this work would not have been possible; and on the other hand the management of the graduate school, namely Prof. Gisela Klann-Delius and Dr. Markus Edler, who supported the development of this work in a benevolent manner and did their utmost to further it.

My final thanks go to my wife Judith, who has not only supported me in my work on this book and who sees me like nobody else.

https://doi.org/10.1515/9783110580761-001

1 Splitting the Spectator

1.1 Introduction

An Affective History

This book poses two related questions. First: how is affective experience in the cinema produced? What, exactly, are spectators referring to when exhibiting emotional reactions, feeling scared, barely withstanding the tension, bursting into tears? Are spectators moved by the fate of the characters or the moral implications of the narrative's events? Are spectatorial feelings pre-determined by the genre of the film? Or do perhaps processes exist that precede such considerations and determine the connection between film and spectator in a subtler and simultaneously more far-reaching way? Second: on what basis might a history be written of the relationship thus implied? What would a history, whose subject is the conditions of affective experience in the cinema, look like and what would be the primary focus of its attention? The present work argues that the answer to both these questions can be gleaned from the analysis of cinematic movement – movement in all its myriad facets, from the way its nuances can be precisely graduated, to its ability to overwhelm in almost violent fashion.

The following pages reveal the full panorama of New Hollywood cinema as a distinct period of film history that can be characterized in two different ways: by its entirely new way of conceiving of and utilizing cinematic movement, on the one hand, and its radical re-definition of the affective relationship between film and spectator, on the other. The underlying hypothesis here is that these two characteristics are in fact closely intertwined – which, as a *theoretical* claim, is not actually a new idea. The benefit of my approach is rather to combine the first question with the second, requiring film history to be written as an *affective history*.

With this as its central motto, this book aims to demonstrate through concrete analysis that movement and emotion are indeed intertwined (a relationship that, theoretically, has already been posited to excess), and to allow this connection to be grasped in concrete terms. The sort of history I am seeking to write here is neither structured as a psychological history of American cinema, nor as a re-construction of historical cinema experiences. The focus is therefore neither on establishing how historical events and developments are reflected in the films of New Hollywood, nor about ascertaining how actual historical audiences might have experienced a trip to the cinema around 1973. My initial intention

https://doi.org/10.1515/9783110580761-002

with this work is actually a simple one: to explore the very real possibilities[1] of affective experience that have been *de facto* open to spectators, and which are characteristic of this film historical period. As far as these possibilities of affective experience can be described systematically, this undertaking can be seen as compiling a phenomenology of New Hollywood.

Yet the true scope of the present work only becomes apparent in light of the title of this introduction: *splitting the spectator.* This title is linked to a hypothesis regarding the importance of affective experience in the constitution of the film spectator's subject position. This hypothesis states that, for the films of New Hollywood, the act of perception is experienced by the spectator as a splitting of their subject position. There are two prerequisites to this hypothesis, the first of which is: what is termed subjectivity – a specific way of being-in-the-world – can be defined in temporal terms, as the lived experience of time. The second prerequisite is that the meaningful experience of time is nothing other than the affective process itself, in that affect organizes this experience in terms of form. Both of these assumptions will be discussed in detail below in reference to film perception and over the course of this book.

Film perception is a process that unfolds in time. The time in question here takes the form of series of movements on screen. The specific composition of movements that constitute what happens in the film becomes an affective experience for the spectator through perception, which thus establishes a spectatorial subjectivity. In the cinema of New Hollywood, however, the spectator is prevented from being able to create a unified affective connection to the film's events and/or occupy a consistent, coherent position in a number of different ways. This idea is of interest in both theoretical and historical terms: if the hypothesis of the splitting of the spectator is taken as our basis here, the two questions posed at the beginning certainly cannot be regarded as trivial. They, in fact, reveal two additional ideas: first, that a proper description of how the affective relationship between film and spectator is organized during the concrete process of film perception is still, to a large extent, lacking; and second, that this sort of broadly phenomenological approach may well be able to open up new perspectives on film history.

---

1 I use the term possibility here (in relationship to reality) in line with Henri Bergson: "[...] it is the real which makes itself possible and not the possible which becomes real." In this understanding, the real is not the realization of a program already laid out in possibility; rather, the real that takes place in time, the free creation of the new, is the source of possibility. Henri Bergson: The Possible and the Real. In: id.: The Creative Mind. An Introduction to Metaphysics, New York 1968, pp. 107–125, here p. 122.

In the previous research carried out on New Hollywood, two interpretations dominate. The period is understood either as an anomaly within the framework of ongoing processes of industrial adaptation or as a canonical collection of masterpieces, as American auteur cinema's finest hour. While there are clear justifications for both of these interpretations, neither is particularly well-suited to gauging New Hollywood's historical relevance. While the former – if it does indeed even grapple with the films themselves – attempts to explain New Hollywood based on its influences and thus tends to reduce films to these influences, the latter operates by subjecting the works to retrospective appreciation, as a kind of backlash to the former. Both thus fail to engage with this cinema directly, favoring instead a teleology, conceived in either positive or negative terms, or (in the case of the former), a functionalism that describes the system as capable of infinite assimilation and adaptation.

Unlike these previous attempts, the approach suggested here operates based on the assumption that this cinema cannot be defined *a priori* as a historical formation, whether in terms of economical and production constraints, lists of stylistic influences, or normative value judgments. The parameters for categorizing and systematizing these films must instead be derived from the concrete experience of the films themselves. An approach such as this is not so much concerned with describing the "before" or "after," as with seeking to focus attention on the films' critical potential, by grasping crisis as a moment of decision and change.[2] To put it simply, the idea is to introduce a particular idea of *movement* into the writing of film history.[3] With this in mind, whenever the present work refers to New Hollywood as a distinct period in American film history, this should not be understood in an essentialist way. What is truly distinct about this period is the specific way it transformed the existing, by fracturing that which previously appeared coherent; its distinction lies in the fact that the end of the crisis produced something new, which did not represent a return to a starting point before the crisis took place. New Hollywood changed American cinema, and the reverberations of this change still echo today.

Maurice Merleau-Ponty formulated what is at stake with this idea in his discussions of the problem of movement: "If we want to take the phenomenon of

---

2 For an elaboration of the concept of crisis with regard to film history, see Michael Wedel: Filmgeschichte als Krisengeschichte. Schnitte und Spuren durch den deutschen Film, Bielefeld 2011, pp. 14–17.

3 As Maurice Merleau-Ponty writes, "movement is not limited to submitting passively to space and time, it actively assumes them, it takes them up in their basic significance [...]." Merleau-Ponty: Phenomenology of Perception [1945], London/New York 2002, p. 117.

movement seriously, we shall need to conceive a world which is not made up only of things, but which has in it also pure transitions. The something in transit [...] is to be defined only in terms of the particular manner of its 'passing'."[4] Relating this type of manner or *mode* to the cinema of New Hollywood is what I seek to engage with in the present work. This entails neither grasping the films as fixed artifacts nor as ensembles carrying particular characteristics (such as a series of film historical influencing factors or a series of film-critical attributes), but rather as arrangements aimed at shaping affective experience, whose result is not pre-determined. Merleau-Ponty exemplifies this difference in reference to a stone being thrown through the air: "We shall not find in the stone-in-movement everything that we know in other ways about the stone. [...] The moving object, as object of an indefinite series of explicit and concordant perceptions, has properties, the mobile entity has only a style."[5] Style is thus not (only) what is typical, but above all a generative principle, which Merleau-Ponty paraphrases by way of the concept of the pregnant (in the sense of the productive and the fruitful).[6] If style thus concerns the way in which something appears, analyzing it enables a level of discourse to be reached where form and content cannot be separated and where the meaning of words such as "subject" or "emotion" is not necessarily clear from the outset. In this specific sense of the word, the present work thus explores the style of New Hollywood – by making the same dual reference to history and affectivity already contained within Merleau-Ponty's conception of style.[7] Another theoretical resource for this approach is what Raymond Williams has termed "structures of feeling."[8] Williams attempts to describe how each concretely lived historical constellation of social relations shapes and delimits possibilities of affective experience: "What really changes is something quite general, over a wide range, and the description that often fits the change best is the literary term 'style.'"[9] The emphasis here is on style not as a means of classification, but as connected to the phenomenon of historical transformation. It is no coincidence that Williams conceptualizes

---

4 Merleau-Ponty: Phenomenology of Perception, p. 275. Vivian Sobchack has laid the groundwork for the film theoretical engagement with Merleau-Ponty's philosophy, see Sobchack: The Address of the Eye. A Phenomenology of Film Experience, Princeton 1992.
5 Merleau-Ponty: Phenomenology of Perception, pp. 273 – 274.
6 See Merleau-Ponty: The Visible and the Invisible. Followed by Working Notes, edited by Claude Lefort, Evanston 1968, pp. 216 – 217.
7 See Merleau-Ponty: Phenomenology of Perception, p. 529. For the relationship between style and affectivity, or style and expression, see ibid., pp. 211 – 212.
8 Raymond Williams: Marxism and Literature, Oxford/New York 1977, pp. 128 – 135.
9 Williams: Marxism and Literature, p. 131.

this connection with reference to affectivity. Style is thus not meant in the sense of the revelation of some specific authorial position (a position cited by many as a characteristic of modern cinema), nor in the sense of a classification mechanism to mark a particular art historical era. Instead, the concept of style directly concerns the affective-corporeal process of film perception, as will be discussed in detail below.[10] According to Hermann Kappelhoff, this process can be described as a "stylization"[11] of the spectator's perceptual activity.

The goal of this undertaking is to stop the nexus of emotion and movement from being taken for granted in two respects. First, it is necessary to analyze the function of and meaning behind the use of movement-generating procedures for the spectator's affective experience at the level of individual films. Second, at the level of historical processes, it is precisely this shaping of affective experience which makes it possible to properly address the motion/emotion of the New Hollywood era or rather its critical potential. For it is only by articulating this potential that we are able to capture its ongoing relevance to this day. The idea of "splitting the spectator" refers to this idea of being moved as a specific, affect-poetic strategy.

Fissured Feeling

An impression of this particular tendency can already be gained by looking at the film generally regarded as spearheading New Hollywood: BONNIE AND CLYDE (Arthur Penn 1967).[12] Let us recall, for example, the end of the film: a medium long shot places the viewer on the side of a country road. The birds are singing and a barely perceptible wind moves through the grass. A middle-aged, slightly rotund man in overalls tinkers with his truck, trying to change one of the tires. Once the tire is on the ground, he stands up and turns around, scanning the road with a nervous, searching gaze. A reverse shot follows, a wide shot of the road in bright sunlight, which is bordered by a field to the left and

---

10 This conception can thus easily be brought into connection with Panofsky's discussion of cinematic style, which he derives from the fact that film links together time and space by way of movement. See Erwin Panofsky: Style and Medium in the Motion Pictures [1947]. In: id.: Three Essays on Style, edited by Irving Lavin, Cambridge 1997, pp. 91–128.

11 Hermann Kappelhoff: Matrix der Gefühle. Das Kino, das Melodrama und das Theater der Empfindsamkeit, Berlin 2004, p. 169.

12 A note on the films listed in the text: Unless otherwise stated, the country of production is always the USA. The director and year of production (which refers here to the year in which the film premiered) are usually only included at the first mention of a particular film.

bushes and trees to the right. The road disappears behind a bend a few hundred meters away. The man gets back to work.

A cut follows: into the interior of a moving car (which is moving across the frame from the right to the left), with a close-up of the upper bodies of the two people inside: a man at the steering wheel, a woman in the passenger seat, both in their mid- to late twenties. A subtle tension can initially be detected in their bearing and conversation; it soon gives way, however, to joyful abandon. The woman takes a pear from the shopping bag on the back seat, bites into it, and then passes it to her companion so he can take a bite. The air rushing through the car windows blows her medium-length blond hair across her face. The couple is none other than Bonnie and Clyde; and although their names alone are enough to make clear what must follow, even with everything that has already happened over the course of the film, we are still not prepared for what will now ensue. There is no way of repairing the fissure that will open up between two different spectatorial positions in this scene: the one that shares the protagonists' perspective, on the one hand, and the one that recognizes them as mere bodies, as objects of destruction, on the other. This is the sort of fissure that comes to the fore when I talk about "splitting the spectator."

A cut then follows, back to the man at the truck, who is now pumping up the tire. He looks up at the road again, searching, waiting. His second look is answered by another reverse shot; this time of a car coming around the bend in the distance. After a brief cut back to the man, a second cut directs us back to the interior of the car to confirm that the two cars are one and the same and that it still carries the couple we are already familiar with. Supported by the shot/reverse shot structure of the montage, their gazes meet that of the man, with the couple smiling happily as they recognize him as a friend before stopping the car next to him. The man indicates that he has a flat tire and needs assistance. Clyde gets out of the car, while Bonnie remains seated inside. An over-the-shoulder shot of Bonnie from inside the car follows, with the view through the windscreen accentuating the couple's spatial separation, generating a sense of quiet unease that thus foreshadows what is coming: the two of them will not be reunited. A small breeze once again ruffles Bonnie's hair.

From this point on, the montage accelerates and it feels like it is the acceleration itself that is responsible for the subsequent development of the scene – and in a key sense, this impression is entirely justified, as it is indeed the montage where the fissure between the two spectatorial positions is made manifest. We move first from a medium shot of the two men to a close-up of Bonnie, now looking somewhat skeptical, before Clyde is also isolated within a second close-up. The older man is agitated and distracted and casts repeated glances at a bush on the other side of the road. Suddenly, three birds flutter up out of the bush with a clattering of wings, followed by the camera and the gazes of the three characters. A rapid pan follows the birds' flight, until the sun is shining directly into the camera. Their gazes jump from the birds back to the bush, whose leaves and branches are swaying and rustling in the wind. All at once, the old man hurls himself under the truck. At that moment, the couple realizes what is happening: they have been ambushed. Their gazes connect once again across the few meters that separate them, which now feel like an abyss, alerting each other of their awareness of the situation and bidding farewell in equal measure, in a set of rapid alternations between a head and shoulders shot of him and a close-up of her. Once Clyde starts moving towards Bonnie, there is a final cut back to the ominous bush, from which machine gun fire now erupts with an ear-splitting bang, shredding its leaves.

The film switches into slow motion and the speed of the montage increases once again, in order to depict the effect of the hail of bullets on the couple's bodies. The sound of the guns does not abate; Bonnie's occasional screams actually up the intensity. The force of the impact robs their bodies of any self-control, the convulsive twitches and contortions of their arms and legs reminiscent of the lifeless movements of puppets or marionettes, particular in Bonnie's case. The combined effect of the editing and slow motion both extend Clyde's fall to the ground and break it into fragments, while the bullets shred the clothes and faces of the two outlaws. The pear in Clyde's hand explodes with a squirt of juice, the single bite he took of it still in his mouth. Bonnie's torso is now hanging out of the open car door, while Clyde convulses before rolling onto his stomach, enshrouded in the swirling sand and dust. Finally, Bonnie's right arm slips out of her lap and now dangles in front of her face. Her hair still moves in the breeze, but otherwise everything is still. The birds have also fallen silent. A medium long shot from above sums up the result of the scene, as the last cloud of dust dissipates.

Those responsible for the attack slowly emerge from their hiding places; the older man also approaches, as do the two farm hands who have been following events from the distance. The camera initially frames the characters' movements through the window of the open car door, before moving along the bullet-riddled bodywork to behind the car and bringing the characters back into view through the shot-to-pieces back window. The protagonists' perspective, which originally integrated the spectator into the plot, is now replaced by the empty perspective of the car. The men drop their guns and a hard cut to black follows almost immediately, whereupon the credits appear, accompanied by a slow guitar number.

Through these movements, the spectator experiences a radical transformation in their relationship to what is happening in the film. One key factor of this transformation is the relationship between the movement within the image and the montage. While the montage seems to service the characters' movements at the beginning of the scene, it takes command shortly before the firing begins, rapidly increasing pace and simultaneously fragmenting the space by isolating the two protagonists in tight to very tight framings.

In the process, the camera's eye for detail remains essentially unchanged, which may well be one of the main reasons for the disturbing effect of the scene. During the car journey, how the juice from the pear runs down Clyde's cheek and the wind plays with Bonnie's hair can already be seen. When the bullets subsequently rip through the protagonists' faces and clothes, this happens at exactly the same level of description but receives an entirely different emphasis, due to the sound of the machine guns, the high frequency of cuts, and the use of slow motion. The feeling of control slipping away, already made manifest by the spastic convulsions of the bodies as they are riddled with bullets, is repeated for the spectator as a corporeal experience of the image's own jarring, arrhythmic convulsions, which tear open the spatiotemporal context. The image shifts from a rhythm of anthropomorphic or automobile movement to a destroyed rhythm or a rhythm of destruction. What is disturbing here is not just the murder of the protagonists. What is disturbing is the shift from a perspective seemingly operating in harmony with the characters as they perform their actions, to an inhuman, destructive perspective that the protagonists are subjected to – and which remains our own perspective all the same.

This attack on the integrity of the spectatorial position thus does not just feed on violent images. Instead, a sort of aesthetic short circuit is responsible, connecting two different modalities of vision, of a kind with those described by Kappelhoff: "[Films like BONNIE AND CLYDE] allow the dirty images of the other cinema [i.e., underground cinema, author's note] to parade around in the magnificent garb of fancy cinematography and opulent directorial style linked to a new auteur cinema."[13] Formulated in abstract terms, the splitting of the spectator is thus realized in the form of a short circuit between contradictory perceptual orders. In the film analyses that follow, it will be necessary to examine this operation in detail, keeping in mind that the parameters of and conditions for such a short circuit are often very different when viewed across the whole of New Hollywood. This book aims to provide a theoretical clarification and systematization of these parameters and conditions. What is created in the process, is the history of an upheaval in feeling, whose repercussions still affect us today.

---

13 Kappelhoff: Realismus. Das Kino und die Politik des Ästhetischen, Berlin 2008, p. 161. All quotes from German sources have been translated by James Lattimer.

The Shock of Freedom

On December 8, 1967, *Time Magazine* titled its cover story: "Hollywood: The Shock of Freedom in Films."[14] In the accompanying article, Stefan Kanfer sketches an overview of a new Hollywood cinema, which contains a whole series of factors, setting it apart from the cinema characteristic of the decade until that point. He sees BONNIE AND CLYDE as paradigmatic of this shift: "In both conception and execution, BONNIE AND CLYDE is a watershed picture, the kind that signals a new style, a new trend."[15] Yet the focus here is on more than just a trend; the focus is, in fact, on an entirely new "style," very much in the spirit of Merleau-Ponty, understood as a reordering of the perception and expression through which film is experienced. Kanfer's essay represents perhaps the first attempt to grasp something still emerging at the time, which would only receive a name in the mid-1970s: New Hollywood.

Kanfer's title is entirely apt. If taken literally, it opens up an initial perspective on the present work: the relationship between cinematic movement and the feeling of the spectator in the cinema of New Hollywood. The idea of exploring this theme is born from the theoretical premise that: how every film is staged puts into practice a particular idea of how the affective relationship between the film and the spectator should be formed. This means that analyzing a particular film makes possible assertions, regarding how it positions, addresses, and conveys affect to its spectator, or, to put it more succinctly, regarding how the film shapes the spectator's perception as an affective experience. I will use the term "affect poetics" to refer to the systematic context that forms the basis for the development of such relationships; a context that can be verified via film analysis. This work is thus dedicated to exploring the affect poetics of New Hollywood as a distinct period in American film history.

The title of the *Time Magazine* article can be read in two different ways, with the main emphasis placed on either shock or freedom, respectively. Yet a third reading is equally possible, which links together the implications of these two other readings.

Let us begin with shock. By employing this concept, Kanfer highlights, on the one hand, the radicalism of the transformation he identifies. This corre-

---

14 Stefan Kanfer: Hollywood: The Shock of Freedom in Films. In: Time Magazine, December 8th, 1967, URL: http://www.time.com/time/printout/0,8816,844256,00.html, last accessed June 5th, 2019.

15 Kanfer: Hollywood. For an account of how BONNIE AND CLYDE came to be seen as this kind of watershed picture, see Mark Harris: Pictures at a Revolution. Five Movies and the Birth of the New Hollywood, New York 2008, pp. 337–351 and pp. 366–371.

sponds to the first fundamental hypothesis of the present work, which states that: New Hollywood created something *genuinely new* in American cinema, something that cannot be reduced to the sum of its influences and forerunners. To prove this hypothesis, it is essential, from the outset, to avoid applying any sort of normative perspective, which might restrict the films' analysis; whereby any transformation, regardless of how radical, is always represented in negative terms, based on either deviation from or agreement with tradition. Instead, therefore, the approaches employed by the films must be described with regard to how they modulate and transform the affective relationship to the spectator – not least when the films in question actively reference other films. This is what may be achieved with the concept of affect poetics. The approach is based on the conviction that films are not to be grasped as naive documents of factual constraints, whether social, historical, or film historical in nature; but rather that they, in fact, position themselves toward these contexts in a certain manner.

On the other hand, the term shock already represents one initial affect-poetic principle. Kanfer describes this principle as a tearing of the boundaries previously separating expressive and aesthetic registers. This assessment can be expanded into the second initial hypothesis of the present work: the films of New Hollywood follow a strategy aimed at *challenging and overwhelming* the spectator, with respect to the affective-corporeal act of perception. They attack the various demarcations that ensure the integrity and stability of the spectatorial position with respect to a film's perception. The categorial ordering of the classical genre system is one main target of these tactics of border violation. It becomes increasingly difficult to ascribe the films of New Hollywood to distinct genres, in the classical sense; or rather, the attempt to ascribe them to certain genres does them increasingly little justice.

This point leads directly into the other reading of Kanfer's title, which places an emphasis on the idea of freedom. Kanfer speaks explicitly of freedom from formula, convention, and censorship. This alludes to a decisive 1966 development, namely the end of the Motion Picture Production Code, the so-called Hays Code, which had set the guidelines for moral self-censorship on the part of the Hollywood studios from 1930 onwards, primarily regarding sexuality, violence, and the relationship to public institutions. The end of the Hays Code and the introduction of a ratings system based on age in 1968 opened up cinema to a whole new field of aesthetic possibilities, which could now be explored step-by-step.[16]

---

16 See Bergson: "If we put the possible back into its proper place, evolution becomes some-

Freedom thus also refers here to the range of different poetic approaches, already noted by Kanfer in 1967. This diversity is further reflected in the third hypothesis of the present work: the cinema of New Hollywood *does not represent a homogenous structure* and equally cannot be described in terms of a universal poetic program encompassing all of its films. Furthermore, the films of New Hollywood do not constitute a canon of retrospectively compiled masterpieces, especially with regard to the big names that emerged during this period (such as Stanley Kubrick, Martin Scorsese, Steven Spielberg, and Francis Ford Coppola, to mention only the most prominent figures). Rather, engaging with this period requires addressing the subject in suitable breadth, to avoid simply affirming what one has already allegedly known from the beginning. In the present work, this is ensured by the decision to expand the corpus of films viewed to over 400,[17] and echoed by the title of this introduction. "Splitting the spectator" is not a universal program but rather an attempt to express, on several different levels, the tendency toward diversification and disintegration so characteristic of this period. Hence, it does not just aim to characterize the specific affect-poetic alignment of individual films, but also points to the fact that, beyond classical genre cinema, no new, unified system of relations is (yet) available, which might allow the spectator to find some degree of orientation. This is further reflected by the use of the plural form in the title of this book. (This is, in a way, inverting the standard point of view, motivated by economic production, whereby the diversification of films on offer represents a reaction to the splintering of audiences).

As Kanfer's text also implies, freedom can equally be described as an affect-poetic strategy, in that it may refer to the expansion and refinement of the expressive register of the films in question (which is not meant here as a value judgment). Mainstream, commercial cinema suddenly began tapping into techniques and approaches used rarely or not at all before, such as the use of handheld cameras, natural lighting and real settings, deliberate blurring effects, slow motion, time lapse, and split screen. These were complimented by new conceptions of acting, in evidence since the 1960s, which increased the scope of physical expressivity and emphasis on characters' tics and peculiarities. This also applied, for example, to the use of different linguistic dialects. At the same time, spoken dialogue lost its previously unchallenged aural dominance and entered into competition with music and background noise on the sound-

---

thing quite different from the realisation of a program: the gates of the future open wide; freedom is offered an unlimited field." See Bergson: The Possible and the Real, p. 122.

17 As a rough means of orientation, the Internet Movie Database lists 4806 US feature productions for the period from 1967–1980. URL: imdb.com, last accessed June 1st, 2019.

track. As rock music soundtracks replaced classical scores, a whole world of new rhythms gained entrance into cinema, including, in particular, the use of contemporary classical music in horror films. Against this backdrop, the pace of montage also changed, tending towards ever smaller units, edited together in rapid acceleration, on the one hand, and sustained, insistent framings and extended tracking shots and pans, on the other. This *expansion of the possibilities of cinematic movement* is significant on all levels and stands in direct relationship to the affect-poetic transformation carried out by New Hollywood – my fourth hypothesis. Over the course of the work, the direct relationship between cinematic movement and the spectator's feeling posited here will first be given theoretical grounding and then be explored across various exemplary film analyses.

And thus, we arrive at the third reading of the title, which brings together the two readings discussed above. From this perspective, the "shock of freedom" can be understood as the description of a spectatorial experience, characterized by the irresolvable contradiction between a new diversity of emotional experience and the more or less violent undermining of the embodied viewing position. This is the conflict that arises when the use of a greater range of more differentiated, expressive registers is combined with a strategy of the deliberate shattering of boundaries. The result here is three new affective modes, which run counter to the classifications of the classical genre system and each shape their own, new relationship between film and spectator. The modes in question are those listed in the title of this book: suspense, paranoia, and melancholy. These are not generic categories, within which the films operate, but rather each of the modes is realized in a specific manner during the actual perception of a particular film. As previously discussed, this is the reason they do not constitute a homogenization of New Hollywood, in the sense of generating an all-encompassing container or universal poetic program. For all their differences, what these modes do have in common is that they address the spectator's active and passive capacities in equal measure: both in terms of the ability to experience and perceive in a nuanced, differentiated manner, as well as in terms of opening oneself up to attack and vulnerability. Exploring the interplay between these two aspects is the ultimate goal of my fifth and most important hypothesis, regarding what connects New Hollywood's various affect-poetic maneuvers, namely: the *splitting of the spectator* in terms of affective experience. To now grasp what might be meant by this process of splitting, it is necessary to formulate a theoretical basis for connecting cinematic movement and spectator emotion.

1.2 Cinematic Expressivity

Emotion in Film Theory

As already mentioned, the idea of connecting movement and emotion in film perception is not new. Yet once we move beyond the things usually taken for granted,[18] which form the standard basis for relating these three terms to one another, there is a considerable lack of clarity in this field. Many of the numerous more recent studies of spectator affect in the cinema[19] thus grasp movement merely as some sort of rationalizing context, employed metaphorically, which does not itself require any further investigation (this can also be gleaned from some of the titles in question here, such as "Moving Pictures," "Moving Viewers").[20] Frequently lurking behind such titles is a refusal to recognize film's temporal dimension and its specific manner of shaping movement as genuine prerequisites for the spectator's emotional experience.[21] Instead, attempts are made to determine the source of this experience by other means.

---

18 Kappelhoff: Die vierte Dimension des Bewegungsbildes. Das filmische Bild im Übergang zwischen individueller Leiblichkeit und kultureller Fantasie. In: Anne Bartsch, Jens Eder, and Kathrin Fahlenbrach (eds.): Audiovisuelle Emotionen. Emotionsdarstellung und Emotionsvermittlung durch audiovisuelle Medienangebote, Cologne 2007, pp. 297–311, here p. 297.

19 Since the 1990s, there has been increased interest in the subject of emotion in the field of film studies. The vast majority of research conducted to this end is aligned with a cognitivist understanding of psychology, which largely link the film's emotional effect on the spectator to the characters and plots depicted within it. Central representatives of this trend include Noël Carroll: The Philosophy of Motion Pictures, Malden 2008; Torben Grodal: Moving Pictures. A New Theory of Film Genres, Feelings, and Cognition, Oxford 1997, and Embodied Visions. Evolution, Emotion, Culture, and Film, Oxford 2009; Carl Plantinga, and Greg M. Smith (eds.): Passionate Views. Film, Cognition and Emotion, Baltimore 1999; Plantinga: Moving Viewers. American Film and the Spectator's Experience, Berkeley 2009; Murray Smith: Engaging Characters. Fiction, Emotion, and the Cinema, Oxford 1995; Ed Tan: Emotion and the Structure of Narrative Film. Film as an Emotion Machine, Mahwah 1996. In addition to these monographs, there are also several anthologies dedicated to the connection between film and emotion. See, for example, Matthias Brütsch et al: Kinogefühle. Emotionalität und Film, Marburg 2005; Fabienne Liptay, and Susanne Marschall (eds.): Mit allen Sinnen. Gefühl und Empfindung im Kino, Marburg 2006; Bartsch, Eder, and Fahlenbrach (eds.): Audiovisuelle Emotionen.

20 Carroll, for example, is satisfied with merely pointing out the fact that films generate affect in their viewers, visible in their commercial success, their cultural significance, and the strategies used to market them. Carroll: The Philosophy of Motion Pictures, p. 147.

21 See, for example, Noël Carroll: The Paradox of Suspense. In: Peter Vorderer, Hans J. Wulff, and Mike Friedrichsen (eds.): Suspense. Conceptualizations, Theoretical Analyses, and Empirical Explorations, Mahwah 1996, pp. 71–91, here p. 72 and p. 87.

There are three standard approaches employed to this end, which are sometimes combined.[22] The first of these is based on an understanding of emotion as the effect of the cognitive assessment of a situation, referred to as appraisal: "An emotion may be defined as a change in action readiness as a result of the subject's appraisal of the situation or event."[23] According to this definition, emotions are thus fundamentally object-related. The fact that this understanding of emotion stems from individual psychology generates a problem: that, if one wants to be able to explain the spectator's emotional engagement, the staged plot of a film (whose dramatically condensed situations carry an attendant reduction in complexity) must be equated with situations from real life. As a consequence of this dilemma, Ed Tan distinguishes between emotions relating to the fictional context and those relating to its status as an aesthetic construction, its character as an artifact – a differentiation that has proved enormously influential for the creation of cognitive theories. This distinction ultimately boils down to the separation of form and content, which are installed as mutually exclusive aspects of film experience. A relationship of total transparency (or total illusion) is thus created, on the one hand, whereby the results of the narration are presented to the spectator as corresponding with reality. On the other hand, however, film is represented as an entirely hermetic spectacle, an aesthetic firework display, which prohibits any reference to questions of content. Attention is usually lavished here on the apparent "standard case" of commercial movie-making, offered by the linear, mainstream narrative, based on production and economic considerations; a case allegedly characterized by precisely the sort of interplay that thus relegates "aesthetic" emotions to the status of a special case.[24] In this respect, the concept is oddly reminiscent of the critical reception dealt to many of the New Hollywood filmmakers, who were repeatedly accused of favoring style over substance.[25] This already suggests that this approach is not suitable for examining

---

22 See Hermann Kappelhoff, and Jan-Hendrik Bakels: Das Zuschauergefühl. Möglichkeiten qualitativer Medienanalyse. In: Zeitschrift für Medienwissenschaft, No. 5 (2011), pp. 78–95, here pp. 80–83, for a summary.

23 Tan: Emotion and the Structure of Narrative Film, p. 46. See also Carroll: The Philosophy of Motion Pictures, pp. 147–191, and Plantinga: Moving Viewers, pp. 48–77.

24 See Plantinga: Moving Viewers, p. 62. For a critique of the distinction between the understanding of narrative contexts, on the one hand, and aesthetic enjoyment on the other, see Robin Curtis: Narration versus Immersion. Die Falschen Fährten der Analyse. In: Maske und Kothurn Vol. 53, No. 2 (2007), pp. 341–352, here pp. 341–342.

25 See, for example, the argumentation of Victor F. Perkins in the discussion conducted by Ian Cameron, Perkins, Michael Walker, Jim Hillier, and Robin Wood: The Return of *Movie*. In: Movie, No. 20 (1975), pp. 1–25.

the contexts at issue in the present work. I will demonstrate the shortcomings of the cognitivist theories in more detail in the chapter on suspense.

Another tendency, closely linked to the principle of appraisal, is the attempt to explain the spectator's emotions based on the relationships they form to the characters represented in the film. The spectator forms a bond with these characters via a selection of different relationships: empathy,[26] sympathy,[27] simulation,[28] or combinations of all three.[29] This bond, which functions "within cognitive film theory as an almost axiomatic consensus,"[30] also seems to be a consequence of the concept of emotion carried over from psychology, which demands a strict reference to a particular object. Much like separating content and aesthetics, the problem here is that film characters – once again those that appear in the "standard case" of films, hoping for success at the box office – are thus furnished with a generally understandable, everyday psychology without further ado: "Inasmuch as popular or mass fictions, like movies, are designed to *maximize accessibility*, they gravitate naturally toward the use of the schemas, prototypes, exemplars, [...] and other heuristics that abound in the cultures of their target audiences."[31]

Yet film characters are not simplified versions of "people like you and I," for whom one can automatically feel empathy or concern, or whose motivations one can support or reject. In particular, they do not possess any emotions that could be imparted to the spectator in such a manner. Inasmuch as they are relevant for a film's experience, all of these effects are the result of far more fundamental processes – precisely the ones of interest for the present work. Simply eliding the relationship between movement and emotion, in order to incorporate an ill-considered conception of a film's characters into the analysis of film experience, is a short-cut that carries serious consequences. Film characters do not exist independently of the affective modes which create and modulate the relationship between film and spectator at a primary level. It would appear, that these various cognitivist approaches are incapable of grasping form and content together in relation to the affective experience of the film spectator.

---

26 See Hans J. Wulff: Empathie als Dimension des Filmverstehens. Ein Thesenpapier. In: montage/av, Vol. 12, No. 1 (2003), pp. 136–161.

27 Murray Smith: Altered States. Character and Emotional Response in the Cinema. In: Cinema Journal, Vol. 33, No. 4 (Summer 1994), pp. 34–56.

28 See Grodal: Embodied Visions, pp. 181–204.

29 See Plantinga: Moving Viewers, pp. 102–111.

30 Kappelhoff, Bakels: Das Zuschauergefühl, p. 81.

31 See Carroll: The Philosophy of Motion Pictures, p. 175, emphasis my own.

In this respect, Greg M. Smith's so-called mood cue approach at least represents a step in the right direction.[32] While Smith does not grapple with the fundamental question of the contexts related to film perception, he does, however, incorporate such parameters as camerawork, lighting, music, etc. into his model for examining how cinematic affect is generated. Yet he fails to develop an adequate conception of temporality in the perceptual process, which forms the basis for affect's generation. Over the course of the film, mood cues essentially accumulate one after another, without it being made clear how a mutual context might develop between them, which would form the basis for the spectator's relation to them. Ultimately, behind this concept is a more complex version of the stimulus/response model,[33] which remains indebted to the principle of appraisal.

Cinematic Movement and the Spectator

Before I now move on to outlining my own position, I would like to explain the terminology used in the present work. Recently, the debate surrounding questions and conceptualizations of emotion and affect has intensified to such a degree that the two terms have been placed in a dichotomy,[34] on the one hand, and claimed as indistinguishable from one another, on the other.[35] Neither of these arrangements seems particularly desirable, in light of the fact that the focus here is clearly on related subjects. In the present work, my intention is thus not to play emotion off or against affect, but rather to relate the two concepts to one another. Emotion serves as the more comprehensive term here, which connects movement and feeling; or, to be more precise, emotion can be understood as a process whereby an affective dynamic (in this case modulated by a film) is brought into relation with the spectator's feelings, in order to generate a new quality as a result. This feeling component is located on the side of the spectator; while affect and its generation describe the dynamic between form and feeling,

---

32 Greg M. Smith: Film Structure and the Emotion System, Cambridge 2003.

33 See Smith: Film Structure and the Emotion System pp. 39–40. For a critical evaluation of Smith's model see Kappelhoff, Bakels: Das Zuschauergefühl, pp. 83–85, and Robert Sinnerbrink: Stimmung. Exploring the Aesthetics of Mood. In: Screen, Vol. 53, No. 2 (Summer 2012), pp. 148–163, here pp. 152–154.

34 See, for example, Brian Massumi: Parables for the Virtual. Movement, Affect, Sensation, Durham/London 2002.

35 See Ruth Leys: The Turn to Affect. A Critique. In: Critical Inquiry, Vol. 37, No. 3 (Spring 2011), pp. 434–472.

my primary concern. It is this latter dynamic that makes change possible in the first place. Affects (in the plural) are thus not a purely physiological, pre-linguistic, raw mass that always precede our thoughts and feelings. For, if this were the case, how could different affects be distinguished from one another? Affects are instead produced, circulated, and modulated via discourses and media, with different affects and feelings, further, permanently interacting with one another. To this end, to now come to grips with New Hollywood as a distinct film historical period, it is also essential to specify and qualify the spectator's unique feelings in order to define what I mean by the splitting of their viewing position. I thus understand affects as contributing to a process that is generally geared towards this kind of spectatorial qualification.[36] The concept of affect poetics is also to be understood in the same sense.

The two other concepts central to my undertaking have already been mentioned; namely, "affective mode" and "style." It seems to me that, along with the theoretical concept of style derived from Merleau-Ponty, the concept of the affective mode is well-suited to specifying both style and affect poetics in historical terms, with regard to the cinema of New Hollywood (not least because of the way it grapples with the concept of genre). An affective mode is neither an affect nor a feeling, but rather a poetic principle of ordering, which regulates the dynamics of affect as they unfold in time, in relation to a film's perception. The affective modes of suspense, paranoia, and melancholy, examined in detail in this book, are specific to this film historical period in their concreteness and configuration.

Hermann Kappelhoff's study on the melodramatic in cinema is the central point of reference for developing the concept of the affective mode in the present work. At the very beginning, Kappelhoff makes a clear distinction between the melodramatic mode and the film genre of the same name:

> The concept of *melodramatic representation* is not determined here by the generic grouping linked to the 'melodrama' [...], but rather relates to a particular pattern of aesthetically mediated perceptual processes. This pattern can be gleaned from the representational structure [...] if one grasps these structures as the basis for the temporal modeling of spectatorial perception.[37]

---

36 Referencing the process of qualification indicates the extent to which affect and style are connected; namely in that "the experience of quality is that of a certain mode of movement or of a form of conduct" – in other words, of a style. Merleau-Ponty: Phenomonology of Perception, p. 234.

37 Kappelhoff: Matrix der Gefühle, p. 29. All emphases are taken from the original text unless otherwise stated.

I will draw on this theoretical basis in what follows, in order to develop a conceptualization of affective modes which grasps them as sites for germinating historical change – a change that, in the case of New Hollywood, deliberately positions itself against the categorizations of the classical genre system.

Raymond Bellour remarks on the degree to which the concept of emotion converges with the concept of affect, when it is brought into alignment with movement and states of motion. In much the same way, Gilles Deleuze defines the affective process, in reference to Henri Bergson, as "a motor effort on an immobilised receptive plate."[38] It should be emphasized here that the present work is not a history of emotions, in the sense of specific entities that can be given discrete names (a history of sadness, of revulsion, etc.), but rather a history of feeling, in the sense of the spectator's concrete, felt experience as it unfolds in time.

The starting point of the present work is an awareness (to be further developed in the following) of the fact that emotions in cinema are neither generated independently from the aesthetic dimension of the film experience, nor do they simply "appear" in films and find their way to the spectator. Rather, emotions can only be conceived of under the conditions of the affective experience of film perception. For this reason, starting from a fixed definition of what constitutes an emotion and then attempting to find examples within individual films is not a suitable approach.[39] The focus must instead be on developing a suitable concept of emotion through the films themselves; such as Deleuze, for example, suggests: "In creative works, there is a multiplication of emotion, a liberation of emotion, and even the invention of new emotions. [...]."[40] First of all, therefore, the conditions of the experience of film perception, and how these relate to the affective experience of spectators, must be clarified. Of these conditions, movement and time are the first and foremost to be taken into consideration.

There are two necessary conditions, which, taken together, are sufficient for the perception of a film in the cinema: 1. The movement of the film strip through

---

38 Raymond Bellour: Le Dépli des Émotions. In: Trafic 43 (September 2002), pp. 93–128, here p. 100; or Gilles Deleuze: Cinema 1. The Movement-Image, Minneapolis 1997, p. 68. See here also Merleau-Ponty's description of the body as "an intertwining of vision and movement." The Primacy of Perception. And Other Essays on Phenomenological Psychology, Evanston 1964, p. 162. **39** This is the problem with approaches that over-emphasize phenomenological accounts of film-viewing, without bringing them into contact with the destabilizing force of affect. See e.g. Julian Hanich: Cinematic Emotion in Horror Films and Thrillers. The Aesthetic Paradox of Pleasurable Fear, New York/London 2010. **40** Deleuze: The Brain is the Screen, [1986]. In id.: The Brain is the Screen. Deleuze and the Philosophy of Cinema, edited by Gregory Flaxman, Minneapolis 1986, pp. 365–374, here p. 370.

the projector and 2. The physical presence of a spectator with an awareness of the fact that something is perceived. How is movement thus perceived in film? According to one popular misunderstanding, the creation of the illusion of movement is due to the eye's physical inertia, which allegedly generates an afterimage as its effect.[41] In actual fact, the impression of movement evoked by film is only possible due to *active mental involvement* on the part of the spectator. As Albert Michotte remarks, in relation to Max Wertheimer's corresponding investigations, the issue is not whether the spectator believes something against their own better knowledge; it is, rather, simply impossible to "discriminate between the real movement of an object [...] and stroboscopic movement, the basis of cinema."[42] The reality of cinematic movement is thus beyond debate.

From the very outset, the spectator is thus more than just a passive receiver of transmitted, visual stimuli; their act of perception is essential for the existence of movement in the cinematic image on the screen. How can the relationship between the spectator and the movement perceived in film now be described in more precise terms? There are two main answers to this question, which are both important for the theoretical project of this book. One is by Gilles Deleuze, the other by Vivian Sobchack.

The Whole and the Duration

According to Deleuze, "cinema does not give us an image to which movement is added, it immediately gives us a movement-image."[43] This statement can certainly be connected to gestalt theoretical considerations: the movement is not added to a photogram afterwards, but is always created as an "intermediate image" that cannot be divided further. But, as Deleuze writes further, movement has "two aspects. On one hand, that which happens between objects or parts; on the other

41 On the "tradition" of this widespread fallacy and for more on the conditions for the perception of movement in the cinema see Joachim Paech: Der Bewegung einer Linie folgen... Notizen zum Bewegungsbild. In: id.: Der Bewegung einer Linie folgen... Schriften zum Film, Berlin 2002, pp. 133 – 161, here pp. 149 – 161.
42 Albert Michotte van den Berck: The Character of "Reality" of Cinematographic Projections. In: Michotte's Experimental Phenomenology of Perception, edited by Georges Thinés, Alan Costall, and George Butterworth, pp. 197 – 209, here p. 198. He continues in the footnote on the same page: "The movement itself should be considered as a perceptual form, which is spontaneously established when the appropriate configuration of stimulation occurs."
43 Deleuze: Cinema 1, p. 2. See Merleau-Ponty: Phenomenology of Perception, p. 318: "in so far as there is movement, the moving object is caught up in that movement."

hand that which expresses the duration or the whole."[44] Deleuze explains what this means with Henri Bergson's famous example of sugared water. The dissolution of sugar in water has two aspects: firstly, the diffusion movement of the individual sugar particles, secondly, "a qualitative transition from water which contains a sugar lump to the state of sugared water"[45]. The critical insight is "that my waiting, whatever it be, expresses a duration as mental, spiritual reality"[46]. This duration is exactly the duration of the transformation, the change from one state to another. Like a melody, it describes a whole, a process that is equally realized in each of its points – and this whole is realized in the viewer's perception, as a "spiritual reality." Thus at the same time the subject position of this spectator, the consciousness or temporality of this specific waiting, is constituted.

However, the whole cannot be understood as a sum, as a totality of relationships. Within such a system, real movement would not be possible. Jean-Luc Nancy illustrates this fact in a commentary on Deleuze:

> Motion is not a displacing or a transferring, which may occur between given places in a totality that is itself given. On the contrary, it is what takes place when a body is in a situation and a state that compel it to find its place, a place it consequently has not had or no longer has. I move (in matter or mind) when I am not – ontologically – where I am – locally. Motion carries me elsewhere but the "elsewhere" is not given beforehand: my coming will make of it the "there" where I will have come from "here".[47]

Movement is not a process that occurs between two pre-existent points. Rather, the movement in its performance itself creates a specific relationship between these points. The whole, whose change expresses movement, is therefore, according to Deleuze with Bergson, the "open":

> The whole and the 'wholes' must not be confused with *sets*. Sets are closed, and everything which is closed is artificially closed. Sets are always sets of parts. But a whole is not closed, it is open; and it has no parts except in a very special sense, since it cannot be divided without changing qualitatively at each stage of the division.[48]

This dynamic unity of the whole is expressed in what Merleau-Ponty calls "style." It is the uniformity of style as a certain way of ordering time (and

---

44 Deleuze: Cinema 1, p. 11.
45 Deleuze: Cinema 1, p. 9.
46 Deleuze: Cinema 1, p. 9.
47 Jean-Luc Nancy: Abbas Kiarostami. The Evidence of Film, Paris 2001, p. 28.
48 Deleuze: Cinema 1, p. 10.

space) that establishes the unity of form.[49] Again, the comparison with a melody is instructive: it is never given in advance, but must always be experienced in a concrete duration. At the same time it changes as soon as one changes or takes away only one note. Likewise, emotion, the "outward movement," is not a movement from a predetermined inner space to a predetermined outer space. Rather, the emotion always generates a new specific relationship between inside and outside. (I will discuss the equation of the whole with the open in more detail in Chapter II on suspense.)

Expression and Experience

As we have seen, movement is realized in both of its aspects in the spectator's active perception. But how can this relationship be described in more detail with regard to the spectator's possibilities of experience? Vivian Sobchack has given an answer to this question by attempting to relate Merleau-Ponty's theories of perception to the cinema apparatus. Sobchack's core statement concerns the relationship between experience and expression, which she sees mirrored in each other in film perception:

> More than any other medium of human communication, the moving picture makes itself sensuously and sensibly manifest as the expression of experience by experience. A film is an act of seeing that makes itself seen, an act of hearing that makes itself heard, an act of physical and reflective movement that makes itself reflexively felt and understood.[50]

Two things are thus said: First, the relationship between viewer and film cannot be reduced to the dichotomy of subject and object of perception. Rather, the film (*each* film) represents its own way of perceiving the world and of behaving towards it, a way to which the viewer in turn relates when he sees a film. Secondly, the perceptual impression of cinematic movement does not simply arrive at the viewer, who then translates it into sense and meaning. Instead, cinematic movement – as movement that is always perceived in a certain way – is always already meaningful and significant, inasmuch as it becomes "a concrete physical-sensu-

---

49 "There remains to understand precisely what the being for itself of the *Gestalt* experience is – It is being for X, not a pure agile nothingness, but an inscription in an open register, in a lake of non being, in an *Eröffnung*, in an *offene*." Merleau-Ponty: The Visible and the Invisible, p. 206.
50 Sobchack: The Address of the Eye, pp. 3–4.

al experience for the viewer as a foreign mode of perception on his own body"[51]. It is this significance, this meaningfulness of a mode of perception – i.e. a subjectivity that relates to the world in this and not another way – with which the viewer deals. Film and audience are thus always interwoven in a reflexive relationship:

> Without an act of viewing and a subject who knows itself reflexively as the locus and origin of viewing as an act, there could be no film and no 'film experience'. Thus, a description of the film experience as an experience of signification and communication calls for a *reflexive turn* away from the film as 'object' and toward the act of viewing and its existential implication of a body-subject: the viewer.[52]

The fact that the viewer is implicated in the act of seeing does not mean that his subject position is given from the outset. Rather, it is constituted through the interplay of film and viewer in what Sobchack describes as "address of the eye," which simultaneously addresses the physical situation of seeing as well as its visual "transcendence," its reaching out beyond itself:

> [...] the visual transcendence in bodily immanence that is the 'address of the eye' enables both the spectator and the film to imaginatively reside in each other – even as they both are discretely embodied and uniquely situated.[53]

The act of film perception interweaves film and audience in the reflection of a specific way of being-in-the-world, precisely what Merleau-Ponty calls style. This interdependence – from which the relationship between viewer and film is first constituted – is the basis on which a concept of affect poetics, as I introduced it above, can be meaningfully developed: if film as an expression of experience through experience always implies an actively perceiving viewer, then it becomes possible to think about how the subjectivity of this viewer is constituted in the concrete experience of film, and to what extent this position can be described as an affective relationship to film.

Cinematic Movement and Emotion

Starting from the statement that the movement perceived while watching a film is produced mechanically and made manifest between the conflicting poles of

---

51 Kappelhoff, Bakels: Das Zuschauergefühl, p. 86.
52 Sobchack: The Address of the Eye, p. 51.
53 Sobchack: The Address of the Eye, p. 261.

three interconnected apparatuses – the spectator's bio-physiological apparatus and the recording and playing devices – Gertrud Koch[54] emphasizes that the idea of an anthropomorphic matrix for film movement (as appears occasionally in the work of Vivian Sobchack amongst others)[55] does not go far enough. Koch distinguishes between two dimensions of movement, namely *representation* and *generation* – the latter of which is of primary interest for us here – and highlights the camera as a movement-generating factor. While the camera is capable of taking a mimetic approach, modeled on the human body, it also contains an "optical" potentiality unique to film. This potentiality neither requires a narrative legitimization nor can it be broken down in reference to the mental states of fictional characters. It can be inferred from this argument that the system of so-called basic emotions developed from evolutionary biology (which include happiness, fear, anger, repulsion, grief, and surprise, depending on the classification) is hardly suitable to cover the entire spectrum of experience for perceiving a film – because it does not take the conditions of this experience into consideration. Yet cinematic movement is *real*;[56] the way it becomes enveloped in an emotional quality is linked to the spectator's perception. Koch draws on the work of Michotte[57] to conceptualize this enveloping process as a theory of empathy, not linked to any sort of character, which forges ahead as a kind of contagion transmitted via the spectator's physical sensation. Imagining this (individual) movement, i.e., the experience of emotion, would thus be a secondary representation in the spectator's consciousness.[58]

---

54 Gertrud Koch: A lecture series at the Freie Universität Berlin during the winter semester 2004/2005 entitled "Movement," held together with Gabriele Brandstetter and Gunter Gebauer.
55 For a critique of Sobchack's tendency to conceive of film experience as an affirmation of the anthropomorphic corporeality of the spectator, see Drehli Robnik: Körper-Erfahrung und Film-Phänomenologie. In: Jürgen Felix (ed.): Moderne Film Theorie, Mainz 2002, pp. 246–280, in particular p. 260. For the differences between everyday perception and film perception see Rudolf Arnheim: Film as Art, Berkeley/Los Angeles/London 1957, pp. 8–34.
56 See also Tom Gunning: Moving Away from the Index. Cinema and the Impression of Reality. In: Gertrud Koch, Volker Pantenburg, and Simon Rothöhler (eds.): Screen Dynamics. Mapping the Borders of Cinema, Vienna 2012, pp. 42–60.
57 Albert Michotte van den Berck: The Emotional Involvement of the Spectator in the Action Represented in a Film. Toward a Theory. In: Michotte's Experimental Phenomenology of Perception, edited by Thinés, Costall, and Butterworth, pp. 209–218.
58 Koch refers in this context to the so-called James/Lange theory, whose central hypothesis is that emotions are the effects of physical states and not the other way round: "My thesis [...] is that *the bodily changes follow directly the perception of the exciting fact, and that our feeling of the same changes as they occur is the emotion.* Common sense says, we lose our fortune, are sorry and weep; we meet a bear, are frightened and run; we are insulted by a rival, are angry and strike. The hypothesis here to be defended says that this order of sequence is incorrect, that

The seeming contradiction of an artificially evoked feeling expressed in "physically real" terms, which Gertrud Koch addresses, is at the heart of Hermann Kappelhoff's study on the genealogy and phenomenology of the melodrama: "What is this lively 'human' and 'fellow' feeling if this feeling is not only capable of being deceived on a grand scale but can itself also be based on deceptions and illusions?"[59] This question points to the "paradox of passive activity"[60] on the part of the spectator, who, after being given over to the illusion of the world represented, appropriates it as an inner state. This process of appropriation transforms the real cinematic image into a "factual psychic reality,"[61] which ultimately may have a physical reaction as its consequence – in the case of melodrama, crying.

Kappelhoff subsequently refines this model by introducing the concept of *expressive movement*, drawing on the work of Helmuth Plessner,[62] on the one hand, and grappling with the theoretical considerations of Sergei Eisenstein, on the other[63] (whose inclusion here is of particular relevance for the present work due to his reception by the filmmakers of New Hollywood[64]). This concept enables the connection between movement and emotion to be grasped in systematic fashion, because it explains the basis for how the spectator's concrete perception becomes a feeling. Expressive movement is not to be understood here as a "*type*

---

the one mental state is not immediately induced by the other, that the bodily manifestations must first be interposed between, and that the more rational statement is that we feel sorry because we cry, angry because we strike, afraid because we tremble, and not that we cry, strike, or tremble, because we are sorry, angry, or fearful, as the case may be. Without the bodily states following on the perception, the latter would be purely cognitive in form, pale, colourless, destitute of emotional warmth. We might then see the bear, and judge it best to run, receive the insult and deem it right to strike, but we could not actually *feel* afraid or angry." William James: What is an Emotion? In: Mind, Vol. 9, No. 34 (April 1884), pp. 188–205, here pp. 189–190. Bellour points out that this model is also of significance for Deleuze's concept of emotion, see Bellour: Le Dépli des Émotions, p. 100.

59 Kappelhoff: Matrix der Gefühle, p. 11.

60 Kappelhoff: Matrix der Gefühle, p. 13.

61 Kappelhoff: Matrix der Gefühle, p. 13.

62 See Helmuth Plessner: Die Deutung des mimischen Ausdrucks. Ein Beitrag zur Lehre vom Bewußtsein des anderen Ichs [1925]. In: id.: Gesammelte Schriften VII. Ausdruck und menschliche Natur, edited by Günter Dux, Frankfurt 2003, pp. 67–130.

63 See Sergei Eisenstein: The Fourth Dimension in Cinema. In: id.: Selected Works Vol. 1 Writings 1922–34, edited by Richard Taylor, London 1988, pp. 181–194.

64 See, for example, Stephen Prince: Savage Cinema. Sam Peckinpah and the Rise of Ultraviolent Movies, Austin 1998, p. 57, in reference to Sam Peckinpah; Michael Pye, Lynda Myles: The Movie Brats. How the Film Generation took over Hollywood, London/Boston 1979, p. 154, in reference to Brian De Palma.

of movement but rather a specific *dimension* of movement which is rooted in the perception of a temporal form"[65] – a temporal form that integrates the various parameters of cinematic staging (the movement of the characters, the camera, the music, etc.) in meaningful fashion. This is what is meant by Gilles Deleuze, when he talks of movement expressing change "in duration or in the whole"[66].

> The duration of a film thus does not just simply describe the time it requires to be watched. It is also the same time in which a specific sensuality is revealed and made complete as the law of a world in the corporeal presence of the spectator's gaze. Over the duration of this process, each shot describes a change in, an extension to, a new perspective on the perceptual world of the film; and every single shot here is already always related to this perceptual world in its entirety, like each tone in a musical composition.[67]

What unfolds over the duration of a film's perception is a world as a *whole*, which, in line with Deleuze, is not to be understood as the totality of this world's elements, but rather as the law that regulates how they are organized and how they change. For this reason, it is not permissible to distinguish between so-called fictional emotions and artifact emotions: film is not an artifact but rather the specific way in which a world is perceived. The spectator's "passive activity" is involved in how the perception of this world unfolds, as Kappelhoff explains in reference to Eisenstein's conception of montage: "When edited together with others, the movement image creates on the one hand a veritable racecourse of physiological stimuli, impacts, and effects which the spectator passes through. On the other hand, this image is the matrix of a process of permanent feedback in which precisely these impacts and effects are taken up as a figure of expression and realized as spectator emotion."[68] In the expressive movement, the temporal unity of this process of passing through is organized into a sense-producing whole. This can be brought into direct connection with the work of Raymond Bellour, who defines the "reality effect of emotion in cinema" as "being seized by an idea via the body itself being seized."[69]

The ongoing connection between these two approaches stems from the fact that they both systematically include all registers of cinematic expressivity; in Kappelhoff's case combined in the temporal form of expressive movement, in Bellour's case (or rather the concept by Daniel Stern Bellour appropriates for

---

65 Kappelhoff, Bakels: Das Zuschauergefühl, pp. 84–85.
66 Deleuze: Cinema 1, p. 8.
67 Kappelhoff: Die vierte Dimension des Bewegungsbildes, p. 309.
68 Kappelhoff: Realismus, pp. 30–31.
69 Bellour: Le Dépli des Émotions, p. 100.

his film theory) justified by the concept of amodal perception. This concept abstracts from the modalities of the individual senses and thus arrives at "the manner in which the elements of an artwork are arranged," a manner to which Stern himself assigns the term style[70] – the same concept of style whose analysis forms the basis of this book. Bellour comments that:

> The *translation of perceptions into feelings* requires the artistic style "to transform perceptions 'faithful to reality' (color harmonies, lines etc.) into virtual forms of feeling, for example the feeling of silence". From this, the concept of 'expressive form' is also derived, with which Stern then describes aspects of social behavior in the early phase of reconciling affect and from which "a forerunner of the experience of art" is made.[71]

The basic outline of a model has thus been laid out, which is capable of connecting the concept of style, introduced at the beginning, with the previously discussed approaches to expressivity in film. We have used these initial theoretical considerations to develop a foundation that enables the affect poetics of a film to be described as a specific mode of placing the spectator in relation to a world, and whose order is revealed through the manipulation of the duration of the embodied perceptual process. According to Merleau-Ponty, there exists something akin to "a temporal style of the world,"[72] and it is this temporal style that I will attempt to isolate and systematize in each of the film analyses to follow. Cinematic movement is always to be examined here in terms of the dual aspect described by Kappelhoff: on the one hand, in terms of its direct impact on the senses; on the other, in terms of how it organizes time. At both of these levels, each analysis taps into the specific connection between movement and emotion in the films of New Hollywood.

---

70 Daniel N. Stern: The Interpersonal World of the Infant: A View from Psychoanalysis and Developmental Psychology, New York 1985, p. 159.

71 Bellour: Le Dépli des Émotions, p. 117, emphasis my own.

72 Merleau-Ponty: Phenomenology of Perception, p. 422.

1.3 The Cinema of New Hollywood

The Term New Hollywood

As mentioned at the start, the new American cinema was only given a name towards the middle of the 1970s: New Hollywood.[73] Nearly simultaneously, the debate began as to whether this name was actually fitting, based around two questions: first, how to place it within a particular historical period and second, how to categorize it in critical terms.

Peter Krämer's overview of "postclassical Hollywood,"[74] for example, names three possibilities for its historical periodization: a "postmodern" perspective, which grasps the entire second half of the 20th century as one, while locating the key films of postmodern cinema largely in the 1980s;[75] another interpretation, inspired by André Bazin's concept of classicism, identifies 1939 as the starting point and CITIZEN KANE (Orson Welles 1941) as the first example of modern cinema before 1967 is eventually reached over the course of the "New Movie" (1950s) and "New American Cinema" (early 1960s); finally, and most potently, the notion that 1967 represented a rupture and moment of true modernist intervention into the context of mainstream cinema. Common between these last two possibilities is their assertion that this period comes to an end around 1975 – through either a transition into the postmodern or a return to neo-classicism.[76]

Krämer remarks that the arrival of the term New Hollywood had the effect of dramatically extending the classical period in film historiography, from 1920 – 1939 all the way into the 1960s.[77] This meant largely ignoring aesthetic changes which had occurred between the late 1940s and mid-1960s and their accompanying social, cultural, and industrial factors; replacing them, instead, with a tele-

73 See Axel Madsen: The New Hollywood. American Movies in the '70s, New York 1975; Hans Blumenberg (ed.): New Hollywood, Munich/Vienna 1976; Steve Neale: New Hollywood Cinema. In: Screen, Vol. 17, No. 2 (1976), pp. 117–122.
74 Peter Krämer: Post-classical Hollywood. In: John Hill, and Pamela Church Gibson (eds.): The Oxford Guide to Film Studies, Oxford 1998, pp. 289–309.
75 One example of this tendency is the approach taken by Timothy Corrigan: A Cinema Without Walls. Movies and Culture after Vietnam, New Brunswick, NJ 1991.
76 Krämer: Post-classical Hollywood, p. 303. Several researchers take a comparatively neutral approach to such questions of period, such as by drawing on the decade as a means of categorization, like Peter Lev: American Films of the 70s. Conflicting Visions, Austin 2000, or by taking an even more schematic path, such as that followed by the anthology by Lester D. Friedman (ed.): American Cinema of the 1970s. Themes and Variations, Oxford 2007.
77 Krämer: Post-classical Hollywood, p. 300.

ology, redirecting all these movements as leading into the rupture of 1967.[78] Krämer further detects repetitions in the criteria used to assert these various film historical shifts: European influences, stylistic innovation, the breaking of taboos, a new understanding of heroism and masculinity, and a socially critical agenda were already the subjects of critical discussion in the 1940s and 1950s; as were the influence of youth culture, technological improvements, event-oriented trends, and the alleged disappearance of narration in favor of spectacle.[79] Against this backdrop, Krämer is of the view that recent research on New Hollywood (both in a broader and more narrow sense) has overemphasized the new:

> [...] in general, critical debates about developments in post-war American cinema have dealt with stylistic change only in a cursory, abstract, and unspecific fashion, quickly moving from observations about individual film examples to claims about fundamental shifts in the overall aesthetic and industrial system.[80]

For Krämer, these various conflicts over periodization are partially the result of how film history itself is conceived. While the approaches linked to production aesthetical considerations tend towards longer-term perspective, auteurist critics concentrate on a small group of directors, who are regarded as being at the center of a short-lived artistic "renaissance"[81].

Krämer addresses a whole series of important points here, regarding which my own approach also must take a position. Unfortunately, however, in his monograph published several years later on the same subject, he does not do justice to the demands formulated in his essay. This monograph argues primarily from the point of view of production aesthetics, and explains the changes characteristic of New Hollywood through corresponding changes in American society – a

---

78 Krämer: Post-classical Hollywood, pp. 300 – 301.

79 Krämer: Post-classical Hollywood, p. 303.

80 Krämer: Post-classical Hollywood, p. 307.

81 The alternative term Hollywood Renaissance already came into play in 1977 but was unable to gain wide acceptance and still carries conflicting connotations, see, for example, Diane Jacobs: Hollywood Renaissance, Cranbury 1977; Glenn Man: Radical Visions. American Film Renaissance 1967–1976, Westport 1994; Geoff King: New Hollywood Cinema. An Introduction, London 2002, pp. 11–48; Peter Krämer and Yannis Tzioumakis (eds.): The Hollywood Renaissance. Revisiting American Cinema's Most Celebrated Era, New York 2018. While Jacobs and Man bring their discussions into alignment with canonical auteurs and films, King essentially argues based on production aesthetics and uses the concept of renaissance to distinguish this period from a longer one that stretches all the way into the present. For a critique of the concept of renaissance (what is it that is allegedly being *re*born here?) see Lars Dammann: Kino im Aufbruch. New Hollywood 1967–1976, Marburg 2007, pp. 11–12.

relationship that consistently follows the logic of supply and demand. As a consequence, any view of the aesthetic autonomy of the individual films is lost, while their significance is derived simply from their commercial success:[82] successful film "models" are copied; though what exactly constitutes such a model is only defined in unsystematic fashion, or even trivially: Many successful films were based on novels, more films used pop songs on the soundtrack than previously, and successful actors were a key factor in films' success. Overall, a relatively incomplex model of the cinemagoer is utilized; Krämer works based on the assumption that cinemagoers endeavor to repeat the enjoyment they experienced watching films in the past and thus look for similar ones.[83] This amounts to a perfectly circular argument, which must regard any change in the area of cinematic expressivity as an anomaly.

Krämer's monograph is only one of the most recent in a long series of attempts to describe New Hollywood in terms of either its autonomy or its historical context. It is also a straightforward example of what Thomas Elsaesser has termed, in another essay on the historiography of New Hollywood, as a "canonical story."[84] Such stories function based on an understanding of Hollywood cinema as an industry, making the most important moments across its history the antitrust case of 1948, the arrival of television and the fall in cinema audiences as a result, and the restructuring of many studios at the end of the 1960s. From such a perspective, New Hollywood represents an exception in an already narrow (1967–1976) or even narrower (1969–1972) sense, read as either a failed intervention (from the standpoint of an ideological critique or rather cinephile perspective) or a phase of adaptation (as Elsaesser suggests and discusses in detail), which indirectly created the prerequisites for the sort of blockbuster cinema identified with the 1980s.

David Cook's worthy, comprehensive summary refers, for example, to the 1970s as an era of illusion, which came to an abrupt end on November 7, 1980, when Ronald Reagan was elected president:

First was the illusion of a liberal political consensus created by the antiwar movement, the Watergate scandal, and the subsequent resignation of Richard Nixon [...]. The second illusion, intermingled with the first, was that mainstream American movies might aspire to the

---

82 Peter Krämer: The New Hollywood. From BONNIE AND CLYDE to STAR WARS, London 2005, p. 4.

83 Krämer: The New Hollywood, p. 11.

84 Thomas Elsaesser: American Auteur Cinema. The Last – or First – Picture Show? In: id., Alexander Horwath, and Noel King (eds.): The Last Great American Picture Show. New Hollywood Cinema in the 1970s, Amsterdam 2004, pp. 37–69, here pp. 42–44.

sort of serious social or political content described above on a permanent basis. This prospect was seriously challenged when the blockbuster mentality took hold in Hollywood in the wake of JAWS (Steven Spielberg, 1975) and STAR WARS (George Lucas, 1977), and it was shattered by the epochal success of the Spielberg-Lucas juggernaut of the early Reagan years.[85]

A remarkable gesture of disappointment is used here to revoke the historical validity of an entire decade. Robert Phillip Kolker takes a more indifferent tone, stating New Hollywood's ideological failure from the point of view of cinephile film criticism: "During the late sixties and early seventies, some film [sic] questioned assumptions, as some directors became more independent and more in control of their work. In the eighties, American film once again became a great affirming force [...]."[86] Yet this indifferent tenor also seems to indicate a deep-seated disenchantment. What is often implied by such assessments is the lack of radicalism displayed even by the films at the heart of New Hollywood, a position that is particularly apparent in the work of James Bernardoni.[87] His version of New Hollywood, which comes across as essentially little more than a pale imitation of classical cinema, consists above all in listing all the fallacies to which newer films succumbed in relation to older ones. In his view, only their external look and feel was copied and burnished via new technologies; the substance was lost in the process.

This hypothesis of a supposed lack of radicalism (setting aside questions of normative value judgment) invokes a fundamental debate on the historiography of American cinema, also addressed by Krämer, sparked by the question of the extent to which one can even talk of a post-classical cinema. As Murray Smith remarks in an essay on this debate, the focus here is less on claiming that the classical Hollywood system remains entirely unchanged to this day (that is, in its aesthetic, production-economical, and socio-political aspects),[88] and more

---

85 David Cook: Lost Illusions. American Cinema in the Shadow of Watergate and Vietnam, 1970 – 1979, Berkeley 2000, pp. xv–xvi.

86 Robert Phillip Kolker: A Cinema of Loneliness. Penn, Kubrick, Scorsese, Spielberg, Altman (2nd Edition), New York/Oxford 1988, p. 14. In this second edition, Kolker goes as far as to replace the section on Francis Ford Coppola with one on Spielberg, as the former was not apparently able to fulfill the expectations placed on him: "Francis Ford Coppola's fall from effective filmmaking has been so great that I have replaced the chapter on his work with one on Steven Spielberg." ibid. p. x.

87 James Bernardoni: The New Hollywood. What the Movies Did with the New Freedoms of the Seventies, Jefferson, NC/London 1991.

88 See Smith: Theses on the Philosophy of Hollywood History. In: id., and Steve Neale (eds.): Contemporary Hollywood Cinema, London/New York 1998, pp. 3 – 20, here p. 5.

about debating the scale of any such changes. Whereby, Smith agrees with Krämer that: "It is not that change has not occurred, but that the scale of change has consistently been overestimated."[89]

From this kind of long-term perspective, (allegedly permanent) change ultimately becomes a characteristic of continuity. A paradigmatic model of this type of long-term perspective can also be found in the writings of David Bordwell, Kristin Thompson, and Janet Staiger.[90] They emphasize the ability of the Hollywood system to adapt to altered circumstances and/or to assimilate outside influences. Smith summarizes this standpoint as follows:

> From this point of view, historians of the 'New' or post-classical Hollywood, while correctly recognizing new phases or trends in product differentiation, are not warranted in positing a break with classicism. Indeed, the very regularity with which declarations of new epochs have been made, the sheer number of 'New Hollywoods' that one finds posited over the course of film history, recommends this more sober view: if things are always 'new', nothing is ever really new. There *is* a constant process of adjustment and adaptation to new circumstances, but this is an adaptation made on the basis of certain underlying and constant goals: the maximizing of profits through the production of classical narrative films. Rather than looking for a fundamental break between classicism and a putative post-classicism, we would do better to look for smaller-scale changes and shifts, at both the institutional and aesthetic levels, within a more broadly continuous system of American commercial filmmaking.[91]

Further representatives of this point of view include film historians such as Robert Ray[92] or Geoff King,[93] who see no essential changes exhibited in the cinema of New Hollywood, according to my historical grasp of the period (1967–1980), when compared to classical cinema. The films are primarily viewed from the standpoint of the influences visible in them (above all from the Nouvelle Vague and classical Hollywood).[94] Yet even the treatment of these actual

---

89 Smith: Theses on the Philosophy of Hollywood History, p. 14.

90 See David Bordwell, Janet Staiger, and Kristin Thompson: Classical Hollywood Cinema. Film Style and Mode of Production to 1960, London 1988. See also Bordwell: On the History of Film Style, Cambridge 1997; Thompson: Storytelling in the New Hollywood. Understanding Classical Narrative Technique, Cambridge 1999.

91 Smith: Theses on the Philosophy of Hollywood History, p. 14.

92 See Robert B. Ray: A Certain Tendency of the Hollywood Cinema, 1930–1980, New Jersey 1985.

93 See Geoff King: New Hollywood Cinema.

94 A particularly crass example of this approach is provided by Noël Carroll: The Future of Allusion. Hollywood in the Seventies (and Beyond). In: October, Vol. 20 (Spring 1982), pp. 51–81. Carroll primarily uses the concept of allusion to discredit the artistic value of the films of New Hollywood. According to him, these films invoke older ones in order to ennoble themselves or to

or alleged influences is not analyzed as a poetic approach in its own right, but rather explained away in view of commercial necessities: the radical techniques employed by the cinema of the Nouvelle Vague, for example, were supposedly watered-down for the more conservative American market.[95] Yet it is not sufficient to just demonstrate or suggest influences. The (indisputable) fact, for example, that the end of MCMABE & MRS. MILLER (Robert Altman 1971) references the end of TIREZ SUR LE PIANISTE (François Truffaut, France 1960), hardly helps to explain the specific atmosphere of Altman's film;[96] a description is needed here that focuses on the manner of the images' sensory appearance, a description including all the various factors that remain unaddressed when the emphasis is merely on tracing lines of iconographic tradition. It should also be remembered that such lines can lead in the wrong direction – sometimes only slightly, but sometimes significantly. When Elsaesser, for example, traces the end of TWO-LANE BLACKTOP (Monte Hellman 1971) back to the end of LE DÉPART (Jerzy Skolimowski, France 1967),[97] while Hellman himself talks of PERSONA (Ingmar Bergman, Sweden 1966) as his model,[98] then the difference is perhaps not so decisive, even if important tactile elements of TWO-LANE BLACKTOP are possibly obscured by Elsaesser's reasoning. But when Robert Ray derives the use of slow motion in BONNIE AND CLYDE, EASY RIDER (Dennis Hopper 1969), and THE WILD BUNCH (Sam Peckinpah 1969) from films such as JULES ET JIM (François Truffaut, France 1962) or even ZÉRO DE CONDUITE (Jean Vigo, France 1933),[99] it represents an emphatic distortion of film history; to say nothing of the fact that just referring to the "actual" influence in question (in this case Kurosawa,

---

satisfy the personal obsessions of the new filmmakers. It is only the shell of these old films that is being reproduced in the process; this cinema is entirely dependent on references to other films to generate "genuine" emotional effects. Carroll's polemic ignores the range of different treatments of film history which characterize New Hollywood and which are to be demonstrated over the course of the present work.

95 See, for example, Kolker: A Cinema of Loneliness, p. 29; Ray: A Certain Tendency of the Hollywood Cinema, p. 350.

96 See Hauke Lehmann: Becoming-Texture: New Hollywood Melancholy in MCCABE & MRS. MILLER. In: mediaesthetics No. 1 (2016), URL: https://www.mediaesthetics.org/index.php/mae/article/view/43/144, last accessed March 7th, 2019.

97 See Elsaesser: The Pathos of Failure. American Films in the 1970s. Notes on the Unmotivated Hero [1975]. In: id., Horwath, and King (eds.): The Last Great American Picture Show, pp. 279–292, here p. 292.

98 See Kent Jones: "The Cylinders Were Whispering My Name." The Films of Monte Hellman. In: Elsaesser, Horwath, and King (eds.): The Last Great American Picture Show, pp. 165–194, here p. 184.

99 See Ray: A Certain Tendency of the Hollywood Cinema, pp. 288–295.

for Penn and Peckinpah at least) hardly does justice to the innovative character of these American films anyway.

In American research in particular, the aesthetic aspect is nearly always conceived of as dependent on the context of production, a tendency most marked in the work of Justin Wyatt, whose model of the high concept film, without this organizing principle, would be in danger of merely enumerating arbitrary stylistic characteristics.[100] However important and correct it might be to keep sight of this interdependency between money and aesthetics, overemphasizing it can create a warped view of the very films that generated talk of New Hollywood in the first place. With this in mind, it is too convenient a short cut to confuse the institutional weakness of studios with the weakness of the genre system: both are represented differently within their respective historical dynamics, concern different time-periods, have different causes, and have different effects on the films themselves. Both are also not identical to, nor do they simply mirror, the social upheavals of the 1960s and 70s. This is the core insight from which an affective history of New Hollywood must begin. The three modes of affectivity which are the subject of this book create their very own histories by referring to and modulating ever specific paradigms of aesthetic experience.

A similar diagnosis also applies to the apparent end of New Hollywood: there is something premature about identifying the commercial success of, say, STAR WARS or JAWS as the end of the New Hollywood "experiment." Films made between 1975 and 1980 not corresponding to this pattern are quickly declared anomalies, as in this summary by Smith:

> Although some 'arty' projects continued to be supported by the studios into the late 1970s – DAYS OF HEAVEN (1978), APOCALYPSE NOW (1979), ALL THAT JAZZ (1979), HEAVEN'S GATE (1980) – the direction of the industry had been set by the monumental success of those 'hyperbolic simulations of Hollywood B-movies', JAWS [...] and STAR WARS.'[101]

While, on the one hand, any sort of descriptive precision for distinguishing between films is thrown out of the window in favor of popular critical labels ("arty"), two individual films are attributed the power of changing the historical course of an entire cinema, on the other.[102] It would seem as if the balance of overemphasis has tipped to the other side here.

---

100 See Justin Wyatt: High Concept. Movies and Marketing in Hollywood, Austin 1994.

101 Smith: Theses on the Philosophy of Hollywood History, pp. 11–12.

102 For a critique of this idea, see Peter Lev, who notes two things: first, the emphasis on action and speed in JAWS und STAR WARS is not an exclusive feature of these films, but can already be found at the beginning of the 1970s. Second, Lev also emphasizes that other poetic projects also

There is one line of research in the debate surrounding New Hollywood that turns such talk of a long-term perspective against its initiators, in order to apply it to the canonical status of several New Hollywood films; an argument that operates as an apologia in the broadest sense. Prominent examples here include the monographs by Glenn Man,[103] Todd Berliner,[104] and Jonathan Kirshner,[105] and, to a lesser extent, by Lars Dammann,[106] who attempts to retain a more or less non-partisan perspective, as far as the critical assessment of the period is concerned. When discussing the selection of films analyzed (around 16), for example, Man explicitly comments: "It may be too obvious to say that my choice of each film relies on its status as a classic of the period."[107] While this certainly does not lack irony, it is also indicative of a canonical approach that applies the concept of the "classical" to an often decidedly anti-classical aesthetic, without seeing this as a problem. In this way, a whole new continuity is created, which, when taken to the extreme, potentially results in a negation of film history.[108] Correspondingly, it is no surprise that the periodization of New Hollywood included in these works is not only superficially justified, but also sometimes highly arbitrary, such as the decision by Berliner to exclude not just the end of the 1970s from his corpus but also the end of the 1960s: "The earlier group [before 1970], however, presages a movement that hadn't yet taken hold in mainstream American cinema and the later movies [after 1977] are more isolated examples of a kind of film that starts to peter out about the time of ROCKY (1976) and STAR WARS (1977)."[109]

The logical consequence of this approach is that the criteria used to attest the purported novelty of New Hollywood end up being extremely vague. Both Man and Berliner work from a dichotomous distinction between mainstream,

---

coexisted alongside STAR WARS towards the end of the 1970s. See Lev: American Films of the 70s, pp. 167–168.

103 See Man: Radical Visions.

104 See Todd Berliner: Hollywood Incoherent. Narration in Seventies Cinema, Austin 2010.

105 See Jonathan Kirshner: Hollywood's Last Golden Age. Politics, Society, and the Seventies Film in America, New York 2013.

106 See Lars Dammann: Kino im Aufbruch.

107 Man: Radical Visions, p. 5.

108 "The 'appreciation' or apology strives to cover over revolutionary moments in the course of history. For it, what matters is the reconstruction of continuity. It lays stress only on those elements of the work which have already become part of its influence." See Walter Benjamin, Lloyd Spencer, and Mark Harrington: Central Park. In: New German Critique, No. 34 (Winter, 1985), pp. 32–58, p 33.

109 Berliner: Hollywood Incoherent, p. 6. Lev also only begins his investigation from 1969 onwards.

narrative cinema and art cinema, a backdrop used to frame New Hollywood as an example of the former moving towards the latter, or rather incorporating certain principles of so-called art cinema.[110] The actual analysis does not, however, reflect this hypothesis and continues to proceed as if recapitulating the plot and describing the characters and their actions in psychological terms did justice to the films – as if the focus were still on the standard case of classical narrative cinema, postulated by neo-formalist film theory. One also looks in vain for a single, overarching idea about the unique character of this cinema. Glenn Man restricts himself to a claim of originality, which he does not specify any further. For Berliner, the key feature of the films he analyzes is their current popularity, which he proves amongst other things by pointing to the scores they have received on the Internet Movie Database (IMDb). Looking at such approaches makes criticism of the proliferation of "New Hollywoods" feel understandable, as the criteria for a non-normative description of New Hollywood as a period in American film history, which could be distinguished from both classical cinema and the cinema of the 1980s alike, are still widely lacking.

Peter Lev's study[111] sets itself apart from the canonical approach by connecting the specific complexity that he postulates for the films to a film historical hypothesis. According to Lev, this complexity does not just extend to individual films, but concerns the cinema of the 1970s in its entirety. This means both the "sheer diversity of ideological and aesthetic approaches,"[112] and the fact that these approaches are also correlated in diverse, often contradictory fashion. Against this backdrop, Lev emphasizes that the generally accepted dramatic structure of this period of film history – an initial phase of experimentation, followed by the dominance of the so-called "movie brats," which finally leads to commercial consolidation and the end of any such experimentation – can only be put together if a whole series of tendencies are ignored which can be observed over the course of this process (and which can neither be easily incorporated into a teleology nor into a functionalistic model).[113]

Lev's study is thus not only characterized by the fact that he deals with a large number of films, but also in that he takes films into account that normally fall through the cracks of canonization, such as COOLEY HIGH (Michael Schultz 1975), LEADBELLY (Gordon Parks Sr. 1976), BETWEEN THE LINES (Joan Micklin Sil-

---

110 Berliner's work can at least be praised for the fact that it is restricted to only a few examples and thus attains a degree of precision in its description, while Man only has a few pages at his disposal for the films he deals with and Dammann's overview even fewer.
111 Lev: American Films of the 70s.
112 Lev: American Films of the 70s, p. xvii.
113 Lev: American Films of the 70s, pp. xviii–xxii and pp. 181–183.

ver 1977), and GIRLFRIENDS (Claudia Weill 1978). Yet this important contribution to the debate's differentiation has certain downsides. The broad grasp of the subject – a total of 40 (!) films are discussed – generates the methodological problem that little space is available for the analysis of individual films. Plot descriptions and brief critical assessments are thus often all that remains; valuable observations are seldom pursued any further.

This problem of adequate representation highlights a more fundamental difficulty, namely the widespread tendency for the content of the films to form the main point of orientation. This leads to the creation of such categories as hippie, vigilante, or feminist films, which offer relatively few insights with respect to the purported originality of New Hollywood, merely replacing old genre descriptions with new ones with little systematic justification for doing so. A similar approach can be observed when films are grouped according to their alleged political orientation.[114] The decisive question here is whether this range of categories is further justified from a formal standpoint. This question also remains unanswered in Lev's work due to the lack of corresponding theoretical foundation. The historically distinct character of New Hollywood cannot be grasped in such fashion.

The Incoherent Text

Even when an effort is made to emphasize the specificity of New Hollywood, there are still repeated echoes of negative determination in talk of conflict,[115] incoherence,[116] and contradictions;[117] my own work is no exception. It is by no means my intention to question the fact that deviations of this kind do indeed exist. But it is not sufficient to simply state that a degree of deviation exists; such deviation must be examined in its own right and according to its own standards.

With this in mind, one work should be highlighted that takes a step in this direction: Robin Wood's groundbreaking study *Hollywood from Vietnam to Reagan*. Wood is rightly seen as one of the first critics to consistently subject the cinema of New Hollywood to serious intellectual engagement, taking a critical perspective on society that draws on Marxist theories, on the one hand, and

---

114 See, for example, Ray: A Certain Tendency of the Hollywood Cinema, p. 301.

115 See the subtitle of Lev's monograph: Conflicting Visions.

116 See Robin Wood: Hollywood from Vietnam to Reagan... and Beyond [1986], New York 2003, within it: The Incoherent Text. Narrative in the 70s, pp. 41–62.

117 See Alexander Horwath: A Walking Contradiction (Partly Truth and Partly Fiction). In: id., Elsaesser, and King (eds.): The Last Great American Picture Show, pp. 83–105.

Freudian ones, on the other. Wood can take true credit for recognizing the central role of the modern horror film in the cinema of the time; an insight I will address at length in the final chapter of the present work, where the focus will be on the newly created forms of expression, including the new horror film, alongside the road movie and police film. The tendency towards psychoanalytical interpretations of this genre, and above all its protagonist: the monster, remains influential to this day and can, to a large extent, be attributed to Wood's writings.

My primary interest here is, however, another idea, namely the concept of the "incoherent text" established by Wood.[118] This term describes Wood's belief that a large number of the films of the 1970s cannot (any longer) be read and understood in a coherent manner: they throw up irresolvable contradictions, which cannot simply be put down to plot holes but rather challenge the entire way in which films create their worlds: "I am concerned with films that don't wish to be, or to appear, incoherent but are so nonetheless, works in which the drive toward the ordering of experience has been visibly defeated."[119] Although, to point out this incoherence, Wood mainly argues on the level of plot and the psychology of the characters, the way in which he arrives at the theme alludes to an idea that is relevant for my argument: namely the conflict between energy and its repression, which has always characterized Hollywood cinema:

> The American cinema has always celebrated energy, a tendency one normally associates with the Romantic; the energy, however, can only be celebrated when it has undergone a very thorough process of repression, revision, sublimation, displacement. The Classicism of Hollywood was always to a great degree artificially imposed and repressive, the forcing of often extremely recalcitrant drives into the mold of a dominant ideology typified at its simplest and crudest, but most clarified and regulated, by the Hays Office Code. The need for the code [...] testifies eloquently, of course, to the strength and persistence of the forces it was designed to check: its requirements, passively accepted by studios and audiences, corresponded neither to the films people wanted to make nor to the films people wanted to see. Insofar as Classicism stands for control and Romanticism for release, the Hollywood cinema expresses in virtually all its products, but with widely varying emphases, the most extraordinary tension between the Classical and the Romantic that can be imagined.[120]

Wood describes Hollywood cinema as a dynamic constellation, a constant back and forth between pressure and counter pressure. Wood locates the energy, which must be held in check by institutions such as the Hays Code, in the wishes

---

118 Wood: Hollywood from Vietnam to Reagan, p. 41. Berliner also seems to refer to this term in his book, albeit without making explicit reference to Wood.
119 Wood: Hollywood from Vietnam to Reagan, p. 42.
120 Wood: Hollywood from Vietnam to Reagan, p. 43.

and desires of spectators and filmmakers – obviously with Freud in mind. In the 1960s, this energy reaches a level that overwhelms the system's possibility to control it: "By the mid-60s, the circumstances that had made possible (in LIBERTY VALANCE, in RIO BRAVO, in PSYCHO) the transmutation of ideological conflict, such as necessarily exists in any Hollywood movie, into a significantly realized thematic, no longer existed."[121] To stay with this image, the *de facto* end of the code released a large amount of energy, leading classical cinema's already tenuous balance into open revolt. The concept of incoherence, which, in the work of Berliner, is relegated to an arbitrary measure of cinephilic quality, thus attains both a theoretical and (cultural) historical relevance. Wood names TAXI DRIVER (Martin Scorsese 1976), LOOKING FOR MR. GOODBAR (Richard Brooks 1977), and CRUISING (William Friedkin 1980) as particularly charged examples of incoherent texts. Incoherence is produced, for example, when Scorsese's film is unable to clearly distance itself from its protagonist; when LOOKING FOR MR. GOODBAR makes no obvious declaration on feminism; or when CRUISING avoids positioning itself clearly regarding the conflict between hetero- and homosexual forms of socialization.

In relation to the last two films, in particular, Wood's early insistence on their narrative, psychological, and ideological complexity (which runs counter to and against their original assessment, within critical discourses, as misogynistic and homophobic, respectively) represents a significant step in the historical engagement with New Hollywood. Yet, regardless of how astute his approach is, it still ultimately remains tied to questions of interpretation and the effort required to translate these films into a political statement: they are incoherent because they "don't know what they want to say."[122] Wood thus somewhat undermines the implications of his own argumentation, based on the idea that art, in general, is geared toward the ordering of experience.[123] My objection here is that experience encompasses far more than just political and ideological views and, at the same time, cannot be grasped directly through propositional statements. The ordering of experience, in particular, cannot be equated with the elimination of contradictions. In this sense, order and coherence are not the same thing. The majority of the following discussions consist in describing films as blueprints for ordering experience that not only contain contradictions but also implicate the spectator's own position with regard to how these contradictions unfold.

---

121 Wood: Hollywood from Vietnam to Reagan, pp. 43–44.
122 Wood: Hollywood from Vietnam to Reagan, p. 42.
123 Wood: Hollywood from Vietnam to Reagan, p. 41.

The reason Wood equates coherence and order is that he does not pursue his own model to its logical conclusion: he forgets the energy (of motion) made manifest by the interplay of pressure and counter pressure which had formed his starting point (a figure of thought that appears to make his ideas compatible with more radical approaches[124]). When he, for example, distinguishes between subtle graduations of irony at work at the end of TAXI DRIVER,[125] he does not understand irony to be a dynamic principle for the dramatization of affect, but rather as the fixing of "actual" meaning, which deviates from those propositionally constituted statements that can seemingly be extrapolated from what happens in the plot. Questioning the presence of irony thus becomes a rigid either/or, used to decide on which side the critical assessment falls. Yet the very essence of irony is to *destabilize* meaning by introducing a specific temporality into the process of perception. In this manner, it also directly affects the position of the spectator. According to this perspective, the ever-growing doubt regarding the ironic character of what is depicted, as described by Wood, would constitute a dramatization of affect in its own right. Once again, Merleau-Ponty's argument regarding the relation between movement and the object in motion is effective here: irony is not to be understood as a static quality, but rather as a style,[126] as a specific way of being in the world and thus also in motion. In cinema, this style itself is not necessarily tied to the semantic logic of psychoanalysis, but potentially independent of it, as Félix Guattari explains:

> Commercial cinema is nothing else but a simple, inexpensive drug. Its unconscious action is profound. More perhaps than that of psychoanalysis. First of all, at the level of the session. Cinematographic performance affects subjectivity. It affects the personological indi-

---

124 Wood's argumentation is not necessarily beholden to its Freudian foundation; it becomes more convincing if it is linked to other considerations, made at the same time, about the relationship between cinema, desire, and the energy of desire: Félix Guattari's *The Poor Man's Couch:* "Film has become a gigantic machine for modelling the social, while psychoanalysis will forever remain a small cottage industry reserved for selected elites." Guattari: The Poor Man's Couch. In: id.: Chaosophy. Texts and Interviews 1972–1977, pp. 257–267, here p. 258. Cinema's potential for mobilizing and reproducing the subjectivisation process, as described by Guattari, is at the very heart of the idea presented here of splitting the spectator. On the relationship between Guattari's discussions and the theoretical perspective developed here, see Kappelhoff: Matrix der Gefühle, pp. 289–291.
125 Wood: Hollywood from Vietnam to Reagan, pp. 48–49.
126 Here, it is to be noted once again that the concept of style I am using must be strictly set apart from the meaning it carries in everyday usage, whereby style is seen as revealing an authorial presence. See, for example, Kolker: A Cinema of Loneliness, p. 9, or Man: Radical Visions, p. 2. This latter usage of style also carries the danger of trivializing the fact of aesthetic innovation by relating it to a director's personal preferences.

viduation of enunciation and develops a very particular mode of conscience. Without the support of the other's existence, subjectivation tends to become hallucinatory; it no longer concentrates on one subject, but explodes on a multiplicity of poles even when it fixes itself on one character.[127]

The dynamic of such an explosion "into a multiplicity of poles" encapsulates the idea of splitting the spectator. The three affective modes analyzed in this book thus represent three different possibilities for shaping this dynamic. Therein, they directly address the problem of producing the new, also suggested by Deleuze, when he writes that, while "affect is independent of all determinate space-time," it is nonetheless "created in a history which produces it as the expressed and the expression of space or a time, of an epoch or a milieu (this is why the affect is the 'new' and new affects are ceaselessly created, notably by the work of art)."[128]

The New in New Hollywood

A word here regarding the use of the concept of "classical" and, in particular, "classical Hollywood cinema": I am well aware of the danger of reducing cinema before 1967 to a monolithic block and one of my concerns is to, in fact, emphasize the dynamics of this older cinema's development. I would, therefore, suggest the concept primarily be understood as a function of marking a historical crisis: "classical" thus refers less to the cinema before 1967 in its entirety, but rather serves as a starting point for exploring the diverse, often radical tendencies toward revision characterizing the cinema of New Hollywood. Over the course of the present work, by tracing the shockwaves produced by this upheaval in detail, a much more differentiated picture of classical cinema emerges implicitly, positioned in relation to these innovations. The concept of the classical thus does not establish a dichotomy, but rather makes it potentially possible to unfold hidden perspectives contained within this period, keeping in mind that these are only in effect wherever they appear concretely. Understood in this way, the classical thus also describes the specific dynamic of creation of generic forms, not some sort of pre-established mental horizon, beyond which the post-classical already awaits: "Such a way of approaching a work would not deny the figure of classicism itself, but would understand that the specificity of specific classical instances mandates understanding [...] classicism as difference, not as something entirely pre-

---

127 Guattari: The Poor Man's Couch, p. 264.
128 Deleuze: Cinema 1, p. 101.

determined."[129] In this way, it is possible to grasp both the ongoing development of Hollywood cinema alongside a clear discontinuity, decidedly related to this regime of continuity, first made manifest in selected films from 1967 onwards.

If, in this manner, one avoids describing classical genre cinema as a rigid, traditional system of rules, it becomes equally clear that the sheer violence of the upheaval of 1967 can not only be grasped as a rebellion against this system and thus, drawing on it alone, explained *ex negativo*. Rather, a whole series of additional factors must be taken into consideration. The following chapters go into considerable detail about precisely how this relationship should be conceived.

Ultimately, the debate in film research thus boils down to one, central question: what is new about New Hollywood? This question is connected to another, superordinate question: how can the new be conceived of in film history anyway? Two paths tend to dominate the previous discussions, neither of which leads to our desired end. The first allows the new to be merged with its origin,[130] reducing films to their influences and assessing them from a normative perspective, determined by their deviation from or agreement with existing lines of tradition. The second grounds the new in the visionary power of the filmmaker and thus tends to isolate it from its historical context.

One frequently expressed criticism of New Hollywood is that the films failed to reveal a viable alternative to the classical genre systems and to the classical model of formally closed narration.[131] Instead, innovations supposedly exhausted themselves in manipulating or undermining the old forms, with which, in keeping with Audre Lorde's well-known adage, one will never be able to dismantle the master's house.

In my view, however, the genre/genre negation or narration/anti-narration dichotomy is misleading. It goes without saying that a narrative can be tracked in these films (for which fiction films is that not that case?) and, since they do not exist in a historical vacuum, regardless of how directly or obliquely, they ob-

---

129 William D. Routt: [Review] De la figure en général et du corps en particulier: l'invention figurative au cinéma. In: Screening the Past, No. 9 (2000), URL: http://www.screeningthepast.com/2014/12/de-la-figure-en-general-et-du-corps-en-particulier-linvention-figurative-au-cinema/, last accessed March 11th, 2019.

130 This approach is based on precisely the same misunderstanding that Bergson demonstrates in his discussion of possibility and reality. See Bergson: The Possible and the Real.

131 See Neale: New Hollywood Cinema, pp. 120–121; Ray: A Certain Tendency of the Hollywood Cinema, p. 294; David Cook is even of the view that the 1970s are actually characterized by a return to genre cinema, see Cook: Lost Illusions, pp. 159–299.

viously reference the genre system, which has left its mark on the American film landscape since the 1930s. Linking the radicalism (in other words, the critical value) of the films of New Hollywood to the extent to which they correspond to a modernist ideal of auteur cinema (of the kind implemented in the critical treatment of the Nouvelle Vague or Neo-Realism, for example[132]) merely side-steps the actual problem. This creates another circular argument: as the films are examined before the backdrop of classical genres, one can only ever arrive at relative degrees of deviation or agreement.

The new can, however, only be conceived of when serious attention is given to the problem of movement and, accordingly, when the points of reference for the investigation are not set out in advance – if one thus allows for the possibility that the primary goal of the films is *not* to do away with genre or even narration. If the debate is dominated by the view that the new in New Hollywood is overstated, this is, to put it bluntly, simply an indication that one is looking for the new in the wrong place. This brings us back to the opening of the introduction: the narrative and genre-related dimensions of a film are both ultimately based on the processes I am interested in exploring in the present work; *it is at this base level of film experience where the transformation takes place* that characterizes New Hollywood as a distinct film historical period. The effect of the shift represented by New Hollywood is, therefore, at once subtler and more fundamental than generally assumed, for it has an impact on both the level of narration *and* the classical genre system. Yet the sort of secondary effects at issue here are far harder to systematize, visible to a certain extent in the proliferation of often overlapping, contradictory categories and sub-categories one comes across in the research (road movie,[133] buddy movie,[134] police film,[135] vigilante,[136] blaxploitation,[137] hippie horror film,[138] acid western,[139] neo-noir,[140] to name just a few).

---

132 Leo Braudy points out that this modernist ideal is itself a myth. See Braudy: The Sacraments of Genre. Coppola, De Palma, Scorsese. In: Film Quarterly, Vol. 39, No. 3 (Spring 1986), pp. 17–28, here pp. 18–19.

133 See Elsaesser: The Pathos of Failure.

134 See Wood: Hollywood from Vietnam to Reagan, pp. 202–218.

135 See Todd Berliner: The Genre Film as Booby Trap. 1970s Genre Bending and THE FRENCH CONNECTION. In: Cinema Journal, Vol. 40, No. 3 (Spring 2001), pp. 25–46.

136 See Elsaesser: The Pathos of Failure, pp. 282–283.

137 See Novotny Lawrence: Blaxploitation Films of the 1970s. Blackness and Genre, New York 2008.

138 See Matt Becker: A Point of Little Hope. Hippie Horror Films and the Politics of Ambivalence. In: The Velvet Light Trap, No. 57 (Spring 2006), pp. 42–59.

139 See Jonathan Rosenbaum: Dead Man, London 2000, pp. 47–62.

140 See Mark T. Conard (ed.): The Philosophy of Neo-Noir, Lexington 2007.

Keeping in mind the radicalism of this upheaval, the present work opposes the hypothesis that New Hollywood represents an exception and, in particular, that there was a return to neo-classicism around 1980, which cashed in, as it were, on the achievements of the 1970s. The present work insists, to the contrary, that the 1967 rupture not only could never be undone, but also that the phase around 1980 has to be grasped as an additional transformation, which took this rupture as its starting point. From this perspective, however low its standing may be in cinephile circles, the cinema of the 1980s cannot be understood without the cinema of New Hollywood. To access this historical dynamic, it is now necessary to explore in greater detail what exactly is new about New Hollywood.

Shock and Freedom: Affective Modes

Set against the processes that will form the focus of the following chapters, questions of genre assignment and narration are actually secondary. My primary interest is the change in the affective relationship between film and spectator, a change expressed in the establishment of particular affective modes. These modes correspond to neither classical genres nor to newer, hybrid forms: rather these forms emerge via combinations of these modes.[141] Modes are not categories, according to which films can be classified[142] but are instead in each case realized in the concrete act of film perception.

Seen in this way, the concept of affective modes has both theoretical and historical components. In theoretical terms, it describes a specific way of ordering the relationship between movement and emotion. This means that the modes of suspense, paranoia, and melancholy are not themselves emotions, but rather organize how the spectator's emotions connect to the audiovisual stagings employed by the film. My main focus here (via the concept of affectivity) is on the dynamic unfolding in time, by means of which the film form is transformed into concrete, spectatorial feeling. The respective modes each provide different conditions for this dynamic unfolding.

The link to the historical is provided by the notion that these modes produce this dynamic differently than the affectivity of classical Hollywood cinema. The

---

141 It is only when the new forms are derived from these combinations that the difference between New Hollywood and classical cinema can be grasped. Otherwise, the argument that there have always been road movies, police films, horror films etc. still very much applies.

142 Amongst other things, this avoids the often questionable practice of categorizing films according to politically "left-wing" or "right-wing" cycles as suggested by various historians, see, for example, Ray: A Certain Tendency of the Hollywood Cinema, pp. 298–299 and p. 328.

modes cannot produce orientation with regard to content or ideology and do not follow the internal periodization suggested for New Hollywood: the suspense mode, for example, determines both Steven Spielberg's DUEL (1972) and Robert Altman's 3 WOMEN (1977). Paranoia is not just to be found in ROSEMARY'S BABY (Roman Polanski 1968), but also in PUNISHMENT PARK (Peter Watkins 1971), while melancholy ultimately pervades New Hollywood cinema all the way from THE GRADUATE (Mike Nichols 1967) to THE DEER HUNTER (Michael Cimino 1978). This allows for – and in fact demands – the suspension of the majority of critical demarcations thus far applied to investigating and assessing the films of New Hollywood. Instead of such demarcations, attention can now be focused on cinematic movement as the decisive condition for the spectator's emotional experience. In this way, the model of affective modes indeed becomes a way of rewriting film history – as an affective history.

So, what is new about New Hollywood? There is no one answer; rather, the answer is immanent to the multiplicity of historical, aesthetic, and poetic relations the films themselves establish to other images. That is, it lies in the ways these films allow and enable us to think film history.

2 Suspense:
Forms of Cinematic Thinking

2.1 Theoretical Basis

The first of the three affective modes at the heart of this investigation is suspense. Unlike the two other modes, paranoia and melancholy, suspense is a concept already well established in film theory, which does not, however, seem to possess a great deal of relevance outside of film aesthetical contexts. With this in mind, it does not make a great deal of sense to start by striving to establish a cultural historical connection to the state of society in the USA in the 1970s, as is so essential for paranoia and melancholy. The focus in these opening remarks must instead be on ascertaining the prerequisites for an affect poetics of suspense in New Hollywood in theoretical terms. The work of Alfred Hitchcock, including his comments in interviews, forms a central point of reference here, both with respect to film studies research as well as the films of New Hollywood themselves. We are thus concerned with a strand of cinema that creates its own independent poetological genealogy.[1]

There is also a gap in research, decisive for us here: while Hitchcock is widely recognized as an important forerunner of New Hollywood,[2] this connection either lacks theoretical substance in relation to the concept of suspense or, as in the work of Deleuze, it actually leads away from precisely this historical object: American cinema openly drawing on Hitchcock. In neither case is the phenomenon of the suspense mode in 1970s cinema treated as an independent theoretical or historical problem.

There are two main reasons for this: first, the transformation of the classical genre system has yet to bring about an update in the necessary critical vocabulary. For the films addressed here, this means that they are grasped either as belonging to some altered form of the horror genre, such as in the work of Robin Wood,[3] or attempts are made to do justice to them by creating new hybrid cate-

---

1 For the concept of genealogy, see Michel Foucault: Nietzsche, Genealogy, History. In: The Foucault Reader, edited by Paul Rabinow, New York 1984, pp. 76–100, in particular pp. 83–91. For the relationship between genealogy and film history, see Kappelhoff: Matrix der Gefühle, pp. 19–20.

2 See Robin Wood: Hollywood from Vietnam to Reagan, pp. 44, 78 and 86; Thomas Schatz: Old Hollywood/New Hollywood. Ritual, Art, and Industry, Ann Arbor 1983, p. 22; Deleuze: Cinema 1, pp. 200–211.

3 See Wood: Hollywood from Vietnam to Reagan, pp. 85–119.

https://doi.org/10.1515/9783110580761-003

gories and sub-genres. For example, CARRIE (Brian De Palma 1976), the subject of analysis in this chapter, is referred to by Pauline Kael as a "lyrical thriller"[4] – a legitimate attempt to categorize the film based on how its complex emotional impact renders traditional categories largely meaningless. Yet the fact that this film and others like it actively subvert the classical categorial systems, and use suspense as a means of doing so, can only be gleaned indirectly from such statements.

Second, the emergence of New Hollywood is historically linked to the appropriation and redefinition of Truffaut's concept of the *auteur* by Andrew Sarris and other film critics after him.[5] In line with this new auteur theory's religiously canonical approach, references to particular patterns and directorial techniques from Hitchcock's films can be rapidly declared as quotes, homages, or plagiarisms, such that any analytical exploration of the actual affect-poetic implications of each respective technique is eclipsed by the glow of superficial recognition. Put briefly, "Hitchcock" as a discursive element thus takes the place of suspense.

Among the filmmakers of New Hollywood, Brian De Palma felt the effects of this trend most acutely, with his deliberately overemphatic attempts to subvert such processes of recognition generating a severe backlash.[6] When, in the following, CARRIE is analyzed as one of De Palma's most important films and a paradigmatic example of the function of suspense in New Hollywood cinema, the goal is not to rehabilitate De Palma, a task which others have already taken upon themselves for some time.[7] The focus is equally not on looking for

---

4 Pauline Kael: The Curse. In: The New Yorker, November 22nd, 1976, pp. 177–183, here p. 177.
5 See John Caughie (ed.): Theories of Authorship [1981], London/New York 2001, pp. 61–67.
6 The following comments may as well be representative for an entire branch of American film writing focused on De Palma's work "[...] the director has made an entire career of imitating earlier movies, most notably [...] those of his idol Hitchcock. Like Hitch, De Palma is famed for his elegant camera movements, shock cutting, use of lurid colour (especially red), and meticulously staged set-pieces of violent action – in short, technique – but unlike the master he lacks originality and ideas. [...] There is a cold, clinical misanthropy (and indeed, misogyny) to much of De Palma's work, evident in his readiness to subordinate his thinly drawn characters to flashy visual effect." Geoff Andrew: The Director's Vision. A Concise Guide to the Art of 250 Great Filmmakers, Chicago 1999, p. 59. It goes without saying that more substantial statements on De Palma's alleged plagiarism and misogyny can be found, even if these also jump to the same sort of premature conclusions collected here in concentrated form.
7 One of the first American critics to deal with De Palma's oeuvre independently is Robin Wood. See Wood: Hollywood from Vietnam to Reagan, pp. 120–143. See also Eyal Peretz: Becoming Visionary. Brian De Palma's Cinematic Education of the Senses, Stanford 2008, pp. 19–20, pp. 184–185, and pp. 188–189; Chris Dumas even goes as far as putting the rejection of De Palma in academic discourse down to structural reasons and those relating to the history of aca-

and qualifying the references to Hitchcock's oeuvre in De Palma's film – above all to YOUNG AND INNOCENT (1937) and PSYCHO (1960) – but rather to draw on the affect-poetic principles of suspense, realized in these films and others, to derive how CARRIE positions the spectator in a unique manner.[8] This corresponds to the film's approach, in that (much like other representatives of the suspense mode in New Hollywood) it does not so much reference other films as part of a pre-existing film history, but rather isolates and adapts the various expressive operations and figurations they contain.[9] The result is a sort of abstract version of film history, which proceeds based on the idea of *cinematic thinking* as a form of dialogue between films. Cinematic thinking does not refer here to the incorporation of philosophical concepts, but rather how reflexivity unfolds as an experience for the spectator. Involving the spectator and his or her emotional reactions in the cinematic process itself is the key business of suspense. The goal of this reflexivity is less concerned with recognizing allusions and references and more about modifying the conditions that determine the relationship between film and spectator. When, say, CARRIE references YOUNG AND INNOCENT, this reference is to be understood as the modification of a highly specific manner of directing the spectator's attention. The main focus of the analysis of CARRIE will thus address how its notorious references to other films generate an entirely unique quality of feeling during the concrete act of perception, which is further characteristic of the cinema of New Hollywood of a whole. An adequate concept of suspense must, however, first be developed to this end.

The State of Research on Suspense

Since the 1990s, in particular, we can observe an increase in studies on suspense in film, although the majority of the research published to this end stems from

---

demia, yet then gets bogged down for his own part in inaccuracies and generalizations. See Dumas: Un-American Psycho. Brian De Palma and the Political Invisible, Chicago 2012. For a more measured assessment of De Palma's current critical status see Adrian Martin's review of Dumas's book: To Wax Zizekian. On *Un-American Psycho: Brian De Palma and the Political Invisible*. In: Screening the Past, July 2012, URL: http://www.screeningthepast.com/2012/07/to-wax-zizekian/, last accessed April 30th, 2019.

8 See also Sarah Greifenstein and Hauke Lehmann: Manipulation der Sinne im Modus des Suspense. In: Cinema, Vol. 58 (2013), pp. 102–112, primarily in relation to YOUNG AND INNOCENT. The reference to YOUNG AND INNOCENT even eludes the somewhat over-eager listing of De Palma's "robberies" compiled by Thomas M. Leitch in How to Steal from Hitchcock. In: David Boyd: After Hitchcock. Influence, Imitation, and Intertextuality, Austin 2006, pp. 251–270.

9 See Peretz: Becoming Visionary, pp. 184–185.

the field of cognitive film theory.[10] What all these approaches have in common is that they mainly grasp suspense as a phenomenon related to (film) narration, which the spectator also plays a part in creating. This entails the spectator formulating questions, whether consciously or unconsciously, which relate to how the narration will proceed: "Will the hero appear in time?," "Will the bomb explode?" etc. According to theories of this kind, films generate suspense by leaving the spectator in the dark as to the answers to these questions. Narratively linear films, constructed according to this question-and-answer model, thus serve cognitive theories by establishing the norm, leaving all other forms of dramatic construction to be treated as deviations.[11] This narrative model enjoys such a degree of dominance that even the distinction between film and other media becomes insignificant – they may all be addressed together via the concept of "text."[12] This focus on narration and, even more narrowly, on spoken dialogue is sometimes so entire that a sort of baseline for the "average" narrative film is postulated, addressing all other staging factors in such a way that they almost completely disappear from the field of investigation (Carroll summarizes these as "non-verbal factors" and categorizes them as "stylistic decisions" that are frequently redundant when brought into connection with the spoken word).[13]

At the same time, it is established that suspense is only generated when the spectator is interested in the story or on some level engaged. This represents a notable distortion of what actually happens in this situation. According to my hypothesis, suspense is not based on spectator engagement, but is rather the very thing which generates this engagement in the first place; it itself represents a particular way of *affectively involving the spectator in the film's events* as a *spe-*

---

10 See, for example, Noël Carroll: Toward a Theory of Film Suspense. In: Persistence of Vision, No. 1 (Summer 1984), pp. 65–89; Marie Annette de Wied: The Role of Time-Structures in the Experience of Film Suspense and Duration. A Study on the Effects of Anticipation Time upon Suspense and temporal Variations on Duration Experience and Suspense, university dissertation at the University of Amsterdam, 1991; Hans J. Wulff: Spannungsanalyse. Thesen zu einem Forschungsfeld. In: montage/av, Vol. 2, No. 2 (1993), pp. 97–100; Peter Wuss: Grundformen filmischer Spannung. In: montage/av, Vol. 2, No. 2 (1993), pp. 101–116; see also the anthology by Peter Vorderer, Hans J. Wulff, and Mike Friedrichen (eds.): Suspense. Conceptualizations, Theoretical Analyses, and Empirical Explorations, Mahwah 1996. A more recent approach can be found in Aaron Smuts: The Desire-Frustration Theory of Suspense. In: The Journal of Aesthetics and Art Criticism, Vol. 66, No. 3 (Summer 2008), pp. 281–290.
11 See Carroll: Toward a Theory of Film Suspense, pp. 69–70.
12 See Wulff: Suspense and the Influence of Cataphora on Viewers' Expectations. In: id., Vorderer, and Friedrichsen (eds.): Suspense, pp. 1–17, pp. 1–2.
13 See Carroll: Toward a Theory of Film Suspense, p. 68 and p. 85.

cific mode of cinematic expressivity. By neglecting the aesthetic dimension, cognitive theories are faced with the problem of having to explain this involvement in some other way. Many of them thus link the generation of suspense to a relationship of empathy, identification, or, at the very least, sympathy between the spectator and the characters represented in the film.[14] Here we come across a fundamental problem for a large number of cognitive theories in particularly acute form: with no further ado, film characters are equated with real people, for whose life or wellbeing one must now fear (even if the "knowledge" of the conventions of mainstream cinema, so sought after by cognitive theories, in particular, should make this fear unnecessary). The objection raised by Hitchcock that the "fear of a bomb" about to explode is more powerful than any alliance with a film character[15] already contradicts this idea, as does the well cited example from PSYCHO, where the spectator hopes (with Norman[16]) that the incriminat-

14 See Dolf Zillmann: The Psychology of Suspense in Dramatic Exposition. In: Vorderer, Wulff, and Friedrichsen (eds.): Suspense, pp. 199–231, here p. 201. According to Zillmann, film characters function like everyday people with whom one can enter into an affective relationship without further ado. Empathy becomes the description of every form of emotional reaction linked to a person, pp. 214–215 ("feeling with, feeling for", p. 215). Zillmann's example may be particularly blatant, but its directness is very much representative. See, for example, William F. Brewer, who links suspense to a "concern for the plight of the character." Brewer: The Nature of Narrative Suspense and the Problem of Rereading. In: Vorderer, Wulff, and Friedrichsen (eds.): Suspense, pp. 107–127, here p. 123.

15 "[Hitchcock:] I might go further and say that with the old situation of a bombing properly presented, you might have a group of gangsters sitting around a table, a group of villains. [Truffaut:] As for the instance the bomb that was concealed in a briefcase in the July 20 plot on Hitler's life. [Hitchcock:] Yes. And even in that case I don't think the public would say, "Oh, good, they're all going to be blown to bits," but rather, they'll be thinking, "Watch out. There's a bomb!" What it means is that the apprehension of the bomb is more powerful than the feelings of sympathy or dislike for the characters involved." François Truffaut: Hitchcock (Revised Edition), New York 1985, pp. 58–59. Whether more powerful or not: the "apprehension of the bomb" (which, as Hitchcock adds directly afterwards, is *not related in any way to the object being represented*, but rather, as my hypothesis would have it, to the instability of the situation) is a feeling of a different nature than sympathy.

16 The role played by the character of Norman in this scene becomes clearer when he is placed in a long series of Hitchcock characters who are either damned to watch or who move from being a spectator to being actively involved, that is, who themselves become objects of the gaze: L.B. Jefferies in REAR WINDOW (1954), Josephine McKenna in THE MAN WHO KNEW TOO MUCH (1956), Scottie Ferguson in VERTIGO (1958), or Melanie Daniels in THE BIRDS (1963). The frequency of such characters in Hitchcock's film indicates that they fulfill a formal function for the generation of suspense. This implies that this formulation actually has to be turned on its head: suspense does not depend on identification with a character, but rather the aesthetic mode of suspense creates a specific relationship between the spectator and the character.

ing car carrying Marion Crane's corpse will disappear completely into the swamp.

The attempt to link the generation of suspense to any sort of moral question runs into similar, if not even greater difficulties, such as the approach suggested by Carroll: "[...] I am holding that, in the main, suspense in film is a) an affective concomitant of an answering scene or event which b) has two logically opposed outcomes such that c) one is morally correct but unlikely and the other is evil and likely."[17] The origin of this dualistic concept of morals remains mysterious: Does every film establish its own moral system or do spectators simply make moral judgments at their own discretion? Carroll's argument seems to boil down to the idea that some sort of baseline should be introduced here, too, in relation to what "the" audience generally sees as "good" and "bad."[18] The questionable nature of such an enterprise is apparent even without reference to the example from PSYCHO mentioned above.

While deriving suspense from moral considerations appears entirely superfluous, the actual difficulty lies deeper. In relation to suspense, in particular, the problem is that nearly all cognitive theories are based on the concept of information:

> The unsatisfied need for [...] pragmatic information is in any case the source of emotional tension. Yet the degree of tension depends quantitatively on both the strength of this need as well as on the difference between the amount of information seen as necessary for satisfying the prognosis in question and the amount one actually receives.[19]

This argument still forms the basis for the concept of emotion in cognitive film theory to this day, albeit in modified form.[20] On the one hand, it conceives of a calculating spectator who weighs up probabilities,[21] for whom control and the

---

17 Carroll: Toward a Theory of Film Suspense, p. 72.

18 Carroll: Toward a Theory of Film Suspense, p. 76. Zillmann goes as far as to totally decouple the question of morals from cinematic poetics and to leave it to the spectator's judgment. See Zillmann: The Psychology of Suspense in Dramatic Exposition, p. 207.

19 Wuss: Grundformen der Spannung, pp. 102–103.

20 In Smuts's work for example, the need for control is still regarded as one of the prerequisites for the generation of suspense. See Smuts: The Desire-Frustration Theory of Suspense, p. 286. On the relevance of the concept of information, see, for example, Robert J. Yanal: The Paradox of Suspense. In: The British Journal of Aesthetics, Vol. 36, No. 2 (April 1996), pp. 146–158, here p. 146; Richard J. Gerrig: Is there a Paradox of Suspense? A Reply to Yanal. In: The British Journal of Aesthetics, Vol. 37, No. 2 (April 1997), pp. 168–174, here p. 172; see also Torben Grodal: Embodied Visions, pp. 158–204; Carl Plantinga: Moving Viewers, pp. 92–93.

21 Zillmann, for example, postulates that the intensity of tension is dependent on relationships of chance that can be numerically represented without it ever being made clear how such rela-

elimination of knowledge deficits are basic needs. This spectator corresponds to the norm, posited by Carroll, of a narration that functions according to a question/answer schema; the sort of information theoretical vocabulary used in the quotation above should not distract from the parallels to newer models, which draw on considerations from evolutionary theory to arrive at their own conception of the film spectator:[22] both are ultimately about processing stimuli in the most economical way possible.

The problem here is that this perspective turns film perception into an apparent process of information allocation and processing, no longer based in duration, and in fact offers no conception of time that might be linked to the spectator's experience. The dramatic structure of suspense thus ends up as a binary schema, pieced together from questions and answers, which robs complex staging procedures of their temporal composition and, in abstract fashion, spits them out as a series of points of fixed "information." In as much as they can be ordered according to the linear progression of the narration, these points of information are nothing more than the events represented in the film. Anything located between question and answer is either aimed at taking the question further or regarded as a deviation. The empirical intuition, that the amount of time between "question" and "answer" would seem to be hugely significant for the generation of suspense, has no place in this logic; with Carroll, for example, explicitly rejecting this idea. According to him, the delay in resolution is not significant in itself, but rather in terms of the information that could potentially be added during this period of time, which thus might affect the probability of one of the two alternative outcomes.[23] Carroll makes a strict distinction here between form and content by separating film suspense from comparable musical structures, for example,[24] conceding that it "might be said of this paper that it is a theory of narrative suspense in film rather than a theory of film suspense."[25] This separation of form and content does not simply result in an incomplete description, it moreover impedes any actual solution of the problem, since factors of time and movement cannot simply be added after the event, as it were.

---

tionships might be derived from the visual forms concerned. See Zillmann: The Psychology of Suspense in Dramatic Exposition, p. 206.

22 See in particular Grodal: Embodied Visions, but also Carroll: The Philosophy of Motion Pictures.

23 Carroll: Toward a Theory of Film Suspense, p. 78. See also his The Paradox of Suspense, pp. 83–84.

24 Carroll: Toward a Theory of Film Suspense, p. 77. According to this point of view, even the ticking of a time bomb merely refers to the successive increase in the likelihood of an explosion.

25 Carroll: Toward a Theory of Film Suspense, p. 88.

Marie Anette de Wied's work gives its full attention to the factor of temporality, approaching the problem from a standpoint of experimental psychology. It is, in fact, the only work from the field of cognitive film theory taking as its starting point that suspense is not generated at individual moments on the part of the spectator, but rather unfolds across a concrete period of time. Her arrangement of film perception differentiates between screen time (the real time passing in the cinema auditorium) and story time (the progression of the events of the narrative) and postulates that suspense is generated by a shift in the "standard" relationship between these two temporalities (i.e., a delay in the story) such that screen time and story time converge.[26] There are two difficulties in this approach. On the one hand, de Wied introduces the idea of a normal relationship between temporalities. This is not only a relationship that could only ever be determined imprecisely (only in exceptional cases can it even be said how much narrated time a story actually encompasses), but it is also hardly possible to prove what might represent the norm here, regardless of what corpus of films one might choose as an example. On the other hand, de Wied's approach lacks a suitable concept of duration. What she terms duration does not actually constitute a temporal form, but merely correlates to the tempo of the narrative.[27] Grasping suspense as delay, however, is only of explanatory use if one is capable of determining what this delay actually relates to.

It would appear that the cognitive theories, which presuppose the norm of a linear narrative film, still leave much to be explained; this can be seen, for example, in the discussion of the so-called suspense paradox, which these theories appear entirely incapable of solving.[28] Hence, a different path must be taken, which links suspense back to the problem of cinematic time and movement. This will enable a more precise and comprehensive picture to emerge, which will fully reveal the complex connection between spectatorial perception and cinematic staging.

---

26 De Wied: The Role of Time-Structures in the Experience of Film Suspense and Duration, p. 40.

27 See De Wied: The Role of Time-Structures in the Experience of Film Suspense and Duration, p. 15.

28 See Carroll: The Paradox of Suspense; Gerrig: Is there a Paradox of Suspense?; Yanal: The Paradox of Suspense; Smuts: The Desire-Frustration Theory of Suspense, pp. 284–289; Christy Mag Uidhir: An Eliminativist Theory of Suspense. In: Philosophy and Literature, No. 35 (2011), pp. 121–133. Over the course of this chapter, my own position regarding this so-called "paradox" will become clear.

Suspense and Cinematic Movement

As discussed in the introduction, Nancy, in his commentary on Deleuze, defines movement (or, in this case, motion) as follows:

> Motion is not a displacing or a transferring, which may occur between given places in a totality that is itself given. On the contrary, it is what takes place when a body is in a situation and a state that compel it to find its place, a place it consequently has not had or no longer has. I move (in matter or mind) when I am not – ontologically – where I am – locally. Motion carries me elsewhere but the "elsewhere" is not given beforehand: my coming will make of it the "there" where I will have come from "here."[29]

To be in motion is understood in this case as no longer having solid ground under one's feet, as being suspended somewhere between the place left behind and the one yet to be found. Nancy expresses this via the use of the future perfect tense; here related both to space and time. Or, as put by Deleuze: "The whole is not a closed set, but on the contrary that by virtue of which the set is never absolutely closed, never completely sheltered, that which keeps it open somewhere as if by the finest thread which attaches it to the rest of the universe."[30] This openness, for Deleuze, is closely linked to the concept of relation – the latter he identifies, more than any other, with the oeuvre of Alfred Hitchcock in his taxonomy of images. Deleuze is not the only one to characterize Hitchcock as the first, in the history of cinema, to involve the spectator in the way the cinematic process unfolds in time. As Truffaut writes:

> The art of creating suspense is also the art of involving the audience, so that the viewer is actually a participant in the film. In this area of the spectacle, film-making is not a dual interplay between the director and his picture, but a three-way game in which the audience, too, is required to play.[31]

To the spectator, the camera (or, in Truffaut's case, the director as an authorial presence) becomes an instrument of mediation, revealing to them privileged access to the events of the film, pointing the spectator to them; creating a triangle between spectator, camera, and film. While, according to Deleuze, Hitchcock's involvement of the spectator aims at the creation of a "mental image,"[32]

---

29 Nancy: The Evidence of Film, p. 28.
30 Deleuze: Cinema 1, p. 10.
31 Truffaut: Hitchcock, p. 14.
32 "When we speak of mental image, we mean something else: it is an image which takes as objects *of* thought, objects which have their own existence outside thought. [...]. *It is an*

which, for the film characters, splits apart into a "varied play of experienced conjunctions,"[33] my own focus in the following is the concrete affective quality of the spectatorial feeling linked to such a mental image. The question is: how the "figures of thought,"[34] as Deleuze calls them, in Hitchcock's oeuvre were modified by New Hollywood cinema and designated as a poetics of affect. Karl Sierek formulates the basis for such an approach as follows:

> The sensation of tension is an extremely physical feeling. It proves the close relationship between understanding and one's own body image [...]. Anyone who squirms in the cinema initially creates a relationship to themselves, establishing a relationship between one's own recollection or desire and the frame of reference of one's body – between a previous image or (virtual) afterimage and an image-now; a pre-image (the film) and a body image.

> The dynamic model of movement of the tension in the body of the viewer is repeated in the relationship between the body and the sounds and images on the screen [...]. As a symptom of speaking to oneself, tension both updates and intensifies first the spatial relations and then the temporal ones laid out in the film. The field of reference in both cases is and remains the current body image of the viewer and what encases it, the cinema auditorium.[35]

According to Sierek, the tension induced by the film – the modification in the relationship between the image body and the "body image"– reveals the connection between corporeal-affective experience and logical understanding. In both senses, suspense is closely, even essentially linked to the creation of relations. But what does it mean to create relations? In this context, Pascal Bonitzer differentiates between two varieties of suspense, tracking one back to Griffith and the other to Hitchcock:

> Suspense is thus indeed achieved through editing, but Hitchcock, in contrast to the Griffithian acceleration of parallel actions, employs an editing of convergent actions in a homogenous space, which presupposes slow motion and is sustained by the gaze, itself evoked by a third element, a perverse object or a stain.[36]

---

image which takes as its object, relations, symbolic acts, intellectual feelings." Deleuze: Cinema 1, p. 198.

33 Deleuze: Cinema 1, p. 207.

34 Deleuze: Cinema 1, p. 207.

35 Karl Sierek: Spannung und Körperbild. In: montage/av, Vol. 3, No. 1 (1994), pp. 115–121, here pp. 116–117.

36 Pascal Bonitzer: Hitchcockian Suspense. In: Slavoj Žižek (ed.): Everything You Always Wanted to Know About Lacan (But Were Afraid to Ask Hitchcock), London/New York 1992, pp. 15–30, here p. 28.

For Bonitzer, montage is the fundamental process for generating suspense and thus the decisive operation for creating relations: Griffith's parallel montage is described as a dyadic arrangement, Hitchcock's brand as a triadic one.

This links back, on the one hand, to the assertion that Hitchcock involves the spectator in the mechanism of the cinematic process. Bonitzer also takes this idea further, describing the triangular arrangement as a specific connection between concrete visual structures and the spectator's perceptual activity. Fundamental, and representative of one decisive difference with the Griffith model (another difference will be discussed later on), is the creation of a visual relation between the gaze, conveyed by the camera, and the conspicuous "perverse object." The act of *showing* establishes a relation that presupposes temporal and spatial continuity ("convergent actions in a homogenous space"). This continuity is by no means a function of a one-to-one realism,[37] but, instead, always relates to the spectator's perceptual activity. The spectator's hearing and seeing become the location in which the relation is constituted. For montage does not just operate in abstract terms, nor does it just create semantic connections. Rather, it generates concrete spatial and temporal relations, realized in the act of perception. In this way, Bonitzer's idea of "convergent actions" can be expanded to the following: suspense *relates movement to movement* or, more precisely, movement is perceived through its relation to a temporally constituted, formal context.

Many of Hitchcock's typical techniques can be traced to this primacy of continuity: his preference for "flexible" acting styles, which can be inserted into various possible relations;[38] the removal of "unnecessary" space of the characters' surroundings,[39] so the spectator's attention may be directed more easily; or the principle of the wandering close-up, not interrupted by the movement of the characters;[40] "Our primary function is to create an emotion and our second job is to sustain that emotion."[41] Bonitzer describes how even the shower scene montage in PSYCHO serves to extend a moment whose suddenness could hardly be grasped otherwise.[42] The use of shot-reverse shot and structures of looking in general (understood as a function of what Deleuze refers to as the

---

37 "[Hitchcock:] The placing of the images on the screen, in terms of what you are expressing, should never be dealt with in a factual manner." Truffaut: Hitchcock, p. 223.
38 "[Hitchcock:] In my opinion, the chief requisite for an actor is to do nothing well [...]." Truffaut: Hitchcock, p. 89.
39 Truffaut: Hitchcock, p. 222.
40 Truffaut: Hitchcock, p. 225.
41 Truffaut: Hitchcock, p. 89.
42 See Bonitzer: Hitchcockian Suspense, p. 28.

"mental image"[43]) involves the spectator's vision in the process of transformation between shots and is thus of fundamental significance for Hitchcockian suspense. Assisted by the weaving together of individual shots, relations are incessantly inscribed in the image space, that is, ratios of tension in all their variations.[44]

Suspending: Delaying

Only through emphasizing these relations' concrete adherence to time and space, can the full meaning of the principle of continuity be revealed: its meaning first becomes apparent when contextualized with the desire for *discontinuity*. Therein lies the meaning of the "perverse object": it sticks out from the series of natural signs as a "demark," as Deleuze puts it.[45] Discontinuity thus always presupposes a continuous context from which it can emerge. Sierek describes the consequences of this principle for the spectator's affective involvement:

> Neither control nor knowledge *as such* could be hypostatized as primary systems of reference and used as means of explaining the specific feeling of tension in the cinema. Suspended *between* control and its loss, knowledge and a lack thereof, the body finds itself in both states simultaneously: in control *and* not in control, knowing *and* unknowing, in the dynamic, non-linear interplay between these extremes, the poles of tension and release.[46]

Vivian Sobchack attributes this interplay between continuity and discontinuity, and thereby, the prerequisite for the emergence of the perceptual relationship characterized by suspense, to film's general capacity for movement: "[...] the

---

43 "What Hitchcock thus brings into cinema is, then, the mental image. It's not a matter of the look, and if the camera's an eye, it's the mind's eye" Deleuze: On the Movement-Image. In: id.: Negotiations 1972–1990, New York 1995, pp. 46–56. As a function of the mental image, I regard the structure of looking as enormously important, albeit less as a description of the actions of the characters being represented and more in the sense of a perspective, a directional power being inscribed into the image space.

44 The image space refers to the space in the film as it appears as an image, that is, initially independent of its indexical or diegetic functions. Its parameters are light, color, form, and movement. On the theoretical concept of the image space and the distinction between the image space and the plot or narrative space, see Hermann Kappelhoff: Der Bildraum des Kinos. Modulationen einer ästhetischen Erfahrungsform. In: Gertrud Koch (ed.): Umwidmungen. Architektonische und kinematographische Räume, Berlin 2005, pp. 138–149.

45 Deleuze: Cinema 1, p. 203.

46 Sierek: Spannung und Körperbild, p. 118.

very motility of vision structures the film and the spectator as always in the act of displacing themselves – if not in space, then in time; if not in time, then in attention and intention."[47]

Suspense thus presents a problem for cognitive theories of emotion: when movement is related to other movement, allowing for no determination of a particular, objectifiable stimulus, the audience's emotional activity, the way their feelings are created and how they become affectively engaged, cannot be described as a stimulus-response reaction. In its place, *stimulation* appears, or what Bonitzer variously describes as the erotic dimension of suspense, closely related to the process of delay and postponement:

> This subjective stretching, this viscosity of time, is related to eroticism, and it concerns the eroticized time in the prolonged, necessarily disturbing undecidability of an event. Suspense is the erotic prolongation of the trajectory of a coin thrown up in the air, before it falls on one side (tails: yes) or the other (heads: no).[48]

In another text, Bonitzer describes this in even stronger terms: "suspense consists in varying this satisfaction, in order to feed it."[49] However, suspense does behave in far more complex manner than just that "strange, yet banal identification, according to which an onscreen meal can trigger real hunger or sexual images an erection."[50] One, initial indication of this is provided by Bonitzer's use of the term "viscosity," which Maurice Merleau-Ponty also uses to describe the "adherence of the perceived object to its context,"[51] ultimately describing, thereby, a formal whole; a whole that, in this case, is temporally constituted. This temporal context, this formal unity is nothing but the form of aesthetic experience itself. Suspense therefore relates to (and manipulates or distorts) the spectator's experience of lived time.

Eyal Peretz picks up on the aspect of disturbance, which Bonitzer mentions in passing, and places it at the heart of his own considerations, developed in his examination of the films of Brian De Palma: "If De Palma is essentially a director of horror and suspense, it is because his work emerges from the insight of their essential co-belonging and origin in the discovery – the cinematic discovery par

---

47 Sobchack: The Address of the Eye, p. 299.
48 Bonitzer: Hitchcockian Suspense, p. 28.
49 Bonitzer: Deframings. In: Cahiers Du Cinéma, Vol. 4, 1973–1978, pp. 197–203, p. 199. See also Jean Epstein: "Waiting for the moment when 1,000 meters of intrigue converge in a muscular *dénouement* satisfies me more than the rest of the film." Epstein: Magnification [1921]. In: October, Vol. 3 (Spring 1977), pp. 9–25, here p. 9.
50 Bellour: Le Dépli des Émotions, p. 101.
51 Merleau-Ponty: Phenomeonology of Perception, p. 12.

excellence – of *movement as suspension of a presupposed center of orientation and of stable meaning and as unmasterable fall.*"[52] When related to the interplay between control and lack of control, which Sierek identifies as being at the core of how tension is felt, eroticism and horror thus appear as two sides of the same coin.

At the same time, it is likely more than mere coincidence that Bonitzer emphasizes the corporeal dimension of this feeling, while Peretz highlights the problem of how meaning is constituted. One may directly infer that the relationship between these two dimensions, body and meaning, can be demonstrated through suspense in paradigmatic fashion. It is important to note that eroticism and horror don't only refer to affective modalities; each can further be defined as a specific manner of comprehensively ordering film perception. Linda Williams's concept of body genres,[53] which categorizes the temporality of the horror film – or, to be more precise, the slasher film – as "too early" and that of the pornographic film as "right now,"[54] is instructive here, and not only in relation to cinematic time. The connection between suspense and the third body genre, the melodrama – a mode that, as will be shown, is particularly relevant in the case of CARRIE, though not restricted to it – has yet to be theoretically explored. Williams characterizes all three of her conceptualized forms of excess as displacing a body no longer in control, a body "'beside' itself with sexual pleasure, fear and terror, or overpowering sadness," as the aural dimension's focus shifts from speech sounds to inarticulate screams and cries.[55]

As remarked upon at the beginning of this chapter in relation to the horror film, however, it is important to keep in mind the difference between these genres and the mode of suspense. Suspense is always generated through the *creation of a relationship* between the modalities described by Williams – between the "here" and "there," the "now" and the "not yet." This is how Williams explains the concept of fantasy, with reference to her conception of body genres as "genres of gender fantasy," summarizing the aspects mentioned by Bonitzer and

---

52 Eyal Peretz: Becoming Visionary, p. 29. A look at De Palma's filmography makes entirely clear that he also sees horror and the erotic, or rather the erotic and suspense, as closely related: one only has to think of films such as SISTERS (1973), DRESSED TO KILL (1980) or BODY DOUBLE (1984), see also Peretz: ibid., p. 189. Bonitzer also assumes a relationship between horror and suspense, even though he conceives of horror (or rather crimes) as more closely connected to the psychoanalytic category of desire, see Bonitzer: Hitchcockian Suspense, pp. 17–20.

53 Williams adapts this concept from Carol Clover and extends it accordingly, see Linda Williams: Film Bodies. Genre, Gender, and Excess. In: Film Quarterly, Vol. 44, No. 4 (Summer 1991), pp. 2–13, here p. 4.

54 Linda Williams: Film Bodies, p. 9.

55 Linda Williams: Film Bodies, p. 4.

Peretz, respectively, as she does so: "For fantasies are not, as is sometimes thought, wish-fulfilling linear narratives of mastery and control leading to closure and the attainment of desire. They are marked, rather, by the *prolongation of desire*, and by the *lack of fixed position* with respect to the objects and events fantasized."[56] As will become evident, this radical perspective of a poetics of suspense – which is not subsumed by the body genres, but rather moves asymptotically towards them – is only achieved in the cinema of New Hollywood.

2.2 Analysis

CARRIE

According to the assessment of film criticism, Brian De Palma finally developed a distinct aesthetic profile with CARRIE[57] – however negatively this profile may have been seen at time.[58] There is indeed no overlooking the fact that this film brings about a transformation in De Palma's *oeuvre*. In the following, I wish to discuss this transformation, not merely in relation to Hitchcock (whether

---

56 Linda Williams: Film Bodies, p. 10, emphasis my own.

57 See Roger Greenspun: Carrie, and Sally and Leatherface Among the Film Buffs. In: Film Comment, Vol. 13, No. 1 (January/February 1977), pp. 14–17; Royal S. Brown: Considering De Palma. In: American Film, Vol. 3, No. 4 (July/August 1977), pp. 54–61; Paula Matusa: Corruption and Catastrophe. Brian De Palma's CARRIE. In: Film Quarterly, Vol. 31, No. 1 (Fall 1977), pp. 32–38; Dmetri Kakmi: Myth and Magic in De Palma's CARRIE. In: Senses of Cinema, February 2000, URL: http://sensesofcinema.com/2000/cteq/carrie/, last accessed March 27th, 2019.

58 The central point of criticism is the film's alleged misogyny, which feeds on the connection between Carrie's menstruation and her telekinetic powers, which are deemed destructive. The critique is frequently mixed together with polemics against De Palma's apparent technophilia. See Serafina Kent Bathrick: CARRIE Ragtime. The Horror of Growing up Female. In: Jump Cut, No. 14 (1977), pp. 9–10; Shelley Stamp Lindsey: Horror, Femininity, and Carrie's Monstrous Puberty. In: Journal of Film and Video, Vol. 43, No. 4 (Winter 1991), pp. 33–44. For a consistent and comprehensive rejection of the misogyny accusation, see Bruce Babington: Twice a Victim. Carrie meets the BFI. In: Screen, Vol. 24, No. 3 (1983), pp. 4–18. For a detailed discussion of this subject, see Kenneth MacKinnon: Misogyny in the Movies. The De Palma Question, Newark 1990. For a current summary of the debate surrounding the film, see Alexandra Heller-Nicholas: Life in the Old Girl Yet. CARRIE (1976) and the Unbearable Lightness of De Palma Bashing [September 5th, 2008], URL: http://filmbunnies.wordpress.com/category/alex/depalmas-carrie/, last accessed March 27th, 2019. This debate is relevant in the sense that it throws up the question of what position the spectator takes on in relation to the film and the events and characters represented within it. The question of such spectatorial positioning forms a main focus of the analysis. By clarifying these fundamental relationships, the following discussions can thus be understood as making an implicit contribution to this debate.

it moves toward or away from his work);[59] but would like, rather, to describe De Palma's approach primarily based on its concrete qualities of audiovisual composition: in terms of a mode of suspense specific to the cinema of New Hollywood.

To start with a quick recapitulation of the plot: Carrie is a highly reserved girl, around seventeen, who attends Bates High School, where she is an outsider, a constant target of teasing and maliciousness. She is also further repressed at home by her fanatically religious mother. At the start of the film, Carrie gets her first period, an event for which she is entirely unprepared and which places her in a state of panic, rendering her defenseless against the ridicule of her classmates. In this situation of extreme emotional stress, her telekinetic powers emerge for the very first time. These powers reach their full force when Carrie falls victim to a secret plot initiated by her classmate Chris at the prom. After the vote is rigged to crown her prom queen, at the very moment she believes all her dreams have come true, a bucket of pig's blood is dumped over her in front of the entire school. Carrie unleashes her powers and transforms the prom into a veritable inferno, slaughtering all the attendees, with the exception of one girl, Sue. When Carrie returns home, her mother is already waiting, planning to kill her. In a further orgy of destructive energy, the house collapses on both of them and sinks into the ground. The film ends showing Sue, the sole survivor, waking with a scream from a nightmare, in which Carrie's hand bursts out of the grave and grabs her.

The Prom Night Sequence

CARRIE also marks a step towards a new concentration on form within De Palma's filmography. Almost from the very beginning, everything in the film,

---

59 This would also be inappropriate, since the staging patterns the film draws on and begins to transform relate to a much wider spectrum of cinematic expressivity; worthy of mention here are the B-horror films and youth melodramas of the 1950s and the beach party films of the early 1960s (or rather the nostalgic return to them in the 1970s in the form of AMERICAN GRAFFITI [George Lucas 1973] and its successors), and not least the radical theater of Richard Schechner: various commentators have pointed out the proximity to the destruction sequence in De Palma's DIONYSUS IN '69, which is based on a stage play by Schechner. David Greven uses CARRIE as an example to explore the continuity between woman's film and modern horror, see Greven: Representations of Femininity in American Genre Cinema. The Woman's Film, Film Noir, and Modern Horror, New York 2011, pp. 91–115. Hermann Kappelhoff also points out the connection between sentimentality and horror which forms the justification for the continuity examined by Greven, see Kappelhoff: Matrix der Gefühle, pp. 236–238.

from dialogue to production design, is geared towards the dramatic highpoint of the prom night sequence, to which the analysis that follows is dedicated. This formal coherence, typical of the suspense mode in New Hollywood, is accompanied by an enormous degree of temporal expansion of the scene's dramatic units. In a film barely 100 minutes long, the whole prom night sequence takes up nearly half an hour, posing a problem for analysis in consideration of space alone.

One main point of reference for the sequence, in terms of the kind of cinematic thinking discussed at the beginning of this chapter, is the ballroom scene from Hitchcock's YOUNG AND INNOCENT. CARRIE borrows several key arrangements, techniques, and motifs from this sequence and places them in relation to one another in novel ways. Three elements, which I will return to later, deserve particular attention: first, the arrangement of the stage and audience, second, the technique of the tracking shot, which produces the relationship between these spaces, and finally, the motif of the (radiant/defiled) face.

The main focus of our investigation is the prom sequence's climax: the moments surrounding the bucket's fatal fall. Before the sequence begins, the apparatus used to mount the bucket above the stage has already been established. Further, it is not introduced as an abstract "piece of information," but rather through a rapid, concentrated run-through of precisely the same camera movement which will show the bucket's use during the prom night sequence: a tracking shot along the rope that Chris pulls at the sequence's climax in order to empty the contents of the bucket over Carrie. Therein, the film quite literally relates one movement to another (figs. 1–3).

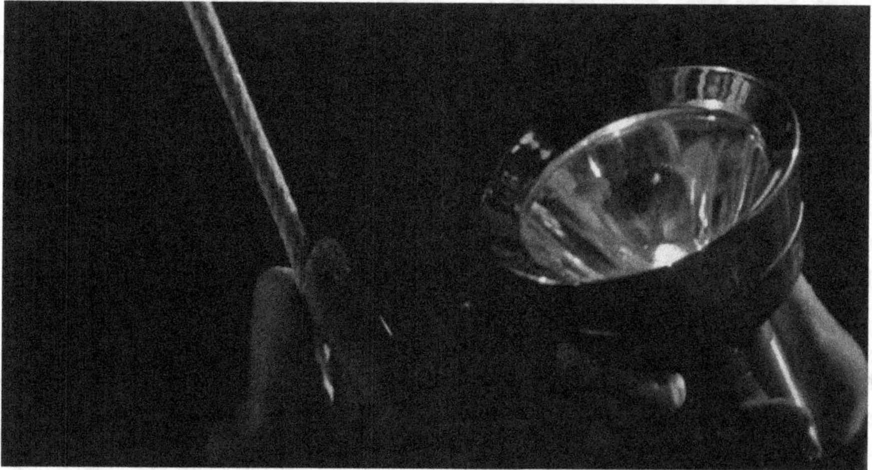

Figs. 1–3: From blood to bucket.

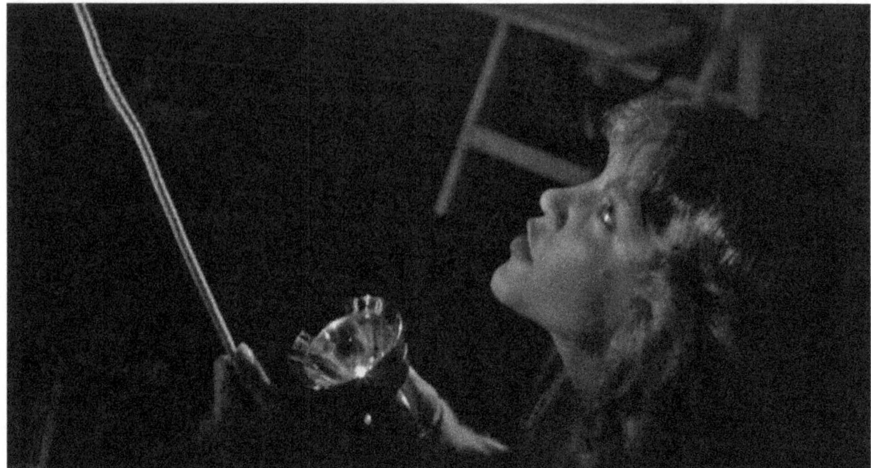

Fig. 2

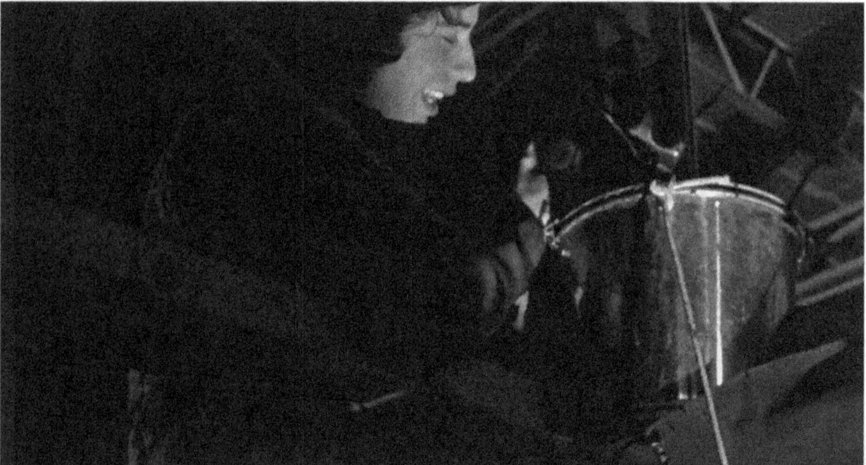

Fig. 3

In this way, everything that follows is not only relevant in its own right, but also stands in constant relation to what has already occurred, and to how these previous events are then invested into future developments. Accordingly, the entire prom night sequence unfolds as a process wherein different but related figures of movement are increasingly interwoven with one another, reaching a point of culmination in the seconds preceding the bucket's fall. But let us take one thing at a time: the sequence as a whole can be broken down into five parts or, to be more precise, into an introduction, three main sections, and a coda.

The short introduction (around a minute and a half) shows Carrie and Tommy in the car in front of the gymnasium, as the soundtrack segues into their arrival at the prom itself. Their arrival and Carrie's experience of the prom form the subjects of the second section (just under 11 minutes), which ends with Carrie and Tommy filling out slips, secretly voting for themselves as prom king and queen. The third section (just under nine minutes) begins following a short intermezzo (Margaret White at home in the kitchen) and initiates the climax: the voting slips are collected, setting the plot against Carrie into motion. This section ends with the bucket's fall, followed in the fourth section by the massacre of the prom attendees after a grand pause of shocked silence. The fourth section (four minutes) ends with the gymnasium's doors slamming shut once Carrie has left the building. Thereafter, the coda (almost a minute) shows the death of the co-conspirators Chris and her boyfriend Billy, who attempt to run Carrie over in their car as she heads home; the explosion of the car releases the remaining pent-up energy and the film moves toward its first finale.

As is indicated here, on one level, the dramatic structure may be described as a series of states of tension, following a pattern of tension – release – intensification of tension to a point of climax – discharge – and finally disintegration. Shorter phases and figures are inscribed within this overarching, compositional structure, including the climax in the third section, to which we shall now turn.

The Tracking Shot

This third section is around nine minutes in its entirety (including the fall of the bucket) and can be broken down into two further parts: the roughly two-minute long tracking shot that connects all the relevant elements of the scene's construction and Carrie's subsequent walk to the stage, which culminates in her coronation and humiliation.

The tracking shot is announced via a close-up of Carrie's adversary Chris, whose face, as the protagonist's antithesis in the context of this scene, announces that the plot against Carrie has been set in motion. The tracking shot then begins with a glimpse of Carrie's voting slip, accompanying it on the way to the stage, and then moves over the stage (where the bucket is located), and back to Carrie, who, together with Tommy, is declared the winner of the rigged vote at precisely this moment (figs. 4 – 11).

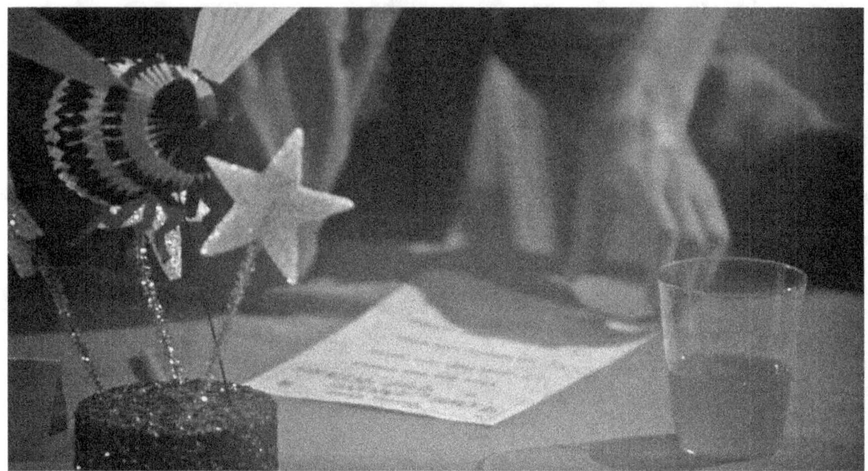

Figs. 4–11: The omniscient tracking shot.

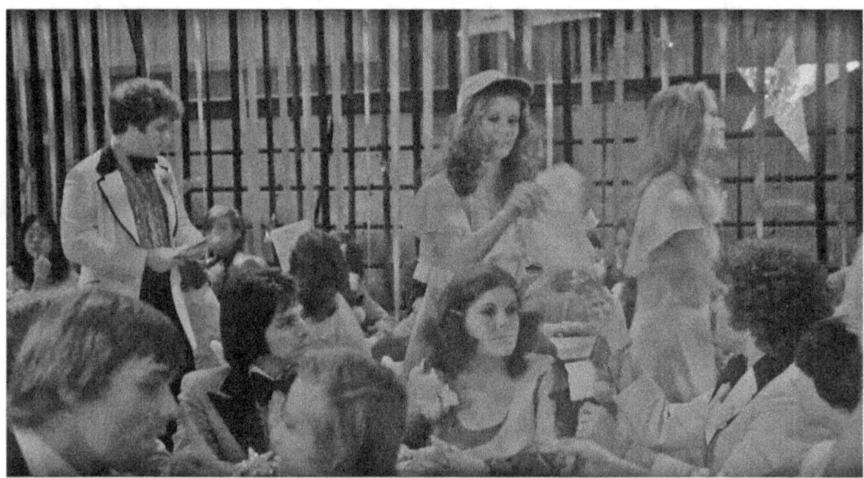

**Fig. 5

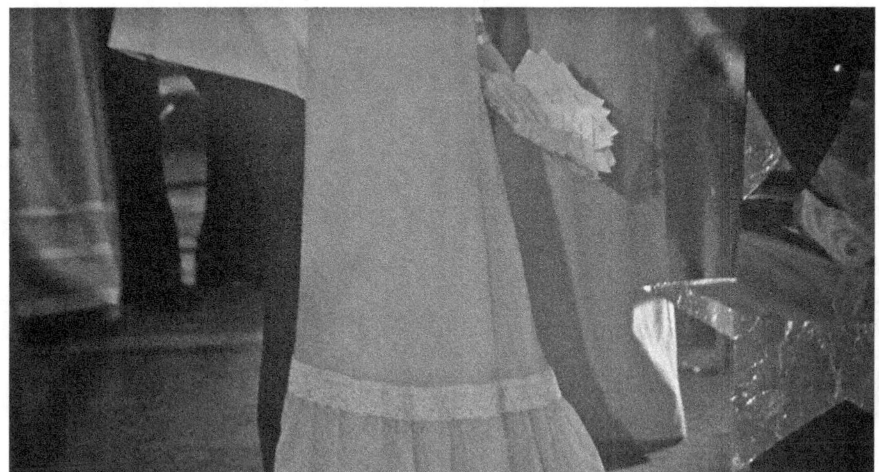

Fig. 6

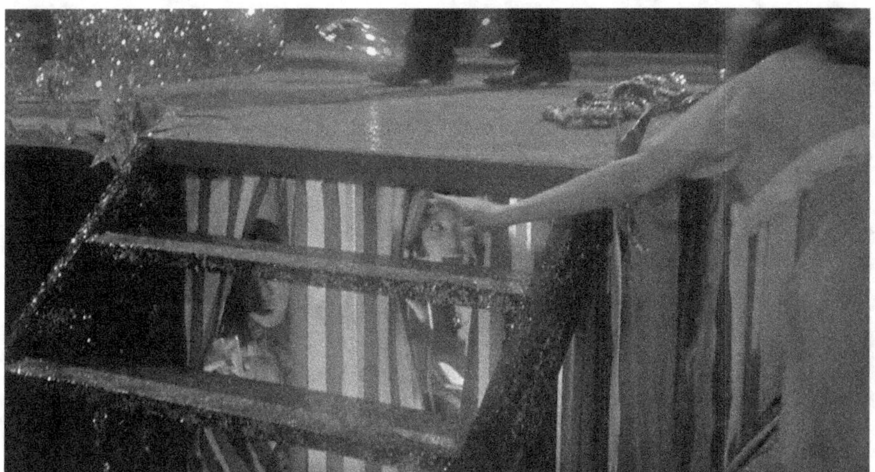

Fig. 7

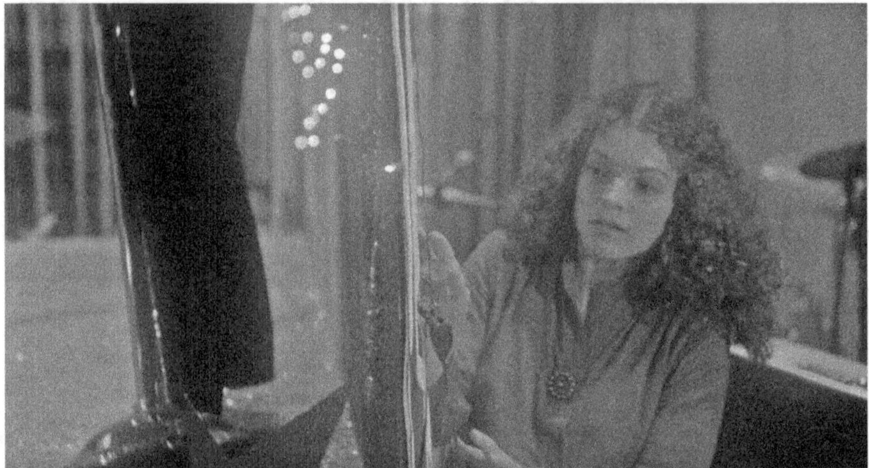

Fig. 8

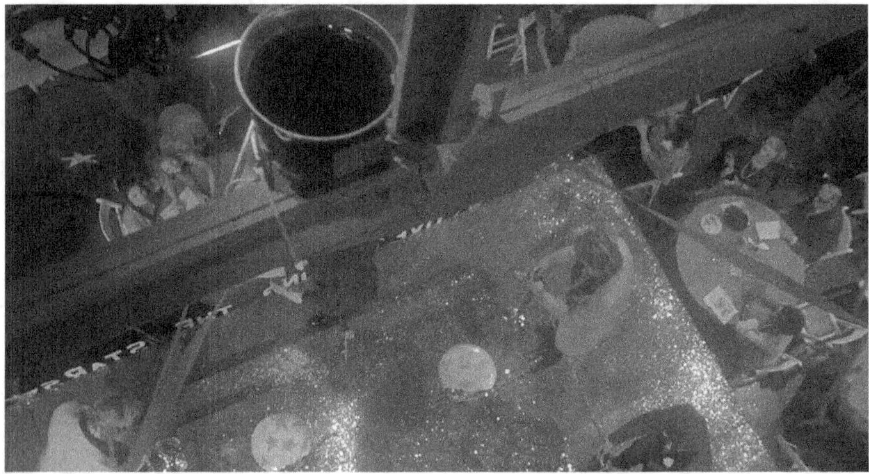

Fig. 9

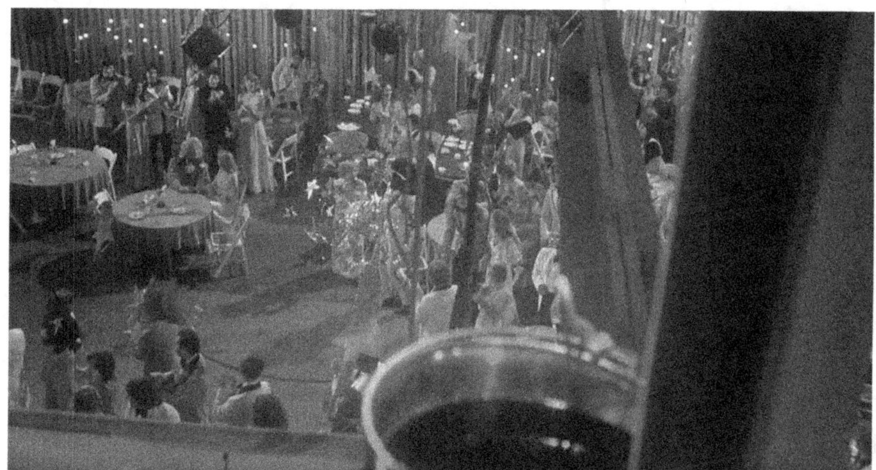

Fig. 10

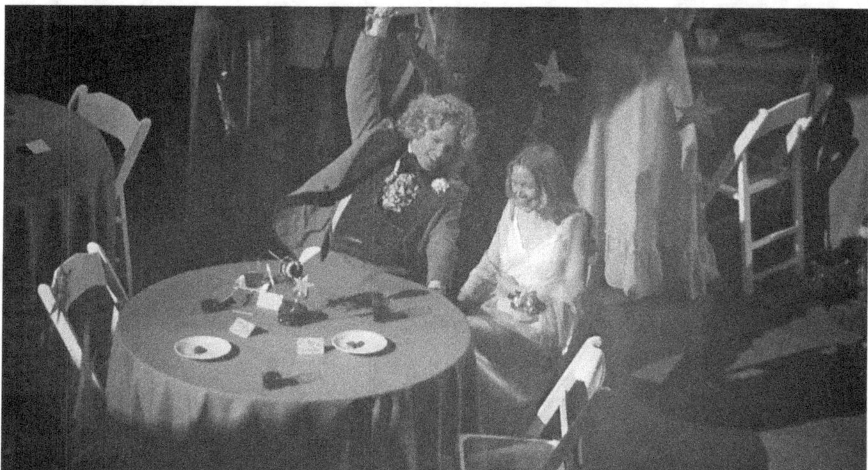

Fig. 11

As mentioned, the shot opens with the image of the voting slip, inscribed with Carrie and Tommy's secret agreement (fig. 4). Norma, the girl collecting the votes, is party to Chris's plot and, after she catches sight of the slip, Carrie's (and Tommy's) secret is already no longer a secret. Norma collects the slip with the others and walks through the gymnasium in the direction of the stage (fig. 5). The slip takes a leisurely course to its goal – that is, toward its place in the plot: Fig. 6 shows the slips shortly before they are thrown away and substituted with forged ones.

The camera follows the slips as they are collected in the gym and the two individuals collecting them, slowly moving towards the stage. The distance between the camera and the characters continuously oscillates, much like the camera itself, occasionally pausing briefly, before gently beginning to move again. At the same time, the space between the camera and the characters is repeatedly crossed by secondary characters who momentarily block the line of sight. Once the vote-collectors arrive next to the stage at the front, the camera comes to a proper stopping place for the first time. This pause is underlined by the dramatic, descending strings on the soundtrack, which play exactly as the slips fall to the floor and then continue in a deep, constant tone, accompanying Norma the rest of the way.

Norma now delivers the slips to the jury, which includes Miss Collins, Carrie's physical education teacher. With the camera still in pursuit, Norma then walks along the stage and knocks on its side to signal to Chris, who is hiding beneath it (fig. 7); here the string figure returns for the second time. But instead of dying away, this time it serves as the basis for further string progressions, layered on top of one another, as the camera moves, first, alongside the stage and then follows the rope connecting Chris to the bucket aloft. As the camera arrives at the stage's rear wall, Sue suddenly appears, taking up the position of an observer to the events (fig. 8). At this moment, the music gains new intensity: the melody is shortened into a series of two-note figures, which gradually increase in pitch as if climbing a ladder, while the camera moves up the back wall of the stage, now closely following the rope, in an almost hysterical gesture. Having arrived at the top, the camera floats freely and independently over the stage, now only loosely oriented by the rope, while on the soundtrack, a glockenspiel performs the film's title theme, underlaid with a continuous high tone played by the strings. Finally, the bucket enters the camera's field of vision, framing it in relation to the chairs on the stage, obviously arranged for the winning couple (fig. 9). At this point, the camera makes a lengthy pause for a second time; the strings fade away, while onstage preparations are made for the announcement of the voting results. Before the winning couple is announced, the camera starts moving again, creating one, final, decisive connection: between the bucket and Carrie (fig. 10). There, the shot ends where it began, with Carrie und Tommy, now picked out from the masses of tables with a zoom, just as they start walking towards the stage (fig. 11).

Rhythm and Perspective

This tracking shot is a prime example of what Deleuze calls a "figure of thought" – both in itself and in the way it reworks the tracking shot from YOUNG AND INNOCENT. By connecting all the elements that will be involved in the sequence's further development in a single movement, it creates the conditions for everything that ensues – Carrie and Tommy, co-conspirators Chris and Billy, Miss Collins, Sue, and finally the bucket containing the pig's blood. This manner of *creating relations*, as already discussed, is the suspense mode's first and most fundamental operation. But how are such connections established in CARRIE? The shot begins with a close-up of the voting slip collected by Norma; from this tight framing, the camera immediately zooms out to capture Norma together with Carrie and Tommy in a fleeting tableau (fig. 12).

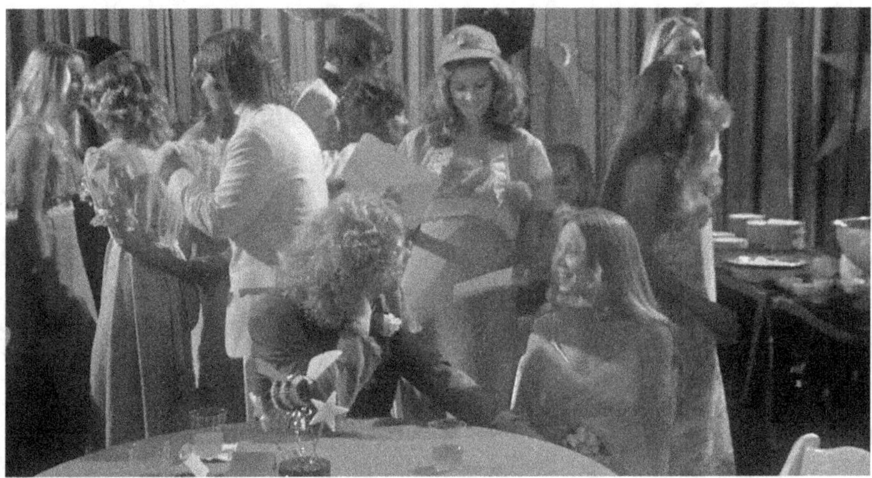

Fig. 12: Looking and knowing.

The irony of Carrie voting for herself as prom queen, and thus unknowingly accepting her own fate, is clearly visible in Norma's facial expression. The movement of the zoom-out reproduces the disclosure of this secret: starting from an intimate, close proximity and shifting toward a kind of public visibility, specified in greater detail below. At this point, the film reconfigures its structure of knowledge, both between the characters and in their relation to the spectator; not, however, in the sense of interjecting abstract information, but precisely in how Norma *knowingly* grins (and grinningly knows) and how this one voting slip moves with all the others through the room: that is, according to a specific *rhythm*, generated in relation to the movement of the camera and the characters. This rhythm can be described as a sort of leisurely swinging motion; a steady fluctuation akin to a musical legato that shifts back and forth between serene panning movements and lingering pauses, between waiting and pressing onwards. This unobtrusive, almost wave-like stopping and starting is further complemented by the way the view is constantly obstructed and cleared again as secondary characters cross the frame, and the continual modulation of the distance between Norma and the camera. Before eventually reaching its epicenter, the one element upon which everything quite literally hangs – the swinging bucket that will eventually tip over and fall – this swaying motion is manifest in a range of forms as the sequence progresses.

Another central feature of the tracking shot is activated by this swinging or swaying, specifically, by the quality of the camera's movement, its elasticity and viscous malleability. It is as if a rubber band were tied between the lens and its object (first loosely, then increasingly tightening). The band not only ensures that the connection is never broken, and that every even mild deviation is answered by a return to the object of our attention; rather on account of these factors, every increase in distance charges the constellation with a kind of free-floating, suspended energy, which is never fully resolved, even when the objects in question approach one another. This energy, initially restrained in the tracking shot and intensifying later, precisely correlates to the aforementioned rhythm. It is no accident that the elastic gesture of the camera, which seems to almost cling to the objects of the mise-en-scène before letting go of them, differs from the comparatively stiff camera movement in YOUNG AND INNOCENT. Rather, a question of the precise control over a sequence of movement, it goes straight to the heart of the intimate relationship between the agency of the omniscient camera and the spectator. In YOUNG AND INNOCENT, the camera's superficial gesture of searching first morphs into targeted movement and then into an intimate approach towards a face, progressively carving everything superfluous from the field of vision, in order to align the remaining elements with each other, as if they, too, were organized like a face.[60] The tracking shot in Carrie does not merely depict this focusing

---

60 See Greifenstein, Lehmann: Manipulation der Sinne im Modus des Suspense, p. 106.

process once or twice, but oscillates nearly the entire time between rarefying[61] the field of vision and allowing it to generously expand, constantly recalibrating the relationship between individual elements and the whole. This play of singling out points of focus, this creation of a privileged, intimate perspective, which addresses the viewer directly as it grants insight, is the second criterion for an affect poetics of suspense. It is grasped as the introduction of discontinuity or as *a breakdown of a seemingly coherent perceptual context*.

As such, if we can talk of a dynamic of knowledge distribution, then it is precisely in the sense that knowledge is formulated as a specific rhythm. The way this rhythm alternates between stopping and forward motion is, in turn, the result of another temporal entanglement, defined above as the future perfect, which in concrete terms refers to the fact that *the bucket will have fallen.*[62] Two temporalities intersect here: first, the time relating to the various lingering pauses, repeatedly made manifest over the course of the prom night sequence in almost pure form: in Miss Collins's nostalgic reveries, or even more clearly in the arc shot around the dancing Carrie and Tommy, which seems to never want to end. It is during these lingering pauses that suspense is brought into relation with the mode of melodramatic fantasy investigated by Hermann Kappelhoff: time as an "accumulation of eternities."[63] The second temporality in question is linked to Chris's plot, whereby B must inexorably follow A, with all the cruelty this entails: the collection of the voting slips is followed by the announcement of the results, the walk on to the stage by the tipping of the bucket.

When Norma grins knowingly, *seeing* the X on the piece of paper, the respective acts of looking, knowing, and grinning coincide. This means that the camera – which was itself taking an intimate look at the voting slip just previously – now watches an act of seeing and, in the same way, constructs a relation, a visual-spatial constellation, which corresponds precisely to the temporal entanglement between the protection of Carrie's intimacy and her greatest possible humiliation. At this juncture, one perspective thus splits off from an assumed

---

61 With regard to Hitchcock, Deleuze speaks of "rarefied images." See Deleuze: Cinema 1, p. 12.
62 It is precisely this temporal linkage that enables suspense to create a feeling of *possibility* in the viewer. This feeling does not relate to the idea of allowing different alternatives to pass through one's mind (it is not in question whether or not the bucket will fall), but is rather generated via the way in which a retrospective gaze is inscribed into the future development: "As reality is created as something unforeseeable and new, its image is reflected behind it into the indefinite past; thus it finds it has from all time been possible, but it is at this precise moment that it begins to have been always possible, and that is why I said that that its possibility, which does not precede its reality, will have preceded it once the reality has appeared." Bergson: The Creative Mind, p. 82.
63 Kappelhoff: Matrix der Gefühle, p. 12.

continuum. The other positions of differing knowledge, which are now established over the course of the tracking shot and will be related to one another in the
section that follows, are thus to be understood as different perspectives in a
quite literal sense: as different bearers of the look, progressively splintering
the relationship between the viewer and what is happening in the film. One of
these bearers is the bucket itself.

Look, therefore, does not refer here to the represented activity of a character
(it does not, for example, relate to Norma's sneering grin as a psychological object), but rather functions by inscribing a specific rhythm into the entire set-up.
The tracking shot is thus not merely content to create one single relationship, but
rather multiplies the number of perspectives and relationships to such an extent
that the scene's entire set-up becomes highly charged.[64] This is what brings the
swinging motion's growing intensity to its climax in the next section.

The Crowning and the Humiliation

In the section that follows, the central role of the look and its intimate correla-
tion to the rhythm now become even clearer, as the section unfolds almost entirely in a series of shots and reverse shots, with the movement of the tracking
shot (from Carrie to the blood and then back again) now emphatically recon-
structed in Carrie's walk onto the stage. As different carriers of the look are
added one by one, a sort of web is created, drawing ever tighter as the sequence
progresses.

As already seen, the tracking shot ends with a zoom, ultimately capturing
Carrie and Tommy, bathed in brilliant blue, in a medium long shot (fig. 11).
With the cut that follows, the camera jumps closer and captures them in a medium close-up, switching to slow motion as they stand up from the table to begin
their walk to the stage. In combination with the use of slow motion, the music
also marks a shift in the relationship between the two temporalities. While the
tracking shot maintained a precarious balance between the modes of conspiracy
and nostalgia, here the pendulum has clearly swung in favor of "lingering here,"

---

64 Luc Lagier notes that De Palma's films always work to transform appropriated images by
augmenting them with a range of additional perspectives. Examples of this include the museum
sequence in DRESSED TO KILL (whose starting point is the museum scene in VERTIGO), or the assassination footage in BLOW OUT (1981). Lagier ascribes this process to one of the founding documents of New Hollywood: the Zapruder film, whose single, restricted perspective is perceived as
fatal. Lagier: Les mille yeux de Brian De Palma, Paris 2008, p. 99. See also the discussion on
paranoia in the third chapter of this book.

accompanied by an equally melodramatic ostinato, signifying the fact that "it's too late." To provide elegiac emphasis, the film's title theme swells into a tutti, played by the entire string section (repeatedly unfolding in harp arpeggios and later supplemented by woodwinds), while the slow motion, framing, and editing bathe the walk to the stage in the applause of the clapping mass. The constant shifting back and forth, between looking and being looked at, between Carrie's face and those of the people cheering her on, denies any impression that she is actually moving forward, instead swaying back and forth between radiant, pale, blue moonlight and dull-colored ochre (figs. 13–14).[65]

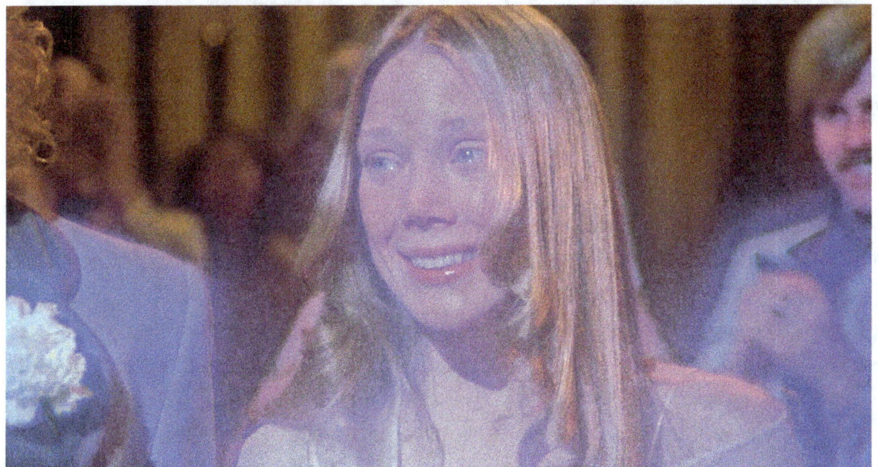

Figs. 13–14: Color, look and time.

---

65 In its use of color, the film most obviously references the poetics of classical melodrama and the youth melodramas of the 1950s in particular. See Kappelhoff: Matrix der Gefühle, pp. 162–168 for more on the melodramatic use of color. Of particular significance here is the discussion on concepts of "firstness" and the virtual, to which I will return in the following.

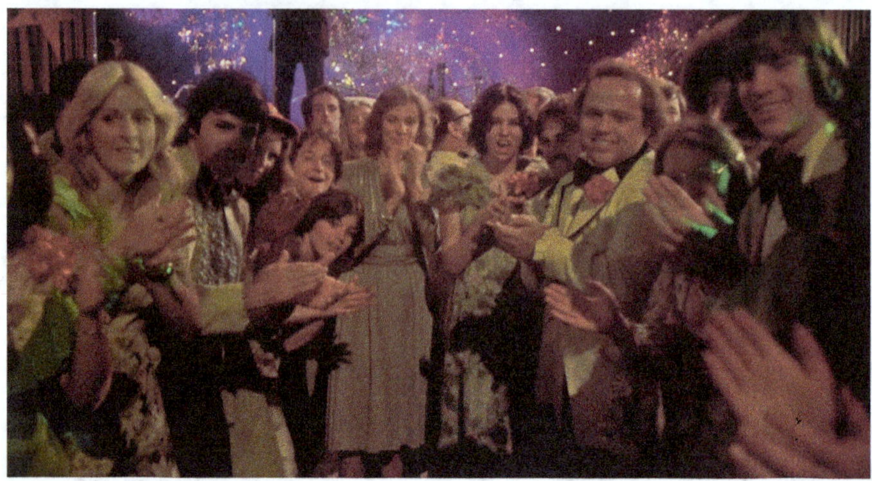

Fig. 14

It is, of course, no accident that the image swings between these particular colors; but is due, instead, to the entirely systematic translation of space into time. The looks directed at Carrie elevate her to a luminous, ethereal figure, freed from all transience, while those in the direction of the stage are already inclined towards the shade of red that awaits her in the bucket and that will soon dominate the entire scenery.

It is thus only logical in terms of cinematic thinking that when the second of these two looks is extended, it leads to Chris's face waiting under the stage, which returns Carrie's gaze, unseen. When Chris appears in close-up, the sumptuous air of the title theme, in a major-key, and its layers of high-pitched violins are countered by a dark, minor-key figure, played on cello and double bass, which, in phrasing that now tends towards the staccato, reinterprets the first theme's extreme legato swell; sudden stabs at a higher pitch now accentuate the metallic edge of the violins. The grand arc of the first theme, initially held to the downbeat, disintegrates into a series of syncopated, almost percussive interjections. As such, the music also generates an enormous formal contradiction, which corresponds to the one apparent at the level of color. Both themes alternate for the next minute and a half: gentle fluctuation within the music thus now expands to fluctuate between two, conflicting themes. This corresponds to the fact that the close-ups on Chris remain at normal speed and thus subtly interrupt the flow of the slow-motion images (subtly, as the fixed shot keeps movement within the image to a minimum anyway, reducing the degree of contrast between the images shown at normal speed and those in slow motion). This alternation is not to be understood as a rapid oscillation between two moods; rather, over the course of the scene, the swaying motion also inscribes a sensation of temporality, suspended between two opposing poles.

Carrie and Tommy have now arrived at the stage and walk up the steps. Stretched out by Chris's inclusion, the web of looks expands further with the addition of Sue's perspective, who is following events from near the back wall of the stage. Moments later, the bucket's perspective is also added, beneath which, in the meantime, the radiant pair has finally arrived. With the shot of the bucket swinging back and forth at normal speed, the figure of swinging motion – which, as a continuous, rhythmic principle made manifest in various forms, pervaded the entire sequence since the start of the tracking shot – now finally comes into focus (fig. 15).

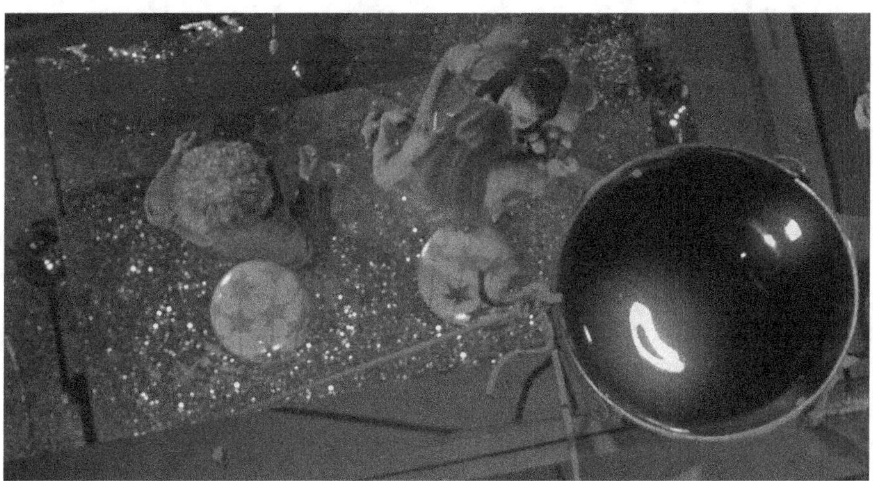

Fig. 15: The swinging is actualized.

In the words of Deleuze, one could speak here of a sudden shift from the virtual to the actual: the image as a whole swings before the bucket itself does. Deleuze distinguishes between

> two states of power-qualities, that is, affects: as they are actualised in an individuated state of things and in the corresponding *real connections* (with a particular space-time, *hic et nunc*, particular characters, particular roles, particular objects) and as they are expressed for themselves, outside spatio-temporal co-ordinates, with their own ideal singularities and their *virtual conjunction*. The first dimension is essential to the action-image and to medium-shots; but the other dimension constitutes the affection-image or the close-up. The

> pure affect, the pure expression of the state of things in fact relates to a face which express-
> es it (or to several faces, or to equivalents, or to propositions).[66]

I will discuss the function of the face below, but first, it is necessary to register two decisive insights. On the one hand, when the swinging focuses on the bucket, it is only a *momentary* shift. For immediately after the bucket has been shown, the swinging motion is detached from it and permeates the scene's entire configuration like a virus: in the close-up of Chris's hands shaking the rope, in the clattering of the rope against the stage's rear wall, in the back and forth between shot and counter shot, between the audience and the stage. These shots don't constitute an action-image in the Deleuzian sense; rather the montage refers to the image's duration itself. That is, on the other hand this swinging is not merely part of the staging, the affection-image's "meaning," but also denotes the dynamic of motion that disrupts the equilibrium of the cinematic image as a whole. This means, the affection-image is not constituted in itself but according to its relational aspects. In a nutshell, the swinging does not build toward the bucket's fall, but rather the bucket's fall fulfills the swinging motion as the movement that annuls the previous perceptual order and establishes a new one in its place.

This loss of equilibrium is materialized in the remaining events of the sequence. Whereas Carrie's walk to the stage was characterized by a near complete standstill of temporal progress, with the introduction of a second musical theme, the tempo is now upped slightly: the rate of cuts increases from an average shot length of around seven seconds to around five – 20 shots within a minute and a half. The true *accelerando*, however, only begins near the end of the next sequence (87 shots in 3:20 minutes or an average of 2.3 seconds per shot), again marked by a change in the music. Here, the alternation between the two themes gives way to a new one, which now combines the high and low string figures. Deep bass lines shift the title theme from a major to a minor key, almost like a tango rhythm, decelerated into slow motion; brass, additionally and significantly, now enter. The surging, *sforzato* figures press forward, capturing an energy, yet to be channeled into acceleration. With its severe appoggiatura, the restless bass contrasts heavily with the sharp violin accents, as the music grows steadily more percussive. As the climax approaches, the rate of the cuts increases to less than one second per shot, while the violin *staccato* continues to speed up. The montage itself, together with the music, is thus an essential factor in the dynamic escalation.

---

66 Deleuze: Cinema 1, pp. 102–103.

By the start of the *accelerando* section, all perspectives have been established; the section begins with a close-up of Chris and a detail shot of her hands pulling at the rope. This movement continues, as the rope whacks against the back of the stage, noticed in turn by Sue. Until now, all shots have been more or less repetitions from the previous section; mobilizing Sue's point of view, the sequence now gets properly underway. The establishment of the connection between Carrie and the bucket for the benefit of the spectator, previously performed by the tracking shot, is now carried out by Sue via shot reverse shot (figs. 16–17). The camera's brief tracking movements, in the point-of-view shots, function as a precise translation of Sue's searching gaze; additionally, Sue now also moves through the scenic space, like the camera had before, constructing the relationship between Carrie, the bucket, the rope, and Chris.

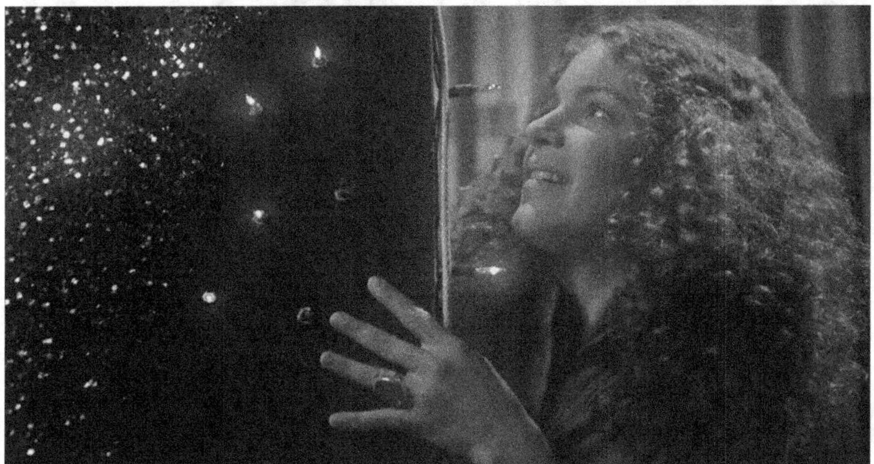

Figs. 16–17: Sue discovers the rope.

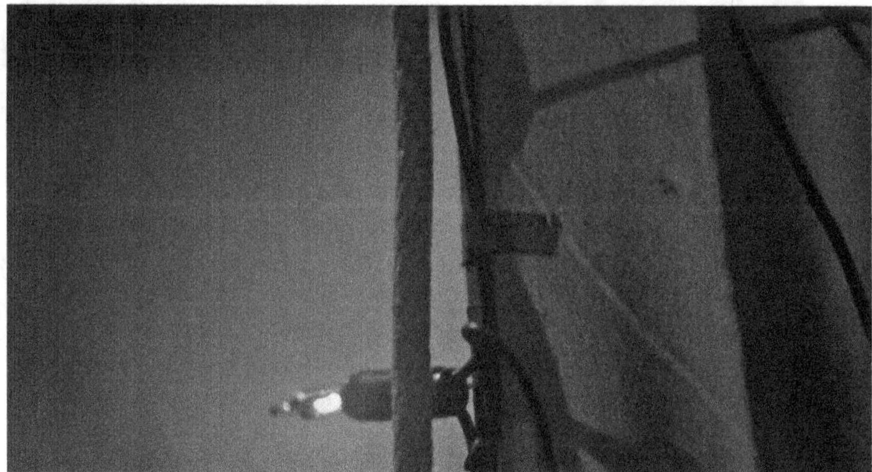

Fig. 17

Sue's actions set the scene's entire structural configuration in motion – a contagious dynamic, beginning from the tiny detail of the clattering rope, eventually grips the entire room. The first step in this progressive expansion occurs with the translation of the swinging rope into Sue's movement along the side of the stage; this movement, in turn, catches the attention of Miss Collins, drawing an ever-larger orbit. In the process, it is progressively disengaged from coherent plot connections and transferred into the dynamics of the music and montage. Put more precisely, at this level, there is no longer any categorical difference between individual elements of the staging. A huge detail shot of Chris's mouth appears alongside a medium close-up showing Sue and Miss Collins together; an accent in the string section carries the same value as the slap in the face Chris gives to Billy. The movement has completely freed itself from its representational obligations. The general back-and-forth becomes faster and faster, eventually spirals out of control, and discharges as the bucket crashes down, accompanied by a dramatic downward *glissando* in the strings, which peters out in the sounds of blood splattering and dripping and the crowd's shocked, sharp intake of breath. No sound can be heard during the tortuously long 45 seconds that follow, except for the banging bucket and the pattering of blood. This silence is connected to a state of shock conveyed in slow motion. Once the sound (and the normal speed) are finally restored, the spectator does not encounter them directly but now as filtered through Carrie's subjective, hyper-sensitive perception, bringing about a decisive shift in perspective that ushers in the destruction sequence.

Swinging Escalation

Let us return, once again, to the moment when the swinging movement's escalation takes on a life of its own, before finally spiraling out of control. At this point, a principle asserts itself, with all power at its disposal – one we have already attempted to grasp with Deleuze's concept of virtuality: not just *one* kind of swinging, but rather universal swinging. As formulated by Sergei Eisenstein, inasmuch as techniques of staging are characterized as "taking full account of all the stimulants in the shot," film perception becomes, thereby, "a direct physiological sensation."[67] Eisenstein explains this idea as follows:

> Because, while a shot is a visual *perception*, and a tone is a sound perception, *both visual and aural overtones are totally physiological sensations.*
>
> And, consequently, they are *of one and the same kind*, outside the sound of acoustic categories that serve as guides, paths to its achievement.
>
> For the musical overtones (a beat), the term 'I hear' is no longer strictly appropriate.
>
> Nor 'I see' for the visual.
>
> For both we introduce a new uniform formula: 'I feel.'[68]

The swinging bucket is no longer just seen or heard, but rather affectively, physically experienced as a movement – this is the decisive point that goes beyond Eisenstein's words – the consequences of which inexorably bring the entire configuration crashing down. Hence, the movement is directly related to the temporality of the formal context and, thereby, to the process of perception itself. In line with Eisenstein, this movement is transmitted to the spectator as a motor-infection – not to be understood as a spatial back-and-forth, but rather as a sensual urge to lose one's balance, to achieve a moment of weightlessness that suspends the normal motor-sensory order. This swinging overrides the scene's previous order and segues into the subsequent destruction. Suspense, at least

---

67 Eisenstein: The Fourth Dimension in Cinema, p. 191 (Writings 1922–32). Eisenstein's comment on this phenomenon, which he refers to using the concept of the overtone, is notable here: "Here it is a question of the same kind of de-individualisation of the *character* of a category of feeling as you find, for instance, in a different 'psychological phenomenon': when you feel the pleasure that derives from extreme *suffering*. Stekel writes of this: 'In cases of affective hypertension pain ceases to be regarded as pain, but is felt as nervous tension... But any powerful nervous tension has a tonic effect, and the heightened tone provokes a feeling of satisfaction and pleasure.'" Eisenstein: Footnote to The Fourth Dimension of Cinema, p. 186. The sensation of suspense is closely related to this principle of stimulation.
68 Eisenstein: The Fourth Dimension in Cinema, p. 186.

primarily, does not refer to the spatial order, the narrative, or the configuration of the characters, but rather to time itself, wherein movement spirals out of control.

In this sense, it can be said that suspense reflexively references what I defined in the introduction as expressive movement. Insofar as it inscribes a different rhythm into this expressive movement, for example, by pushing towards a climax, it challenges this movement's organic context.[69] When expressive movement is realized as a temporal form, to the same extent "at every point along its path,"[70] suspense introduces a sort of gestural dimension to the movement at a meta-level, aligning this movement with a vanishing point.[71] At stake here is clearly not the theoretical concept of expressive movement itself; rather, the description of just such a reflexive relationship is precisely what reveals its actual value. What is addressed here is the organic relationship between discrete, formal units, characteristic of classical Hollywood cinema – this can already be seen, as previously mentioned, in the extreme elongation of individual sequences in CARRIE, or even more clearly in Steven Spielberg's DUEL (1972), which extends the format of the chase sequence to feature length.[72]

The Time of the Imagination

But what does this undermining of organic, contextual associations mean for the spectator's concrete, affective experience? To answer this question, it is necessary to take a step back and return to the lengthy tracking shot, which sets in motion this escalating, swinging dynamic. As we have seen, the tracking shot begins with an image of intimate knowledge, which is then immediately destroyed. To a certain extent, this conflict is acted out over the entire course of the tracking shot, reaching an initial climax at the moment the voting slips are exchanged. Once again, the camera is a privileged spectator, but intimacy

---

69 "Wherever movements appear in the realm of the organic, they proceed according to a *unified rhythm*, exhibit a dynamic shape that can apparently also be detected via experiment. They [...] don't form a temporal mosaic, but rather a certain integrity is predetermined, within which the courses of individual movement are variable." Helmuth Plessner: Die Deutung des mimischen Ausdrucks, p. 77, emphasis my own.

70 Kappelhoff, Bakels: Das Zuschauergefühl, p. 85.

71 See Merleau-Ponty's comment on viscosity as an expression of a connection to a formal context. In: The Phenomenology of Perception, p. 12.

72 "Le cinéma moderne [...] a défait les émotions organiques pour travailler des plans plus subtils, il a ouvert le cinéma sur les dimensions plus grandes et plus petites." Bonitzer: Système des émotions [1982]. In: id.: Le champ aveugle. Essais sur le réalisme au cinéma, Paris 1999, pp. 95–102, here p. 102.

has given way to secrecy: it is no longer about the contrast between sensitive introspection and the harsh glare of the public eye, but rather about the scheme's presence in the midst of alleged innocence. It is almost astounding, however, how subtly this reevaluation takes place: only a small step separates a feeling of wounded intimacy from the desire for this intimacy's destruction.

A key factor contributing to this reevaluation is the fascination with the mechanics of the conspiracy, with its frictionless execution, and thus, above all, with the virtuosity of the camera in motion, able to move seemingly weightlessly and effortlessly through the space, focusing on one detail here and another there, before regaining its synoptic view. The interplay between the tension's ebb and flow, which will later characterize Carrie's walk to the stage in extremely magnified form, can already be found here in numerous small figures of movement; for example, once the rapid tracking shot up the stage's rear wall, tightly linked to its orienting object (the rope), arrives at the top, the accumulated tension is discharged through the camera's movement, which gradually comes to a standstill, and the renewed expansion of perspective.

In this context, it is worth briefly returning to the concept of the erotic that Bonitzer employs in reference to suspense. As already mentioned, this is not about the images' erotic content; it pertains, rather, to a specific, perceptual relationship, which Bonitzer traces back to the elasticity and viscosity of time. According to Laura Marks, one can likewise speak of an erotic dimension to the experience of space, analogous to that of time. The common denominator is the interplay between control and its loss, which Sierek recognized as fundamentally important for suspense. Marks writes: "What is erotic? The ability to oscillate between near and far is erotic. In sex, what is erotic is the ability to move between control and relinquishing, between being giver and receiver. It's the ability to have your sense of self, your self-control, taken away and restored – and to do the same for another person."[73] The oscillation between intimacy under threat and the cruelty of the plot (each of which understood as temporal relationships) analyzed above in CARRIE is closely linked to the back-and-forth between activity and passivity and/or subject and object, described by Marks: "What is erotic is being able to become an object with and for the world, and to return to being a subject in the world [...]."[74]

Marks sees this interplay as primarily realized in a perceptual relationship which she refers to as "haptic visuality." This form of visuality is manifested

---

73 Laura U. Marks: Touch. Sensuous Theory and Multisensory Media, Minneapolis/London 2002, p. xvi.
74 Marks: Touch, p. xvi.

in an inclination toward the suspension of the relationship between figure and ground and thus positions the spectator in a particular way:

> The term haptic *visuality* emphasizes the viewer's inclination to perceive haptically, but a work itself may offer haptic *images*. Haptic images do not invite identification with a figure so much as they encourage a bodily relationship between the viewer and the image. Thus it is less appropriate to speak of the object of a haptic look than to speak of a dynamic subjectivity between looker and image.[75]

Haptic visuality thus plays with the affective ambivalence that accompanies both a loss of control and a loss of distance. If we now return to the example of the rapid, vertical tracking shot up the back of the stage, for a few moments, the image becomes a line, before the camera reestablishes its greater authority and opens up to the space in front of it. This tracking shot is accompanied by dramatically ascending string figures, which, along with the decelerating movement, subsequently allow the built-up tension to fade away in a resounding, high-pitched tone. The flexibility and agility of the camera places the spectator in a relation of intimate familiarity with the objects, before again providing an overview of the scene. In Marks's words, once again:

> The point of tactile visuality is not to supply a plenitude of tactile sensation to make up for a lack of image. [...] Rather it is to point to the limits of sensory knowledge. By dancing from one form of sense-perception to another, the image points to its own caressing relation to the real and to the same relation between perception and the image.[76]

According to Marks, the camera's choreography outlines both a relationship to the scene's configuration and one between film and spectator. To emphasize once again: the erotic does not refer to reveling in sexually charged imagery (it is rather the other way round). Instead, as already discussed, these remarks directly connect the erotic dimension of suspense to the dimension of knowledge.

The decisive element of this connection is that, for suspense, the "dance" of the camera does not simply refer to a reversible, inconsequential back-and-forth between tactility and a synoptic view. Rather, as explained above, the moment of increased focus introduces an element of discontinuity into the continuous – a discontinuity which only *appears* reversible. As Luc Lagier remarks, in view of the relationship between Carrie and her mother, the figurative umbilical cord

---

75 Marks: Touch, p. 3.
76 Marks: Touch, p. 20.

is finally severed with the appearance of blood, making any return impossible.[77] When the camera thus returns from the "perverse object," to use Bonitzer's term, to the configuration as a whole, its view is no longer the same but has now, in fact, shifted (as in the example with Norma's look at the ballot). This split or shift in perspective introduces distortion into the larger, general context, a hidden current that relates to both the duration of the image and its ultimate collapse. Bonitzer speaks of suspense as an *anamorphosis of cinematographic time*, a perspectival distortion, initially perceived as an irritation, which can only produce new meaning through a shift in the standpoint of the observer.[78]

(To make a brief digression here, precisely this concept of an irreversible shift determines the relationship between CARRIE and other films, in terms of cinematic thinking. To name one obvious example, just as the divergence of a privileged perspective cannot be undone, the spectrum of cinematic expression was irrevocably changed by the methods for directing attention introduced by Hitchcock in YOUNG AND INNOCENT.[79] And just as this shift in the dramatic structure of suspense moves towards an inversion of the old order, it is possible to further develop the principles of staging from YOUNG AND INNOCENT in such a manner that these would, in turn, place the order of this very film in question.[80] By combining both faces into one figure, CARRIE thus challenges the distinction made in YOUNG AND INNOCENT between the radiant face of the heroine and the grotesque countenance of the killer. In a similar manner, the function of the look – already important in YOUNG AND INNOCENT but only alluded to selectively

---

77 See Lagier: Les mille yeux de Brian De Palma, p. 85.

78 See Bonitzer: Hitchcockian Suspense, p. 20. Roland Barthes also describes suspense as a form of distortion, which he brings into connection with the principle of relation and the opening of the (narrative) sequence, see Barthes: An Introduction to the Structural Analysis of Narrative [1966]. In: New Literary History, Vol. 6, No. 2 (Winter 1975), pp. 237–272, here pp. 267–268. Barthes does mention the "obvious" communicative function of suspense, that is, to secure contact to the reader and their ambivalent, affective reaction ("consumed with that particular anguish tinged with delight"); yet he emphasizes the logical dimension here above all, the reflexive play with structure, and thus comes to the conclusion that suspense addresses reason, not the "viscera."

79 See Greifenstein, Lehmann: Manipulation der Sinne im Modus des Suspense, p. 105. See also Francesco Casetti: Eye of the Century. Film, Experience, Modernity, New York/Chichester 2008, pp. 39–43.

80 As a genealogical force, suspense thus explicitly demonstrates the same temporal relationship which Bergson formulates as an implicit relation between the real and the possible: "That one can put reality into the past and thus work backwards in time is something I have never claimed. But that one can put the possible there, or rather that the possible may put itself there at any moment, is not to be doubted. [...] The possible is therefore the mirage of the present in the past." Bergson: The Creative Mind. p. 118.

in this earlier film – is radically applied to the configuration between stage and audience in CARRIE. These transformations constitute the major difference between the two films, specifically in terms of their affective positioning of the spectator: while YOUNG AND INNOCENT meticulously balances the relation between control and its loss, treading a fine line of subtle irony, CARRIE brings extreme opposites literally face to face and thus, from a comparable initial set-up, creates a much greater discrepancy between sentimental intimacy and infernal chaos.[81])

The connection between these two dimensions, the erotic and knowledge, lies in the temporality of the process of perception. To illustrate this, let us return, once again, to Carrie's walk to the stage: as previously described, this scene is concerned with the temporal (and spatial) entanglement between lingering stasis and pressing forward. But, in terms of the spectator's experience, how is this time filled qualitatively? Obviously, this time is not about reenacting the plot, nor collecting information potentially relevant for how the scene plays out. To the contrary, we're dealing here with an entirely unreal time, filled with imaginative activity, during which Carrie's radiant smile and the looming, blood-filled bucket are played off of one another. Time opens into a dimension no longer tied to the organic progression of the scene's units but rather almost entirely detached from them. This time is *given* to the spectator by the film. As Roger Greenspun notes, the film constantly transforms dream into nightmare;[82] the spectator's resulting experience is an emotional balancing act, that registers, alongside the complete indulgence in the beauty of appearances, a subtle undercurrent, which threatens to sweep them away.[83]

---

81 It goes without saying that this is not a value judgment, but rather a distinction between affect poetic strategies.

82 Greenspun: CARRIE, p. 17.

83 Against this background, Pauline Kael spoke of De Palma's satirical approach and sadism, the latter term finding broad echoes in feminist criticism of De Palma's films (which hardly can have been Kael's intention), see Kael: The Curse, p. 177. For all the justification of such a point of view, it still makes things too easy by failing to take seriously one of the two sides of the coin (the nostalgic reverie and the sadness for the loss of innocent intimacy) and relegating it, instead, to the status of a joke. It is, however, a misleading conclusion to assume that the truth of suspense lies below the surface, in terror; terror is to be taken just as seriously and lightly as nostalgia. Ultimately, it comes down to the veering back and forth between two temporalities. Certainly, when David Greven chalks up the hypervaluation of sadism to Kael, he, in turn, can be accused of failing to recognize the extent to which the film's ambivalence he identifies also draws on this question of temporality. See Greven: Representations of Femininity in American Genre Cinema, p. 108.

The staging of the suspense mode is thus naturally not directed at withholding information from the spectator: the outcome is clear from the very beginning. As Royal Brown rightly points out, for example, the poster for the film already employs the contrast between the radiant and blood-spattered Carrie.[84] The intention of the corresponding techniques in the film itself consist in conjuring up the latter image, superimposing the grimace onto the radiant visage. The idea is not to scare the spectator by fabricating a terrifying image; to the contrary, the subject of this fear is the instability of experience itself:[85] the leap from one face to another.

Face and Grimace

By contrasting these two faces, as I have already mentioned, CARRIE appropriates a motif from YOUNG AND INNOCENT. Although, in the earlier film, this confrontation seems at first glance almost accidental, in CARRIE, it forms the very core of the scenic construction, closely connected to the theme of the look. (If we want to know how suspense creates histories, it is such a retroactive reversal from the margins to the center of a film's poetic logic that we might regard as paradigmatic.)

YOUNG AND INNOCENT dramatizes a relationship of (ostensible) reversibility between the face and the ballroom (the tracking shot through the ballroom segues into a close-up of a face, while, in its reversal, the eyes' twinkling is detached from this face and transposed onto the entire hall); in the prom night sequence, the face initially functions in a similar manner, as a hinge between intimate and public realms. This function does not begin with the tracking shot (introduced by Chris's face in close-up), but in fact much earlier. Schematically speaking, the film works over the entire course of the sequence to convey Carrie's introverted face, occasionally bashfully concealed in her hands, to the stage and, once there, to expose it to the gazes of the assembled crowd, until this confrontation unleashes Carrie's own gaze, in turn.

The spectator is incorporated into this process in a complex way: not only in relation to their advanced knowledge of the plot against Carrie, but also in how Carrie's facial expression is repeatedly made the focal point for a number of contagious effects as the sequence unfolds – for example, as she responds with a

---

84 See Brown: Considering De Palma, p. 60.
85 See Robert MacLean: The Big-Bang Hypothesis. Blowing Up the Image. In: Film Quarterly, Vol. 32, No. 2 (Winter 1978/1979), pp. 2–7, here p. 5.

smile to Miss Collins's story or when she buries her face in her hands in faux-shame after voting for herself on the slip. In these moments, the spectator is emphatically linked to Carrie's perspective. The film's rhythm melodramatically translates this perspectival bond into the spectator's temporal experience: the cut from the brief scene in the car to inside the hall is like being thrown into the deep end; the initially rapid cuts at the start correspond to a state of nervous intensity; as Carrie gradually acclimates to her surroundings, the montage also calms down, until it halts entirely in the endless arc shot around Carrie and Tommy as they dance together.

The tracking shot provides contrast, not only as it is influenced by the face of Carrie's rival; it furthermore identifies the face's new significance for the film's staging in general. This significance is established in the detachment of the rhythm from Carrie's perspective, as it passes on to connect Norma, Chris, Billy, Sue, and the bucket – in other words, as it becomes autonomous.[86] In precisely this sense, the image itself becomes a face through the tracking shot, possessed of its own perspective and rhythm. The image organizes itself into a face by bringing its collected elements into alignment and placing them into relationship with one another – it is assembled into a whole. During the process of its constitution, however, the movement points preemptively to the thing that will prevent closure of this whole: the relation between Carrie and the bucket.

Hence, to adopt a distinction made, with recourse to Merleau-Ponty, by Vivian Sobchack: the spectator's attention is, on the one hand, directed to the intended *object* of the tracking shot and, decisively on the other, to the intentional *act* of redirecting attention.[87] The initiation of suspense is thus based on a dual reference: a self-reflexive gesture of showing. The shift in the spectator's attention is nothing other than the experience of a physically palpable resistance, a stubbornness set against the cinematic process that is most clearly revealed in the movement of the camera: "It is at moments of disjunction that the moving camera reveals itself most obviously as an 'other's' intentional consciousness."[88]

---

86 On the question of the standpoint of the spectator, Greven writes: "To take CARRIE as an example, points of identification with Carrie undergo so many radical changes and challenges throughout the film that our own spectatorial position can only be described as liquid." Greven: Representations of Femininity in American Genre Cinema, p. 190. This idea of a standpoint in flux appears appealing, but neglects the fact that conflicts emerge between these different positions; they do not simply follow one another, but are rather brought into relation with one another.

87 See Sobchack: Toward Inhabited Space. The Semiotic Structure of Camera Movement in the Cinema. In: Semiotica, Vol. 41, No. 1/4 (1982), pp. 317–335, here pp. 322–323.

88 Sobchack: Toward Inhabited Space, p. 324.

If film perception always rests on the doubled relationship of the spectator to the intended object and the intentional act, suspense heightens the tension between these two aspects until a new perspective splits off entirely. At these moments, the accumulation of tension in the body of the spectator is measurable in the camera's shifting of the image space, together with its continuous realignment and refocusing of perspective. Suspense thus orchestrates the spectator's entanglement in cinematic seeing and hearing, in which each individual movement is not apprehended by their perception, but continuously and emphatically perceived in relation to the whole; in other words, in relation to the fact of transformation.

Simultaneously, the camera stakes out the course, subsequently traversed in the following sequence of Carrie walking to the stage. In the process, the spectator becomes part of a configuration of movements that successively slip out of their control – until the bucket finally falls.[89] While the tracking shot organizes the image into a face, the walk to the stage and the coronation are staged as the gradual derangement of its facial features – an idea condensed at various points in the expressions of Sue, Miss Collins, and Tommy. At various points, their faces each convey the loss of balance and apparent order in expressive, mimetic gestures (in the case of the two women, the movement from radiant smiles to confusion, for Tommy, the outrage when faced with Carrie's total humiliation); all of which, like Carrie's visage earlier in the scene, possess similar contagious effects. The relationship between stage and audience (that is, the preconditions for the face's visibility) increasingly splinters into fragments, which are reassembled by the montage with virtually no regard for their actual spatial position. In the process, elements of Chris's face, isolated in various close-ups – eye, mouth, tongue – also evolve into elements of the climactic dynamic of swinging escalation, striving towards a new order, exceeding that of the face.[90]

The destruction of the face, in a dual sense, ensues in truly emphatic fashion: in the torrent of blood as it gushes out over Carrie; a vertical, downward movement (accompanied by a violin glissando) diametrically opposed to both the weightless sensation conveyed by the slow motion and the dynamic of swinging escalation (figs. 18–19).

---

89 See here and on the following: Greifenstein, Lehmann: Manipulation der Sinne im Modus des Suspense, pp. 108–109.

90 William Paul remarks that this fragmentation of the face refers back to the fragmentation of Carrie's body in the shower scene at the start of the film. See Paul: Laughing Screaming. Modern Hollywood Horror & Comedy, New York 1994, p. 360.

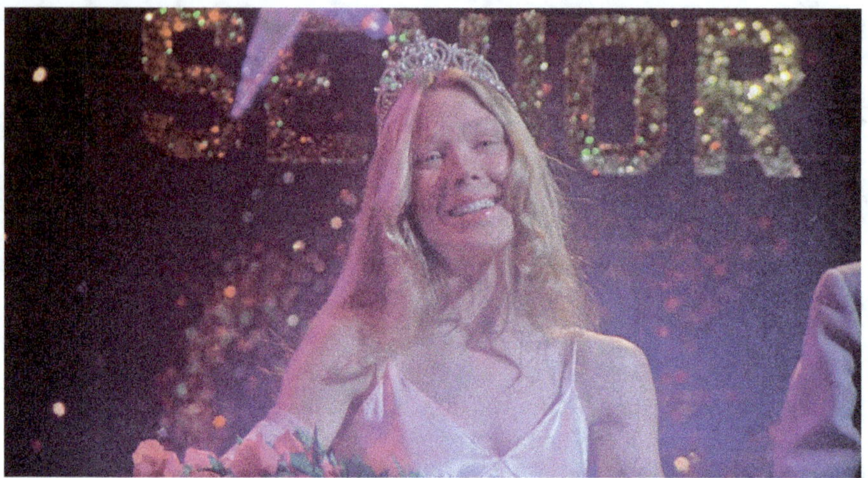

Figs. 18–19: The red breaches the blue.

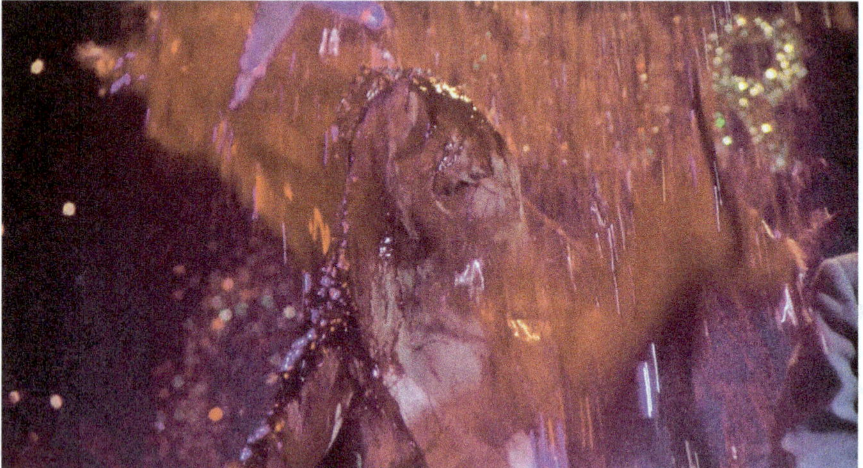

Fig. 19

This violent impulse tears apart the contextual associations created by the escalating, swinging movement and induces a state of shock. As a temporal interruption, this arrest determines the abyss, portended by the diametrical opposition,
which now opens between stage and audience. In the process, the spectator is
yanked out of the reenactment of movement, in which they appeared fully integrated only moments before. Unfolding in time, the dynamic of suspense now
drives towards the vanishing point, a point of radical reversal, imaginarily pre-

sent throughout: blue becomes red, weightlessness yields to gravity, the radiant face is transformed into a grotesque. The perceptual order is turned on its head.

The *inversion of the previous order* is the third and final core-criterion of the affect poetics of suspense, following the production of relations and the divergence of a privileged, scopic authority. Precisely as the movement finally spins out of control, the principle of its uncontrollability is isolated, objectified, and fixed (that it may then be played out, in the destruction sequence, to its final, logical conclusion). Carrie herself embodies this principle, manifested in her telekinetic powers. Brian De Palma identifies this power as emotion: "I felt the telekinesis was basically a device to trick, and I wanted to use it as an extension of her emotions – her feelings that were completely translated into actions, that only erupted when she got terribly excited, terribly anxious and terribly sad. It was always a little out of control [...]."[91]

Telekinesis is elevated into a metaphor for suspense itself, in this remark, as it invokes precisely the same fear-craving balancing act between control and its loss which is constantly performed by the spectator. Nicole Brenez also interprets telekinesis in terms of its connection to suspense, specifically in the relation between shot and reverse shot:

> La télékinésie dans CARRIE n'est pas du tout un force surnaturelle satanique comme dans le roman homonyme de Stephen King, mais un pouvoir formel logique. Carrie, c'est le principe intérieur du contrechamp, son étrangeté constitutive, elle l'anime à sa guise, en faisant tomber les cendriers, en faisant voler les couteaux qui vont crucifier sa mère, en faisant s'effondrer les maisons: puisqu'elle y est toujours déjà. Elle est toujours au fond de toute image, comme ici la douche au fond de l'espace, le flou au fond du net et l'ombre au fond du corps.[92]

Brenez's comments initially reinforce the idea that CARRIE's approach cannot be derived from classical horror film traditions – a distinction that De Palma also makes himself.[93] She draws instead on the concept of logic, which links her con-

---

91 Brian De Palma in: Mike Childs, Alan Jones: De Palma has the Power! [1977]. In: Brian De Palma. Interviews, edited by Laurence F. Knapp, Jackson 2003, pp. 37–45, here p. 41.

92 Nicole Brenez: De la figure en général et du corps en particulier. L'invention figurative au cinéma, Paris/Brüssel 1998, p. 329. From this perspective, Brenez primarly sees CARRIE as taking PSYCHO a step further by seeking to get to the bottom of what Marion Crane has to do with Norman Bates: "Carrie figure ainsi le développement de cette hypothèse que l'autre, Norman Bates, le corps synthétique, est le plus intime du même, Marion Crane apparemment en train de se laver du Mal au moment où elle déchaîne la mort." Ibid.

93 "I've made so many films and people still keep saying 'The Horror Genre.' They never seem like horror films to me! Horror films are 'Hammer Films' – vampires and Frankenstein. I love

siderations to what Deleuze calls a "figure of thought." On the other hand, and this is the decisive point for us, the function of the gaze and the face are transposed in abstract terms into the arrangement of the montage and the relation between shot and reverse shot. From this perspective, it seems only logical that the contrast between stage and audience and between seeing and being seen (equated here with being laughed at), expressed by the pairing of the frontal shots/reverse shots, does not just result in the unleashing of Carrie's telekinetic powers, but further in the division of the image itself into split screen. The omniscience, staged and celebrated by the tracking shot, is thus opposed by the destruction of any coherent spectatorial position and the denial of knowledge, the disintegration of any sort of space which could be met with a gaze of contemplative distance and mastery. When the face meets its antithesis, however, this nevertheless does not mean the suspense has come to an end. To the contrary, from here on the film piles layer upon layer, gathering up the numerous threads of the suspense's dramatization, one after another, conclusion atop purported conclusion, without ever allowing the spectator to definitively come to rest. As Lagier writes,[94] Carrie's return to her mother's house is already an illusion, no less than Sue's final dream. Accordingly, De Palma describes the meaning of the famous shock effect of this (actually final) scene: "A sad little scene, and all of a sudden, we're never going to let you go."[95]

2.3 Conclusions and Historical Outlook

Telekinesis and Emotion: Shock and Suspense

If grief is understood as a disposition toward time and impermanence that accepts "the circumstance of loss [...] in its entire brutality or cruelty,"[96] then De Palma describes, in very precise terms, the shifts connected to this shock from one temporal relationship to another and from activity to passivity. The final scene depicts an act of farewell – only to emphasize at the last moment that not only will there never be a farewell, but that it is the spectator who will never be released (figs. 20 – 21).

---

those pictures but I don't feel it's exactly what I'm doing. Maybe I'm trying to hammer out a new genre, somehow..." De Palma in: Childs, Jones: De Palma has the Power!, pp. 44 – 45.

94 See Lagier: Les mille yeux de Brian De Palma, p. 85.

95 De Palma, quoted by Brown: Considering De Palma, p. 61.

96 Ludwig Binswanger: Melancholie und Manie. Phänomenologische Studien, Pfullingen 1960, p. 124. See also the discussion on melancholy in the 4th chapter.

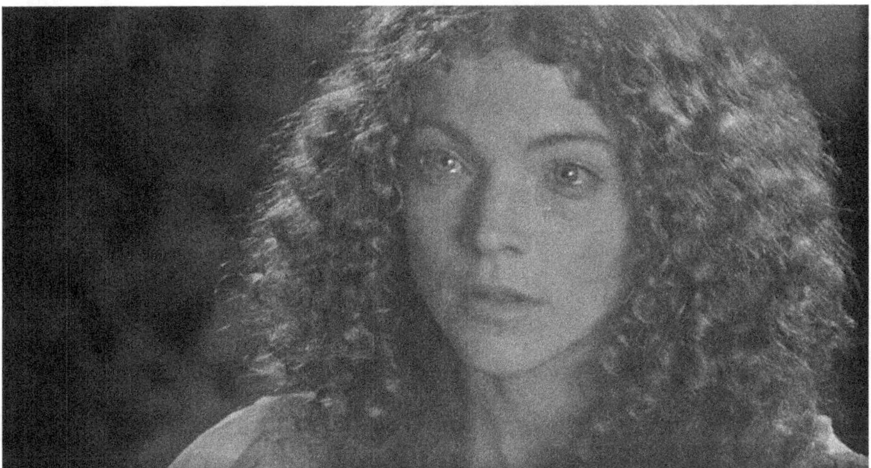

Figs. 20–21: Tears flow and the order is torn apart.

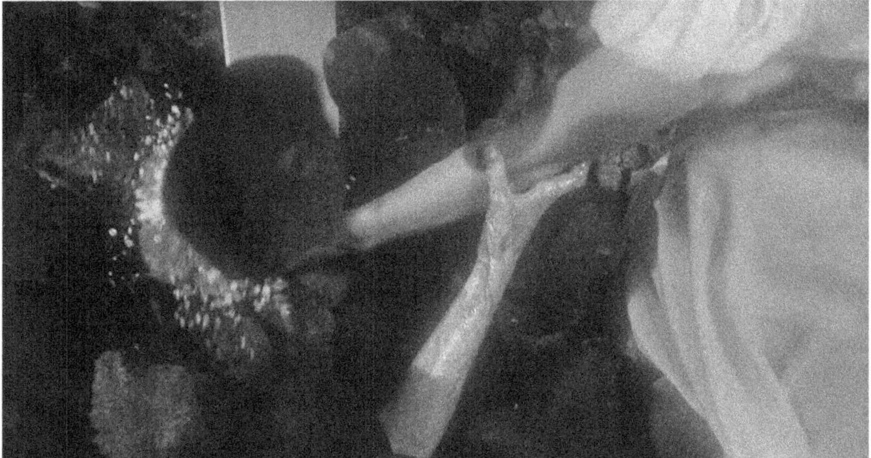

Fig. 21

Once again, the final scene concentrates the dramatic structure of suspense that has shaped CARRIE throughout. In closing, I would like to attempt to reconstruct this scene as the navigation of a concrete, affective experience; simultaneously, this reconstruction will incorporate the insights collected over the course of the chapter, bringing us to a conclusion. I wish to contextualize these insights via a series of comments by Maurice Merleau-Ponty on the perception of shapes (*Gestalt*), which can be perfectly applied to this final scene. Merleau-Ponty writes (in connection to the question of the relationship between feeling and meaning):

> If I walk along a shore towards a ship which has run aground, and the funnel or masts merge into the forest bordering on the sand dune, there will be a moment when these details suddenly become part of the ship, and indissolubly fused with it. As I approached, I did not perceive resemblances or proximities which finally came together to form a continuous picture of the upper part of the ship. I merely felt that the look of the object was on the point of altering, that something was imminent in this tension, as a storm is imminent in storm clouds. Suddenly the sight before me was recast in a manner satisfying to my vague expectation. Only afterwards did I recognize, as justifications for the change, the resemblance and contiguity of what I call 'stimuli' – namely the most determinate phenomena, seen at close quarters and with which I compose the 'true' world. [...] But these reasons for correct perception were not given as reasons beforehand. The unity of the object is based on the foreshadowing of an imminent order which is about to spring upon us a reply to questions merely latent in the landscape. It solves a problem set only in the form of a vague feeling of uneasiness, it organizes elements which up to that moment did not belong to the same universe and which, for that reason [...] could not be associated. By placing them on the same footing, that of the unique object, synopsis makes continuity and resemblance possible [...].[97]

Merleau-Ponty illustrates here how a figure is constituted in collaboration with the perceptual activity of an observer. One fundamental point of this illustration, for our purposes, is the element of unease, which, according to Merleau-Ponty, is present at the start of this process. He describes it as a feeling of indeterminate, unlocalized tension, aligned with something imminent – in both a spatial and temporal sense. This unease is characterized by the fact that it can only be retrospectively traced back to clearly defined causes, specifically because these causes relate to the process as a whole as it unfolds in time. Hence, when Merleau-Ponty speaks of placing the elements of an object on the same footing, he is referring to the process of change itself. This process of transformation (duration) advances to consciousness precisely to the degree by which the accumulated tension proceeds, at the same time, towards its climax and – in suspense – its tipping point.

In this sense, the structure of the image at the beginning of the scene is understood, to use Merleau-Ponty's words, as a latent question or, as formulated by Peretz,[98] as a spectatorial address, provoked by the specific manner of perception. This is precisely what Bonitzer means when he writes of "the gaze, itself evoked by a third element, a perverse object or a stain."[99] Here we find the formal equivalent of what eludes cognitive theories in the relationship between the

---

97 Merleau-Ponty: Phenomenology of Perception, p. 17.
98 Peretz: Becoming Visionary, p. 26.
99 Bonitzer: Hitchcockian Suspense, p. 28.

spectator and a film's characters: precisely because the image is structured as a question we are justified in establishing a spectator's engagement.

In this context, Sierek speaks of the spectator's eye settling into the empty spaces of the image: "Tension is created in this gaping, brittle 'in-between.' It expands the space between two points and empties it instead of making it solid. Tension is extensive rather than intensive. It is only once these gaps have been emptied that they can be filled with the body of the observer, sucking him or her into the vacuum [...]."[100] This is precisely the function of slow motion and the gradual ebb and flow of the music on the soundtrack in the prom night sequence. Therein we can explain why the unease described by Merleau-Ponty cannot be clearly localized: it spreads out in relation to the whole and does not pertain to any clearly definable intensity. Further, this indeterminate quality is not simply a lack of a clearly attributable localization: "We must recognize the indeterminate as a positive phenomenon. It is in this atmosphere that quality arises. Its meaning is an equivocal meaning; we are concerned with an expressive value rather than with logical signification."[101] In the case of tension, we are dealing with a quality of unease, which suffuses space and time; we are not concerned, thereby, with "pure" feeling, but always with a meaningful context.[102] Precisely in the moment at which unease focuses on a clearly defined intensity – the moment of shock, as it were – suspense reaches its tipping point: "Emotion always means, as Daney put it, 'the shift from one register into another.'"[103]

We thus return once again to the question of the connection between telekinesis and suspense and between suspense and emotion, respectively. Brown paraphrases De Palma's own stance regarding this question: "'The telekinesis,' De Palma said, 'is just an extension of Carrie's own adolescent emotionality, basically. It has no good or evil attached to it; it's just an extension of her subconscious desires. And, unfortunately, it's used in a kind of very emotional sense. She has no control over it; it just sort of erupts.'"[104] Regarding the final scene

<hr>

100 Sierek: Spannung und Körperbild, p. 117.
101 Merleau-Ponty: Phenomenology of Perception, p. 6.
102 "Analysis, then, discovers in each quality meanings which reside in it." Merleau-Ponty: Phenomenology of Perception, p. 5.
103 "L'émotion serait en chaque cas *le basculement d'un registre à un autre*." Bellour: Le Dépli des Émotions, p. 108.
104 Brown: Considering De Palma, pp. 58–59.

and the shock effect produced by the arm bursting out from the grave, this idea of "eruption" is of particular interest.[105]

How is the shock effect created in the final scene, a sort of negative "order which is about to spring upon us a reply to questions merely latent in the landscape"? If one takes De Palma's suggestion seriously, then it is emotion itself, entirely consuming the plot, which shakes the entire configuration of the world like a kind of seismic quake and allows it to appear in a new light.[106] This "e-motion," as an outwardly-directed movement, necessarily raises the question of the possibility of control – not just for the character but, given that it consistently plays on the boundary between activity and passivity, above all, for the spectator.[107] If one follows Merleau-Ponty's description, the shock transporting the old order into the new is based in the spectator's feeling that, "the look of the object was on the point of altering" – the shock thus certainly does not arise from nothing. The "eruption" of emotion, from this point of view, represents the tipping point in a balancing act. In this sense, in reference to CARRIE's staging, Royal Brown discusses an awareness that the most profound effects on the spectator are not produced by the sudden outbreak of casual violence; rather they arise from modulated variations (however extreme), which are all cut from the same cloth.[108] To reuse a formulation from the beginning of this chapter: discontinuity always remains related to continuity.

---

105 I am aware that telekinesis does not, strictly speaking, play a role at the level of the plot here; however, what I'm interested in is a specific principle of how movement is composed.
106 "Our deepest emotional experiences intervolve changes in our identities and changes in the patterns of our perceptions. They are usually accompanied by realizations that we are perceiving the world or our selves in a new or different 'light'." Sue Cataldi: Emotion, Depth, and Flesh. A Study of Sensitive Space. Reflections on Merleau-Ponty's Philosophy of Embodiment, New York 1993, p. 151.
107 See, for example, Kappelhoff: Matrix der Gefühle, p. 13.
108 Brown goes on to explain that the film itself has already presented the model of dramatic structure applied here in almost blatant fashion: "De Palma fits CARRIE's finale into the film very much the same way a composer would close a musical composition, by reusing a 'progression' that has been solidly established within the artistic structure. Each of the film's three climactic scenes – the locker room scene leading up to Carrie's first menstruation; the sequence where Carrie and Tommy Ross are crowned queen and king of the senior prom and then doused in pig's blood; and the concluding sequence – are all shot in slow motion. So by the time the third sequence of slow-motion lyricism begins, the audience is well acquainted with the inevitable modulation to blood, whether menstrual, pig or, ultimately, the blood of death." Ibid. Brown's cloth metaphor refers in advance to Deleuze, according to whom Hitchcock's conception of the image does not refer to painting or theatre, but rather to weaving. See Deleuze: Cinema 1, p. 204.

Bill Schaffer (employing PSYCHO as an example) describes the emotional experience of suspense as a state of temporal and physical conflict, whereby the direction of the spectator's gaze through the movement of the camera is manifested as a compulsion to face the unavoidable fate of one's own affect[109] – entirely in the sense of presentiment described by Merleau-Ponty:

> Suspense plays on the helplessness of my point of view; I am being rushed towards thoughts that are not my own. At the narrative level in suspense I am too early – I must wait to see what happens – but in terms of the privacy of my perception I am too late from moment to moment. I can do no better than meet the fate of my affect. [...] *The organ the director plays upon is the organ of my lateness.*[110]

The disruption of the subject position described by Schaffer ultimately stems from the recognition of the affect as one's own, as something the spectator cannot renounce because its self-evidence is generated within their own emotions. Schaffer thus grasps the emotional dimension of suspense, in the last instance, as a transformation of corporeal self-relation:

> What I really hope/fear may emerge, at any instant whatever, is an image of my own secret body, an image of my fate, the body that is seen by time but does not appear in space: the virtual body which expresses me as pure possibility. [...] The question which plagues me as I put myself in Hitchcock's hands is finally not just 'what will happen next?', but 'what will I have become?'[111]

The so-called paradox of suspense, usually broken down by cognitive theories into an over-simplified dichotomy of knowledge versus its lack, reveals itself to be a question of the bodily experience of perception, which is recreated with each viewing and which can never be completely traced back to an earlier experience:

> What remains indeterminate even when the narrative outcome is certain, what may have changed in the interim since my first viewing and which may now be ready to reveal hith-

---

109 Schaffer is referring here to the moment where a visual limit is crossed in the opening scene of PSYCHO – a process that demonstrates the interplay between continuity and discontinuity par excellence, whereby the "screen" that splits the space in two (the window frame and the blind) is crossed in one continuous camera movement (it is this pattern of movement that is referenced in the title of the essay: Cutting the Flow). Bill Schaffer: Cutting the Flow: Thinking PSYCHO. In: Senses of Cinema, No. 6 (2000), URL: http://www.sensesofcinema.com/2000/6/psycho/, last accessed March 12th, 2019.
110 Schaffer: Cutting the Flow.
111 Schaffer: Cutting the Flow.

erto unknown dimensions, is not something in the film itself considered as an object kept at a distance, it is the film *in me*, as it lives in me. Ultimately, it is myself.[112]

If suspense is a form of cinematic thinking that shapes reflexivity as the spectator's corporeal-affective experience, this thinking is aimed at insistently destabilizing the integrity of the spectator's position. From this perspective, splitting the spectator refers to nothing else than the spectator's involvement in a process which confronts them with the inevitable fact that their own feelings are outside of their control. This dimension of the unknown inside the self is renewed by the shock each time. But this principle of shock does not operate arbitrarily; ultimately at stake is a question of balance.[113] The idea of suspense as a state of uncertainty concerns the spectator's sense of balance, their feeling for proportion and rhythm, in a very direct and literal way – one that includes all the implications of the complex relationship between different temporalities already discussed. In the destruction sequence, even the denial of an authoritative perspective belongs to the web of relations which constitute the dramatic structure of suspense. Moreover, in its specific duration, this denial occupies a well-calculated place in the progression of tension and release, which structures CARRIE in quasi-musical fashion. The image of balance created over the course of the entire film is highly unstable – thus the goal of the final scene is to pull the rug from under the spectator for one, last time.

Suspense in New Hollywood: Subverting Genres

CARRIE is not the only New Hollywood film to try its hand at keeping the spectator up in the air. Based on the criteria for the suspense mode that have already been discussed – the creation of relations, intertwining of temporalities/divergence of particular perspectives, and inversion of order – we may assemble a small panorama of relevant films. Additionally, these criteria can now be developed further, in order to characterize the specific character of suspense in New Hollywood. Examining these films reveals the explosive, affective power of a poetics which operates using both imperceptible convergences and shock-like inversions. One object of this explosive power is the categorial order of the classi-

---

112 Schaffer: Cutting the Flow.

113 On the connection between suspense, shock, and balance, see also André Bazin: A Bergsonian Film: THE PICASSO MYSTERY. In: Bazin at Work: Major Essays & Reviews from the Forties & Fifties, edited by Bert Cardullo, New York/London 1997, pp. 211–219.

cal genre system; time and again, of primary concern are both the undermining of dichotomies and the sudden recognition of the other in the self.

As was already apparent with CARRIE, one possible way of further developing the fundamental operation of suspense – the creation of relations – consists in multiplying these relations. This applies to various other De Palma films, as well; aside from CARRIE, above all in SISTERS (1973), OBSESSION (1976), and, of course, DRESSED TO KILL (1980), which, in terms of interweaving different relations, remains his most complex and dense film, alongside RAISING CAIN (De Palma 1992) and FEMME FATALE (De Palma, France 2002). THE OTHER (Robert Mulligan 1972) works with the old motif of the doppelgänger, but relates this to fundamental problems of cinematic form in highly original fashion. The film is about a pair of twins, one of whom is dead but, however, still seems to exist for the other; the relationship is instituted in the film through the consistent establishment of shared lines of sight between the two characters (even within one and the same shot), but without ever including both within the image-frame simultaneously. Relations are thus not multiplied here; rather, one and the same relation is constantly varied over the course of the film. Other films markedly allow relations to proliferate, as in THAT COLD DAY IN THE PARK (1969) and 3 WOMEN by Robert Altman. In both films, Altman's primary focus is on small shifts in the power structures between different characters, which eventually snowball into dramatic upheavals and, thereby, import elements of psychological and dramatic ambiguity into suspense. These films, as a result, convey a far less obvious impression of their attention to form than "mid-period" De Palma. On the other hand, suspense becomes an incredibly subtle medium and integrates even the most delicate registers of cinematic expressivity; hence, especially in 3 WOMEN, changes in light and nuances of facial expression are bestowed with enormous significance. The dense atmosphere created by these films functions like a web, in which the spectator becomes increasingly entangled. Proliferating relations are also evident in WILLARD (Daniel Mann 1971), which explores pathological relationships in similar fashion to Altman, albeit more tinged with horror – the relationships, in this case, are between a reclusive bachelor named Willard and his rats. Similar to the role of telekinesis in CARRIE, the rats function as an extension of Willard's state of mind; and, like in CARRIE, this extension is a blessing and a curse in equal measure. Deleuze and Guattari dedicate a short discussion to the film in *A Thousand Plateaus*, in connection with the idea of becoming-animal.[114]

---

114 See Gilles Deleuze, and Félix Guattari: A Thousand Plateaus. Capitalism and Schizophrenia, New York 2004, p. 257 and p. 268.

The films that interweave different temporalities usually proceed in substantially more direct fashion – for example, through the extreme prolongation of this process of interweaving, so that, occasionally, it even encompasses the entire film. The prime example of this tendency is Steven Spielberg's DUEL (1972).[115] This film embodies two trends, which each left a considerable mark on New Hollywood: the development of the modern horror film into an affect-poetic arrangement that annihilated the boundaries of classical genres ("the infiltration of its major themes and motifs into every area of 70s cinema")[116] and the road movie's emergence as a new, expressive form that connected diverse configurations of classical genres while maintaining a decidedly anti-genre sensibility.[117]

DUEL draws on the old format of the chase sequence (between a passenger car and a 40-ton truck) and allows it to take over the entire film. In clear contrast to CARRIE, for example, here the tension barely ever lets up, so that, towards the end of the film, the spectator may experience symptoms of fatigue, cramping, and exhaustion. In places, the chase slogs up a mountain pass with tortuous slowness, like a race between two snails, before accelerating again into hysteria. Here, the dramatic structure of suspense is materialized in the linkage between the spectator's perspective and the lines of sight generated by the car – which is a shared characteristic with the road movie.[118] The car and film converge here as two locomotive apparatuses or machines, especially in their positioning of their respective "passengers" – for better or worse, the driver/spectator is glued to their seat, at the mercy of the vicissitudes of the dramatic structure in its composition of affective intensities.

One consequence of this state of helplessness is that the focus is notably displaced onto the characters' physical state. In DUEL, and similarly in films like SORCERER (William Friedkin 1977) or ALIEN (Ridley Scott 1979), close-ups of hands and faces dripping with sweat are more than just centers of gravity for the staging. Rather, New Hollywood's pivotal refinement of expressive registers (camerawork, lighting, editing, acting, sound design) constitutes a new relationship between the spectator's body-image and the images of bodies in film, whereby the mechanisms employed by suspense to involve the spectator zero-in on beads of sweat or the delicate play of muscles – an approach famously carried to extremes much later in MISSION: IMPOSSIBLE (Brian De Palma 1996).

---

115 For a comprehensive analysis of the film, see Hauke Lehmann: Schrecken der Straße. Steven Spielbergs DUEL als Road Movie-Horrorfilm. In: Uta Felten, and Kerstin Küchler (eds.): Kino und Automobil, Tübingen 2013, pp. 159–185.

116 See Wood: Hollywood from Vietnam to Reagan, pp. 44–45 and pp. 63–143.

117 See David Laderman: Driving Visions. Exploring the Road Movie, Austin 2002, p. 3.

118 See Kolker: A Cinema of Loneliness, in reference to BONNIE AND CLYDE, pp. 40–43.

This focus on the body sets up the last of the fundamental transformations carried out by the cinema of suspense on classical Hollywood, namely the clear accentuation of the moment of inversion. This moment usually forms the point of introduction into the visual world of horror, for example, in the notorious scene in JAWS where the shark devours Quint, the opening of IT'S ALIVE (Larry Cohen 1974), or the dog attacks in WHITE DOG (Samuel Fuller 1982). This principle is clearly applied in systematic fashion in the so-called slasher film, whose prototypes include such films as BLACK CHRISTMAS (Bob Clark, Canada 1974) and COMMUNION/ALICE, SWEET ALICE (Alfred Sole 1976), before the paradigm took on a definite form several years later in HALLOWEEN (John Carpenter 1978). Here, the boundaries to more "pure" forms of horror are fluid. In view of the structure of the suspense mode, which works against temporal closure, it should come as no great surprise that the slasher film tends toward seriality more than any other form of film expression, as it allows for the shift from dream to nightmare to be played out in near-infinite variations and layerings – for example, this is quite literally the operating principle of A NIGHTMARE ON ELM STREET (Wes Craven 1984), both at the level of the film's own dramatic structure as well as in relation to its sequels.

Even in films that can be directly attributed to this quasi-genre, however, the reversal can also appear in different forms, like in WHEN A STRANGER CALLS (Fred Walton 1979), which changes perspectives in the middle of the film to give the murderer a face and a story. The *Be Black Baby* sequence in De Palma's HI, MOM! (1970) works with the spectator's social prejudices and expectations regarding dramatic structure, triggering them through specific aesthetic signals (black and white, handheld camerawork, the type of lighting), to highly disturbing effect; at one point, during a television program within the film, even the film's tacit fictional status seems to suddenly be in question. Finally, the inversion at the end of PRETTY POISON (Noel Black 1968), whereby the alleged protagonist finds himself to be a character manipulated by someone else's plot, is totally perplexing. The effect of this inversion is not based on a step in the direction of body horror but, rather, on the subversion of classical plot conventions. The actual shock connecting these various examples derives from the realization that the context of experience is itself unstable – whether in relation to the body, everyday psychological conventions, or film historical socialization.

The fascination with instability indeed seems to be the common thread running through the films of this cinema of suspense – from Hitchcock's *oeuvre* via the cinema of De Palma (the final shot of PASSION [2012] is a pointed example of the balancing of dream and nightmare), to one of its more recent incarnations in Christopher Nolan's INCEPTION (2010), whose own final shot encapsulates this fascination in none-too-subtle fashion. While one can certainly find, in this film, a focus on the body and the multiplication of relations to near-delirious levels, the passage linking the suspense film to horror seems only recently to have been opened up again in films like PROXY (Zack Parker 2013) and IT FOLLOWS (David Robert Mitchell 2014). Thus, raising the question of whether, in spite of all systematic considerations, this connection between suspense and horror is, in fact, something historically specific. Keeping this question of historical dimension in mind, let us now turn to the next affective mode.

3 Paranoia: Forms of Mediatization

3.1 Historical Context and Theoretical Basis

If you were to ask for the best description of the dominant mindset in American society at the time of New Hollywood, you'd invariably encounter one central concept: paranoia.[1] Ordinarily – and unsurprisingly – this result, and likewise the paranoia film's heyday in New Hollywood, is ascribed to several decisive events of the 1960s and early 1970s (including the assassinations of John F. Kennedy, Lee Harvey Oswald, Malcolm X, Martin Luther King Jr., and Robert Kennedy, and, naturally, also the Watergate scandal). Yet, these events cannot be conceived of apart from their communication through the media and, as such, cannot be separated from this mediation. This indicates that the concept of paranoia can redirect our attention to how television and cinema themselves shape perception, rather than merely reflecting such historical developments[2] – this is this chapter's main objective.

---

1 See Hendrik Hertzberg, and David C.K. McClelland: Paranoia. An Idée Fixe Whose Time Has Come. In: Harper's Magazine, June 1974, pp. 51–60; John Carroll: Puritan, Paranoid, Remissive. A Sociology of Modern Culture, London 1977; Joan Didion: The White Album. In: id.: The White Album. Essays [1979], New York 2009, pp. 11–48, here p. 12; Peter Knight: Conspiracy Culture. From Kennedy to the X Files, London/New York 2000, pp. 28–35; Andreas Killen: 1973 Nervous Breakdown. Watergate, Warhol, and the Birth of Post-Sixties America, New York/London 2006, pp. 227–260; Francis Wheen: Strange Days Indeed. The 1970s: The Golden Age of Paranoia [2009], New York 2010.

2 As an example, one can consider here the numerous ramifications of the assassination of JFK (i.e., the erosion of trust in the government, the arrival of conspiracy theories), some of which only came into effect years after the actual event – in reaction to and as part of the arguments surrounding the correct interpretation of the evidence, particularly the Zapruder film: "John Kennedy's death may not be the most significant aspect of his assassination. What was of crucial importance was the struggle over its framing." Art Simon: Dangerous Knowledge. The JFK Assassination in Art and Film, Philadelphia 1996, p. 5. This fact makes me hesitate to use the term "trauma" in relationship to these events. On the role of media representation in the story of the Kennedy assassination, see also Fredric Jameson: The Geopolitical Aesthetic. Cinema and Space in the World System, Bloomington/Indianapolis/London 1992, p. 45, and Manfred Schneider: Das Attentat. Kritik der paranoischen Vernunft, Berlin 2010, pp. 427–481. On the connection between psychopathology (in particular schizophrenia), the modern, and modern art in general, see also Louis A. Sass: Madness and Modernism. Insanity in the Light of Modern Art, Literature, and Thought, New York 1992, particularly pp. 355–373. One further relevant development at the intersection of media and social culture in the 1960s and 1970s is the increasing emergence of diverse forms of surveillance, see Stephen Paul Miller: The Seventies Now. Culture

https://doi.org/10.1515/9783110580761-004

Since its very foundation, the USA seems to have offered favorable conditions for the growth of a "paranoid style."[3] The potency of this worldview, whereby society and history are exploited by the imaginary activities of impersonal, anonymous powers, it could also be argued, can likewise be detected in Hollywood cinema, at the very latest, since its so-called classical phase in the 1930s.[4] Since the end of the Second World War and since the 1960s, in particular, paranoid thinking and the attendant notion of the conspiracy theory have not simply reached levels of popularity previously unknown, but have also obviously undergone a qualitative change.[5] According to Timothy Melley, it appears less likely that one individual historical event (such as those mentioned above) or political constellation (such as the Cold War, whether in relation to the fear of Communism or the atomic bomb) is responsible for this development but, rather, an overarching impression or feeling of "diminished human agency."[6] Among other things, Melley connects this new feeling to a sense of unease, related to the effects of mass media:

> After all, to suggest that *conspiracies* are perpetrated through the mass media is to rethink the very nature of conspiracy, which would no longer depend wholly upon private messages, but rather upon mass communications, messages to which anyone might be privy. This

as Surveillance, Durham/London 1999; Paul Cobley: "Justifiable Paranoia". The Politics of Conspiracy in 1970s American Film. In: Xavier Mendik (ed.): Shocking Cinema of the Seventies, Hereford 2002, pp. 74–87.

3 See Richard Hofstadter: The Paranoid Style in American Politics. In: id.: The Paranoid Style in American Politics and other Essays, New York 1965, pp. 3–40, here p. 7; Peter Knight: Introduction. A Nation of Conspiracy Theorists. In: id. (ed.): Conspiracy Nation. The Politics of Paranoia in Postwar America, New York/London 2002, pp. 1–17. Even though Knight (by referring to Hofstadter and others) emphasizes that the United States by no means has the monopoly on conspiracy theories, he does, however, advocate the view that the fear of subversion and invasion has been and continues to be instructive for the constitution of an American identity defined by race, class, and gender, ibid. p. 3–8.

4 See George Wead: Toward a Definition of Filmnoia. In: The Velvet Light Trap, No. 13 (Fall 1974), pp. 2–6.

5 See Simon: Dangerous Knowledge; Knight: Conspiracy Culture, p. 32; Timothy Melley: Empire of Conspiracy. The Culture of Paranoia in Postwar America, Ithaca/London 2000, pp. 2–3, and passim. Melley is explicitly against conceptualizing paranoia, in line with Hofstadter, as a transhistorical phenomenon and instead traces the popularity of the concept in post-war America back to specific historical events, which will be discussed in the following. See also Knight: Introduction, pp. 5–8. See in contrast to this Schneider, who primarily seems to assume a consistency of "paranoid reason" across the centuries. See Schneider: Das Attentat, p. 478.

6 Melley: Empire of Conspiracy, pp. 11–12. See also Leerom Medovoi: The Cold War and SF [Review]. In: Science Fiction Studies, Vol. 27, No. 82 (November 2000), pp. 514–517, here pp. 515–516.

new model of "conspiracy" no longer simply suggests that dangerous agents are secretly plotting against us from some remote location. On the contrary, it implies, rather dramatically, that whole populations are being *openly* manipulated without their knowledge. For mass control to be exercised in this manner, persons must be significantly less autonomous than popular American notions of individualism would suggest.[7]

What Melley describes (without naming it explicitly as such) is nothing less than a crisis of perception: individual consciousness is apparently no longer even capable of recognizing the subtle exertion of influence on body and spirit alike, let alone defending itself against it. Melley quotes American journalist Vance Packard, who describes practices of the advertising industry at the end of the 1950s: "Typically [...] these efforts take place beneath our level of awareness; so that the appeals which move us are often, in a sense, hidden. The result is that many of us are being influenced and manipulated, far more than we realize, in the patterns of our everyday lives."[8] Described here in concrete terms is perception's inability to overcome the impressions to which it is subjected (intended here, among other things, as the notorious subliminal messages and images). Melley names the feeling produced by this configuration "agency panic." This feeling springs from the fear that individuals are not (or no longer) capable of acting in a socially meaningful way or, in extreme cases, even of controlling their own behavior.[9] Despite losing sight of the role of mass media over the subsequent course of his argumentation, in favor of concentrating on written texts (although he does at least continue to name examples from film and television), Melley's diagnosis creates the prerequisites for both grasping the colorful concept of paranoia in concrete terms, as it relates to the mediation of perceptual experience, and for deriving what is new about its post-war incarnation, precisely from this perceptual experience. Accordingly, determining an affect poetics of paranoia in the cinema of New Hollywood not only contributes to a more exact description of this film historical period; rather, it is furthermore helpful for positioning this period in a considerably broader cultural-historical context that reaches all the way into the present, referred to in various settings as mediatization.[10]

---

7 Melley: Empire of Conspiracy, pp. 2–3.

8 Vance Packard: The Hidden Persuaders, quoted by: Melley: Empire of Conspiracy, p. 1. See also Paul Jensen: The Return of Dr. Caligari. Paranoia in Hollywood. In: Film Comment, Vol. 7, No. 4 (Winter 1971), pp. 36–45, here p. 37.

9 Melley: Empire of Conspiracy, pp. 11–12.

10 Mediatization is understood here as the movement of the media into the center of social processes and their increasing interconnection with forms of cultural self-understanding. See Jay G. Blumler, and Dennis Kavanagh: The Third Age of Political Communication. Influences

Definition Difficulties

It seems necessary, at this point, to clarify more precisely the relation between the terms employed here, to do justice to the complex set of connections between clinical psychology, cultural studies, and film aesthetic terminology, which all intersect in this context. Commonly, the concepts of "paranoia" and "conspiracy theory" are used synonymously or at least without a clear distinction. Furthermore, the use of "paranoia" draws variously on contemporary clinical psychology,[11] the theories of Freud (in which case the connection is often loose and more associative in nature)[12] and Lacan (usually with a large degree of interpretation),[13] respectively, or sociological approaches, separate from both of these.[14] It would appear that, especially following Richard Hofstadter's famous use, the term's application in politics has since mutated into a battle cry, running the risk of (or making possible in the first place) pathologizing the political convictions of the opposite camp.[15] In clear distinction from this, a universalist interpretation has also been developed, which uses the term to describe the state of modern and post-modern subjectivity.[16]

---

and Features. In: Political Communication, Vol. 16, No. 3 (1999), pp. 209–230. Blumler and Kavanagh detect the growing influence of mediation via the press since the 1960s, primarily contingent on the arrival of television.

11 See Robert S. Robins, and Jerrold M. Post: Political Paranoia. The Psychopolitics of Hatred, New Haven/London 1997.

12 See, for example Dana Polan: Power and Paranoia. History, Narrative, and the American Cinema, 1940–1950, New York 1986; see also Cyndy Hendershot: Paranoia, the Bomb, and 1950s Science Fiction Films, Bowling Green 1999. According to Knight, Hofstadter and Pipes implicitly draw on a Freudian projection model, see Knight: Conspiracy Culture, pp. 14–15.

13 See Jacqueline Rose: Paranoia and the Film System. In: Screen, Vol. 17, No. 4 (1976), pp. 85–104. According to Eyal Peretz, the early theoreticians of the suture in the wake of Lacan and Jacques-Alain Miller conceptualized classical Hollywood cinema in general as paranoid and the corresponding spectator as a paranoiac. Peretz: Becoming Visionary, pp. 59–61.

14 See Robert Alan Goldberg: Enemies Within. The Culture of Conspiracy in Modern America, New Haven/London 2001.

15 Hofstadter already acknowledges the term's pejorative connotations and notes their intention. See Hofstadter: The Paranoid Style in American Politics, p. 5. See also Skip Willman: Spinning Paranoia. The Ideologies of Conspiracy and Contingency in Postmodern Culture. In: Knight (ed.): Conspiracy Nation, pp. 21–39, here p. 23. By contrast, in many more recent approaches, the concept of the conspiracy theory opens up the perspective of a relatively neutral engagement with the phenomenon, see Goldberg: Enemies Within, pp. xi–xii; and also primarily Knight: Conspiracy Culture, pp. 7–9.

16 See Fredric Jameson: Postmodernism, or, The Cultural Logic of Late Capitalism, Durham 1991; Patrick O'Donnell: Latent Destinies. Cultural Paranoia and Contemporary U.S. Narrative, Durham 2000. The tendency to generalize the concept and thus render it abstract also appears

In view of this confusing mélange, a degree of definitional clarity is evidently necessary. To begin with, it should be noted that the widespread association of paranoia, almost exclusively, with conspiracy theories is a representative result of transferring a clinical term into the realm of social and cultural studies and the latter's advocation for an often narrow conception of politics. In clinical descriptions of the condition, however, "recourse to unjustified thoughts of conspiracy" is merely one of seven symptoms of a paranoid personality disorder, regarded in turn as separate from a "delusional disorder" (i.e., paranoia in a strict sense), which would likely refer primarily to a persecution complex.[17] The focus on conspiracy theories in the academic discourse is unsurprising, given that this discourse not only focuses on questions concerning society as a whole but also employs methodologies that emanate from a truly broad conception of what constitutes a text. It is also influential in the scant film and media studies research that exists on paranoia – both with respect to the selection of relevant films and the concentration of respective analyses on plot, action, and characters.[18] One further consequence of the theoretical specialization of these discourses is a tendency to treat this concept in largely abstract terms. This is particularly in evidence for the sort of post-modernist approaches which place the concept of "reality" of any kind in scare quotes, thus robbing the central question of a cognitivist definition of paranoia (along the lines of "who is actually insane, me or everyone else?"[19]) of referential footing altogether. Paranoia thus becomes an epistemological problem, a question of the validity of interpretation in general (to such an extent that the concepts of interpretation and paranoia increasingly converge).[20]

---

to be inherent in Lacan's considerations, see, for example, Carl Freedman: Towards a Theory of Paranoia. The Science Fiction of Philip K. Dick. In: Science Fiction Studies, Vol. 11, No. 1 (March 1984), pp. 15–24, here p. 17.

17 See Horst Dilling, W. Mombour, and M.H. Schmidt (eds.): Internationale Klassifikation psychischer Störungen. ICD-10, Chapter V (F) [5th Edition], Bern 2005, pp. 114 and pp. 227–228.

18 See Wead: Toward a Definition of Filmnoia; Ray Pratt: Projecting Paranoia. Conspiratorial Visions in American Film, Lawrence 2001; Gérard Naziri: Paranoia im amerikanischen Kino. Die 70er Jahre und die Folgen, Sankt Augustin 2003; Marcus Krause, Arno Meteling, and Markus Stauff (eds.): The Parallax View. Zur Mediologie der Verschwörung, München 2011; Eva Schwarz: Visual Paranoia in REAR WINDOW, BLOW-UP and THE TRUMAN SHOW, Stuttgart 2011; Henry Taylor: Conspiracy! Theorie und Geschichte des Paranoiafilms, Marburg 2017.

19 "Either me, or the rest of the whole world is absolutely insane" is how the protagonist of Orson Welles's THE LADY FROM SHANGHAI (1947) formulates this dilemma.

20 "The irreducible elementary phenomenon here is at the level of interpretation." Lacan: The Psychoses: The Seminar of Jacques Lacan, Book III, Trans. Russell Grigg, New York 1993, p. 21. See also Melley: Empire of Conspiracy, pp. 16–25.

To counter these tendencies toward either a narrow or abstract treatment of the term, it should be emphasized that paranoia, as far as it is relevant for the present work, refers neither to the psychological state of a particular individual, nor to a collection of symptoms, but rather to a specific manner of being moved, or, in the words of Deleuze and Guattari: a *process*.[21] This approach allows the concept of paranoia to be related to the dimension of concrete experience, which configures the duration of perception. In this way, Deleuze and Guattari's concept of the (production) process is characterized first by "incorporating recording and consumption within production itself."[22] Rather than presuming a defined subject position, it outlines a chain of connections between "machines," aiming for a subject's "completion" – that is, for the production of subjectivity. Second, this chain does not distinguish between man and nature; it is, rather, primarily concerned with plugging "an organ-machine [...] into an energy-source-machine."[23] Cinema is exemplary of this kind of chain: "In cinema, one no longer speaks; it speaks in one's place: [...] A machine treats you like a machine, and the essential thing is not what it says, but the sort of vertigo of abolition that the fact of being 'machinized' provides for you."[24] The goal of this book as a whole is to describe just this sort of "vertigo."

With this in mind, a film analysis concentrating on the spectator's perceptual experience must, first of all, distinguish between the concept of paranoia used in this setting and all other usages, in order to then examine the (film) historical prerequisites for an affect poetics of paranoia. Thereafter, our next step is to obtain, via film analysis, the criteria for such an affect poetics and, finally, by examining the results of this analysis, to determine to what extent a mode of feeling is manifested, which could then be concretely related to the terminology of clinical psychology. Obviously, this task is entirely distinct from charting a set of symptoms traceable to a psychologically constituted individual. Structuring this investigation in the manner outlined above offers a suitable means for testing the hypothesis, repeatedly postulated in scholarly literature, that the phenomenon of paranoia's new character in the second half of the 20th century is principally to be defined on the basis of the mediation of perceptual experience.

---

21 See Deleuze, Guattari: Anti-Oedipus. Capitalism and Schizophrenia, Minneapolis 2000, p. 4.
22 Deleuze, Guattari: Anti-Oedipus, p. 4.
23 Deleuze, Guattari: Anti-Oedipus, p. 1.
24 Guattari: The Poor Man's Couch, pp. 264–265.

Paranoid Style and Intellectual Feelings

To begin, it should be noted that there are several reasons the concept of the conspiracy theory appears ill-suited to grasp the full scope of paranoia. First, as previously mentioned, it reduces the phenomenon to a single aspect, meaningful only in its sociological and politological context. Second, it neglects the aesthetic dimension, our clear focus here, which can be analyzed in terms of how it shapes perception. The concept of paranoid style, informed by Richard Hofstadter, thus seems promising by comparison: "When I speak of the paranoid style, I use the term much as a historian of art might speak of the baroque or the mannerist style. It is, above all, a way of seeing the world and of expressing oneself."[25]

While, as a historian, Hofstadter largely refers to actual people and situations in the text, his approach still offers a starting point for our investigation – not least because it explicitly declares a dual perspective on perception and expression, similar to the one formulated by Vivian Sobchack for film theory, in connection to Merleau-Ponty.[26] In this sense, paranoid "style" – as Lacan also observes, applying the same term[27] – is defined less as a personal peculiarity, an excess in the constitution of meaning but, rather, as a way of being in the world,[28] on the very basis of which something like a subject position is constitut-

---

25 Hofstadter: The Paranoid Style in American Politics, p. 4.

26 See Sobchack: The Address of the Eye, p. 3. For her concept of style, see pp. 212–219.

27 See Lacan: The Problem of Style and the Psychiatric Conception of Paranoiac Forms of Experience, trans. Jon Anderson. In: Critical Texts, Vol. 5, No. 3 (1988), pp. 4–6. Through the concept of style, Lacan links the domain of artistic creation to that of psychiatry, explicitly under the aspect of emotional expression. In contrast to his later writings, here he emphasizes "that the world characteristic of these subjects is transformed even more in its perception than in its interpretation [...]." The problem of interpretation merely follows from this transformation: "Indeed, on the one hand the field of perception is stamped for these subjects with a character, both immanent and imminent, of 'personal signification' (the symptom called 'interpretation'), and this character is exclusive of the affective neutrality of the object that at least virtually demands rational knowledge. On the other hand, the alteration, notable among them, of spatiotemporal intuitions modifies the scope of the conviction of reality [...]." Ibid., p. 5.

28 In view of this formulation by Merleau-Ponty ("[...] which means that we recognize a certain common structure in each person's voice, face, gestures and bearing and that each person is nothing more nor less to us than this structure or way of being in the world."), Lacan's idea is also of note here, who establishes a "homology between insanity and personality" in his dissertation on paranoia. Merleau-Ponty: The Film and the New Psychology. In: id.: Sense and Non-Sense, trans. H. Dreyfus, and P. Dreyfus, Evanston 1964, pp. 48–59, here p. 53; Lacan: De la psychose paranoïaque dans ses rapports avec la personalité, Paris 1975, p. 56.

ed in the first place. It is therefore possible to obtain the criteria for an affect poetics of paranoia from the analysis of exemplary films.

This kind of poetics must also consider what Lacan, in reference to Pierre Janet, calls "intellectual feelings": "Sentiments d'imposition, d'influence, de pénétration, de substitution; de vol, de devinement et d'echo de la pensée, d'étrangeté du monde extérieur."[29] Intellectual feelings are not simply correlatives of cognition. Rather, they concern the very limits of understanding and expression: "[...] pour le malade comme pour l'observateur, il faut concevoir les *sentiments intellectuels* comme des état affectifs, presque ineffables, dont le délire ne représente que l'explication secondaire." Lacan continues, "Ces sentiments paraissent aussi indispensables non seulement à la théorie du souvenir et de l'identification du passé, mais même à la théorie de la perception elle-même."[30] Paranoid style thus has to be understood as an operational connection between perception and expression or, rather, as an entirely specific *mode* of connection between them – a mode that resists inclusion in the conventional order of affective categorization but introduces new forms underneath and between these categories.

Grasping paranoia, from a (neo-)phenomenological perspective, as a specific way of interweaving film perception and film expression casts a new light on the approaches specified above, which understand paranoia as a mechanism for safeguarding the integrity of identity and/or narration. Of these conceptualizations, many associate paranoia with schizophrenia, interpreting it as a reaction to the schizophrenic's disintegrating perceptual world.[31] However this relationship is defined, it is of decisive importance for the purposes of our investigation that the two principles are understood as not simply mutually exclusive but, rather, in relation to one another.[32] Indeed, only this connection to schizophrenia prevents the concept of paranoia from withering into a purely abstract construct. Patrick O'Donnell thus writes:

> The work of paranoia is, precisely, to convert contingent, segmented pieces of the real into an observable and interpretable pattern of conspiracy. Paranoia, in this sense, absolutely depends on a schizoid regime of signs with its single sectors, serialities, and points of de-

---

29 Lacan: De la psychose paranoïaque, pp. 133–134.

30 Lacan: De la psychose paranoïaque, pp. 135–136.

31 See O'Donnell: Latent Destinies, p. 11; Melley: Empire of Conspiracy, p. 205. See also Freud's understanding of paranoia as the function of an "attempt at restoration" in so-called paraphrenics, see Freud: On Narcissism [1914]. In: id.: The Standard Edition of the Complete Psychological Works of Sigmund Freud, Volume XIV (1914–1916): On the History of the Psycho-Analytic Movement, Papers on Metapsychology and Other Works, pp. 67–102, here p. 86.

32 See Deleuze, Guattari: Anti-Oedipus, pp. 273–283.

parture that provide the material for paranoid activity. Equally, the work of paranoia is sustained by the simultaneity of haecceity and the ahistoricity of multilinear systems. For the paranoid awaits those unexpected, detemporalized instances of revelation when patterns magically converge into full-blown assemblages [...].[33]

Paranoid style is not simply ascertained through the denial of disintegration but, rather, represents a particular way of ordering what has been fragmented – both spatially and temporally – and acting in relation to it. This is precisely the sense in which Lacan employs the concept of process in its analogy to the development of personality:

> Le *processus psychique* s'oppose directement au *développement* de la personnalité, qui est toujours exprimable en *relations de compréhension*. Il introduit dans la personnalité un élément nouveau et hétérogène. A partir de l'introduction de cet élément, une nouvelle synthèse mentale se forme, une nouvelle personnalité soumise de nouveau aux *relations de compréhension*.[34]

Melley's concept of agency panic indicates a direction of argumentation similar to O'Donnell's, as he grapples with Deleuze and Guattari. Likewise, here, paranoia is linked to schizophrenic patterns of thought: "By agency panic, I mean intense anxiety about an apparent loss of autonomy or self-control – the conviction that one's actions are being controlled by someone else, that one has been 'constructed' by powerful external agents."[35] The concept of agency panic addresses a dual concern of the present work: that emotional states are concretely described (in the sense of Lacan's "intellectual feelings") and, particularly, in the form of their historical concretization – indeed, Melley employs the term to describe the altered quality of the phenomenon of paranoia following the Second World War.[36]

Paranoia and Post-Classical Cinema

The experience of the Second World War and the totalitarian dictatorships of the first half of the 20th century had a marked effect on the development of film and

---

33 O'Donnell: Latent Destinies, p. 29.
34 Lacan: De la psychose paranoïaque, p. 142.
35 Melley: Empire of Conspiracy, p. 12.
36 Melley: Empire of Conspiracy, p. 26.

on the way in which film and film poetics have been understood and discussed since the late 1940s.[37] As such,

> [...] a particular idea of cinema as mass medium had thus become questionable after having been politically instrumentalized on all sides, if not outright discredited. Particularly regarding the idea that the form of film's aesthetic experience, in the tradition of avant-garde poetics, was to be connected to the blueprint for a new subjectivity on the part of mass society beyond the bourgeois individual [...].[38]

Thus, the "unity of a new form of media culture, entertainment industry, and state terror,"[39] especially informed by the Third Reich, anticipates the same unease, formulated at the beginning of this chapter, in the face of the advertising industry's manipulation and monopolization of the individual.[40] This unease was expressed in the film critical and cinephile debates of the 1940s and 1950s, among other things, in the comparison between Italian Neorealism and Soviet montage.[41] According to André Bazin, the former is characterized by "never making reality the servant of some *a priori* point of view," as "compared with the chief schools of realism that preceded it and with the Soviet cinema."[42] Precisely this manner of establishing *a priori* an (ideological, historical) perspective on an event – which, in its distancing from real-life experience, evinces a close affiliation to descriptions of the schizophrenic's relationship to reality[43] –

---

37 See the controversy surrounding Gilles Deleuze's hypothesis of the potency of the experience of the Second World War in his "natural history" of the film image. See Deleuze: Cinema 1, pp. xix–xx and pp. 215–219; Jacques Rancière: Film Fables [2001], Oxford/New York 2006, pp. 107–123.

38 Hermann Kappelhoff, Bernhard Groß, and Daniel Illger: Einleitung. In: id.: Demokratisierung der Wahrnehmung? Das westeuropäische Nachkriegskino, Berlin 2010, pp. 9–21, here p. 11.

39 Kappelhoff: Realismus, p. 55.

40 See the discussion on the relationship between advertising, propaganda, and totalitarianism in the Third Reich, such as in S. Jonathan Wiesen: Creating the Nazi Marketplace. Commerce and Consumption in the Third Reich, Cambridge 2011, particularly pp. 63–117, or in Uwe Westphal: Werbung im Dritten Reich, Berlin 1989.

41 See Daniel Illger: Heim-Suchungen. Stadt und Geschichtlichkeit im italienischen Nachkriegskino, Berlin 2009, pp. 192–195.

42 André Bazin: Vittorio De Sica, Metteur-en-Scene. In: id.: What is Film?, pp. 61–78, here p. 64.

43 This relationship is often determined by the impression that one is perceiving reality like a scene from a film or behaving towards reality like a camera. See Sass: Madness and Modernism, pp. 285–287. Joan Didion relates this distancing technique on the one hand to the state of a film before it is edited and on the other to the historical timeframe of the late 1960s: "I was meant to know the plot, but all I knew was what I saw: flash pictures in variable sequence, images with no 'meaning' beyond their temporary arrangement, not a movie but a cuttingroom experience." Didion: The White Album, p. 13.

is attacked by American theorist Robert Warshow, on the occasion of revisiting several Soviet revolution films in the 1950s: "No death is without meaning; even that baby hurtling in its carriage down the Odessa steps in POTEMKIN is part of the great plan [...]. [...] It was not at all an artistic failure that I encountered in these movies, but something worse: a triumph of art over humanity."[44]

The same basic idea, albeit without the polemic, can also be found in Serge Daney's periodization of film history, summed up by Gilles Deleuze in his introduction to Daney's book. The first era, which, among other things, is identified with Soviet montage cinema, designates the film image's function as linked to the question of what can be seen *behind* this image: "And of course what there is to see behind an image appears only in succeeding images, yet acts as what takes us from the first image to the others, linking them in a powerful beautifying organic totality [...]."[45] The standpoint to which reality is subordinated is thus an invisible one, resisting direct recognition, and only accessible through the connections between its individual elements – a fundamental principle of paranoid thinking. Just like Daney, Deleuze cannot avoid labeling this conception a failure and, simultaneously, associating it with the idea of a grand manipulator: "[...] this form of cinema didn't die a natural death but was killed in the war [...]. [...] The organic whole was simply totalitarianism, and authoritarian power was no longer the sign of an *auteur* or *metteur en scène* but the materialization of Caligari and Mabuse [...]."[46]

In reaction to this, postwar cinema – that is, the second era – newly determines the image's function through the question of what there is to be seen on the surface itself: "What is there to see on the surface of the image? 'No longer what there is to see behind it, but whether I can bring myself to look at what I

---

44 Robert Warshow: Re-Viewing the Russian Movies [1955]. In: id.: The Immediate Experience. Movies, Comics, Theatre & Other Aspects of Popular Culture, Cambridge/London 2001, pp. 239 – 252, here pp. 240 – 241.

45 Gilles Deleuze: Letter to Serge Daney. Optimism, Pessimism, and Travel [1986]. In: id.: Negotiations, pp. 68 – 79, here p. 68. One also thinks here of the programmatic title of an essay by Eisenstein: Beyond the Shot. In: id.: Selected Works. Volume 1. Writings 1922 – 34, London 1988, pp. 138 – 150; see also Eisenstein's concept of the generalized image, which emerges based on the juxtaposition of the individual elements. See id.: Montage in 1938. In: id.: Problems of Film Direction, Honolulu 2004, pp. 10 – 45, here p. 13.

46 Deleuze: Letter to Serge Daney, p. 69. See also Jensen: The Return of Dr. Caligari. On the question of manipulation, Eisenstein's numerous comments to this end are, of course, equally instructive, particularly the notorious phrase that cinema is "a tractor ploughing over the audience's psyche in a particular class context." Eisenstein: The Problem of the Materialist Approach to Form. In: id.: Selected Works. Vol. 1, pp. 59 – 64, here p. 62.

can't help seeing – which unfolds on a single plane.'"[47] Most important for this context, first and above all, is the dwindling of montage's significance, that is, of the connections *between* the images (I will return later to the question of visibility). Deleuze, in his first book on cinema, also lists this aspect, in relation to American film, as one of the characteristics of the "crisis of the action-image." Fundamental, at this juncture, is the parallel between his idea of "a world without totality and linkage" and the schizophrenic's perceptual experience: one of the central characteristics of this experience is fragmentation.[48] Thereby, the connection to two other characteristics, mentioned by Deleuze, is of particular interest for our context: the "consciousness of clichés" and, along with it, the "condemnation of the plot."[49] For Deleuze, the cliché is the antithesis of the image; accordingly, he describes the clichés of "American post-war film(s)" as "sound or visual slogans." These "circulate in the external world, but [...] also penetrate each one of us and constitute his external world, so that everyone possesses only psychic clichés by which he thinks and feels, is thought and felt, being himself a cliché amongst the others in the world which surrounds him."[50] Unlike in the invasion scenarios of science fiction films from the 1950s or post-war film noir,[51] the "occult power is confused with its effects, its supports, its media, its radios, its televisions, its microphones: it now only operates through the 'mechanical reproduction of images and of sound.'"[52] This neatly encapsulates Melley's concept of agency panic as a perceptual experience. A world "without totality and linkage" is held together on the basis of its mediation – although the question presents itself here, as to whether the omnipresent clichés may not have brought about the crisis of the action-image in the first place. Anal-

---

47 Deleuze: Letter to Serge Daney, p. 69.

48 Sass: Affectivity in Schizophrenia. A Phenomenological View. In: Journal of Consciousness Studies, Vol. 11, No. 10–11 (2004), pp. 127–147.

49 Deleuze: Cinema 1, p. 214.

50 Deleuze: Cinema 1, p. 213. See also Jameson: The Geopolitical Aesthetic, p. 49.

51 On the connection between film noir and paranoia, see Polan: Power and Paranoia, in particular pp. 193–249; Wheeler Winston Dixon: Film Noir and the Cinema of Paranoia, New Brunswick 2009. On science fiction, see Hendershot: Paranoia, the Bomb, and 1950s Science Fiction Films. In view of film noir, it should be recalled that this group of films was only consolidated in retrospect and that this retrospective formation of a family grouping was essentially continued in the 1970s – apart from in a few meanwhile-canonical essays, not least in films such as THE LONG GOODBYE (Robert Altman 1973), CHINATOWN (Roman Polanski 1974), NIGHT MOVES (Arthur Penn 1975), and FAREWELL, MY LOVELY (Dick Richards 1975). See Raymond Durgnat: Paint it Black. The Family Tree of the Film Noir. In: Cinema, No. 6/7 (August 1970), pp. 49–56; Paul Schrader: Notes on Film Noir. In: Film Comment, Vol. 8, No. 1 (Spring 1972), pp. 8–13. See also the discussion of this subject in the final chapter.

52 Deleuze: Cinema 1, p. 214.

ogous to the dynamic relation between schizophrenia and paranoia described above, the "condemnation of the plot" thus refers to how the principles of the first era (according to Daney's periodization) are again taken up in the cinema of New Hollywood and related to the principles of the second era. Paranoid style is therefore to be understood as a mode of reflection, which not only relates to the spectator's concrete experience of perception, but also introduces an additional layer of film historical reflexivity.

The film historical and aesthetic parameters for an affect poetics of paranoia have thus been briefly addressed. Hence, the poetic logic of the New Hollywood paranoia film navigates the realm of tension between visibility and invisibility, fragmentation and totality. The location where these conflicts are carried out is the film image itself; that is, here the problem of mediation comes wholly to the fore.

3.2 Analysis

THE PARALLAX VIEW

My next step involves compiling the concrete perceptual, aesthetic criteria for this affect poetics of paranoia through film analysis, namely of the opening sequence of Alan J. Pakula's THE PARALLAX VIEW (1974). This film is indisputably central in the canon of works connected to paranoia and conspiracy, assembled in scholarly research under an enormous range of different conceptualizations.[53] It thus stands to reason that, regardless of what is understood by paranoia in these different approaches, we can glean more than just superficial points of reference for a more precise definition of the concept from this film. In the following analysis, that the film is explicitly about a conspiracy and political assassinations, for example, initially takes a back seat (even if its undoubtedly important for the film's place in the canon), in favor of a focus on considerations, which, after their integration into a meaningful aesthetic program, may be abstracted and applied to other films. Only then (and not via a definition at the

---

53 See Noël Carroll: The Future of Allusion, p. 68; Jameson: The Geopolitical Aesthetic, pp. 45–66; Adam Barker: Cries and Whispers. In: Sight and Sound, Vol. 1, No. 10 (February 1992), pp. 24–25; Peter Lev: American Films of the 70s, pp. 50–54; Drehli Robnik: Allegories of Post-Fordism in 1970s New Hollywood, p. 349; Wead: Toward a Definition of Filmnoia, p. 2; Naziri: Paranoia im amerikanischen Kino, p. 12; Henry M. Taylor: Bilder des Konspirativen. Alan J. Pakulas THE PARALLAX VIEW und die Ästhetik der Verschwörung. In: Krause, Meteling, and Stauff (eds.): The Parallax View, pp. 217–234, here pp. 218–219.

level of themes and motifs), can we test the hypothesis as to whether the shaping of perceptual experience by the media must be understood as a decisive factor for the development of the concept of paranoia following the Second World War.

In describing this film's opening sequence, the analysis will initially proceed in highly detailed fashion, before gradually widening our perspective to ultimately take other films into account as well. One stated goal of this investigation is to render understandable and plausible a disengagement from an entirely too narrow fixation on themes, both for New Hollywood and beyond, thereby significantly expanding the canon of the so-called paranoia film – not arbitrarily but, rather, through strict adherence to developed aesthetic criteria. The result will not be a new genre or comparable structure (such categories are highly problematic when it comes to New Hollywood, as already explained in sufficient depth in the previous chapter), even though the genealogy of the paranoia film is traceable back through the 1930s. To the contrary, according to our preliminary hypothesis, this cinema is defined by nothing but its distinct manner of generating affect, based, in turn, on a series of temporal and spatial, structural formations that shape the relation between film and spectator during the concrete act of perception. Paranoia is used to describe this perceptual relationship that (unlike, for example, the narrative schemata already taken into account) can clearly be distinguished from other poetic forms. On the other hand, particular plot patterns and character constellations are preferentially linked with these structural formations and, thus, while there is a certain value to their recognizability, this should not be assumed to be self-evident. This relation will be explained in further detail, once we have selected our criteria for analysis.

To get our bearings, let us start with a short summary of THE PARALLAX VIEW's plot. It begins with the depiction of an assassination: ambitious Senator Charles Carroll is murdered at a public appearance on Independence Day. The official version of events, ascertained by the investigating commission convened in the aftermath, states that the assassin acted alone, contrary to the spectator's better judgment and the suspicions of the film's protagonist, journalist Joe Frady. As one witness after another meet their deaths in mysterious fashion, he becomes increasingly mistrustful, begins to investigate, and, in the process, comes across the so-called Parallax Corporation, which evidently scouts, trains, and hires out assassins. He attempts to infiltrate the company as a potential assassin, initially seeming successful. Yet the murky organization reveals itself as too powerful and eliminates him by embroiling him in the assassination of another politician and having him shot in the process. After the assassination, the same investigative commission convenes once again and reaches the same conclusion they had at the beginning of the film: Frady was a mentally disturbed lone wolf; there was no conspiracy to speak of.

Let us now analyze the film's opening sequence in detail, which depicts the assassination of the senator and can be understood as a prologue, bringing together the film's principal themes and motifs. The setting is Seattle during the celebration of Independence Day; Senator Carroll is the most prominent guest in attendance, portrayed as an up-and-comer with presidential ambitions. A reporter announces his appearance, noting that he is so independent, some people don't even know which party he does belong to. Carroll arrives with the parade at Seattle's iconic landmark, the Space Needle, and, along with a few selected guests, makes his way to the restaurant at its top. Barely having begun his speech, he is shot by an assassin, who then falls from the roof of the tower, after being chased by security guards. In the tumult unleashed by the fatal shots, a second assassin manages to escape undetected. We then leap forward in time: the investigating commission, established following the event, pronounces their verdict: the assassin was working alone and there are no indications of a conspiracy. The image freezes and the title of the film appears.

The Opening Sequence

Let us begin with a rough outline of the sequence's dramatic structure, which can be extrapolated, at an initial level, from the momentum of the cutting rate. Up until the actual moment of the assassination, the first 13 shots have a combined duration of over four minutes (an average of around 18.6 seconds per shot), while the subsequent 10 shots last for merely 15 seconds (therefore averaging around 1.5 seconds per shot). Afterward, the tempo again slows; the final shot in the sequence lasts nearly a minute and a half before the freeze frame begins. This produces the impression of an overriding organic unit, broken down into three parts: a slow build-up, a climax, and subsequent deceleration of momentum. Yet, looking at the individual shots at a micro-level, this initial impression must be further refined. Setting aside the fact that the very low rate of cuts at the start of the sequence is relativized by the high level of movement within the image, it should further be noted that increases in the cutting rate are not gradual but observable in a wave-like and, in each case, sudden escalation. This still somewhat superficial observation refers, however, to a more complex connection: it is evident that several of the markedly short shots, responsible for the sudden increase in the cutting rate, cannot easily be placed within the ostensible narrative context of the scene. This contrapuntal dynamic coincides with deviations from the ongoing progression of the plot. In consequence, regarding this sequence, there can be no straightforward discussion of cohesion among its elements as homogeneous, temporal forms, that is, expressive movements – understanding expressive movement, with Helmuth Plessner, as a "physical action headed towards an image of the totality of plot, the acting subject and his or her surroundings."[54] Precisely this creation of a totality, to use Eisenstein's words, a generalized image,[55] is here destabilized. This directly raises the question of how and in what manner this sequence is otherwise constituted and, relatedly, how it might be described as the formation of an experience as it takes place in time. To answer this question, it is necessary to perform an analysis at the level of individual shots.

The film's first shot begins as a strictly symmetrical arrangement: a low-angle shot of a totem pole reaching upwards, against the light of a clear, blue afternoon sky, framed such that the pole occupies the exact center of the image (which is very wide, as the aspect ratio is 2.35:1), slicing it in two and extending beyond both the top and bottom of the frame (fig. 1). For the entire duration of the shot, drum beats and cymbal clashes can be heard from afar on the soundtrack in a regular tempo, along with the calls and applause of a jubilant crowd. After a good three seconds, the camera begins to move. The figure it traces is composed of a swift downward pan, combined with a slower pan to the right, so as to rotate around the pole, before segueing into a short, measured tracking shot to the left. Over the course of this complex movement, which is carried out with a degree of elegance and reserve, two structures become visible: a bush or shrub located at the right hand edge of the frame and a futuristic looking tower (the Space Needle) to the left of the pole. It takes about eight seconds to complete the movement; once the shift in frame is finished, the camera stays fixed on the new framing for around two seconds (fig. 5), until, after a total of 13 seconds, the shot ends with a cut. A markedly symmetrical arrangement has given way to a markedly asymmetric one.

---

54 Kappelhoff: Matrix der Gefühle, p. 152. See Plessner: Die Deutung des mimischen Ausdrucks.
55 See Eisenstein: Montage 1938, pp. 162–169.

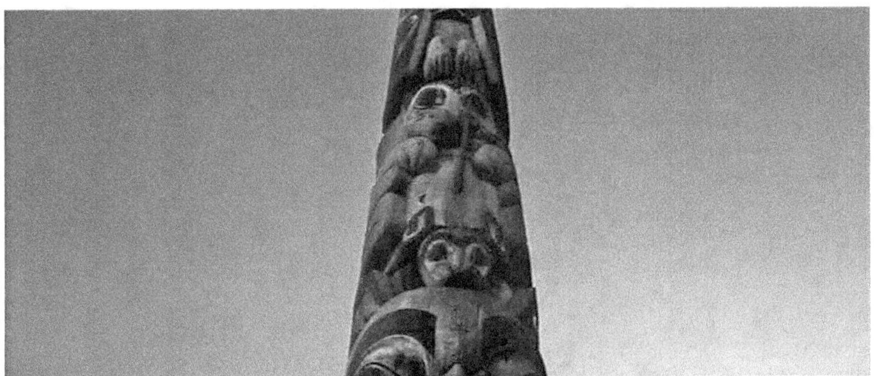

Figs. 1–5: The first parallax shift: the splitting of the image space

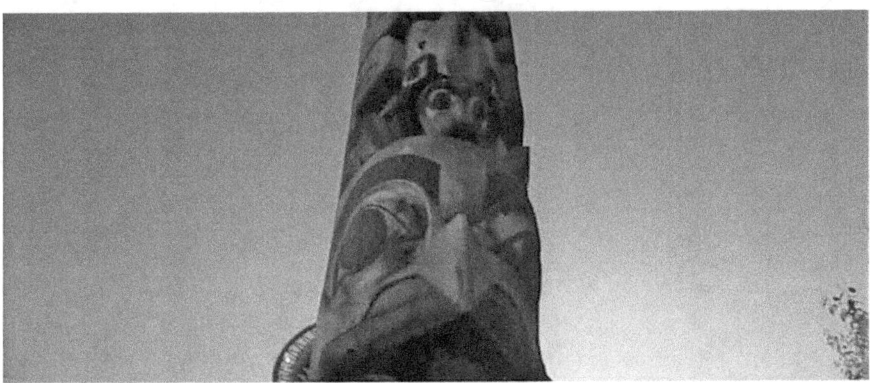

Fig. 2

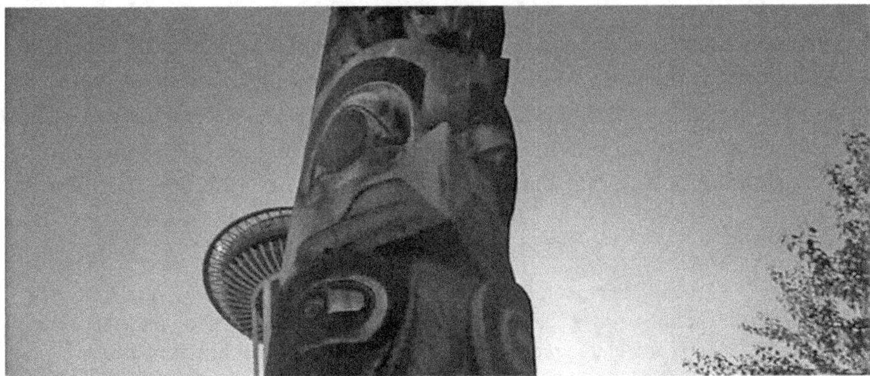

Fig. 3

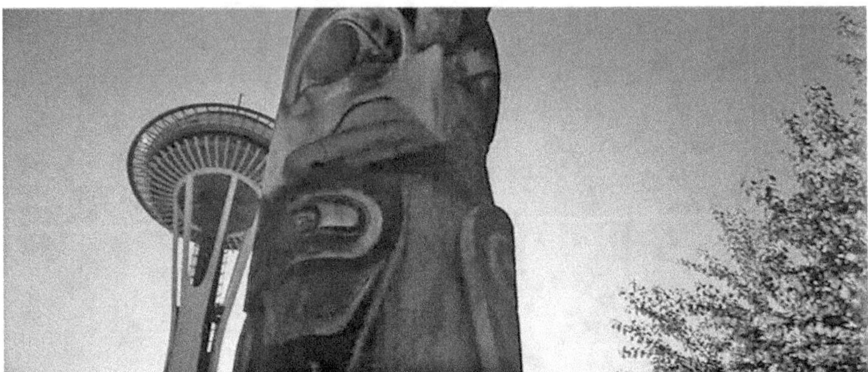

Fig. 4

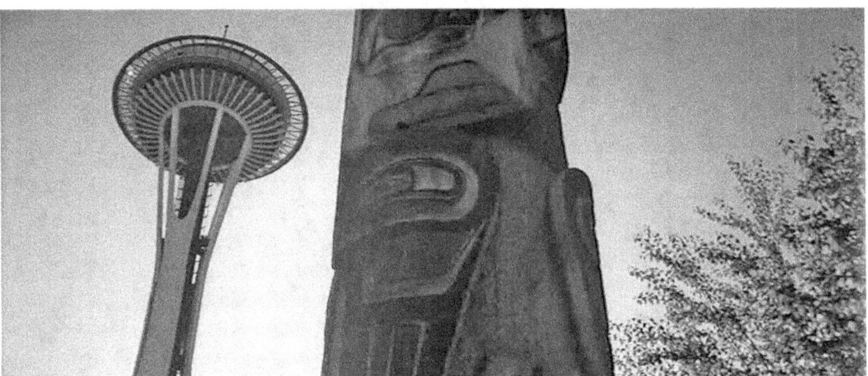

Fig. 5

To use Daniel Stern's words, what does this movement do to change "the implicitly felt intersubjective field" between film and spectator?[56] It is evidently not just the shrub[57] and the Space Needle that have become visible. At a more subtle level of visual composition, it is equally evident that the afternoon sky has changed simultaneously and that the change in light has bathed the mise-en-

---

[56] See Stern: The Present Moment in Psychotherapy and Everyday Life, New York 2004, p. xvi. Present moments "capture a sense of the subject's style," ibid., p. 16. The accentuated position of this shot and its clearly articulated programmatic status permit it to be analyzed as a unit of experience in Stern's sense of the term.

[57] It cannot be definitively ascertained whether these branches belong to a tree or a shrub. What is of decisive importance for the staging here is the fact that the characteristic structural element of a tree is missing, namely the emphasis on the vertical (no trunk can be seen). On the contrary, the twigs and branches do in fact extend in all directions to the same degree.

scène in a decidedly cooler atmosphere. The camera's relationship to the pole has also changed; the original tendency towards abstraction has given way to the impression that, now, some big block is obstructing the view. These comments refer to the level at which individual movements, as events, obtain their expressive quality: at the level of the shot as a temporal form, where movement is redeployed into relations. At the end of the movement, the bush and the Space Needle are not just both in open view but also differ from one another in terms of how they became visible, how they entered the image space. While the Space Needle's staging structures the mise-en-scène around a clearly delineated object, seen from an obviously defined perspective, the bush, only partially reaching into the image, on the other hand, suggests a blurring of the frame's boundary and an invasion of the image from this blurred boundary – precisely because the bush's perspectival relation to the camera's gaze remains unclear. As final adjustments are made to the framing by the camera, we can also observe the Space Needle, now centered in its half of the image, progressively occupying more space; after a certain point in the movement, the same cannot be said of the shrub (compare figs. 4 and 5). In this way, the Space Needle's appearance, seeming to soar elegantly upwards, is bestowed with an additional degree of dynamism, while the bush remains a steady, static force in the image space. Within this shot's dramatic micro-structure, the staging thus establishes an oppositional dyad, which structures the entire following sequence: namely the contrast between the soaring tower and the expansive branches, between (vertical) prominence, on the one hand, and (horizontal) coequal juxtaposition, on the other. Yet this contrast can only be experienced in sensorial terms via the constellation of the camera and the totem pole, which strictly separates the two spatial orders while simultaneously placing them in relation to one another.

While the totem pole still initially functions as the object of the gaze, within a seemingly homogenous and highly stylized ensemble (to be more precise, it actually structures this ensemble), over the course of the shot, it morphs into a sort of pivot point between the two, opposing, spatial realms. As previously described: as the camera pans around the pole, it serves as a mobile anchoring point, first drifting to the left of the frame, before the tracking shot finally brings it back into the center. Over the course of this movement, the pole appears increasingly massive, while the large eyes carved into its surface, which seem to be looking just past the spectator, become increasingly prominent, thus establishing a vector for redirecting the spectator's gaze. As the image space splits, the totem pole thus inscribes onto this process a form of strange, enigmatic activity, an opaque presence, and a sense of resistance. It is precisely this impression of alien activity or, to be more precise, the relativizing effect it has on one's own activity, that is closely linked to both Melley's concept of agency panic and the concept of the parallax, which gives the film its name. The optical phenomenon of the parallax is defined as the apparent shift in an object's position that accompanies an actual shift in the standpoint of the observer. This concept thus does not just reference the possibility or danger of deception but, much more concretely, also addresses the question, negotiated in this first shot and in the entire sequence that follows, of the activity of the object as it is observed, or, to speak more generally, the problem of the *relativity of movement*.[58] As will be shown in considerable detail, the concept thus links the central characteristics of schizophrenia and paranoia, in accordance with a paranoid style.

The sense of resistance mentioned above initially corresponds to a specific impression: the appearance of the Space Needle and branches in the perceptual experience of the spectator does not represent the introduction of a newly accessible space, even a cinematic narrative space – for the totem pole, itself, seems just as involved in the movement as the camera, so that the gesture of revelation corresponds with one of refusal. The soundtrack also plays a fundamental role in creating the impression of alien activity, albeit in a subtle manner: the drumming and clapping audible in the background, like every noise, implicitly raise the question of where these sounds come from,[59] a question that is not abstract but refers to the spectator's concrete, perceptual experience. This question is posed all the more emphatically here, since the sounds can be audibly localized as originating from a certain distance. Dominated by the constant, march-like, propulsive rhythm of the drums and cymbals, the background noise exerts a pull, to which the camera's activity seems to merely respond – even though the camera hasn't come even a single step closer to the source of the noise by the end of the movement.[60] In actuality, it becomes clear that the spectator's

---

58 The most easily graspable example of the parallax effect can be seen by looking at one's thumb while opening and closing each eye in turn. Hereby it seems as if the thumb springs back and forth. On the phenomenon of the resistance of objects, see also Polan: Power and Paranoia, pp. 242–243. On the fundamental relativity of movement in film, see Michotte: The Character of "Reality" of Cinematographic Projections. In: Michotte's Experimental Phenomenology of Perception, p. 203; also Rudolf Arnheim: Film as Art, p. 32.

59 "Whereas images rarely ask: 'What sound did that image make?' every sound seems to ask, unless it has previously been categorized and located: 'Where did that sound come from?'" Rick Altman: Moving Lips. Cinema as Ventriloquism. In: Yale French Studies, No. 60 (1980), pp. 67–79, here p. 74.

60 In this way, the camera disappoints the expectation and/or classical convention, according to which it is on the trail of the sound's origin: "Among the most basic of camera movements, defined as a function of the narrative, is the tendency to move the camera to a sound, to point it at the area from which the sound is coming (thus turning off-screen sound into on-screen sound)." Altman: ibid., p. 71. From his ideologically critical perspective, Altman emphasizes

gaze is no more anchored within the image at the end of the shot than at the beginning; instead, the tension within the image primarily and considerably increases over the same period. The manner by which the image constitutes a dynamic, building up under the surface, justifies the impression of resistance mentioned above. Thus, we reach the *constellation*, suspended between abstraction and concretion, toward which the entire shot has been driving – that is, the fundamental point is that, underneath the apparent character of the situation, there is another level, which cannot be aligned with the first. The potential insight to be gleaned from this shot is, therefore, less the revelation of a kind of truth but, rather, primarily the realization of the ambiguous nature of reality.[61] This *doubling* of the gaze in the form of a parallax – that is, as an internal contradiction that cannot be resolved – determines the activity of cinematic perception for the whole sequence that follows and is then further developed over the entire duration of the film.

The Groundlessness of History

The overt way in which this first shot connects abstract meaning and the generation of sensuous affect is a key characteristic of both its programmatic stance and its desire to succinctly capture the quintessence of the entire film in one movement – the very nature of parallax. If one grasps the movement in this shot (and in the film) in this sense, as a physically experienced method of generating meaning, then the next step to explore is, in Bellour's words, the 'symbolic' dimension of emotion. Thus, the interplay of sound and image immediately and symbolically opens up an historical perspective, from the very first second of the film. This perspective is initially set up by the striking image of the totem pole, which is placed in relation with the noise of drums, sounding from some

---

that this impression is actually deceptive: the camera identifies instead that which the spectator is supposed to regard as the source of the sound (ibid., pp. 71–72.). In our context, what is crucial here is that the accentuation of the lack of the sound's source charges the image with tension.

61 For this reason, it cannot be simply said that the parallax shift leads to "greater insight, objectivity, and truth" (Naziri: Paranoia im amerikanischen Kino, p. 143), or to the discovery of a "reality behind the reality" (Taylor: Bilder des Konspirativen, p. 234). Instead, the shot brings home the impossibility of grasping the reality behind the facade (i.e., in the sense of a propositional statement) by creating a permanent contradiction. Taylor and Naziri's problematic interpretations stem from their incomplete analyses of the shot: it's not just the tower (the Space Needle) that becomes visible via the camera movement but also the shrub. See Naziri: Paranoia im amerikanischen Kino, pp. 123–124, and Taylor: Bilder des Konspirativen, pp. 221–222.

distance away in a regular, march-like rhythm. This sound[62] is clearly marked as non-Western, "exotic" in the broadest sense, located somewhere among the various associations that go hand-in-hand with "world music." The totem pole initially seems to affirm an association with Native Americans and, if one takes Altman's ideas a step further, to serve as the sounds' visual and semantic anchor. But this is proven to be a misjudgment or, rather, a deception: the camera movement certainly does not bring a tepee camp or anything similar into view; instead, it reveals nothing at all, at least nothing in answer to the question of the sound's origin. To the contrary, in that the totem pole itself serves to anchor the movement, the sound's position within the image remains in question.

How does this symbolic dimension unfold over the course of the shot, and how is it connected with the spectator's embodied, perceptual experience? First of all, it should be noted that the initiation of the camera's movement further develops the historical perspective, immediately announced by the opening: the bush and tower appear in the field of vision in sync – this is the Space Needle, we are in Seattle.[63] The tower's previously mentioned, futuristic feel is substantiated by the fact that the Space Needle was built as part of the 1962 world's fair, whose motto was "Man in the Space Age."[64] The building takes futurism quite literally and translates it into science fiction; that is, into the iconographic inventory of the science fiction film (the "flying saucer" at the top of the tower is particularly prominent, a revolving capsule, which houses a restaurant).

If one thus grasps the movement created by the interplay of the camera and the totem pole as constituting a spatiotemporal relationship, in the sense of a historical perspective, it should be emphasized, in turn, the degree to which this symbolic meaning feeds back into the embodied effect of the pattern of movement. While the narrow tower and its dynamic, upward thrust steadily take up more and more space, the proliferation of branches remains static, marooned in a quasi-ahistorical, perspectival vagueness, due to the fact that it does not form a recognizable vanishing point. Both are placed in relation to the totem pole, whereby the composition now seems to firmly strive for imbalance: the totem pole, which conjures up the era of the nation's violent settlement and

---

62 It is worth noting that this sound resists easy categorization as either a noise or music, at precisely the same moment at which its mysterious quality, the question of where it's actually coming from, comes to the fore. As was discussed in previous chapters, this convergence of categories is absolutely characteristic of sound design in New Hollywood.

63 Like the totem pole, the Space Needle functions as a kind of highly charged, visual shorthand, not least for the city in which it is located and for which it forms a key landmark.

64 See Chad Randl: Revolving Architecture. A History of Buildings that Rotate, Swivel, and Pivot, New York 2008, p. 111.

its painful aftermath,[65] conceals the Space Needle behind it, a symbol of the belief in technology and progress. Yet, as the theme of paranoia is already introduced via the reference to science fiction,[66] this symbol has already been subtly corrupted. At the same time, the green branches contribute an additional element, which erodes the alignment with the future (which, by 1974, basically already belonged to the past anyway) and can only be brought into association with the totem pole, if at all. But at the level of symbolic meaning, in particular, the harsh bifurcation of the frame dominates, so that the shot, as an audiovisual form, generates tension on all levels, eventually provoking the film's first cut. It is thus to be emphasized, in turn, that this shot's meaning cannot be pinned down to the mere revelation of a suppressed counter-narrative, as Taylor argues.[67] If this were the case, we would be dealing with the relatively simple case of a "left-wing" cinema of historical rectification. But the implications of THE PARALLAX VIEW are far more fundamental and radical, in that the ground is entirely yanked from under the spectator's feet. The groundless nature of history is realized as a corporeal understanding of parallax, as an intellectual feeling. Precisely this undermining and eventual destruction of a coherent perceptual position is dramatized later in the famous test sequence.

It is also important to mention that no hierarchy whatsoever is established in the relation between embodied and symbolic meaning, temporal or otherwise. To the contrary, a process of constant feedback is established between these two levels, without any one element rising to the level of a trigger or focal point. The reference to America's indigenous peoples is thus just as present as the striking framing at the beginning of the shot; in the same manner, at the end of the shot, the spatial and historical perspectives both possess the same level of complexity. The sequence that now follows develops this complexity into a perceptual and narrative scenario. Its prevailing principles (the relativization of activity, fragmentation, the contrast between flattening and protrusion) are now related to a whole series of cinematic techniques. One focus of the analysis will now be to show how the film itself brings the problem of mediation to the fore.

---

65 One may think here, for example, of the American Indian Movement active since the late 1960s and in particular of the occupation of Wounded Knee in early 1973.

66 This applies in so far as the 1950s science fiction film refers to a genre classically brought into connection with the post-war paranoia of the Cold War. See Hendershot: Paranoia, the Bomb, and 1950s Science Fiction Films.

67 "Society has an obscene underbelly that holds it up and is ultimately always based on a previous violent crime as a foundational act, similar to a political-mythical primal scene, and it is its return of which this scene serves as an implicit reminder." Taylor: Bilder des Konspirativen, p. 222.

Flatness and Protrusion

Unlike the reserve of the first shot, following the cut, the spectator is suddenly directly addressed, simultaneously, in several respects. To begin with, the view jumps from the deeply layered totem pole constellation to a markedly flat tableau, evidently shot with a telephoto lens (fig. 6). But the dominating effect of these first moments is generated by the soundtrack: not only are the drumming and clashing perceptibly, significantly louder and closer, they are augmented by an additional element in the form of an intro given by a reporter, who looks straight into the camera and thus directs her remarks at a dual spectator (both the actual film spectator and the fictional television one).[68]

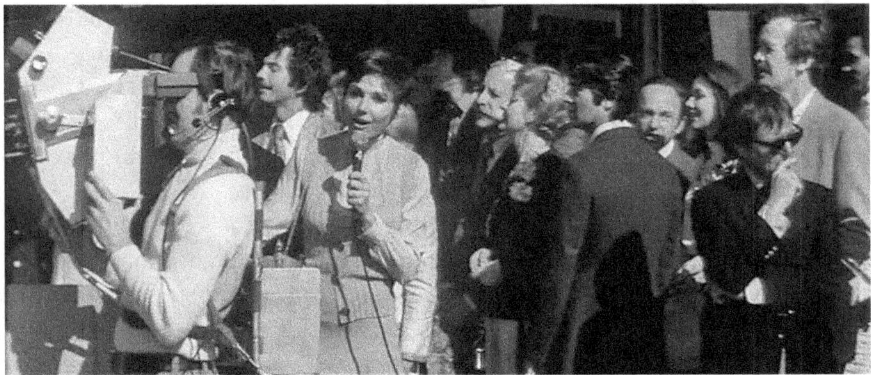

Fig. 6: The tableau as a combination of television and film viewing situations.

The shot's arrangement initially builds on the previous one, albeit with a small shift: the reporter is positioned near the middle of the frame slightly to the left (the space alongside her is held open for the senator's advisor, who will soon join her),[69] standing out from the other figures due to the color of her outfit,

---

68 A shift can equally be discerned here because the fictional television spectator is addressed by an image that is essentially flaunting the fact that it is *not* a television image due its widescreen format. On the other hand, it is the function of how information is conveyed that is, of course, decisive here: it is the *film* spectator who is supposed to be informed about the occasion of the celebrations, not the television spectator ostensibly being addressed.

69 He is initially located at the right-hand edge of the frame. Using the mise-en-scène to anticipate the plot could be understood as simply following classical conventions of staging; within the context of this entirely anti-classical arrangement, it seems instead to be far more a subtle reference to the specific paranoid temporality of latency. See O'Donnell: Latent Destinies, pp. 2–3, who relates the concept of haecceity picked up on by Deleuze and Guattari in *A Thou-*

and meets the camera's gaze from its exact level (not from above or rotated to the side like the totem pole). As far as the space of the action is concerned, the first and second shot bear no understandable relation to one another and, as such, remain isolated from each other; only the soundtrack establishes vague spatial continuity between them. Furthermore, in this second shot, the balance of the audiovisual composition is forfeited already at the outset: for one thing, the visual distinction between figure and ground is already far less clearly delineated than in the first shot, as the background itself consists of various figures (Joe Frady, the protagonist, can already be seen in the shadows at the very back of the image, precisely at the center of the frame). Second, the reporter's voice strains to overcome the noise that surrounds her. And third, after just a few seconds, the parade participants begin crossing in front of the image – exactly as the reporter informs the spectator that we are witnessing a celebration for American Independence Day.

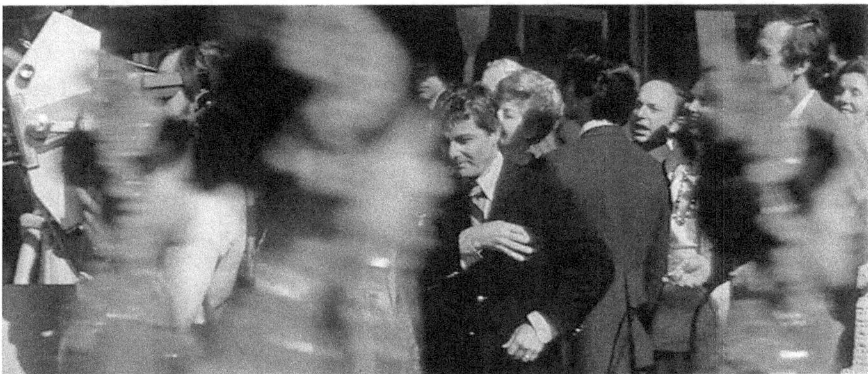

Fig. 7: Adding disturbance and rhythm to the tableau.

These interruptions reveal the flatness of the configuration at two different levels of semantic composition, linked together by the film: on the one hand, they indicate the low depth of field of the lens currently being used; on the other, they consistently intrude upon the camera's concentration on the previously established object of attention. In this sense, the entire second shot can be understood as extracting elements of flatness from the first shot, made manifest in the bush.

The parade participants filing past fulfill an additional function: the irregular and erratic interruptions interact with the regular rhythm of the percussion

sand Plateaus to the concept of paranoia. This form of temporality will be dealt with in more detail below.

and the back-and-forth exchange of dialogue between the reporter and advisor to inscribe a specific duration or arc of tension onto the (27-second long) shot. This arc of tension is formed such that, after the first three to four seconds without any disturbance at a visual level, the subsequent, massive intrusion of the horse and cart, which enters the frame from the left and quickly fills the entire image, ushering in the subsequent interruptions, amounts to a small shock. In the moments that follow, the reporter's lead-in to the interview and first question are repeatedly disturbed by the figures passing by in the foreground of the image (fig. 7), while the advisor's evasive answer, given in the last five seconds of the shot, remains comparatively undisturbed. The reporter hardly has time to re-phrase the question before the cut, this time also on the soundtrack, arrives and the interview is literally cut off.

Several techniques have thus been addressed here, which convey the frag-mentation of the shots in the sequence as a whole. This is first due to the indi-vidual shots' spatial isolation and the fact that they do not adhere to the continu-ity system (i.e., there is no orientation through an establishing shot and no classical series of cuts, according to the principle of shot/reverse shot). Second, the space of the mise-en-scène is often not ordered according to any sort of hier-archy; that is, it remains incomplete, in that it does not reveal the entire process it describes (see fig. 7). It follows, from these two ideas, that an inaccessible space (in the sense of a narrative space) is constructed. Already visible in the first shot, additional, even clearer examples of this principle emerge later over the course of the sequence (figs. 16–17, 18–19). Finally, the fragmentation of space corresponds to a specific temporality, explained in greater detail below, that is not exhausted in the notion of the fragment but includes it as a constit-utive element, as was already alluded to in the discussion of the second shot. This *fragmentary construction of individual shots* and *fragmentation as a general principle* at a formal level are the first and most fundamental criteria for an affect poetics of paranoia. Further criteria will be developed in what follows.

Following a considerable delay, the third shot finally and decisively locates the source of the music and sound in the image *as a source:* namely the parade, bands, and spectators sitting and standing at the side of the road. Although this shot seems to have been recorded from a standpoint nearby the previous one, again the impression of a strong spatial disjunction is created. This is primarily due to the fact that the camera is clearly operating with a far shorter focal length here, meaning the depth of field extends far into the background of the image, where the senator can already faintly be made out.

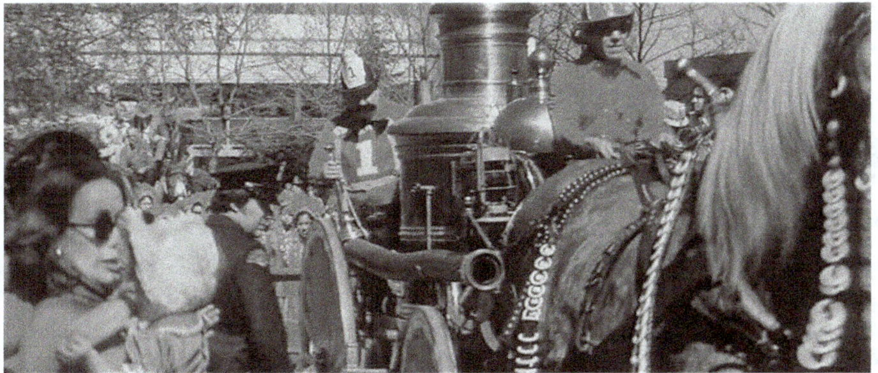

Fig. 8: The parade moving out of the depth of the space, with the senator in the background.

In this way, two directly adjacent shots construct their respective spaces as diametrically opposed to one another, revealing, thereby, the same conflict between flatness and protrusion established in the first shot – as we will see, the third shot ultimately moves towards a low-angle perspective (see figs. 9 – 11). Flatness and protrusion are not simply placed alongside one another in unrelated fashion but, rather, the gesture of protrusion sets the parallax shift onto the next plane in motion.

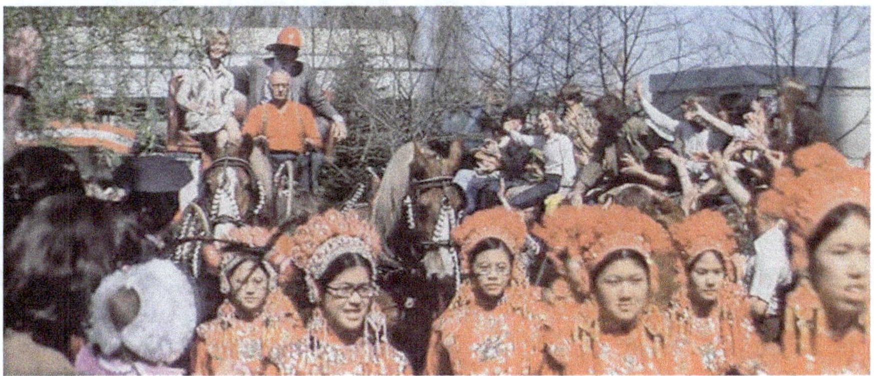

Figs. 9 – 11: Dallas Revisited.

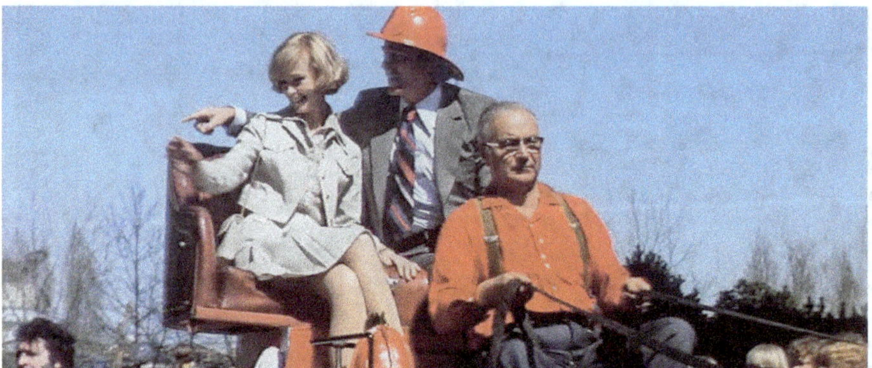

Fig. 10

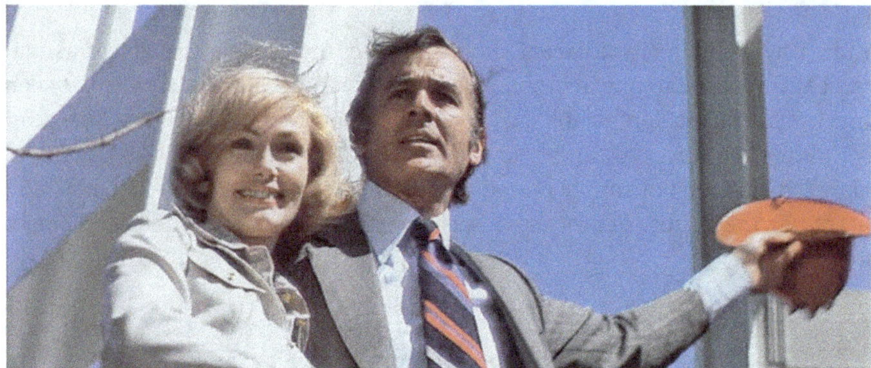

Fig. 11

Hence, the initially abstract contrast between flatness and protrusion now receives an initial concrete meaning over the course of this third shot (which lasts nearly 50 seconds and is thus nearly twice as long as the previous one) through its relation to the senator. And once again, in this sequence, we can see how tightly and complexly embodied meaning is employed to evoke a symbolic dimension: the shot unfolds, on one level, by allowing the senator to progressively appear as a highly vulnerable figure. François Truffaut described what, at first glance, seems like a very similar set-up, namely the murder scene on the staircase in PSYCHO (the murder of Detective Arbogast): "'he [Arbogast] arrived like a flower', which implies, of course, that he was ready to be plucked."[70] The senator and his wife are, indeed, increasingly exposed and iso-

---

70 Truffaut: Hitchcock, p. 273.

lated, until at the close of the seemingly nearly endless shot, only the couple is visible in the frame, seen from a very low angle, entirely unprotected and thus totally at the mercy of the possible assassin (fig. 11). Unlike the scene in PSYCHO, however, a measure of temporal irreversibility is inscribed onto the shot by the regular drumbeat and cymbals, whose continued duration is perceived by the spectator as the clock running down before the fatal gunshot, evoked in the imagination[71] – an effect particularly potent at the end of the shot, when the percussion suddenly stops, as if anticipating the moment of the bullet being fired (still yet to occur), an acoustic echo foreshadowed by the clashing cymbals. While in PSYCHO, as well, we are dealing with a form of anticipation, it is of a decidedly different nature.[72] For this reason, the following question presents itself: how can the mental image of the shot being fired, anticipated by the spectator, be specified in more precise terms?

Zapruder and the Split Spectator

As previously discussed, the building blocks of this question's answer can be found in the linkage of sensorial experience and symbolic meaning. At this level, the way in which the character is exposed, in both structural and iconographic terms, suggests an obvious connection to another politician driving past a camera: shown, namely, in the so-called Zapruder film of the assassination of John F. Kennedy (see figs. 12–15). The panning movement of the camera from left to right is similar here, only the angle of the shot is flipped; the Zapruder film is shot from a high angle and this sequence in THE PARALLAX VIEW from below. Of primary importance is the iconographic and affective reference, produced via the red fireman's helmet, to the blood spurting in the notorious frame 313 of the assassination film (fig. 15).[73] In this sense, the removal of the helmet does not only increase the senator's risk of being shot within the concrete moment of the film's perception, but also connects this moment, via a deictic

---

71 My thanks go to Jan Bakels for making me aware of this.

72 See also Chapter 2 on suspense.

73 This frame and several of the following ones which depict Kennedy's injuries in similarly explicit fashion were left out when *Life* magazine initially printed a section (31 frames in black and white) of the Zapruder film in November 1963. It was only after the publication of the Warren Report in 1964 that the frame (enlarged and in color) was printed in *Life*. The film as a whole was only made available to a wider public in the form of moving images in 1975 via a television broadcast on the ABC show *Good Night, America*. See Art Simon: Dangerous Knowledge, p. 35.

gesture, to the historical moment of the assassination and the reception of its images printed in *Life* magazine.

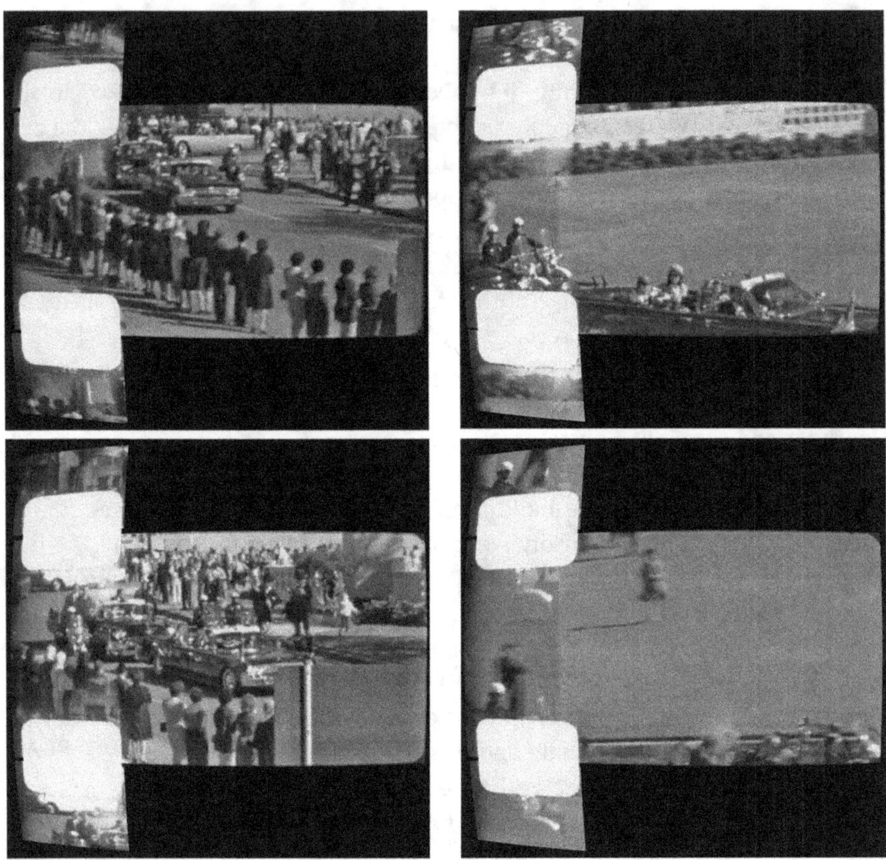

Figs. 12–15: Frames 135, 180, 253, and 313 from the Zapruder film.[74]

In addition, it is not only the documentation of Kennedy's assassination that is addressed with the Zapruder film; instead, this 26-second film also establishes, for its part, a paradigm of paranoid perception. This means that, in THE PARALLAX VIEW, the reference to November 1963 in Dallas does not just serve a memorial purpose but actually lays the groundwork for further poetic development of the paradigm that was formulated with the Zapruder film. Once again, the essen-

---

74 URL: http://www.assassinationresearch.com/v2n2/zfilm/zframe001.html, last accessed March 13th, 2019.

tial principle is fragmentation, the lack of any incorporation into a context. In a short essay about the long take, Pier Paolo Pasolini draws on the idea of montage to describe how, for all the intensity of its expression, the Zapruder film remains incomprehensible and meaningless due to the absence of other, supplementary perspectives (or, more precisely, *any* other perspectives).[75] It is not simply that additional subjective perspectives are missing but, rather, that there is no *coordination* of perspectives around a coherent point of view. Without this coordination, achieved by montage, as Joan Copjec puts it in a comprehensive commentary on Pasolini's text, the material does not possess any viewpoint of its own and thus implies a weakened, reduced form of subjectivity.[76] According to Pasolini, this stems from the fact that Zapruder did not consciously choose his vantage point but began shooting from the position where he happened to be at that moment – such that, to a certain extent, the film shows what Zapruder saw, not the camera lens.[77] In reference to Pasolini's model of a free indirect subjective perspective, Copjec describes this form of subjectivity as a *splitting of consciousness*, which is characteristic of her conception of perversion,[78] as derived from Sartre and Lacan, and which equally gets to the heart of the problem of paranoid perception (following the hypothesis that forms the basis of this chapter): "Perversion seeks to ensure that gaze and vision, desire and law, conscious and unconscious no longer contradict each other but inhabit the same plane, and attempts to force them to coalesce."[79] Unlike perversion, paranoia does not subsist in the desire to force contradictions together but, rather, in the delusional recog-

---

75 Pier Paolo Pasolini: Observations on the Long Take [1967]. In: October Vol. 13 (1980), pp. 3 – 6, here p. 3. Pasolini sees the Zapruder film as a paradigmatic example of the long take.
76 "According to Pasolini's argument, however, the problem is not that the assassination footage cannot be coordinated with any *other* point of view but that, without this coordination, the footage by itself has *no point of view*, properly speaking. Pasolini distinguishes the point-of-view-structure created through montage, and the subjectivity belonging to it, from a different, attenuated or reduced form of subjectivity that is rendered by the long take." Joan Copjec: Imagine There's No Woman. Ethics and Sublimation, Cambridge 2004, p. 199.
77 Pasolini: Observations on the Long Take, p. 3. The Zapruder film thus does not manage to reach "an objectivity of the camera, which follows the self-expression of things," and, therefore, does not connect technical awareness to subjective impression, which, for Pasolini, is the prerequisite for film in the fullest sense. See Bernhard Groß: Pier Paolo Pasolini. Figurationen des Sprechens, Berlin 2008, p. 259.
78 Perversion should not be understood here as sexual deviance, but rather in a structural sense of a manner of being in the world, which, in the case of sadism, which forms Copjec's primary interest here, is characterized by a sort of emotional distancing from the surrounding world – a distancing that we have already encountered, in comparable fashion, in relation to the schizophrenic's approach to the world.
79 Copjec: Imagine There's No Woman, p. 223.

nition of their permanent coexistence. This splitting has nothing to do with ambivalence or indecisiveness (in reference to a cinematic affect poetics, this is exactly where the difference to the horror film lies, above all in its classical incarnation): "For, it is not that some part of [...] experience is split off into the unconscious, but rather that some part, while still remaining conscious, fails to be subjectivized."[80]

Louis Sass described a similar sort of clarity in this splitting process for schizophrenia:

> It is remarkable to what extent even the most disturbed schizophrenics may retain, even at the height of their psychotic periods, a quite accurate sense of what would generally be considered to be their objective or actual circumstances. Rather than mistaking the imaginary for the real, they often seem to live in two parallel but separate worlds: consensual reality and the realm of their hallucinations and delusions.[81]

The lived conflict between objectivity and subjectivity is thus at the core of the problem. Starting from the observation that there are no shots in cinema that are objective in themselves,[82] Copjec compares the subjective perspective of the Zapruder film with the sort of "unattributable shots" which make up the conceptual core of Pasolini's free indirect subjective perspective and in which the camera becomes fixated on a "piece of reality." In this technical fixation, in this "obsession," a form of subjectivity emerges, "which is brought forth objectively, in order to simultaneously allow the poles of subjective and objective to melt into one another until they can no longer be distinguished."[83] Copjec uses Sartre and Lacan to define this latter type of shot as the gaze of the other, which can never be objectified in a character, nor can it transcend the world as an omniscient authority. The Zapruder perspective is thus characterized by the fact that the gaze of the other coincides with the contingent gaze of the voyeur:

> Public ceremony has indeed been converted into a private home movie insofar as the gap between eye and gaze that opens vision to the presence of others as such has vanished. [...] We are no longer in the presence of 'some' (indeterminate) other consciousness, of a public

---

80 Copjec: Imagine There's No Woman, p. 228.
81 Louis Sass: The Paradoxes of Delusion. Wittgenstein, Schreber, and the Schizophrenic Mind, Ithaca/London 1994, p. 21.
82 See also Sobchack: Toward inhabited space, p. 321: "As it is a body in the world, even what we call the 'omniscient' camera is not transcendent in its vision and marks its perceptive senses through direction and perspective. Embodied in the clouds, the camera still has access to the world only from the Here from which it sees and the Now in which it is. It is the world that is transcendent in existence – and not vision, movement, or embodied consciousness."
83 Groß: Pier Paolo Pasolini, p. 259.

with which we maintain a relation of 'uneasy indetermination,' but of an infallible law with which we maintain a relation that leaves no room for doubt. It is the coincidence of eye and gaze that creates the tightly constricted space we observe here and in SALÒ; one is made to look through the eyes of the Other, from which we can take no distance. The possibility of another, contravening look, always left open in the point-of-view-structure, is for structural reasons blocked off. Yet, if the subjective shot doubles with certainty the Other's gaze, it does not afford a view that could be described as pellucid or omniscient, but one, on the contrary, that is stained with obscene enjoyment, with the subjective markings – blurring, shadowing, and the like – of an arbitrary vision.[84]

This contradiction is particularly clearly visible in THE PARALLAX VIEW at the level of camerawork, the attitude of which can be summed up with the formula that, here, chaos is captured with deadly calm. The illusion of omnipotence and grandeur characteristic of paranoia, which is also the underlying basis of its combinatorial procedures, is achieved through the precision in framing and the slow, fateful certainty conveyed by its rhythmic figures, camera pans, and shot length. As previously mentioned, we are by no means just concerned with some "simple" television image here.[85] The almost authoritarian severity of the framing forces the spectator to take on a perspective that is as emphatically insufficient as it is rigid. On the other hand, this gesture of distancing without gaining a synoptic view can also be connected with the schizophrenic's experience of perception, in which power and powerlessness are hotwired together:

> The delusional world of many schizophrenic-type patients is not, then, a flesh-and-blood world of shared action and risk but a mind's-eye-world where emotions, other people, even the patient's own body exist as distant or purely subjective phenomena, mere figments of an abstract imagination *whose power is at the same time limitless and irrelevant.*[86]

---

84 Copjec: Imagine There's No Woman, p. 230.
85 "The cluttered, uncentered shots showing an Independence Day parade, the arrival of a political candidate [...], and his interview by a television reporter combine the documentary qualities of television reporting with the formal rigor and complexity of a formalist art cinema. This formal approach is used to comment on the complex nature of perception, particularly in a world where the moral and political landscape that once was so clear has turned opaque, and any misperception can be fatal." Christian Keathley: Trapped in the Affection Image. Hollywood's post-traumatic Cycle (1970–1976). In: Elsaesser, Horwath, and King (eds.): The Last Great American Picture Show, pp. 293–308, here p. 300. It appears important to insist on two points here: on the one hand, the sequence does not merely combine two expressive registers but rather forces them together into a contradictory configuration: on the other hand, this procedure does not just represent a commentary on the complex nature of perception, but also implements this complexity in the concrete act of the film experience.
86 Louis Sass: The Paradoxes of Delusion, p. 46 (emphasis my own).

With all this in mind, an initial attempt can now be made to sum up what happens in the opening sequence, namely: that perspectives, largely isolated from one another, are strung together without effecting their full coordination. Each individual perspective is not only isolated from the others but also repeatedly and continuously reintroduces the restriction of perceptual possibility (see, for example, figs. 7, 16–19) – however often and seemingly without hindrance the perspective may change, the montage only ever moves from one insufficient view to another: "Each of these presentations of reality is extremely impoverished, aleatory, almost pitiful, if one realizes that it is *only one* among many."[87] The parallax shift is nothing but the precise process whereby one becomes aware of the insufficiency of each individual perspective. Parallax is thus the *principle according to which the fragments are connected*. And just as Pasolini describes how the Kennedy assassination is repeatedly played back from a dozen, (imagined) subjective perspectives, this only results in a multiplicity of presents, which mutually relativize and call each other into question – as a result, no present is created that could ever be transformed into a past.[88] The splitting of the spectator thus concerns a collision of temporal relations.

Ironic Temporality

The memory of an historical assassination, overloaded with meaning, is further enriched by a somewhat less obvious, yet still pertinent reference. The vaguely Asian-identified band (see fig. 9) does not just emphasize the passing of time;[89] their costumes also awaken indeterminate foreign associations, brought together in another Hollywood film whose theme is assassination and paranoia: THE MANCHURIAN CANDIDATE (John Frankenheimer 1962).[90]

---

87 Pasolini: Observations on the Long Take, p. 4.

88 See Pasolini: Observations on the Long Take, p. 3.

89 The idea presents itself here of connecting this moment of rhythmic emphasis with the principle of splitting the Zapruder film into individual frames: each beat of the drum an individual cut.

90 At the very latest by the last sequence of THE PARALLAX VIEW, which makes clear reference to the end of Frankenheimer's film, this comparatively subtle reference turns out to be no coincidence. It seems, instead, as if this type of referential concentration within the visual space itself carries the mark of paranoid thought and is thus a genuine part of the poetic logic of the film. See Andrew Horton: Political Assassination and Cinema. Alan J. Pakula's THE PARALLAX VIEW. In: Persistence of Vision 3/4 (1986), pp. 61–70, which takes a comprehensive look at the relationship between the two films.

Particularly in view of these kinds of references, considering the total absence of any attempted assassination at this point (that is, at the end of the third shot), the film establishes a clearly ironic perspective regarding the events of the plot. Irony is not, however, to be understood here in the everyday sense of the word but, rather and above all, as a specific temporal structure: a highly specialized form of dramatic irony. At this point, this ironic temporality is manifested, on the one hand, as the disappointment of an expectation and, on the other, as the persistent inscription of expectation onto the gestures of the staging nonetheless. This means that the end of the third shot is not connected to a sense of relief that no shot has actually been fired. Instead, it is staged such that the memory of the JFK assassination finds its way into the symbolic level of emotion as a supplementary layer, which does not so much foreshadow the actual assassination that will occur later on but, rather, already preempts it.[91]

The expectation articulated at this point must be clearly distinguished, in its temporal structure – and thus also its affective quality – from the notion of expectation in suspense: rather than the *interplay* between certainty and uncertainty regarding the arrival of a future event, to the contrary, here we are decidedly concerned with a form of *certainty*. In the third shot, the anticipation of the gunshot thus plays out *in the memory of the image itself* and through the actuality of its forward extension into the future. It is in this sense that the concept of the spectator's imagination, mentioned above, must be concretized. Here we find the reason for the difference between this scene and the one, discussed earlier, from PSYCHO. The camera is not out to kinetically model the increase in the level of excitement towards the point of greatest danger; the 'effective moment,' in which present and future are united, is precisely not what the framing strives for.[92] The camera operates, instead, in highly reserved, ponderous fashion, with a sense of calm determination. The moment of the possible gunshot is not prolonged (i.e., via slow motion or montage), as would be constitutive of suspense; rather, it approaches mechanical single-mindedness, corresponding to

---

91 Considered more precisely, the Zapruder film already approaches this temporal structure, as, following a short interruption, it starts up again at the point (frame 133) at which with all probability the first shot had already been fired from Oswald's gun. See Max Holland, Johann Rush: J.F.K.'s Death, Re-Framed. In: New York Times, November 22nd, 2007, URL: http://www.nytimes.com/2007/11/22/opinion/22holland.html?ref=abrahamzapruder, last accessed March 13th, 2019.

92 See also the deconstruction of the effective moment in GIMME SHELTER, which is briefly discussed at the end of this chapter. On the theory of the 'effective moment' in cinema in reference to Lessing and in connection to the *tableau vivant* see Sergei Eisenstein: Laocoön. In: id.: Selected Works. Volume 2: Towards a Theory of Montage, edited by Michael Glenny, and Richard Taylor, London 1991, pp. 109–202; Kappelhoff, Matrix der Gefühle, pp. 144–155.

the uniform division of the Zapruder film into individual frames. The time of the film is not acted upon by any force but, rather, time itself is the power to which everything submits. The duration of the shot is augmented by the static nature of the frames, of the images in which the assassination is frozen for eternity.

In this way, this shot's temporality and the sequence as a whole approach that of *Aeon* (rather than *Kairos*).[93] Deleuze and Guattari write that *Aeon* is "the indefinite time of the event, the floating line that knows only speeds and continually divides that which transpires into an already-there that is at the same time not-yet-here, a simultaneous too-late and too early, a something that is both going to happen and has just happened."[94] But, according to Pasolini, a time that knows only speeds constitutes neither the creation of relations nor, thereby, a present. This *ironic time without a present* is the second criterion for an affect poetics of paranoia.

Perception between Television and Cinema

This ironic temporality is closely related to the principle of fragmentation; taken together, they produce an overriding negative principle, namely the fact that no narrative space emerges. Instead, a space of dissociated perception appears.

---

93 Manfred Schneider draws on the ideas of Giorgio Agamben to bring the temporality of the assassination and how it was conveyed by the media into connection with the concept of *kairos*, as the latter appears in the Pauline epistles. However convincing his analysis may appear and however important it is to incorporate the religious dimension into the discussion, there are still significant arguments against the use of the term *kairos*, which I, following the readings of Daniel Stern and Raymond Bellour, respectively, have related to the experience of the spectator in the concrete act of film perception. Schneider himself thus rightly emphasizes that the time of the assassination is radically separate from the temporality of lived experience and does not form a present, see Schneider: Das Attentat, p. 476. This stands in total contradiction to Stern's conception of the *present* moment, which is based on the *kairos* (unlike Schneider, Stern bases his argument here on pre-Christian antique philosophy). There are also two additional aspects connected to the Zapruder film as a film which are underrepresented in Schneider's work, as he equates the film stills of the stricken John F. Kennedy with the depictions of assassinations by, say, Jacques-Louis David or Vittore Carpaccio from the 18th and 16th centuries respectively without any further ado (on the film image as an intermediate image, see Deleuze: Cinema 1, pp. 2–6). For one thing, there is the relentless *repetition* of the 26-second shot (not only the copy of the film stills) and, for another, in relation to this, the moment of *pre-determination*: unlike the definition of the *kairos* as a moment ripe for action, no action and no change is possible in any way in the Zapruder film; its course of action is instead already set out in advance.

94 Deleuze, Guattari: A Thousand Plateaus, p. 289.

Here, the element of flatness, opposed to protrusion, comes into play: the tendency to reduce the space to two dimensions makes the mise-en-scène appear as if it were beneath a glass dome – a formal characteristic of the image, manifested for the spectator as a feeling of numbness and trepidation (the flipside to the fantasy of omnipotence, expressed in the above-mentioned combinatorial approach). This consequently also applies to the film's protagonist himself, reporter Joe Frady, who repeatedly runs into quite concrete spatial restrictions that stand in the way of his actual function and intention, which is to take action. This corresponds to the fact that the mise-en-scène creates a space devoid of nearly any sort of hierarchy and thus does not privilege the film's protagonist as the object of our attention (see figs. 6, 7, 17). As a result, the character increasingly becomes a spectator himself. Frady thus (at a slightly later point in the sequence) is not even allowed to enter the party in the Space Needle's restaurant where the assassination ultimately takes place: a bodyguard in sunglasses holds him back. At the same time, the shallow depth of field of the shot in question suggests that no further space exists behind the bodyguard anyway, at least not one that actually belongs to the spatial order within the range of the camera's focus (figs. 16 und 17).

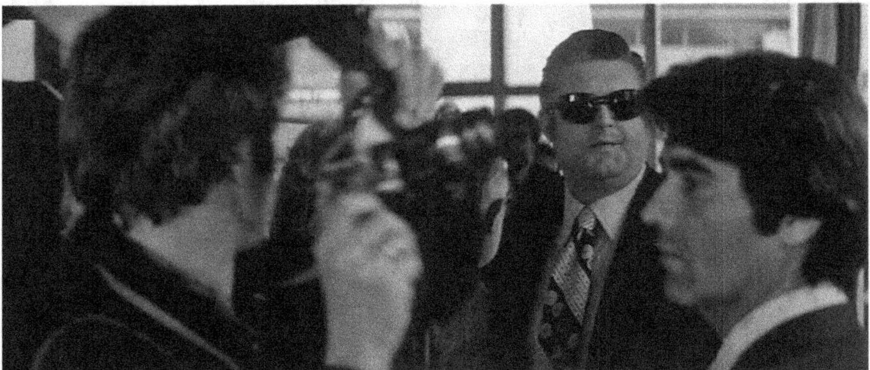

Figs. 16–17: Private party – the space is both overloaded and cordoned off.

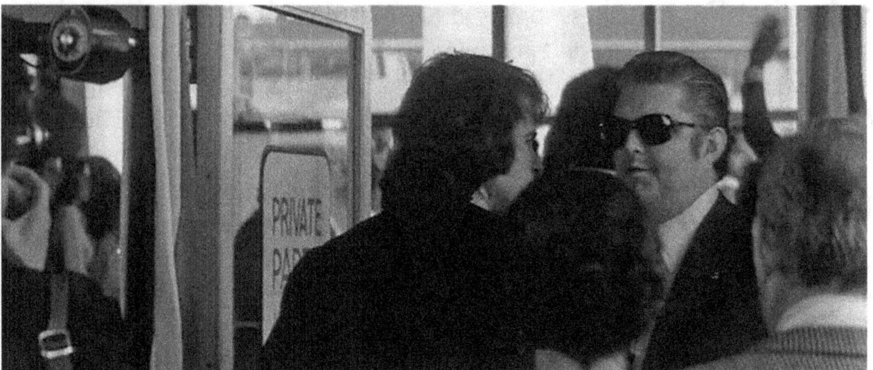

Fig. 17

This principle of dissociated perception, achieved through the flattening of the image space, only gains full significance in the scenes surrounding the actual assassination. It is then that the more deep-seated, symbolic, historical meaning for the film's affect poetics is revealed, namely the complex relationship with television aesthetics already discernible in the second shot of the sequence. Pasolini already links the question of contradictory temporality with the difference between television and film.[95] As was already made clear in the analysis of this shot, addressed here is not simply the fact that corresponding stylistic devices are quoted or reproduced but, rather, the question of the spectator's position. This positioning is depicted in almost emblematic fashion in the shot in which the bullets are fired. The revolving restaurant where the party gathers, located at the top of the tower,[96] is separated from the balcony that encircles it by a panoramic window. The moment of the actual assassination is spatially constructed in such a way that the camera, together with several figures, is located outside and looks through the pane of glass as the senator is struck by the bullets within (figs. 18–19).

---

95 See Pasolini: Observations on the Long Take, p. 3.
96 Taken in tandem with the vertical movement of the elevator, the restaurant can itself be seen as performing its own form of parallax. This, once again, addresses the problem of the relativity of movement and the activity of (non-living) objects.

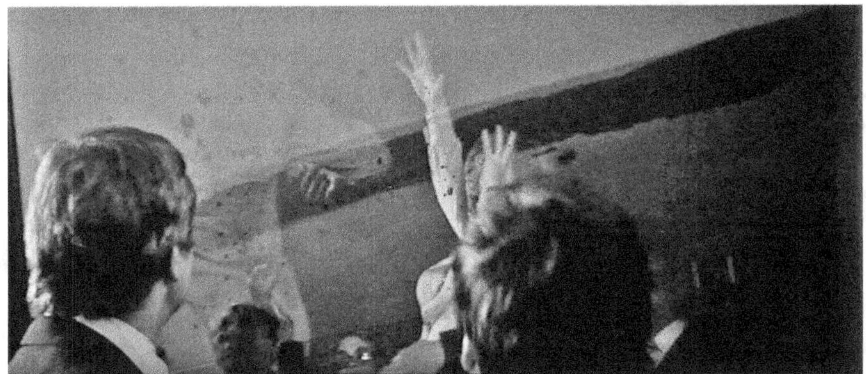

Figs. 18–19: The assassination through glass, splitting the view.

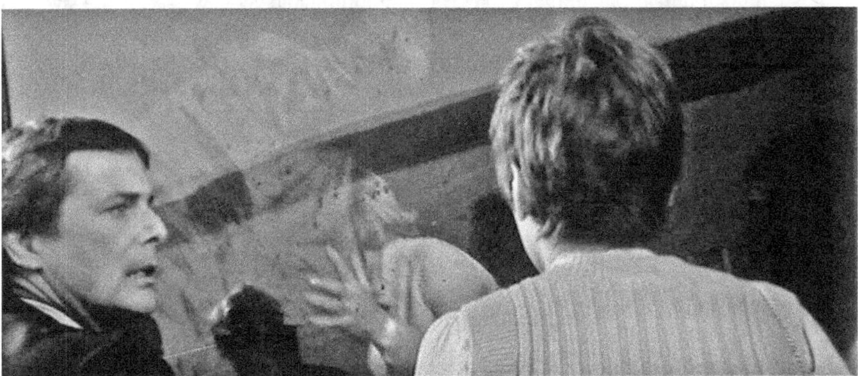

Fig. 19

Once again, we can speak of a doubling of the spectatorial position or, to be more precise, of the splitting of the spectator into two competing perspectives. The pane of glass marks the rupture opening up between the spectator and their double, at once material and intangible.[97] A medial configuration is thus unmistakably established: the spectator watches people watching something which itself recalls a historically charged situation of viewing, in which the images of the diverse assassinations of the 1960s, particularly the Kennedys', are collected and condensed. The *mediatization* of the film image, its construction as the image of an image, is the third, central criterion for the affect poetics of paranoia.

---

97 The pane of glass enters the images as an object primarily due to the traces of violence it carries, namely the drops of the senator's blood that remain stuck to it.

If one talks of a gap between perspectives here, this split is a function of two colliding temporalities, which the poetics of this film strictly differentiates. I already referred to one of these as ironic temporality: already characterized in itself by a splitting or a doubling, in that it always preempts what is to happen. A description of this relationship can also be found in reports of those suffering from schizophrenia, as a concrete perceptual experience that carries a particular affect:

> It is more like gray. It is like a constant sliding and shifting that slips away in a jelly-like fashion, leaving nothing substantial and yet enough to be tasted, or *like watching a movie based on a play and, having once seen the play, realizing that the movie is a description of it* and one that brings back memories and yet isn't real. ... Even a description of it is unreal and tormenting, for it is horrifying and yet seems mild and vague, although it is acute. It is felt in an unreal way in that it isn't constant torture and yet never seems to leave and everything seems to slip away into impressions. ... For what it is, is, and yet *what seems to be is always changing and drifting away into thought and ideas, rather than actualities.* The important things have left and the unimportant stay behind, making the loss only more apparent by their presence.[98]

This temporality pervades large sections of THE PARALLAX VIEW and plays a decisive part in generating the feeling of intractability conveyed by the film. At this particular point in the film, it is, however, joined by another: for a few moments, the film shifts – and tellingly, a specific cut follows here, almost immediately after the shots are fired: a cut into the inside of the tower where the assassination took place. This is a cut into another temporal mode, that of the (repeated) experience of the traumatic moment in the present tense of a television news report: "Live television is a paradigmatic reproduction of something happening in the present."[99] This present tense is also pervaded by shockwaves of the past,[100] although they do not appear here as tension beneath the surface but, rather, emerge for a brief moment from the otherwise dominant feeling of icy distance (achieved primarily through the hectic shake of the hand-held camera and the much higher cutting rate). The moment before, during which the shots are actually fired (after their anticipation during the parade), results in the collision

---

98 Eugene Meyer, Lino Covi: The Experience of Depersonalization, quoted by Sass: The Paradoxes of Delusion, p. 23 (emphasis my own).

99 Pasolini: Observations on the Long Take, p. 3.

100 The depiction of the senator lying on the ground thus precisely picks up on the iconography of the images of Robert Kennedy dying, printed in *Life* and the *L.A. Times* in 1968, among other places. See also Stephen Farber: Movies That Reflect Our Obsession With Conspiracy and Assassination. In: The New York Times, August 11th, 1974, p. 11 and p. 20, which contrasts the two depictions.

of these two temporalities. The surface of the image is represented as an area of tension, over which lines of horror and despair unfurl, just like the various layers and repetitions that anchor the event in medial memory. At the same time, the visual paradigm of paranoia is manifested in the flatness of the pane of glass and in the entire configuration of the scene (which deliberately places the assassin off-screen), namely the *reference to the invisible in the visible.* This element of a traumatic event, insistently evasive in its transmission through the media, provokes the eternal restlessness of suspicion, which, according to Manfred Schneider, only finds calm "when it is allowed to take its place in God's eye."[101] Here, the same compromised subjectivity comes into effect, arising from the recognition that, as Pasolini writes, the chosen perspective represents just one selected at random from all the many other possibilities.[102]

The Combinatorial Linkage of the Elements

The lack of hierarchy implied by a flat surface and the uniform juxtaposition of objects of equal standing in the individual shots, however, does not merely create a sense of deficiency. It simultaneously creates the basis for a montage, capable of selecting elements, seemingly at random, from among all possible, undifferentiated objects (here, once again, we encounter the aspect of power in powerlessness). The division of space thus always implies the creation of a new one, even if the latter is not constituted as a space of narration. The impression conveyed by the montage is, therefore, precisely not one of arbitrariness but, to the contrary, one of highest determinacy. This becomes clear, for example, in the shift from the fourth shot of the film, which returns to the tableau shown in the second shot (see figs. 6 and 7) – we are still at the foot of the Space Needle, before the assassination – to the fifth, a detail shot extracted from this tableau. The cut takes place once the senator has finally arrived to speak to the reporter and she has asked him a question, which he prepares to answer. In the following

---

101 Schneider: Das Attentat, p. 429. On the question of invisibility and God's perspective, see also Copjec: Imagine There's No Woman, p. 216: "For, to be looked at from all sides by a nomadic gaze is to experience ourselves as visible in the world, as sunk within a perspective on which there can be another perspective, whereas to be visible to an all-seeing God would be to experience ourselves as part of some whole. In the first case, the other perspective threatens to demolish or overwhelm our own, while in the second this radical antagonism of perspectives gives way to the sense that God's view enlarges or rectifies our own. In this latter case we are no longer visible in the world, but fully visible only outside it."
102 Pasolini: Observations on the Long Take, p. 4.

shot, the fifth in total, the senator's advisor can be seen smiling opaquely and giving instructions, while the senator's answer to the reporter's question is audible from off-screen (fig. 21).

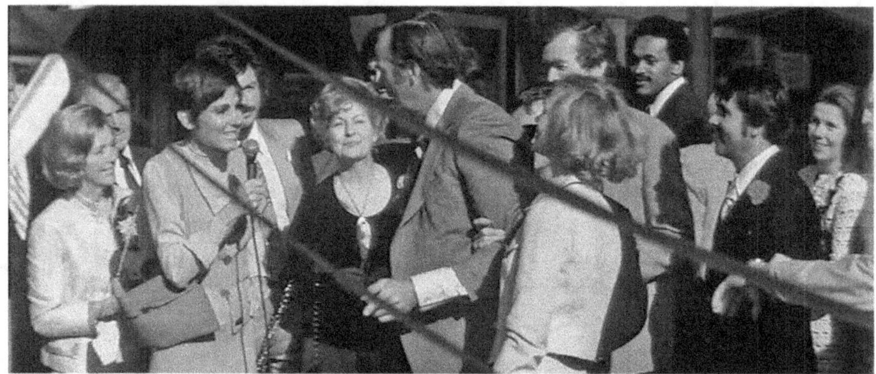

Figs. 20–22: Parallax as the restriction and expansion of the frame.

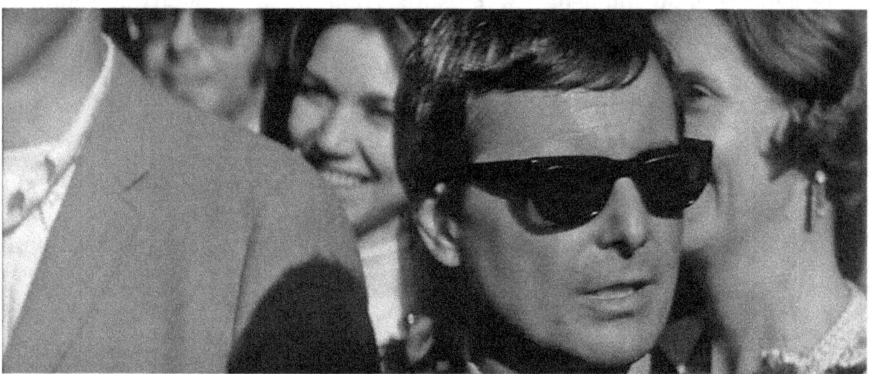

Fig. 21

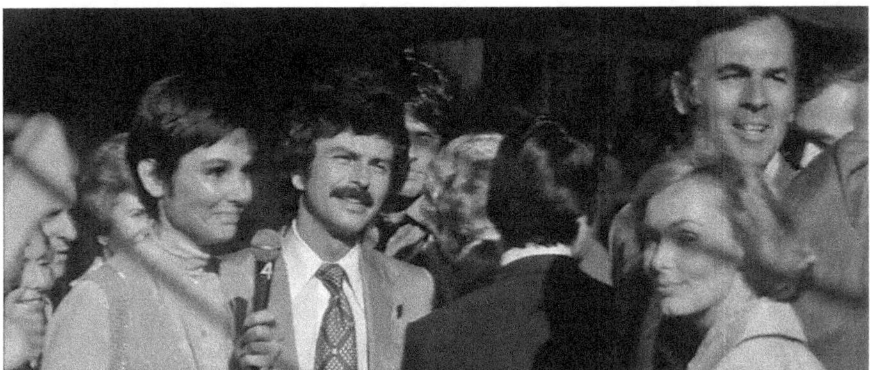

Fig. 22

However simple this operation may appear at first, it is in fact of decisive importance as it pertains to establishing the criteria for an affect poetics of paranoia. This cut, the fourth in total in the sequence, is different from the preceding three, each of which can be legitimately seen, albeit not exclusively, as advancing the ostensible plot (the Independence Day celebrations and the arrival of the senator). In this fourth cut, however, this function is no longer discernible, as the camera's gaze switches to something seemingly incidental. At the same time, the contradictory, dual determination of the tableau shot (merging film and television dispositifs) dissolves and is replaced by a new, independent gaze. Thus, the magnification performed by the cut, like the camera movement in the first shot, opens up a new dimension that follows a divergent logic. Like before, the question emerges as to the agent responsible for this shift in perspective – the very essence of parallax lies in this question. And again, like the first shot, of concern is not simply the isolation or revelation of a particular fragment. The cut-in, to a detail from the previous frame that does not seem to relate directly to the scene's foregrounded plot (the interview), serves instead to *create* such a relationship in the first place – just at a different level than that of the surface-level plot. The relationship between sound and image is once again decisive: the combination of the rhetoric of the senator's answer and his advisor's professional smile not only implies abstractly that the senator is not the author of this speech; rather, this impression ensues automatically, if one takes seriously Altman's hypothesis, that sound inexorably searches for some sort of anchor in the image.

This impression can be described, in Lacan's words, as an intellectual feeling, a "feeling of having something imposed on you, of influence, of being penetrated and replaced."[103] It is no coincidence that Deleuze's description of Hitch-cockian characters also comes to mind. They are "certainly not intellectual, but have feelings that can be called intellectual feelings, rather than affects, in that they are modelled on a varied play of experienced conjunctions."[104] The proximity between Hitchcock and a paranoid perceptual order is grounded in the structural principle of the *relation*, out of which, as we have seen in this case, every anchorage to the present has been expelled nonetheless. Thus, the combinatorics of the elements, through its comprehension by the spectator, may be grasped as the creation of just this kind of intellectual feeling.[105]

Furthermore, the change between shots, already described, possesses an additional, indeterminate surplus value, which ushers from the anti-classical connection of montage and mise-en-scène created at this juncture. In contrast to a classical scene, broken down into shot and counter shot, this configuration offers no formal point of reference for the edit's sequence: the shooting angle in the three, consecutive shots remains at eye level, taken straight-on; with only the field size changing from an American shot (fig. 20), to a close-up, and then finally to a medium close-up (fig. 22). Hence, the detail does not merge with its function, describing the relationship between the politician and his advisor – just as it also does not merge with the logic of the sequence of shots but, rather, remains a singular deviation, a sort of residual that, for the time being,

---

103 Lacan: De la psychose paranoïaque, pp. 133–134.
104 Deleuze: Cinema 1, p. 207.
105 Correspondingly, Théodule Ribot relates the sense of surprise so important for suspense – as a fundamental intellectual feeling – to the subject of the relation: "The first stage is that of *surprise*. [...] It is a special emotional state which cannot be traced back to any other, consisting of a shock, a disadaptation. [...] its special and peculiar character lies in its being without contents, without object, save a relation. Its material is a *relation*, a transition between two states – a movement of the mind, and nothing more." Théodule Ribot: The Psychology of the Emotions, London 1898, p. 369. The parallax shift could be understood analogously as such a relation, as a movement on the part of the intellect, which does not go hand-in-hand with surprise but, rather, with the feeling of losing the ground under one's feet. Unlike Lacan, however, who bases his ideas on Janet, Ribot rejects any sort of fine distinctions; in his "pathology" of intellectual feelings he does, on the other hand, go into detail about the feeling of doubt, which he defines in the following way: "Doubt is a state of unstable equilibrium in which successive contradictory representations neither mutually exclude nor conciliate each other." Ribot: ibid., p. 375. The obvious parallels to the concept of paranoia that I have been developing don't have to be specially emphasized here. It is merely worth noting the similarity between this definition and Pasolini's idea of an entire series of Zapruder films at this juncture. In its more extreme manifestations, this conception of doubt approaches what Louis Sass describes as the schizophrenic's experience of total dissociation from reality.

stays unapprehended. Only its effect, which consists of the shift in the field size from American to medium close-up, is visible.

This interplay between tableau and detail once again takes up the previously described relationship between flatness and protrusion: as the protruding element, the detail shifts attention onto the tableau's arrangement. In this way, the inclusion of the close-up quite literally opens up a new perspective on the otherwise stable organization of the mise-en-scène – similar to what Ludwig Wittgenstein describes as "noticing an aspect" or "seeing-as," whereby seeing and thinking, perception and interpretation cross: "When the aspect changes, parts of the picture go together which before did not."[106]

We thus come closer to the quality of intellectual feelings – the constitution of a privileged perspective in the isolation of detail, a perspective that can, in turn, be brought into direct connection with the delusions of omnipotence and greatness mentioned above; it is thus the affective surplus of the detail, which remains unredeemed, which fuels the combinatorial process, as this detail unleashes an excess of relations.

The parallax's mode of operation can be more precisely specified against this backdrop in film theoretical terms, namely as a connection between the concept of expression and the problem of montage. The *locus classicus* of this connection is the so-called Kuleshov effect, which Naum Kleiman describes as a "transformation of the structure of the material within the image."[107]

For one thing, in the scene in question from THE PARALLAX VIEW, the sequential arrangement of the montage's components plays a role entirely in accordance with the Kuleshov effect: the ominous close-up plainly "contaminates" the shot that follows.[108] Furthermore, the emphasis here is on variations of a vis-

---

106 Ludwig Wittgenstein: Philosophical Investigations, Oxford 1986, p. 208. Wittgenstein also discusses this phenomenon by way of the famous example of the so-called duck-rabbit illusion, an image in which both the head of a rabbit as well as that of a duck can be seen or interpreted. Louis Sass made the connection between this concept of Wittgenstein's and the perception of those suffering from schizophrenia, drawing on the example of Daniel Paul Schreber, from whose memoires Freud developed his concept of paranoia. See Freud: Psycho-Analytical Notes on an Autobiographical Account of a Case of Paranoia (Dementia paranoides) [1911]. In: id.: Collected Papers, Vol. 3, New York 1959, pp. 387–470; Sass: The Paradoxes of Delusion, p. 31.

107 Naum Klejman: Die Einstellung als Montageglied, quoted by Sergej Jutkewitsch: Der große Nigromant. In: Hartmut Albrecht and Christiane Mückenberger (eds.): Lew Kuleschow, Berlin 1977, pp. 112–137, here p. 122. On the relevance of the concept of expression in this context, see Wittgenstein: Philosophical Investigations, p. 198 and pp. 206–211.

108 A comment made by Pudovkin, who was involved in Kuleshov's experiments, is instructive in this context. He writes that: "We took from one film or another several close-ups of the well-

ual-spatial relation; that is, not only do the three shots enter into an abstract, figurative relationship with one another. Rather, and this is of essential importance for the figure of the parallax, the intervals between them can be described as actual movements relating to the image space – leaps between individual frames – comparable to a zoom, for example. Paranoia is thus not simply the arbitrary association of contingent aspects but, rather, the visual space, the "material" of the mise-en-scène, is itself, at its core, susceptible to the seductive power of transformation.[109] Leo Bersani describes this affectively charged relationship between the visible and the invisible in paranoid style thusly: "Paranoid thinking [...] hesitates between the suspicion that the truth is wholly obscured by the visible, and the equally disturbing sense that the truth may be a sinister, invisible design *in* the visible."[110] It is precisely this vulnerability of the visible that connects to the principle of the flat, undifferentiated juxtaposition of elements, which elicits the question of the originator of the parallax shift.

How should one try to envisage the "noticing of an aspect" as a dynamic process? Eisenstein describes it as the creation of a "generalized image":

> What does such a conception of montage really give? In this case, each montage piece is not something unrelated, but becomes a *particular representation* of the general theme which in equal measure runs through all the shot-pieces. The juxtaposition of such particular details in a given montage construction produces that same *whole and general* which has given birth to each of the details, namely the generalized *image* through which the author (and, after him, the spectator) relives the theme.[111]

known Russian actor, Mozzhukhin (Mosjoukine). We chose close-ups which were static and which did not express any feeling at all: quiet close-ups. We joined these close-ups, which were all similar, with other bits of film in three different combinations." Quoted by Amy Sargeant: Vsevolod Pudovkin: Classic Films of the Soviet Avant-garde. London/New York 2000, p. 6. It seems as if a certain expressive under-determination of the individual shot favors both its ability to be combined and the range of aspects it contains in the sense of Wittgenstein.

109 See Freud on the attentiveness of the jealous paranoid: "These attacks drew their material from his observation of minute indications [...]." Sigmund Freud: Some Neurotic Mechanisms in Jealousy, Paranoia and Homosexuality. In: id.: The Complete Psychological Works of Sigmund Freud, Volume 18: Beyond the Pleasure Principle, Group Psychology and Other Works, edited by James Strachey, London 1955, pp. 221–234, here p. 225.

110 Leo Bersani: Pynchon, Paranoia, and Literature, quoted by Melley: Empire of Conspiracy, p. 141.

111 Sergei Eisenstein: Problems of Film Direction, p. 13.

Ultimately addressed here is the concept of expressive movement.[112] Its temporal form recursively acts upon each individual element, by allowing that aspect to emerge on which the cohesion of all elements depends. This is precisely where the intangible quality lies in the noticing of the aspect, explored by Wittgenstein: "Think of the expression 'I heard a plaintive melody'! And now the question is: 'Does he *hear* the plaint?' And if I reply: 'No, he doesn't hear it, he merely has a sense of it' – where does that get us? One cannot mention a sense-organ for this 'sense.'"[113] What Wittgenstein describes in negative terms, Eisenstein, under the concept of harmonic montage, turns into the characteristic of a unique quality of concrete film perception over time:

> Because, while a shot is a visual *perception* and a tone is a sound perception, *both visual and sound overtones are totally physiological sensations.*
>
> And, consequently, they are of *one and the same kind,* outside the sound of acoustic categories that serve merely as guides, paths to its achievement.
>
> For the musical overtones (a beat) the term 'I hear' is no longer strictly appropriate.
>
> Nor 'I see' for the visual.
>
> For both we introduce a new uniform formula: 'I feel.'[114]

The cut-in to the ominous detail, which embodies the principle of fragmentation in its purest form, thus produces an expressive surplus. The utilization of this sort of surplus in a *montage that both grasps everything and is capable of anything* is the fourth and final criterion for the affect poetics of paranoia.[115] The details themselves are to be interpreted from their structural incorporation within new, subterranean contexts. On the one hand, they remain unspecific enough in relation to emotional expression and the represented plot, so that they leave

---

112 We already encountered a very similar principle in relation to the phenomenon of suspense. The difference between the two modalities has already been explored superficially – it lies in the stance taken with regard to the possibility of a cinematic present tense: suspense affirms this possibility, paranoia rejects it.

113 Wittgenstein: Philosophical Investigations, p. 209.

114 Sergei Eisenstein: The Fourth Dimension in Film. In: id.: Selected Works, Volume 1: Writing, 1922–34, edited by Richard Taylor, London 1988, pp. 181–194, here p. 186.

115 "For the paranoid, identity, knowledge, and history are validated by what is out there, and only hidden to the eyes of those who cannot see the *formal* relation between dispersed signs and objects." Patrick O'Donnell: Latent Destinies, p. 16. This establishing of a privileged perspective points to a connection between paranoia and a narcissistic order of perception, see Freud: On Narcissism, and id.: Psycho-Analytical Notes on an Autobiographical Account of a Case of Paranoia. On the significance of montage, see also Adam Barker: Cries and Whispers, pp. 24–25.

space for a range of different interpretations; on the other, they are by no means formed in arbitrary fashion: in each case, they refer to an off-screen space, for example, through the direction of the gaze or movement (see once again fig. 21). Of decisive importance for maintaining the sense of disquiet is that the space referred to always remains off-screen: it forms the Archimedean point of paranoid montage, from which the world can be turned upside down – that area which, according to a book by Stephen King and its eponymous film adaptation, is called "the dead zone,"[116] where history is not yet written and the future can be changed. In this way, the indeterminate component stands for the all-compassing, for the conspiracy. Here, the decisive identifying feature of paranoia, namely the delusional conviction that everything truly is connected,[117] is finally fulfilled.

This feeling that everything is connected, in the sense of what Freud refers to as "relationship delusion," is thus the result of a sort of *virtual* expressive movement that erupts in ominous details, a movement, which, once again, invokes the elements of the ostensible narrative context as if from a second, retrospective point of view.[118] The reason for the claim – noted at the beginning: that the effort to break down the opening sequence into homogeneous units of time quickly encounters obstacles – can now be clearly specified: there is no one "image of the whole," but rather *two competing images*. And there is an even bigger problem: even though, at the end of the sequence, the existence of a conspiracy is no longer in doubt according to the logic of the plot, this certainty is produced from the persistent incompleteness of what can be known at all – for example, when, towards the end of the sequence, the Space Needle's image is taken up again in a sort of a reprise and combined with the figure of the escaped assassin, who – as we must assume, because we are not shown – meets his contact (figs. 23 – 24).

---

116 See Stephen King: The Dead Zone, New York 1979; THE DEAD ZONE (David Cronenberg 1983).
117 Here the analysis touches on the previously mentioned area of suture theory, whose axiom for the paranoia of classical Hollywood cinema is based on precisely the same sort of structures of the gaze produced by the montage. The decisive difference or, if one follows the theorists of suture, the self-reflexivity, of THE PARALLAX VIEW is derived from the fact that the imaginary completion of the structure of reference via a counter shot does emphatically not occur, which thus reveals the underlying schema. See Eyal Peretz: Becoming Visionary, p. 59. It is worth noting in this context that one of the foundational texts of suture theory, namely Daniel Dayan's *The Tutor-Code of Classical Cinema*, was published at nearly the same time as THE PARALLAX VIEW. See Daniel Dayan: The Tutor-Code of Classical Cinema. In: Film Quarterly, Vol. 28, No. 1 (1974), pp. 22 – 31.
118 This retrospective function comes into its own when photos are shown later on in the film, which correspond to the ominous details from the sequence: the moment before the assassination, the second waiter, etc.

The act of looking into the off-screen space, already apparent in the first shot in the carvings on the totem pole, now becomes an emblem of conspiracy.

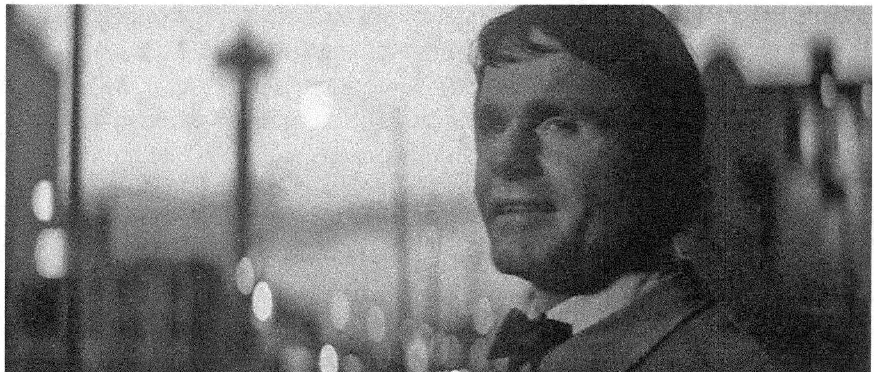

Figs. 23–24: The parallax as a mechanism of conspiratorial linkage.

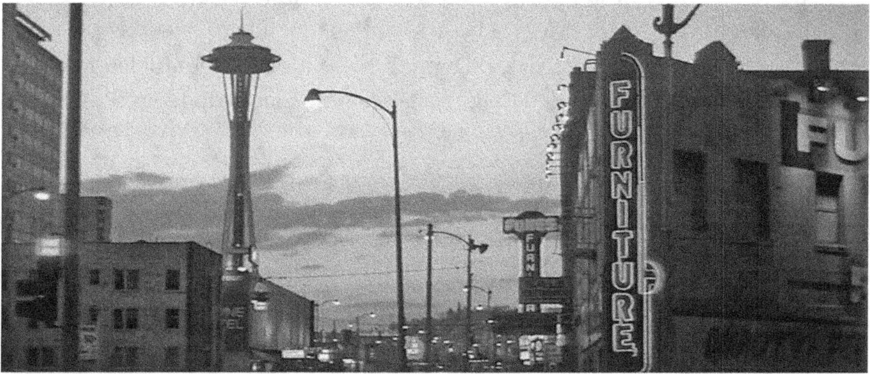

Fig. 24

Thus, the function of the fragment or, rather, the fragmentation fundamental to the affect poetics of paranoia, is revealed here in all its complexity: at the level of individual shots, it introduces a sense of disassociation into the perceptual experience of the represented narrative context; it further makes available each individual shot for the purposes of paranoid combinatorics; it is ultimately to be grasped as a *figure of movement*, at the level of the shots' association with one another. The logic of this movement is based on the figure of the parallax – and, at this final level, addresses both the form of the film and the spectator's affective experience in terms of an intellectual feeling.

The elements of an affect poetics of paranoia can thus be described as the constituent parts of a process, manifested through a film's concrete perception in time. The principle of fragmentation, as already evident in the first shot, stands at the beginning of this process. This principle, as a spatial and temporal structure, can be demonstrated within individual shots and in the relations between them. First only at specific moments and then forcefully towards the end of the sequence, the intrinsic tension between the fragments and the progress of the surface-level plot opens into an additional dimension 'behind the scenes,' which stands in direct opposition to the accentuated flatness of the image compositions.[119] The structuring principle of this dimension is the combinatorial approach, primarily implemented through montage (but also through camera movement, see, for example, figs. 1–5), by means of which fragments may be placed into relation with one another without the resultant creation of any whole (the essence of the paranoid vision of conspiracy is, to the contrary, the continual reference to the invisible that lies beyond the obvious: it feeds upon a basic assumption of incompleteness or, in other words, fragmentation). The dynamics of the combinatorial structure emerge, in turn, from the temporality of irony, the temporality of latency, produced by the "multiplication of presents." The paradox of this temporality can be grasped as the idea of *awaiting the unexpected*, to use the words of Patrick O'Donnell,[120] as a deeply conflicted relationship, in which an experience tied to the vagaries of the immediate present is connected to the distance of retrospection.

---

119 "The perceptual organs of paranoid reason primarily experience the worlds, spaces, and things that unnerve them as surfaces and offer up their own surface images to battle this unnerving feeling. This is the origin of the ambivalent fascination which they see as exuded by images, photos, cards, and written text and which invite them to make artificial interpretations. Even the strongest reason is not capable of interpretating *spaces*, but rather *surfaces* and the signs that appear on these surfaces. But paranoid interpretation doesn't just leave it at that: it pokes through these surfaces [here the relationship between the flat and the protruding is described as a movement, as parallax, H.L.]. It is convinced that these surfaces are diaphragms, from behind which the gaze of the true holders of power and truth might be squinting out." Schneider: Das Attentat, p. 591. This gets to the heart of the relationship between schizophrenia and paranoia, contained within Serge Daney's categories of film historical periodization. See Deleuze: Letter to Serge Daney, p. 69, and the discussion at the beginning of this chapter.
120 "For the paranoid awaits those unexpected, detemporalized instances of revelation when patterns magically converge into full-blown assemblages [...]." O'Donnell: Latent Destinies, p. 29.

3.3 Historical Outlook

Paranoia in New Hollywood

The criteria developed over the course of this analysis enable a new picture to emerge of what is usually understood as paranoia in the cinema of New Hollywood. We are no longer reliant on an imprecise, interpretation-dependent classification, according to plot elements or narrative patterns (such as the uncovering of a conspiracy) but, on the basis of our analysis, are able to establish far more fundamental – and formally verifiable – relationships between films.

If one, for example, proceeds from the manner in which the paranoid perceptual order is constituted by means of a process of fragmentary combination, such films as THE BOSTON STRANGLER (Richard Fleischer 1968), SYMBIOPSYCHOTAXIPLASM TAKE ONE (William Greaves 1971), THE ANDROMEDA STRAIN (Robert Wise 1971), THE CONVERSATION (Francis Ford Coppola 1974), or APOCALYPSE NOW (Francis Ford Coppola 1979) initially come to mind. In THE BOSTON STRANGLER, for example, a distinctive combinatorial procedure appears on the scene, which directly affects the image space of the film; much like in SYMBIOPSYCHOTAXIPLASM TAKE ONE and one sequence from THE ANDROMEDA STRAIN, this space often becomes a black, strangely ill-defined background, on which spaces and actions appear only in partial images, flagged as fragmentary (see fig. 25). In this way, first of all, an emotional distance to the events of the plot is achieved that is specific in each case (with an ironic twist in SYMBIOPSYCHOTAXIPLASM; as the grasping of the rictus of death in THE ANDROMEDA STRAIN); furthermore, the fragments, as THE BOSTON STRANGLER shows in virtuoso fashion, can be combined with one another in infinite fashion.

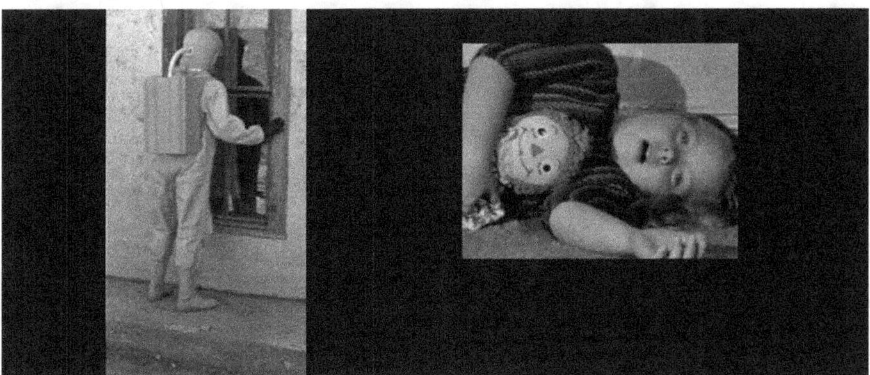

Fig. 25: The creation of the object via looking in THE ANDROMEDA STRAIN.

In THE ANDROMEDA STRAIN, whose plot revolves around a threat to all of human life posed by an alien virus (a telling twist on the invasion motif of the 1950s, as the invaders are now invisible), each act of looking by members of the research team is placed in relation with an emblematic section of their supposed field of view. Thereby, it appears that only this act of looking generates the image in the first place. These visual abbreviations, or slogans, to put things in the words of Deleuze, lack any other embeddedness within the spatial context of the film. Louis Sass describes this strange relationship between the gaze and its object on several occasions, most impressively in the following report on the experience of someone suffering from schizophrenia:

> Whenever I took my eyes off them [the hospital guards], they disappeared. In fact, everything at which I did not direct my entire attention seemed not to exist. There was some curious consistency in the working of my eyes. Instead of being able to focus on one object and retain a visual awareness of being in a room, a visual consciousness of the number of objects and people in that room, all that existed was what was directly in my line of vision.[121]

The phenomenon of the relativity of movement is thus addressed once again: the strange activity of inanimate objects finds its correspondence in the god-like omnipotence of the look that created them, based on a narcissistic perceptual order. In THE ANDROMEDA STRAIN, this procedure is itself embedded within a whole series of two-dimensional imaging procedures, from microscopes to maps and surveillance cameras to electronic graphics. The threat can therefore no longer be separated from its mediated presence, which even has an effect on the depiction of "ordinary" spaces: the use of the split-field diopter lens robs the image of nearly any sort of dimension of depth.

This idea leads to the broad, and central, thematic field of mediation, which is frequently connected with a flattening of space; such films as COMING APART (Milton Moses Ginsberg 1969), THX 1138 (George Lucas 1971), WESTWORLD (Michael Crichton 1973), NETWORK (Sidney Lumet 1976), or CAPRICORN ONE (Peter Hyams 1977) come to mind – merely as representative place-holders for many others. In these cases, cinema itself comes to model the phenomenal reality of paranoid schizophrenic experience as described by patients: "I was myself a camera. The views that people obtained through my own eyes were being recorded elsewhere to make some kind of three-dimensional film."[122]

---

121 Carney Landis: Varieties of Psychopathological Experience, quoted by Sass: Madness and Modernism, p. 277.

122 Morag Coate: Beyond All Reason, as quoted by Sass: Madness and Modernism, p. 286.

The dominant image conjured here, which can be traced back to our discussion of the Zapruder film,[123] is that of an observer *behind* the camera. Joan Copjec can be cited once again to this end: "[...] one is made to look through the eyes of the Other, from which we can take no distance. The possibility of another, contravening look, always left open in the point-of-view-structure, is for structural reasons blocked off."[124] With her interest in perversion, Copjec inverts the configuration: instead of someone looking through our eyes, we are looking through the eyes of the (big) other. Decisive here, however, is the presence of an entity behind the camera. Thereby, what Vivian Sobchack describes as the basic structure of film perception, suddenly affects the perception of reality:

> The schizophrenic disorder, by contrast, often involves something like a shift of conceptual attitudes, as if the mental lives of such people were deprived of the vital ballast provided by engagement in the processes of life. They are characterized by a certain inertia, involution, and self-preoccupation, and seem preoccupied with '*the experience of experience*.'[125]

CAPRICORN ONE implements this idea of an observer behind the camera in a particularly trenchant manner. The film deals with the conspiracy surrounding an alleged NASA mission to Mars. This mission is faked and the apparent Mars landing is shot in a studio – an obvious allusion to the actual conspiracy theory surrounding the authenticity of the moon landing. The scene's climax is formed by a seemingly simple tracking shot that is then revealed to be moving *behind* the (diegetic) camera (figs. 26 – 30):

---

123 See Jean-Baptiste Thoret: 26 Secondes. L'Amérique Éclaboussée. L'assassinat de JFK et le Cinéma Américain, Pertuis 2003. Thoret grasps the Zapruder film as a matrix for an entire series of poetic positions in post-classical American cinema.
124 Copjec: Imagine There's No Woman, p. 230.
125 Sass: Madness and Modernism, p. 166, emphasis my own.

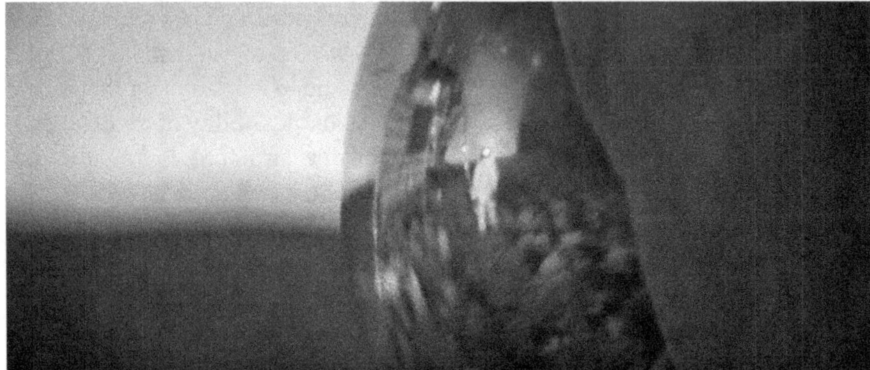

Figs. 26–30: The tracking shot behind the camera as "über-parallax" in CAPRICORN ONE.

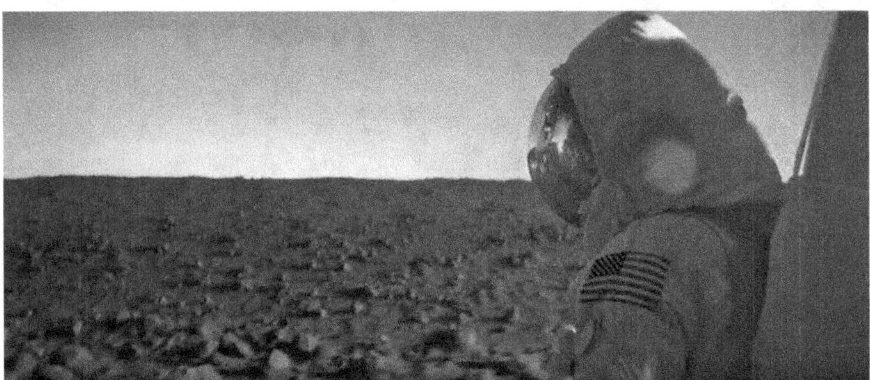

Fig. 27

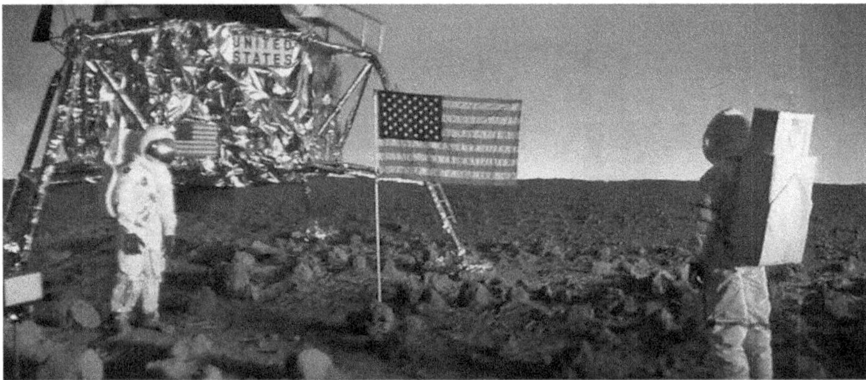

Fig. 28

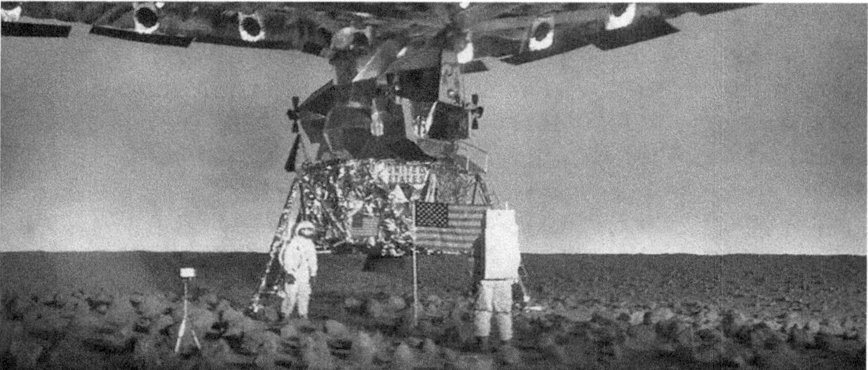

Fig. 29

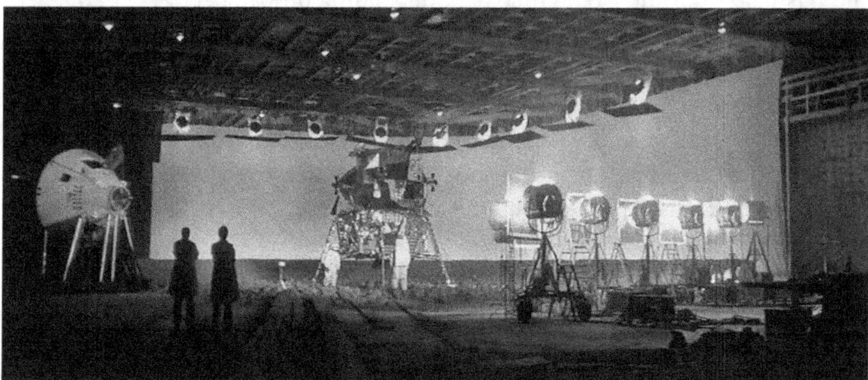

Fig. 30

Finally, the aspect of ironic temporality connects films from such diverse genres as THE SHOOTING (Monte Hellman 1967), ROSEMARY'S BABY (Roman Polanski 1968), GIMME SHELTER (David and Albert Maysles, Charlotte Zwerin 1970), PUNISHMENT PARK (Peter Watkins 1971) or MEAT (Frederick Wiseman 1976). PUNISHMENT PARK, a fake documentary, also reveals how inexpressible affective states, which Lacan links to intellectual feelings, force their way to the surface at the moment when it is no longer possible to implicitly distinguish reality from fiction: mental game-playing is replaced with genuine outrage and frustration, due to the impenetrability of the system. In this way, this film can be used to study the relationship between paranoia and action, in the sense of rebellion and terrorism, much like in ICE (Robert Kramer 1970).

One particularly striking example of the affective impact of ironic temporality is GIMME SHELTER, a film about the Rolling Stones' 1969 tour of the US, which came to a tragic end at the infamous concert on the Altamont speedway. Not far from the stage during this final concert, a man was stabbed to death – an event that happened to be captured on film. Notable about GIMME SHELTER is the temporality of its dramatic structure, which revolves around the moment of the deadly stabbing. The film begins with the tour's opening event at Madison Square Garden, before the second scene jumps to a point in time several months after the Altamont concert: the members of the band are sitting in the Maysles brothers' editing room, watching an early version of the very same film the spectator is currently watching – thus anticipating almost exactly the staging of the assassination in THE PARALLAX VIEW, as described above. Over the course of the film, which initially works through the events of the tour in chronological order, there are repeated cuts back to the editing room, where the Stones (primarily represented by Mick Jagger) comment upon or otherwise react to looking back at what has just – or quite some time ago, depending on perspective – happened. The sentiment of the immediate moment, felt in the present, is thus consistently linked to a retrospective point of view that not only sees the terrible end to come but, over the course of the film, becomes increasingly concerned with establishing connections between this end and even the most seemingly innocuous detail of a previously present moment. In this way, every single cocky remark made by Mick Jagger retrospectively takes on the character of a self-fulfilling prophecy, as if he were delivering a verdict on himself.

This temporal splitting of the act of seeing intensifies when the Altamont concert itself becomes the subject of the staging. The camera constantly picks out small details, which at first glance appear merely mysterious, curious, or perhaps even confusing, but which are retrospectively fused into a nexus of menacing harbingers of the catastrophe: a woman in tears looking at Mick Jagger, a large man in a floppy hat who whispers something into his ear, a sheepdog that walks across the stage, another man who is seemingly having a "bad trip" (fig. 31). The payoff here emerges from the fact that this combinatorial procedure is analogous to the principle according to which the film itself is constructed, since the depiction of the concert is put together from a vast quantity of material collected from different camera teams, each of which operates independently.[126] This means that, from a production point of view, as well, the selection and combination of perspectives is the expression of an awareness that already regards the events as images, while the individual, coherent shots, unavoidably created from the here-and-now of the past-present, repeatedly emphasize the contingent,

---

126 Joan Didion's description of her own experience of reality at the end of the 1960s as a "cuttingroom experience" comes to mind here once again, Didion: The White Album, p. 13.

singular, and unpredictable regarding the concert as a whole and the countless tiny events from which it is composed.[127]

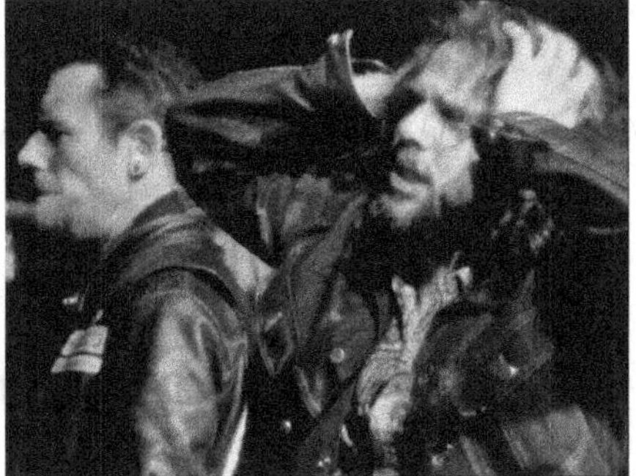

Fig. 31: Like a premonition of the catastrophe.

The adversarial relationship between these two temporal levels is manifested in particularly significant fashion at the moment when the deadly stabbing takes place, which is repeated several times during the film. The first time it is shown at normal speed, evidently from the only camera perspective in which the incident is actually visible: a vantage point behind the stage, which captures the events in a wide shot that manifests the chaos and confusion of the situation.

For a spectator seeing the film for the first time, the fact that a man has just been stabbed only becomes clear afterwards, when Mick Jagger intervenes in voiceover: "Can you roll back on that, David?" At this moment, there is a cut from the concert to the editing room, where Mick Jagger is sitting with David Maysles, one of the directors, at the editing table in front of a sort of movieola (a small video screen). When the scene is played again slower, the music has been removed and all that can be heard is the sounds of the playback mechanics. The film finally stops on a freeze frame, shortly before the knife pierces the neck of the victim (fig. 32).

---

127 For a more thorough analysis of the temporal construction of the film, in particular with relation to the function of the freeze frame and the relationship between the Rolling Stones and their audience, see Hauke Lehmann: Shock and Choreography. Dying and Identity in GIMME SHELTER. In: Snodi 6 (2010), pp. 144–154.

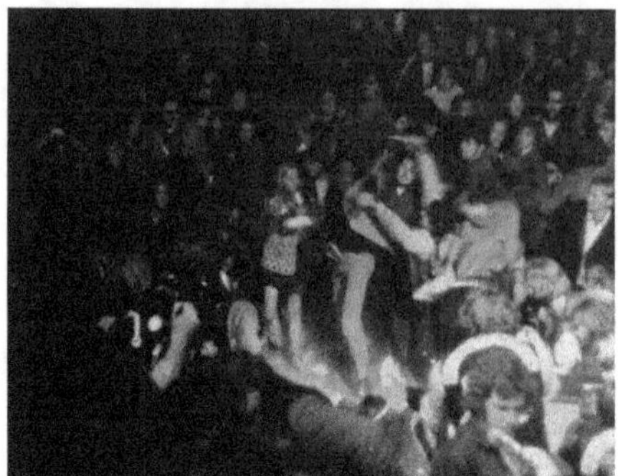

Fig. 32: *Tableau mort.*

The image is stopped several times during the scene and each of the various freeze frames has a different function in the film's poetic structure.[128] Key for the argumentation in this chapter is how a split temporality is made manifest in the freeze frame shown above. The actual incident, which takes place much too fast for the naked eye to recognize, is *repeated* and *frozen*, so that all of a sudden the relationship between the figures involved can now seemingly be grasped. The freeze frame itself and the slowing down of the movements at the editing table, however, change the nature of these relationships in radical fashion: victim and perpetrator come together in an almost graceful gesture, as if performing a precisely composed choreography, and no trace of the attack's violence remains. The key cause of this "transformation of the material within the image" (Kleiman) is the flattening of space via the manipulation of movement: a prison of pre-determination is created, from which no deviation is permitted. The paranoid perspective, anxious to inscribe the decisive moment of the attack within the course of dramatic events as an "effective moment," transforms this moment into precisely such an act of "instrumentalization" and makes it into an image – an image that has been emptied of any "presentness"[129] (inasmuch, as Deleuze and Guattari write, as it has been completely split into that which is to come and that which has already occurred). The focus here is, in fact, on the antithesis of what Lessing referred to as an effective moment.[130]

---

128 See Lehmann: Shock and Choreography, pp. 150 – 151.

129 A discussion of the concept of trauma would lead us too far astray here, and not just for reasons of brevity. It suffices to say that if the relationship between trauma and paranoia were to be determined, then the paranoid style would be that which makes a trauma representable in the first place, that is, an image.

130 "If the artist can never make use of more than a single moment in ever-changing nature, and if the painter in particular can use this moment only with reference to a single vantage

The central aspects of an affect poetics of paranoia in New Hollywood – fragmentation, ironic temporality, the mediatization of the image, and the omnipotence of the montage – not only exist alongside one another but are mutually dependent on and interwoven with each other, as Christopher Lasch already influentially asserted in 1979, in a sort of snapshot of the previous decade. For Lasch, this period is to be viewed under the banner of narcissism, repeatedly emphasized as characteristic of the paranoid style in the form of delusions of grandeur and omnipotence.[131]

> We live in a swirl of images and echoes that arrest experience and play it back in slow motion. Cameras and recording machines not only transcribe experience but alter its quality, giving to much of modern life the character of an enormous echo chamber, a hall of mirrors. Life presents itself as a succession of images or electronic signals, of impressions recorded and reproduced by means of photography, motion pictures, televisions, and sophisticated recording devices. Modern life is so thoroughly mediated by electronic images that we cannot help responding to others as if our actions – and their own – were being recorded and simultaneously transmitted to an unseen audience or stored up for close scrutiny at a later time.[132]

The inability to distinguish between film and life appears again as a *topos* in the reception of THE PARALLAX VIEW: "the society from which it [THE PARALLAX VIEW] takes its material has itself become an epic B picture."[133]

Beyond New Hollywood: Paranoid Cinema of Action

A rather special "B picture" is staged, as a film within the film, at the beginning of THE FURY (Brian De Palma 1978): As if it were a strange reenactment of the

point, while the works of both painter and sculptor are created not merely to be given a glance but to be contemplated–contemplated repeatedly and at length–then it is evident that this single moment and the point from which it is viewed cannot be chosen with too great a regard for its effect. But only that which gives free rein to the imagination is effective." Gotthold Ephraim Lessing: Laocoon: An Essay on the Limits of Painting and Poetry, Baltimore 1984, p. 19.

131 Tom Wolfe has also thrown light on the relationship between narcissism and paranoia, albeit from the side of narcissism. See Tom Wolfe: The Me Decade and the Third Great Awakening. In: id.: The Purple Decades, London 1984, pp. 265–293, in particular p. 280.

132 Christopher Lasch: The Culture of Narcissism. American Life in an Age of Diminishing Expectations. New York 1979, p. 47.

133 Joseph Kanon: The Parallax Candidate, quoted by Horton: Political Assassination and Cinema, p. 62. For more on how fiction and reality flowed into one another in 1960s and 70s American society, see James Hoberman: The Dream Life. Movies, Media and the Mythology of the Sixties, New York/London 2003.

Zapruder film, it shows the assassination of another father figure.[134] The spiral of suspicion continues here insofar as the affective force of this film is exploited for the dark purposes of conspiracy: the staged, i.e. manipulated document serves to brainwash the son of the murdered man, who is equipped with supernatural, extremely destructive abilities. Using THE FURY, Eyal Peretz has described the constitution of a "paranoid cinema of action,"[135] a cinema which he relates on the one hand to the film noir of the 1940s and its successors (e.g. KISS ME DEADLY [Robert Aldrich 1955], TOUCH OF EVIL [Orson Welles 1958] and THE MANCHURIAN CANDIDATE), but which on the other hand also points the way to the 1980s.

This paranoid action cinema in the latter sense ("a cinema that reveals the limits of a cinema of action while showing the roots of its constitution"[136]) emerges as an excessive compensation mechanism for the inadequacies of the image as attested by Pasolini, as a mechanism that quiets the unrest associated with these inadequacies. For Peretz, too, the phenomenon of fragmentation is the basis of an affect poetics of paranoia, which he locates in De Palma as the counterpart to a cinema of "passionate witnessing"[137] (in contrast to the cold observer of the paranoid style). Viewed in a broader film historical context, the paranoid cinema of action can be described as one of the lines of development that determine the transition from New Hollywood to the cinema of the 1980s. Examples for this kind of cinema are films like FINGERS (James Toback 1978), CRUISING (William Friedkin 1980), THE SHINING (Stanley Kubrick 1980), ALTERED STATES (Ken Russell 1980), RAGING BULL (Martin Scorsese 1980)[138], CUTTER'S WAY (Ivan Passer 1981), BLOW OUT (Brian De Palma 1981), THE THING (John Carpenter 1982), BLADE RUNNER (Ridley Scott 1982) or TRON (Steven Lisberger 1982) – films that are all characterized by the fact that they confront the bodies of their characters to an extent previously unknown with the existential situation of paranoid consciousness as it is formed in the paradigm of the Zapruder film.

The beginnings of such a cinema can be traced back to the early 1970s (for example, to Melvin Van Peebles' SWEET SWEETBACK'S BAADASSSSS SONG or to Sam Peckinpah's STRAW DOGS [1971]); its perhaps most concise formulation – alongside films such as TAXI DRIVER (Martin Scorsese 1976) or MARATHON MAN

---

134 Since GREETINGS (1968), the Zapruder film has been an essential point of reference for De Palma, especially obvious in BLOW OUT.

135 Peretz: Becoming Visionary, pp. 54–59.

136 Peretz: Becoming Visionary, pp. 55–56.

137 Peretz: Becoming Visionary, pp. 61–78.

138 See Robin Wood's detailed analysis. In his description of the protagonist, Wood refers very directly to Freud's conceptualization of paranoia. See Wood: Hollywood from Vietnam to Reagan, pp. 219–231.

(John Schlesinger 1976) – can be found in the large test sequence in THE PARAL-
LAX VIEW, in which the protagonist is tested for his suitability as an assassin. The
test consists of a kind of pseudo-avant-garde experimental film. This film, which
Frady and the audience get to see, consists of a sequence of slogans (GOD, FA-
THER, COUNTRY, LOVE, etc.), clichés[139] in Deleuze's sense, whose supposed
meaning can be manipulated in a disturbing way. Each of these slogans is
first illustrated by a series of stills – images that prove to be unreliable and reveal cut after cut, parallax after parallax, an abysmal secondary meaning (the
patriot turns out to be a Klansman, the Pope is staged like Hitler, policemen re-
semble Drag Queens, etc.). After every supposed symbol of psychological, social
or spiritual orientation has successively been corrupted, a figure appears on the
scene that initiates a counter-movement. This is the comic-book character *Thor*,
who appears in the middle of the sequence to condense the accumulated confusion and frustration into violence. The violent outbreak – the assassination attempt, so the overly clear implication – serves to restore the lost order. Thor is
born out of pure agency panic, and he encounters it through a hypertrophy of
the sensomotoric apparatus that foreshadows the action heroes of the 1980s.
In this figure, the enormous affective potential of the paranoid style proves itself
once again in a new way – as a reversal of the desperation and indignation in
PUNISHMENT PARK.

In this way, it would be possible to roughly trace a New Hollywood geneal-
ogy that stretches from the beginnings of a paranoid cinema of action to the present day – from the action protagonists of the 1980s and 1990s in films like FIRST
BLOOD (Ted Kotcheff 1982), DIE HARD (John McTiernan 1988) and THE MATRIX
(Andy and Larry Wachowski 1999) through the first BOURNE trilogy (Doug
Liman 2002, Paul Greengrass 2004 and 2007) up to the superheroes in THE
DARK KNIGHT (Christopher Nolan 2008) and WATCHMEN (Zack Snyder 2009). If,
among the more recent updates of this genealogical complex, one end of the
spectrum is marked by the reissued THOR (Kenneth Branagh 2011) – here doubts
about the individual's ability to perform and act are reduced to a minimum –
then perhaps David Cronenberg's COSMOPOLIS (Canada 2012) would have to be
understood as the other end, a film that with its protagonist Eric Packer, a bil-
lionaire asset manager, presents a very idiosyncratic interpretation of the super-
hero. Deeply buried in the basic constellation of this film (the ride in the limou-
sine, the constant waiting for the inevitable assassination, which finally occurs –

---

139 "Our clichés have all come true in the 70s. We now have only our most cynical metaphors to
live with. And [...] that is a paranoid situation. At no period since Prohibition has it been so easy
to establish immediate paranoia simply by reconstructing or referring to actual events which the
audience has lived through." Wead: Toward a Definition of Filmnoia, pp. 5–6.

albeit differently than expected) the Zapruder film is still recognizable, and the theme of the film could, completely in the sense of the paranoid style, be summarized as "attack of the future on the rest of time," an attack which above all has the destruction of the present as its goal. The question the film deals with now is how this present can find its way back into the high-speed world driven by money trading. In this perspective, the film's dramaturgical arrangement functions as an experimental structure: it is necessary to create a moment that reintroduces the undecidability, the unpredictability of life, and thus not least the possibility of action. From the perspective of this book, the question is how to get from paranoia to something like suspense. Only in its last seconds does COSMOPOLIS attempt to give a clear answer to this question. Perhaps such an answer will only be possible if a third mode is included in the equation: namely melancholy, which I will deal with in the following chapter.

4 Melancholy:
Ways of Perceiving History

What is the talk of the town today will have sunk into oblivion tomorrow;
the cinema voraciously devours its own children.[1]
(Siegfried Kracauer)

Hollywood has always cannibalized itself.[2]
(Kenneth Anger)

4.1 Genealogical Background

Following suspense and paranoia, we now turn our attention to melancholy. My
hypothesis is that, with this mode, the cinema of New Hollywood most emphatically develops an idea of historicity – in reference to both the contemporary
events of the time and its own genealogy, as it relates to classical cinema. If
the suspense mode pursues a project of cinematic thinking and the mode of paranoia interrogates the function of media in shaping the experience of the world,
then the films in the melancholy mode dedicate themselves to interrogating the
foundations on which we can conceive of the connection between the experience
of the world and the experience of film. The concept of melancholy is even less
clearly delineated theoretically than that of paranoia – if that is even possible.
The semantic spectrum of melancholy extends from clinical psychiatry over cultural studies all the way to the history of art. This does not, in itself, represent
anything unique; the specific problem here results from the fact that, in all
these fields, the boundaries between melancholy and its neighboring concepts
are fluid, particularly in the cases of depression, grief, and nostalgia. This conceptual fuzziness is a major reason why research literature on the subject has become increasingly boundless, and not only in the last few years.

The second difficulty that arises in this context may sound contradictory
against this backdrop: while there is no problem demonstrating, on the basis
of film studies research, the relevance of an affect poetics of paranoia for the cinema of New Hollywood, the quantity of discursive evidence is far less comprehensive in the case of melancholy[3] – even though certain cultural diagnostic

---

1 Siegfried Kracauer: Theory of Film. The Redemption of Physical Reality, New York 1960, p. viii.
2 Kenneth Anger: Hollywood Babylon [1975], New York 1981, p. 211.
3 One small exception in film studies research is formed by an essay by Mark Shiel: Banal and
Magnificent Space in ELECTRA GLIDE IN BLUE (1973), or An Allegory of the Nixon Era. In: Cinema

https://doi.org/10.1515/9783110580761-005

findings suggest otherwise, since the first indications consistent with this end are already discernable in the late 1960s. Frank Musgrove, for example, follows in the footsteps of Joan Didion, linking the phenomenon of melancholy to anomie, that is, to the loss of social bonds and norms and the feeling of being uprooted, dominant in the counterculture of the time.[4] A sense of bitter disillusionment regarding the future-oriented idealism and optimism of the 1960s is already alluded to in Didion's work; a feeling that, by the beginning of the 1970s at the latest, runs rampant.[5] This dwindling capacity for social integration unfolds against the backdrop of America's great fall from grace: "Viet Nam is the wound in American life that will not heal," *Time Magazine* wrote in 1971 in reference to the My Lai Massacre,[6] paraphrasing, thereby, Freud's description of the "melancholy complex."[7] In political and economic debates of the same period, theories based on the unavoidable exhaustion of essential human and ecological resources became increasingly influential.[8] The title of one book summarizes this

---

Journal, Vol. 46, No. 2 (2007), pp. 91–116. While Shiel does indeed use the concept of allegory, he does not explore its theoretical implications, particularly in reference to the connection to melancholy established by Benjamin. Garrett Stewart: THE LONG GOODBYE from CHINATOWN. In: Film Quarterly, Vol. 28, No. 2 (Winter 1974/1975), pp. 25–32, is more typical here, which addresses certain, relevant aspects without calling them by name, but also remains at a metaphorical level in its descriptions. Phillip Kolker's *A Cinema of Loneliness* is practically paradigmatic for the reception of New Hollywood as a failed experiment, which does not itself use the concept of melancholy in systematic fashion. Kolker accuses the representatives of New Hollywood of making films that express a general inability to change. In his view, they are thus incapable of formulating an alternative to the dominant ideology. See Kolker: A Cinema of Loneliness, p. 10. Unlike more recent theoretical models, the (implied) concept of melancholy, similar to that of nostalgia, serves a critical rather than a descriptive or even affirmative purpose.

4 See Frank Musgrove: Ecstasy and Holiness. Counter Culture and the Open Society, London 1974, p. 197; Joan Didion: Slouching Towards Bethlehem [1967]. In: id.: Slouching Towards Bethlehem. New York 1981, pp. 94–132. Didion does not speak explicitly of melancholy, but rather evokes the feeling conjured up by the figures of movement of slouching and a non-holding center, respectively, which she borrows from W.B. Yeats, see ibid., p. 94.

5 See Hunter S. Thompson: Fear and Loathing in Las Vegas, London 2005, p. 66, and p. 178 in particular.

6 The Wound Reopened. In: Time Magazine Vol. 97 (April 12th, 1971), p. 15.

7 "The complex of melancholia behaves like an open wound, drawing to itself cathectic energies [...] from all directions, and emptying the ego until it is totally impoverished." Freud: Mourning and Melancholia. In: id.: The Standard Edition of the Complete Psychological Works of Sigmund Freud. Volume 14: On the History of the Post Psychoanalytic Movement, Papers on Metapsychology and Other Works, edited by James Strachey. London 2001, pp. 243–259, here p. 253.

8 See Donella H. Meadows et al.: The Limits to Growth. A Report for the Club of Rome's Project on the Predicament of Mankind. New York 1972; Ernst Friedrich Schumacher: Small is Beautiful.

paradoxical state – one of constant flux between a stubborn past, which cannot be made right, and a barred future – as an experience of disturbed temporality: *The End of the American Future.*[9]

Faced with this set of variables, it is, therefore, telling that one encounters the concept of nostalgia far more frequently than melancholy in research literature on New Hollywood, often applied to films referencing America's recent past.[10] The polemic directed against the assumed thematic or political orientation of these films (or their audiences) tends to water down the structural difference between these two concepts; thus, what is often criticized as nostalgia (namely a sense of longing, primarily for the past), could, instead, be more precisely referred to and analyzed as melancholy (the temporal experience of transience).[11]

Economics as if People Mattered, London 1973; Guido Calabresi, and Philip Bobbitt: Tragic Choices, New York 1978. It was in 1979 that Jimmy Carter finally gave his crisis of confidence speech. See also Kenneth Boulding's description of a "crisis of closure": Kenneth Boulding: The Shadow of the Stationary State. In: Daedalus, Vol. 102, No. 4 (Fall 1973), pp. 89–101, here p. 89.

9 Peter Schrag: The End of the American Future, New York 1973. A sense of stasis is connected to this idea and is frequently asserted as characteristic of the 1970s. See Peter N. Carroll: It Seemed Like Nothing Happened. America in the 1970s, New Brunswick/New Jersey/London 2000.

10 See, for example, Stephen Farber: End of the Road? In: Film Quarterly, Vol. 23, No. 2 (Winter 1969/1970), pp. 3–16, here p. 8 and p. 13; Diane Jacobs: Hollywood Renaissance, South Brunswick/New York 1977, p. 22; Robert B. Ray describes the affective disposition of the period as a schizophrenic alternation between ironic and nostalgic impulses and fails to recognize along the way the close relationship between irony and melancholy, see Ray: A Certain Tendency of the Hollywood Cinema, p. 296. On p. 253, Ray talks of a "sense of lateness" in the 1960s, linked to the loss of the frontier, as postulated by Walter Prescott Webb in reference to Frederick Jackson Turner. Ray identifies this idea of being fundamentally too late without further elaboration in relation to the political stance of "left-wing" films however, see ibid., p. 301. Even a book about the American cinema of the 1960s with such a seemingly pertinent title as "Lost Illusions" uses the concept of nostalgia significantly more often than that of melancholy, see Cook: Lost Illusions, passim. See also Alexander Horwath: A Walking Contradiction, p. 89; Howard Hampton: Everybody Knows This Is Nowhere. The Uneasy Ride of Hollywood and Rock. In: Elsaesser, Horwath, and King (eds.): The Last Great American Picture Show, pp. 249–266, here p. 256 and p. 261; Keathley: Trapped in the Affection Image, p. 303. Timothy Corrigan takes a slightly different approach by situating nostalgia more on the side of the audience. Yet he also neglects to distinguish between nostalgia and melancholy. See Timothy Corrigan: A Cinema without Walls, pp. 11–48.

11 This confusion sometimes moves in the opposite direction, such as when NOSTALGHIA (Andrei Tarkovsky, Italy 1983) is cited as an example of melancholy and analyzed as such, see numerous sections of Margrit Frölich et al: (eds.): Kunst der Schatten. Zur melancholischen Grundstimmung des Kinos. Marburg 2006. While the strategy of ennobling the work takes a back seat here, the inversion of this process can be observed in the critical reception of New Hollywood:

When, on the other hand, the concept of melancholia is indeed related to film, this has recently taken place almost exclusively under the banner of feminist and/or post-colonialist readings of Freud's theories. Within such perspectives, melancholia is either to be overcome in favor of less "patriarchal" ways of dealing with loss[12] or, again according to a more or less anti-Freudian position that frequently mentions the term in the same breath as nostalgia, it is presented as the only way of preserving aspects of one's own history, which have been devalued and negated in social discourse.[13] Both approaches are based on psychoanalytical interpretations of characters in the films in question and their respective behavior: "One examines the melancholy of those in power, and the other examines the melancholy that theorists today are claiming is symptomatic of the racial subject, of women, and of queers."[14]

These approaches leave two aspects unaddressed that are imperative for understanding the problem: first, a notion of how melancholy is connected to cinematic form as a condition of possibility for the spectator's concrete, affective-corporeal experience and how it is expressed via this form; and second, the film historical underpinnings of such an affect poetics of melancholy. That is, it only makes sense to speak of melancholy once it has been explained how

---

here the concept of nostalgia is often used pejoratively. On the criticism of the overemphasis of nostalgia in relationship to New Hollywood, see Peter Lev: American Films of the 70s, p. 182. Such objections to the use of the concept of nostalgia are not intended to suggest that nostalgia did not play a role in New Hollywood; the very opposite is true. Yet it is hard to shake off the impression that the huge financial success of several corresponding films – such as AMERICAN GRAFFITI (George Lucas 1973), STAR WARS (George Lucas 1977) or GREASE (Randal Kleiser 1978) – has led to a lack of differentiation within critical discourse. With this mind, the present chapter is intended to make a contribution to a more differentiated view.

12 See, for example, Tania Modleski: Clint Eastwood and Male Weepies. In: American Literary History Vol. 22, No. 1 (Spring 2010), pp. 136–158. In her attempt to categorize Clint Eastwood's more recent films (such as MILLION DOLLAR BABY [2004] and GRAN TORINO [2008]) as the male equivalent to the allegedly still patronizing genre of the woman's film, Modleski uses the same strategy she herself criticizes to denounce films of this kind (and, at the same time, to denounce those who watch or review them). Further, her considerations result in an incomplex model of the genre system, according to which particular genres are divvied up between the sexes. For its part, Mark Nicholls' approach is far less polemic and far more differentiated: Mark Nicholls: Male Melancholia and Martin Scorsese's THE AGE OF INNOCENCE. In: Film Quarterly, Vol. 58, No. 1 (Fall 2004), pp. 25–35.

13 See David L. Eng: Melancholia/Postcoloniality. Loss in THE FLOATING LIFE. In: Qui Parle 11, No. 2 (Fall/Winter 1999), pp. 137–150. Eng draws on Judith Butler's interpretation of Freud to describe melancholia and the experience of loss as essential for the constitution of any sort of subjectivity.

14 Modleski: Clint Eastwood and Male Weepies, p 142.

this mode places film and spectator in relation to each other; and, furthermore, once we have in place a notion of how films behave towards their own historicity. Precisely these two points form the subject of this chapter. In the context of this investigation, due to concerns of brevity and representational rigor, a precise delineation between melancholy and the neighboring concepts of depression, grief, and nostalgia will be selectively, rather than systematically, conducted. Instead, I will make do with the derivation of melancholy, understood in line with Walter Benjamin, as a phenomenon in which historicity is made manifest as a central component of the experience of the world.[15]

The Voraciousness of Cinema

Melancholy is addressed in the following from two different standpoints: as an affective mode, close to the category of *mood*, and as a mode of *reflection*. The idea is to complement the theoretical approaches of the previous chapters on suspense and paranoia: suspense describes both a perceptual order within certain films and the spectator's affectivity, while not allowing for these two aspects to be considered as terminologically distinct from one another. Paranoia, on the other hand, refers to a perceptual order within certain films, derived from affective states and which itself gives rise to specific feelings, without, however, resulting in actual paranoia on the part of the spectator. By linking together reflection and mood, a more differentiated view is possible, which enables the relationship between film and spectator to be described even more precisely. Thus, the concept of mood enables both cinematic form and corporeal-affective experience to be designated as "melancholy," while the process of reflection represents the temporal dynamic of this connection between form and feeling.[16]

Reflection and mood come into effect on the basis of a specific temporality, which in turn is manifested in the concrete act of film perception and at a macrolevel of (film) historical processes. This means that the way films write history

---

15 "[...] Walter Benjamin saw melancholia as a definitely historical problem related to the experience of modernity. In this view melancholia is no longer a personal problem requiring cure or catharsis, but is evidence of the historicity of one's subjectivity, indeed the very substance of that historicity." Jonathan Flatley: Affective Mapping. Melancholia and the Politics of Modernism, Cambridge/London 2008, p. 3.

16 In this sense, my focus in this chapter is also on honing the concept of reflection, which in previous research on New Hollywood is all too quickly reduced to revealing a film's constructed nature, see, for example, Ray: A Certain Tendency of the Hollywood Cinema, p. 263.

and write themselves *into* genealogical lineages is conveyed to the spectator as an emotional experience. In the comments by Siegfried Kracauer and Kenneth Anger at the opening of this chapter, this temporality ultimately comes down to a *cannibalistic* relationship: cinema devours its own children. In this way, it resembles Saturn or Cronus, the child-eating god of transience, who is, of course, closely linked to the phenomenon of melancholia.[17]

While the differences between these two formulas will have to be explored in greater detail, pertinent at this juncture is that cinema's historical relationship to itself is expressed in each of them. Anger's statement is particularly interesting, as it points to the role played by Hollywood in his own film work. With that said, it appears promising, for the purposes of an adequate discussion of the poetics of melancholy in New Hollywood, to place this cinema in a film historical context that has been insufficiently considered in film scholarship: the American avant-garde and underground cinema.[18] The reappraisal of the relationship between these two formations will primarily take as an example the work of Kenneth Anger, with a few, brief additions regarding other approaches, such as those of Maya Deren, Stan Brakhage, Jack Smith or George Kuchar. Over the course of this contextual repositioning, the concept of mood, in particular, will require additional film-theoretical grounding, which has yet to be developed in any comprehensive manner.[19]

---

17 The standard work on this relationship remains Raymond Klibansky, Erwin Panofsky, Fritz Saxl: Saturn and Melancholy: Studies in the History of Natural Philosophy, Religion, and Art, London 1964.

18 One example of how this genealogical line has been neglected is the way in which New Hollywood is regarded as derived from Nouvelle Vague influences. Alongside Godard and Truffaut, Alain Resnais, in particular, is repeatedly cited in this context, see, for example Carroll: The Future of Allusion, p. 59, or Kanfer: The Shock of Freedom in Films. This conveniently sweeps under the rug that Resnais's treatment of cinematic temporality was in turn heavily influenced by the films of Maya Deren, see Carel Rowe: Illuminating Lucifer. In: Film Quarterly, Vol. 27, No. 4 (Summer 1974), pp. 24–33, here p. 26. One exception to this in previous research is the essay by Leah Hendriks entitled *Beyond the Infinite*, in which Hendriks traces in particularly comprehensive fashion the numerous connections between 2001: A SPACE ODYSSEY (Stanley Kubrick 1969) and EYES WIDE SHUT (Kubrick 1999) to avant-garde filmmakers such as Luis Buñuel, Maya Deren, Kenneth Anger, Jordan Belson, and Stan Brakhage. Leah Hendriks: Beyond the Infinite. In: Offscreen Vol. 6, No. 9 (2002), URL: http://www.horschamp.qc.ca/new_offscreen/kubrick.html last accessed March 13th, 2019.

19 The key recent works worthy of mention here are Sinnerbrink: Stimmung; and Philipp Brunner, Jörg Schweinitz, and Margrit Tröhler (eds.): Filmische Atmosphären, Marburg 2012. What seems problematic to me about the second of these is the lack of delineation of the concept of mood from the less stringently defined concept of atmosphere or, rather, the fact the former is replaced by the latter, see here Margrit Tröhler: Einleitung. Filmische Atmosphären – eine An-

My focus here is not on adding new entries to the list of New Hollywood's influences. My goal is, instead, to describe a configuration in which discourse on cinema's voraciousness is understood as a poetic figure of thought, which the films themselves play an active role in realizing. This means that the genealogical lines in question refer not only to linear relationships of influence or reference but, rather, that these relationships themselves establish a form of temporality which can be described as melancholy or, to use the words of Kracauer and Anger, as cannibalistic. The following first describes this temporal relationship from a macro-perspective (i.e., as a theoretical and film historical relationship), in accordance with an affect-poetic matrix of melancholia, before then exhibiting the concrete, cinematic implementation of this poetics in the subsequent analysis.

The Mirror and the Immediate Moment

In his 1951 essay *Modesty and the Art of Film*,[20] Anger lists all the difficulties with which the urge for artistic expression in film must contend: its instruments are sensitive, inflexible, and require considerable technical knowledge to use; the smallest mistake in a field of mutual dependencies can destroy everything. What is worse, negotiating these complications requires the assistance of human employees, who are themselves even more difficult to monitor. Finally, the artist must also grapple with the most unartistic element in the whole world: namely money.[21]

---

näherung. In: id., Brunner, and Schweinitz (eds.): Filmische Atmosphären, pp. 11–23. Greg M. Smith's "mood cue" approach has also become increasingly influential of late, see Smith: Film Structure and the Emotion System. My own approach, for its part, builds on the work of Hermann Kappelhoff on cinematic expressivity, in particular Kappelhoff: Matrix der Gefühle, and Kappelhoff, Bakels: Das Zuschauergefühl.

20 Kenneth Anger: Modesty and the Art of Film. In: The cover booklet of the Blu-Ray edition of Kenneth Anger: Magick Lantern Cycle, British Film Institute 2009, pp. 1–8.

21 See Deleuze's remarks on the relationship between film and money, which ultimately boils down to the following phrase: "In short: *the cinema confronts its most internal presupposition, money, and the movement-image makes way for the time-image in one and the same operation* [...]. The film is movement, but the film within the film is money, is time." Deleuze: Cinema 2: The Time-Image, Minneapolis 1989, p. 76. It therefore does not seem coincidental that the essential relationship between Anger's work and Hollywood cinema thus situates it at the exact point where the movement-image and the time-image meet: he constantly reincorporates film into his films.

The power to overcome all these imperfections, which appear inherent to film as an art form of the technological age, stems, as Anger puts it, from his love for cinema:[22]

> Of course, we force ourselves to overcome these imperfections and to accept them as the challenge thrown down by this age of technology, since above all else we love cinema. These difficulties can in no way lessen the attraction of this promise of immortality, this certainty that there finally exists a mirror held up to the fleeting face of nature, a means of holding on to 'the inexhaustible flow of visions of beauty' which endlessly die and are reborn and which make the contemplation of beauty a feeling imbued by the sadness of its disappearance, a way of holding on to the moment, a weapon with which to challenge the implacable unfolding of time – there is the miracle, the true miracle of film.[23]

Film is thus the promise of immortality, a means of warding off the transience of earthly beauty: a utopian construction that seems almost designed to do away with melancholy.[24] And yet, as we will see, it manages to sneak in again through the back door – thereby affirming the intuition that Anger's idea of film as nature's mirror bears an affiliation, if an indirect one, to Kracauer's equation of the movie screen with Athena's "polished shield," which allows Medusa's terrifying countenance to be bound by its own gaze.[25]

The historical dynamics of the process in which this kinship is crystallized is, to a large extent, already substantiated by Kenneth Anger's film work itself. It will be shown that what is articulated in New Hollywood as melancholy can-

---

22 One may also compare Maya Deren's plea for the filmmaker to remain an amateur as a countermodel to Hollywood's professionalism, a plea that Stan Brakhage takes up again at the start of the 1970s. Maya Deren: Amateur Versus Professional. In: Film Culture 39 (1965), pp. 45–46. Stan Brakhage: In Defense of Amateur. In: id.: Essential Brakhage. Selected Writings on Filmmaking, edited by Bruce McPherson, Kingston 2001, pp. 142–150. A discussion of the avant-garde's ambivalent relationship to Hollywood cinema in the 1960s can be found in David E. James: Amateurs in the Industry Town. Stan Brakhage and Andy Warhol in Los Angeles. In: Grey Room 12 (Summer 2003), pp. 80–93.

23 Anger: Modesty and the Art of Film, p. 2.

24 See Wolf Lepenies: Melancholy and Society, Cambridge 1992, on the relationship between utopia and melancholia, which was republished in German with a new introduction as "Das Ende der Utopie und die Wiederkehr der Melancholie." This new introduction states that "the intellectual complains about the world and utopian thought emerges from this complaint, which designs a better world and is thus supposed to banish melancholy. For this reason, melancholy has disappeared from utopias. It's more than this though: there is a rigorous ban on melancholy in utopia. This connection is at the heart of Melancholy and Society." Wolf Lepenies: Das Ende der Utopie und die Wiederkehr der Melancholie. In: id.: Melancholie und Gesellschaft. Mit einer neuen Einleitung: Das Ende der Utopie und die Wiederkehr der Melancholie, Frankfurt am Main 1998, pp. vii–xxviii, here p. xxi.

25 See Kracauer: Theory of Film, p. 306.

not simply be grasped as resulting from the failure of the social, utopian projects of the 1960s. Rather, at least from the standpoint of New Hollywood, these projects themselves – along with their failure – are inextricably linked to the question of cinematic form or, to be more precise, the problem of a cinematic understanding of time, movement, and emotion.[26]

Anger's most important idea in this essay concerns the "promise of immortality." It bears noting at the outset that Anger does not speak about immortality in straightforward terms but, rather, leaves the concept in a state of tension, which he conceives of as *attraction* – to be understood here as an allure or stimulation, in a thoroughly erotic sense. His next sentence simultaneously refines and modifies this constellation: now discussing the existence of a mirror, which can be held up to nature's "fleeting face." For Anger, this mirror is a medium for holding on to "the inexhaustible flow of visions of beauty." This notion is less about halting this flow but, rather, rendering it accessible to human perception. Through the reflection in the mirror, the ability to access these visions of beauty becomes a "weapon" against the "implacable unfolding of time."

At first glance, this construction suggests a structural proximity to Siegfried Kracauer's considerations, which also operate with a constellation of flow and mirror. As he puts it in the foreword to *Theory of Film*, "since any medium is partial to the things it is uniquely equipped to render, the cinema is conceivably animated by a desire to picture transient, material life, life at its most ephemeral. Street crowds, involuntary gestures, and other fleeting gestures are its very meat."[27] At the end of the book, this idea of an all-consuming "redemption of physical reality" is linked to the figure of a mirror, as Kracauer discusses the possibilities of film to make "actual horrors" accessible to the spectator's perception: "Now of all the existing media the cinema alone holds up a mirror to nature. Hence our dependence on it for the reflection of happenings which would petrify us were we to counter them in real life. The film screen is Athena's polished shield."[28]

---

26 On the connection between Anger and counterculture, see Matthew Hughes: The Films of Kenneth Anger and the Sixties Politics of Consciousness. University Dissertation at the University of Westminster 2011. URL: http://westminsterresearch.wmin.ac.uk/10179/1/Matthew_HUGHES.pdf, last accessed March 13th, 2019.
27 Kracauer: Theory of Film, p. xlix. In one paragraph on p. 273, Kracauer) dedicates himself to the idea of flow. There he says "Among the cinematic motifs one occupies a unique position – the flow of life. It is the most general of all possible motifs and it differs from the rest of them in that it is not only a motif. In a manner of speaking it is an emanation of the medium itself."
28 Kracauer: Theory of Film, p. 305.

Gertrud Koch makes the following remark on this connection: "Kracauer uses the motif of liberation through memory, the anamnetic solidarity with the dead within a framework in which people and facts are things in equal measure. It seems as if only a world turned ossified into images is one which can be deciphered and experienced as a human countenance."[29] This interpretation is, in turn, reminiscent of Walter Benjamin's description of the melancholic: "Melancholy betrays the world for the sake of knowledge. But in its tenacious self-absorption it embraces dead objects in its contemplation, in order to redeem them."[30]

Yet it also becomes clear here that, in this respect at least, Kracauer and Anger are actually not talking about the same flow or the same mirror. While Kracauer initially brings the idea of random chance to the fore and ends by foregrounding the moment of terror, Anger emphasizes the aspect of beauty. Anger's "visionary" view can also obviously be distinguished from Kracauer's "redeeming" approach, most clearly with respect to the construction of their respective temporal perspectives. The opening passage of Anger's essay is illuminating in this context:

> 'Capturing the immediate moment' is unquestionably the principal condition of artistic creation. The poet who can seize the spark of his inspiration at the very second it strikes and preserve it on the back of an envelope with the stub of a pencil; the native who because he is happily in love takes a bit of clay from the river bank and a few minutes later leaves an insouciant divinity to dry in the sun ... how we envy them, those of us who work with film.[31]

According to Anger, capturing the "immediate moment" is thus the goal of all artistic creation; but, nevertheless, the potential to do so is not automatically feasible for the medium of film. How is it then possible to make good on the "promise of immortality"? Anger's answer lies in the title of his essay: via "modesty." He subsequently advocates moving away from grand designs and the wasteful use of resources in favor of formal concentration: "Breaking through the barrier of these mechanical shortcomings can only be achieved by a conscious return to simplicity, to the direct relationship between the camera and the artist."[32]

---

29 Gertrud Koch: Kracauer zur Einführung, Hamburg 1996, p. 141.

30 Walter Benjamin: The Origin of German Tragic Drama, Brooklyn/London 2009, p. 157. Miriam Hansen has pointed out the connection between Kracauer's concepts and Benjamin's study of the tragic drama, see Miriam Hansen: With Skin and Hair. Kracauer's Theory of Film, Marseille 1940. In: Critical Inquiry, Vol. 19, No. 3 (Spring 1993), pp. 437–469, here p. 444. See also Koch: Kracauer zur Einführung, pp. 139–143.

31 Anger: Modesty and the Art of Film, p. 1.

32 Anger: Modesty and the Art of Film, p. 3.

Seen in this way, Anger's chosen form of expression, namely the poetic short film (conceived as analogous to forms of Japanese poetry like the haiku and tanka), still carries with it the trace of a loss, namely the same loss of immediacy that besets larger-scale versions of this form. It is the fact of this loss that develops into a gateway for melancholy. A second, more subtle line of argumentation should also not be overlooked, alongside this initial, theoretical one: one that could be called the institutional line, in which the love affair with cinema is realized as a love affair with the classical Hollywood cinema of the silent era – a love whose fractured nature is likely expressed most clearly in Anger's film PUCE MOMENT (1949). At this level, Anger's artistic work can be grasped as a counterpoint to classical cinema, a counterpoint born of an experience of loss.

In this sense, PUCE MOMENT, for example, can be read as an incantation to conjure the spirits of the silent film era "goddesses": according to Anger, the film depicts "[...] my love affair with mythological Hollywood... with all the great goddesses of the silent screen. They were to be filmed in their homes; I was, in effect, filming ghosts."[33] The focus here clearly is not to address a nostalgic desire for the good old times; instead, the film's temporality itself, as it unfolds in the spectator's perception, becomes the condition of possibility for these phantoms' resurrection, bound to the present moment. This idea is manifest both in the title and fragmentary form of the film, which lasts around six minutes, as well as in Anger's strategy of filming at 16 images per second, whereby the figure of the silent film diva becomes, to a certain extent, detached from her motionless surroundings, transformed into an unreal, ghostly apparition,[34] an ironically fractured negative image of classical Hollywood.[35] In this respect, the film functions as a forerunner of later works such as Jack Smith's FLAMING CREATURES (1963) or George Kuchar's HOLD ME WHILE I'M NAKED (1966). The latter of these, in particular, fully plays up the irony, so that melancholy is revealed in both its amusing and painful permutations.

This idea of an ambiguous figure, a fun-house mirror that reveals the truth, is expressed even more clearly in the title of Anger's later "chronicle" of Holly-

---

33 A remark by Anger in the sleeve notes to Kenneth Anger: Magick Lantern Cycle, p. 30.

34 The approach used here consisted of getting the actress to move very slowly, so that despite the discrepancy between the speed at which the film was recorded and the speed of playback (when viewed), it is not merely a fast motion that is created but rather a confusing mood of a more subtle nature.

35 "Sexually, politically, aesthetically, cosmologically, Anger has cast himself and his work in a position not only outside the mainstream, but as its negative image." Ed Lowry: The Appropriation of Signs in SCORPIO RISING. In: The Velvet Light Trap, No. 20 (Summer 1983), pp. 41–46, here p. 41.

wood fates and scandals: *Hollywood Babylon.*[36] The chapter of the book dealing with the end of the silent film era and the dawn of the age of talkies – marking one of a long line of deaths, out of which Anger assembles the history of Hollywood (and one which would, indeed, prove fateful for many stars of the previous era) – carries the suggestive title of "Saturn over Sunset."[37] In this chapter, Anger remarks on Hollywood's cannibalism, rendering the reference to melancholy even clearer. The book's final chapter, entitled "Hollywoodämmerung,"[38] depicts the termination of this series of deaths, both large and small, as the arrival of what the present work addresses under the title of "New Hollywood."

Anger's "love affair" with (Hollywood) cinema – understood here not as a biographical or psychological aspect of his life but, rather, as a figure of thought in both his writings and his films – turns out to be intrinsically characterized by what Sigmund Freud, in his essay on *Mourning and Melancholia*, refers to as "the conflict due to ambivalence." Freud explains as follows:

> In melancholia, the occasions which give rise to the illness extend for the most part beyond the clear case of a loss by death, and include all those situations of being slighted, neglected or disappointed, which can import opposed feelings of love and hate into the relationship or reinforce an already existing ambivalence. This conflict due to ambivalence, which sometimes arises more from real experiences, sometimes more from constitutional factory, must not be overlooked among the preconditions of melancholia. If the love for the object – a love which cannot be given up though the object itself is given up – takes refuge in narcissistic identification, then the hate comes into operation on this substitutive object, abusing it, debasing it, making it suffer and deriving sadistic satisfaction from its suffering.[39]

According to Freud, at the onset of melancholy, there exists a fundamental contradiction in the ego's relationship to the love-object, a contradiction that is transferred onto the ego itself following the loss of this object, causing a split: "We see in him [the melancholic] how one part of the ego sets itself over against the other, judges it critically, and, as it were, takes it as its object."[40] This ambivalence generates an initial form of reflexivity, which Freud refers to here as con-

---

36 Kenneth Anger: Hollywood Babylon. If a degree of skepticism should be exercised with respect to the factual nature of his report, Anger's books do at least fit the definition of a chronicle at a formal level: "Anger's *Hollywood Babylon* books, in fact, are chronicles of the ways in which lives have been cursed and destroyed by the demons of film." Mikita Brottman: Introduction. Force and Fire. In: Jack Hunter (ed.): Moonchild. The Films of Kenneth Anger, London 2002, pp. 5–10, here p. 6.
37 Anger: Hollywood Babylon, p. 207.
38 Anger: Hollywood Babylon, p. 401.
39 Freud: Mourning and Melancholia, p. 251.
40 Freud: Mourning and Melancholia, p. 247.

science. This contradiction, which forms the first criterion of the yet-to-be-developed affect poetics of melancholia, is a fundamental hallmark of narcissistic identification understood, according to Freud, as a primitive form of emotional attachment that emerges during the "oral phase." Freud does not merely conceive of this emotional attachment as possessed by ambivalence but, rather, as an explicitly cannibalistic act resulting from this ambivalence.[41] What is therefore the precise composition of Anger's variation on melancholy?

Film as a Mirror of Death

Without question, SCORPIO RISING (USA 1964) is the work from Anger's oeuvre that corresponds to Hollywood's "Götterdämmerung." This film does not simply turn its back on previous objects of desire but, further, in a reflexive inversion, dedicates itself to the *description* of ambivalent love affairs: between bikers and their motorbikes, between bikers themselves, and between bikers and their idols, the rebellious young stars of 1950s Hollywood: Marlon Brando and James Dean. Thereafter, this description is expanded to include the relationship between a religious leader (Jesus) and his flock of believers and between a totalitarian leader (Hitler) and the masses, until it ultimately refers to the constitution of sociality in general – emphatically including the relationship between film and spectator. The conclusive revaluation of the mirror metaphor in Anger's poetics is thus performed by this film. While, in 1951, film still provided Anger with a mirror that promised to capture the transient beauty of nature, speaking retrospectively about SCORPIO RISING, he describes it as a "death mirror held up to American culture."[42] At the latest by this film, the face of nature has been replaced by the omnipresent skull, which had already sporadically appeared in INAUGURATION OF THE PLEASURE DOME (Anger 1954). Put another way, SCORPIO RISING marks the point within Anger's visual logic where he moves away from the sym-

---

41 "Identification, in fact, is ambivalent from the very first; it can turn into an expression of tenderness as easily as into a wish for someone's removal. It behaves like a derivative of the first, *oral* phase of the organization of the libido, in which the object that we long for and prize is assimilated by eating and is in that way annihilated as such. The cannibal, as we know, has remained at this standpoint; he has a devouring affection for his enemies and only devours people of whom he is fond." Sigmund Freud: Group Psychology and the Analysis of the Ego. In: id.: The Standard Edition of the Complete Psychological Works of Sigmund Freud: Volume XVIII (1920–1922): Beyond the Pleasure Principle, Group Psychology and Other Works, edited by James Strachey, pp. 65–144, here p. 104.
42 Kenneth Anger: quoted in Alice L. Hutchison: Kenneth Anger. A Demonic Visionary, London 2004, p. 178.

bol and approaches allegory, in the Benjaminian sense, albeit with one decisive twist: the resurrection, which Benjamin sees as concealed behind the transience inherent to allegory,[43] itself becomes the subject of Anger's process of inversion. The new messiah is called Scorpio, expunging the last remnants of (positive) utopian potential from allegory. This step forms one of the most important prerequisites for an affect poetics of melancholy in the cinema of New Hollywood.

Hence, the new function of the mirror is decisive, inasmuch as it is to be understood as a direct inversion of "Athena's polished shield": revealing the abyss lurking behind the seemingly banal, innocent, or even sacred. Ed Lowry describes this act of disclosure as an "appropriation of signs":

> In a very real sense, Anger's films and SCORPIO RISING in particular, assert themselves as subcultural re-readings of common signs, whereby, as Dick Hebdige has described, "humble objects can be magically appropriated [...]." It is in this way that Anger's reprocessing of culturally manufactured symbols is truly iconoclastic, in the literal sense of destroying sacred images.[44]

Hence, not the use of symbols to visualize interior life (as one could claim for FIREWORKS [Anger 1947], for example) but, rather, the destruction of symbols – the cannibalistic destruction of images via images – forms SCORPIO RISING's agenda. Exactly therein, the film becomes a forerunner of New Hollywood. If, as Benjamin writes, "any object" can "mean absolutely anything else,"[45] if the figure of the biker Scorpio can, for example, be equated not just with Jesus Christ, James Dean, and Marlon Brando, but also with Adolf Hitler, and if the biker scene's affinity with death, through the vector of pop music, extends into the comics of the Sunday papers, then the world is both suffused with meaning and radically emptied of it. According to this interpretation, as a death mirror, film reveals a society that directly and deliberately strives for its own downfall or, at the very least, its unconscious oblivion.[46] This altered reading of the

---

43 See Benjamin: The Origin of German Tragic Drama, p. 223.

44 Lowry: The Appropriation of Signs in SCORPIO RISING, p. 41.

45 "Any person, any object, any relationship can mean absolutely anything else. With this possibility a destructive, but just verdict is passed on the profane world: it is characterized as a world in which the detail is of no great importance. But it will be unmistakably apparent [...] that all of the things which are used to signify, from the very fact of their pointing to something else, a power which makes them appear no longer commensurable with profane things, which raises them onto a higher place, and which can, indeed, sanctify them. Considered in allegorical terms, then, the profane world is both elevated and devalued." Benjamin: The Origin of German Tragic Drama, p. 175.

46 "BLESSED, BLESSED OBLIVION" is tattooed on the arm of the biker killed in the accident at the end of the film.

mirror has a direct effect on the manner by which film and spectator are placed in relation to each other in the concrete act of reception. The emphasis is no longer on a "flow of visions." Rather, from the very beginning, the film announces a logic of self-destruction, according to which every new detail and new thought deepens the play of correspondences and, at the same time, affirms the frivolity and emptiness of the world that is depicted. The difference between symbol and allegory, based on transformation, is famously grasped by Benjamin at the level of temporality:

> The measure of time for the experience of the symbol is the mystical instant in which the symbol assumes the meaning into its hidden and, if one might say so, wooded interior. On the other hand, allegory is not free from a corresponding dialectic, and the contemplative calm with which it immerses itself into the depths which separate visual being from meaning, has none of the disinterested self-sufficiency which is present in the apparently related intention of the sign. The violence of the dialectic movement within these allegorical depths must become clearer in the study of the form of the *Trauerspiel* than anywhere else. [...] Whereas in the symbol destruction is idealized and the transfigured face of nature is fleetingly revealed in the light of redemption, in allegory the observer is confronted with the *facies hippocratica* of history as a petrified, primordial landscape. Everything about history that, from the very beginning, has been untimely, sorrowful, unsuccessful, is expressed in a face – or rather in a death's head. [...] This is the heart of the allegorical way of seeing, of the baroque, secular explanation of history as the Passion of the world; its importance resides solely in the stations of its decline. The greater the significance, the greater the subjection to death, because death digs more deeply the jagged line of demarcation between physical nature and significance.[47]

We thus depart from the lightning-fast intuition of a "mystical instant" and turn towards an immersion in the "depths" between being and meaning. In allegory, these two aspects of the image diverge from one another; they can no longer be reconciled within the moment and, instead, in their dissonance, invite reflexive labor from the observer. The result is a view of history as the history of suffering. If history in SCORPIO RISING can now be understood as a history of suffering, then this suffering is not viewed empathetically but with scornful distance – a stance closely related to melancholy, if one follows the ideas of Robert Burton.[48]

---

47 Benjamin: The Origin of German Tragic Drama, pp. 165–166.

48 "Of the necessity and generality of this which I have said, if any man doubt, I shall desire him to make a brief survey of the world [...] supposing himself to be transported to the top of some high mountain, and thence to behold the tumults and chances of this wavering world, he cannot choose but either laugh at or pity it." Robert Burton: The Anatomy of Melancholy, New York 2001, p. 39. See also Klibansky, Panofsky, and Saxl: Saturn and Melancholy, p. 234: "Melancholic and humorist both feed on the metaphysical contradiction between finite and infinite, time and eternity, or whatever one may choose to call it."

Both attitudes are inscribed with the knowledge of the futility of all human effort in the face of mortality. At the same time, all the calmness of contemplation has disappeared here, leaving an unobstructed view into the "depths," containing the "violence of the dialectic movement." The furious speed of this movement is not, however, aimed at the mystical instant but, rather, at the fact of interchangeability, which is always derived from external correspondence. Benjamin quotes Herbert Cysarz:

> The baroque vulgarizes ancient mythology in order to see everything in terms of figures (not soul): this is the ultimate stage of externalization [...]. There is not the faintest glimmer of any spiritualization of the physical. The whole of nature is personalized, not so as to be made more inward, but, on the contrary, to be deprived of soul.[49]

It is exactly such a process of "soul deprivation" that we encounter in SCORPIO RISING. Carel Rowe writes that "Scorpio's iconoclasm is effected by the critique which the film conducts on itself, demythifying the very myths it propounds by interchanging them with one another and integrating them into a metamyth."[50] A myth to bury all myths.

In this film orbiting death, the "jagged line of demarcation between physical nature and significance" is entirely, fundamentally drawn via the medium of irony (for example, in the relationship between the visual level and the lyrics of the pop songs, in the fixation of the camera on treacherous details, or in the parodic exploitation of the classical continuity system with its parallel montages and inserts). This irony is not unconditionally present but, rather, unfolds across the time of its perception by the spectator, in its cinematic duration, as one of the very factors that torpedoes the symbolic regime. The choice of pop songs is obviously of particular relevance here, as their lyrics serve to both comment on the visual events and, by association with them, reveal new, concealed implications.[51] At the same time, they structure the film in a series of different moods, so that, depending on the character of each song, the comedic, erotic, or violent dimensions of the visual configurations are accentuated.

As a special form of reflection, this irony governs the new temporal measure and, thereby, the relationship between film and spectator. It is no coincidence that SCORPIO RISING is the first of Anger's films to be linked to Shakespeare's

---

49 Herbert Cysarz: Deutsche Barockdichtung, quoted in Benjamin: The Origin of German Tragic Drama, p. 187.

50 Carel Rowe: Myth and Symbolism. Blue Velvet. In: Hunter (ed.): Moonchild, pp. 11–46, here p. 24.

51 See here Lowry: The Appropriation of Signs in SCORPIO RISING, p. 42.

Puck and his derisive motto "What fools these Mortals be!" In the following, the focus will now be on how the conditions for an affect poetics of melancholy in New Hollywood take shape within the historical dynamic of the relationship between Anger and Kracauer, obliquely mentioned above. A central question, here, concerns the particular understanding of the image, which moves between the conflicting poles of symbol and allegory.

Kracauer, Anger, and the Shift Towards the Spectator

Kenneth Anger's films are frequently raised as prime examples of cinematic symbolism,[52] which appears justified for at least the psychosexual drama of FIRE-WORKS and for Anger's 1951 essay. In support of this view are the previously discussed alignment with the immediate moment and the emphasis on visionary perception, as the film flaunts the enigmatic character of its images, beyond which the "truth" of a real event seems to be waiting, as if behind closed doors – as if the spectator only needed the correct key. As already explored, this poetic approach acts in contradiction to Kracauer's point of view. Anger's name thus only appears one single time in Kracauer's book and, indeed, loosely connected to the latter's criticism of the use of symbols in what he terms "surrealist" films of the American post-war avant-garde.[53]

In an interesting parallel to Béla Balázs's critique of Eisenstein around thirty years earlier,[54] Kracauer criticizes the function of signification, "imposed from without" on the images, which "prevents them from unfolding their inherent po-

---

52 See Rowe: Myth and Symbolism, p. 11.

53 See Kracauer: Theory of Film, p. 198. It cannot be easily determined which of Anger's films Kracauer had actually seen before writing this book in 1960; SCORPIO RISING, which was released four years later, clearly was not among them.

54 Balázs refers to Eisenstein's OKTJABR here (OCTOBER, USSR 1927): "It is the Russians who succumb most frequently to the all too obvious danger here, which is that of the hieroglyphic film. When a statue falls from its pedestal in Eisenstein's OCTOBER, this is intended to signify the fall of Czarism. When the broken fragments are reassembled, this is supposed to signify the restoration of bourgeois power. These are signs that have a meaning, just as the cross, the section sign, or Chinese ideograms have a meaning. But images should not *signify* ideas; they should *give shape to* and *provoke* thoughts that then arise in us as inferences, rather than being already formulated in the image as symbols or ideograms. For in the latter case the montage ceases to be productive. It degenerates into the reproduction of puzzle pictures. Images of the filmic material acquire the status of ready-made symbols that are, as it were, imported from elsewhere." Béla Balázs: Early Film Theory. Visible Man and The Spirit of Film, New York/Oxford 2010, p. 128.

tentialities."[55] For him, truly "cinematic" symbols are "a by-product – or an outgrowth, if you wish – of pictures whose main function it is to penetrate the external world."[56] This critique is ultimately based on the contrast between form and material, constitutive of Kracauer's "*material* aesthetic"[57] and, thus, also for his understanding of melancholy:

> This differential treatment of symbols must be traced back to the fact that, unlike cinematic films, surrealistic ones are intended as art in the traditional sense. Accordingly, they are more or less in the nature of a closed composition. And this in turn entails an imagery which exhausts itself in trying to project what its creator believes to have put into it. Since cinematic films on their part explore physical reality without ever completely consuming it, they will not so much feature as release symbolic meanings. Symbols true to the medium are invariably implied.[58]

It is this privileging of the material, of the unformed world of objects, which lies at the core of Kracauer's melancholy poetics.[59] From this standpoint, he cannot endorse the idea of meaning imposed on the material from outside. When Kracauer talks of projection in this context, it is certainly relevant in relation to Anger: this is expressed, however, in the latter's desire to project the film images directly into the heads of the spectators[60] – something quite different from broadcasting them "externally."

It is hard to avoid the suspicion that Kracauer's distinction between form and material is not capable of doing justice to Anger's aesthetic approach. Anger describes his relationships to symbolism as follows: "I suppose my films can be said to have symbolism in them, but I don't see a difference between a symbol and a thing; it's the same."[61] If, as is the case in SCORPIO RISING, not only does everything become a symbol but each symbol can then always be exchanged for another, it is hard to say whether any symbolism actually remains at all. Lowry, for example, argues that Anger's approach is not just a "conception of ideas" (Kracauer) according to Eisenstein's model, but actually has more in common with the principle of collage. Collage "seeks to recover its fragments *as fragments*. In regard to overall form, it seeks to bring out the internal relations of its

---

55 Kracauer: Theory of Film, pp. 190 – 191.
56 Kracauer: Theory of Film, p. 191.
57 Kracauer: Theory of Film, p. viii.
58 Kracauer: Theory of Film, p. 257.
59 See Rudolf Arnheim's critique of Kracauer's theory: Rudolf Arnheim: Melancholy Unshaped. In: The Journal of Aesthetics and Art Criticism Vol. 21, No. 3 (Spring 1963), pp. 291 – 297.
60 See Brottman: Introduction, p. 7.
61 Kenneth Anger, quoted by Rowe: Myth and Symbolism, p. 15.

pieces, whereas montage imposes a set of relations upon them and indeed collects or creates its pieces to fill out a pre-existent plan."[62] The process of working out internal relationships between the film's diverse fragments (Anger's original material, the recording of THE WILD ONE from its television broadcast, the Sunday school film, the comics, etc.) is conducted, for its part, in an ironic mode, insofar as, over the entire film, the formal conventions of classical continuity editing are used or, rather, parodied and attacked – in the production both of spatial connections and, relatedly, of semantic relationships. What opens up in the process are the "depths which separate visual being from meaning," in Benjamin's words: depths far greater than those of mere parody.

With this in mind, it seems somewhat premature to identify Anger's use of symbols as a literary approach, as Kracauer suggests (admittedly without any knowledge of SCORPIO RISING). A greater degree of differentiation seems appropriate, as Balázs, for example, recommends:

> A literary story is [...] transformed from literature to image only by virtue of the shot and the camera lens. [...] The motifs of surrealist films, in contrast, are not realities. Even as motifs they are images, images from our imagination, our inner mental processes. They are not copies, then, but images that are primary realities.[63]

This distinction is vital for no other reason than the fact that, for large portions of SCORPIO RISING, Anger is essentially combining and contrasting (film) images rather than real objects, such as reflections in the mirror, newspaper clippings, posters, comics, images from THE WILD ONE (Laslo Benedek 1953) filmed from a television set, documentary footage, excerpts from a Sunday school film, images from A MIDSUMMER NIGHT'S DREAM (William Dieterle, Max Reinhardt 1935), etc. These images are, furthermore, combined in a manner as indebted to Anger's relationship to classical Hollywood cinema as to his role model Eisenstein: the use of shot/counter shot, parallel montage and axes of looking in formal terms, on the one hand, and their associative, commentarial, and ironizing approach in terms of function, on the other. The result corresponds just as little to the aesthetic of Soviet montage as it does to American genre film and, instead, refers to these forms as conflicting practices for generating both affect and meaning.

The symbolic function is thus not imposed on the images from outside but is, rather, established in the contrast between contradictory images. When, for example, Jesus' disciples from the Sunday school film are equated, via parallel

---

62 Brian Henderson: A Critique of Film Theory, quoted by Lowry: The Appropriation of Signs in SCORPIO RISING, p. 42.
63 Balázs: Early Film Theory, p. 168.

montage, with a horde of half-naked bikers shot by Anger, a convention of classical montage is activated that aims at producing continuity with regard to movement and space. This convention is then used, in turn, to provocative, satirical effect. The satire does not just relate to Christian heritage but, in fact, refers to the classical instrument of parallel montage to the very same degree. On the one hand, the two aspects – Christianity and "Hollywood"[64] – are equated with one another; on the other, this classical technique's potential for comedic as well as sinister effects is made obvious. This complex composition of the image in relation to other images produces the cannibalistic temporality of SCORPIO RISING,[65] and it is precisely such an understanding of the cinematic image that forms the heart of the affect poetics of melancholy in the cinema of New Hollywood.

Having determined the symbol to be an image that stands in relation to other images, we can now reassess Kracauer's hypothesis that it is possible to "see 'the object in itself' before any sort of symbolic character."[66] Anger counters this claim with one no less radical: that there is no difference between object and symbol. According to his view, film images thus gain a different status. As "primary realities," in the sense of Balázs, they target an isomorphism, creating a direct connection between the cinematic apparatus and the spectator's mental activity:

> If [...] symbolic images are introduced into the most absolutely absolute film, however, they are intended not to represent an emotion but to *stimulate it directly* in the spectator. [...] The absolute film does not set out to create a specific artistic representation. It injects its images directly into the eye. Is this still art?[67]

Balázs leaves the answer to this question open, as he regards it as unimportant. Yet the very fact that this question is asked references precisely the point at which a split opens up between Kracauer's criteria and a particular form of effect aesthetics.[68] As quoted above, Kracauer ultimately attests to the idea that "sur-

---

64 The Sunday school film is evidently already a deteriorated form of Hollywood cinema whose unintentional hilarity almost offers itself up to be mocked.

65 Only a perspective such as this provides a way out of the hermetic undertaking of breaking down Anger's films with the help of Aleister Crowley's teachings and enables them to be examined in their historical context. See also Hughes: The Films of Kenneth Anger and the Sixties Politics of Consciousness, p. 11.

66 Koch: Kracauer zur Einführung, p. 137.

67 Balázs: Early Film Theory, p. 168.

68 The fact that there is still something that connects the two approaches despite all their differences is emphasized by Hermann Kappelhoff when he discusses both Eisenstein and Kraca-

realism," in particular, is characteristic of a highly traditional understanding of art and signifies, as a result, a self-sufficiency of form.

The split that appears here is of dual origin: it can, first of all, be explained by how Kracauer derives film from photography. For Kracauer, photography stands at the end of a lengthy process of cultural-historical transformation, whereby "consciousness [...] disengages itself from nature,"[69] thus leading from symbol to allegory: "The more decisively consciousness frees itself from this contingency in the course of the historical process, the more purely does its natural foundation present itself to consciousness. What is meant no longer appears to consciousness in images; rather, this meaning goes toward and through nature."[70] Against this backdrop, neither the symbol nor the allegory can be seen as expressive forms commensurate with the medium of film. To the contrary, through its close kinship with photography, to which Kracauer dedicates himself in his *Theory of Film*, film is itself located in categorical proximity to the realm of melancholy:

> Now melancholy as an inner disposition not only makes elegiac objects seem attractive but carries still another, more important implication: it favors self-estrangement, which on its part entails identification with all kinds of objects. The dejected individual is likely to lose himself in the incidental configurations of his environment, absorbing them with a disinterested intensity no longer determined by his previous preferences. His is a kind of receptivity which resembles that of Proust's photographer cast in the role of a stranger. Filmmakers often exploited this intimate relationship between melancholy and the photographic approach in an attempt to render visible such a state of mind.[71]

According to the second of the two perspectives, Kracauer's rejection of surrealism is rooted in the history of the 20th century. Along these lines, Hermann Kappelhoff traces Kracauer's anti-art argumentation back to the "experience of National Socialist rule as combining a new form of media culture, entertainment industry, and state terror as well as the functionalization of film during the propaganda battles of the Second World War."[72] Based on this experience, Kra-

---

uer in relationship to the concept of realism, see Kappelhoff: Realismus, pp. 16–18. I do not want to contradict this way of seeing things, but would like to point out that such a connection may actually have escaped Kracauer himself.

69 Siegfried Kracauer: Photography, transl. Thomas Y. Levin. In: Critical Inquiry, Vol. 19, No. 3 (Spring 1993), pp. 421–436, p. 434.

70 Kracauer: Photography, p. 434.

71 Kracauer: Theory of Film, p. 17.

72 Kappelhoff: Realismus, p. 55. Miriam Hansen connects this experience with the step beyond allegory: "*Theory of Film* still assumes a postapocalyptic, allegorical landscape, to be sure, but

cauer rejects the project of the avant-garde and "orients himself, if more implicitly than anything else, with a correspondingly 'realistic, narrative approach' to film, which he saw as being realized in Hollywood genre cinema, if anywhere."[73] Decisive in this reorientation is the transformed notion of the spectator in comparison with the pre-war era:

> The image-space of the cinema is no longer the place where a new subjectivity is formed, no longer the utopia of a historical subject; it is instead the place where real individuals try to find their way in a world whose contexts and laws, whose logic and power relations are uncertain.[74]

This melancholic rejection of utopia is thus connected to a utopia of a second order, wherein the freedom to form individual judgements forms the starting point for new hope.

It therefore seems that the relationship between film and spectator marks the point at which it is necessary to differentiate between Kracauer's and Anger's conceptions. If, according to Kracauer, a relationship of "exact correspondence"[75] exists between nature and consciousness, then both thus find themselves in a state of fragmentation – "And we are free to experience it [the material world] because we are fragmentary."[76] For Anger's part, his work turns fragmentation into a spectatorial experience, which the film itself actively works towards. Similarly, in Anger's work, Kracauer's alignment with Hollywood cinema morphs into a strategy of transgressing boundaries at all levels (the boundaries of good taste, between high and low culture), which targets the classical ordering of the spectator's feelings, and functions as a kind of foundational act for the recalibration of the cinematic landscape in New Hollywood.[77]

---

from that landscape even the traces of the demolished subject have disappeared [...]." Hansen: With Skin and Hair, p. 468.

73 Kappelhoff: Realismus, p. 56.

74 Kappelhoff: Realismus, p. 58. See also Koch: Kracauer zur Einführung, p. 139: "The explosion of the false order according to which we used to classify things makes it available for a new order, whose plan must remain unknown."

75 Kracauer: Photography, p. 434.

76 Kracauer: Theory of Film, p. 300.

77 For a greater amount of detail on this strategy of violating boundaries, see Kappelhoff: Realismus, pp. 152–175. This reflexive turn connects such films as A CLOCKWORK ORANGE (Stanley Kubrick 1971), THE LAST MOVIE (Dennis Hopper 1971) or MYRA BRECKINRIDGE (Michael Sarne 1970) with deeply melancholy films about Hollywood like THE DAY OF THE LOCUST (John Schlesinger 1975) or THE LAST TYCOON (Elia Kazan 1976) that appeared slightly later and no longer operated based on the principle of shock, but rather the assumption that the reputation of classical Hollywood was no longer capable of being rehabilitated.

Melancholia and Cannibalism

We now come to the core of the comparison between Anger and Kracauer and the meaning of the difference in their respective expressions of cinema's cannibalism. While Kracauer describes the everyday process of forgetting, particularly inherent to genre cinema, according to which each current film pushes an older one out of the spectator's consciousness (a process that Kracauer's theory, as a project of retrieval, at least implicitly opposes), Anger makes a further, reflexive turn of the screw and depicts Hollywood's unscrupulous treatment of its own history:[78] a history not linked to forgetting but, rather, exploitation to the bitter end – a radical film historical perspective. The intention here is not to admonish Kracauer of having made a mistake. To the contrary, something akin to the cannibalistic logic, on whose basis New Hollywood's melancholy first becomes understandable, is delineated precisely in the relationship between Kracauer and Anger. This logic feeds on the argument that Gertrud Koch sees as both central and critical for Kracauer: namely the primacy of the optical, as was already suggested above in the reflective figure of Athena's polished shield.

The primacy of the optical is crucial in that it must be maintained in the face of "true horrors" – that is, first and foremost, in the face of the mass destruction of the Holocaust. Koch address this idea as follows:

> If "to look" meant "to experience", then the Holocaust could only be experienced if it could be visualized. It is only that which is of concrete character, that which belongs to the world of physical things, that can be visualized. In Kracauer's ontological underpinning of the optical, the image as the "redemption of physical reality", there is indeed an almost boundless trust in the idea that that which is immune to liberation evaporates in the transfer to the image.[79]

This trust reaches its zenith in a sentence contained in Kracauer's study on Nazi propaganda: "The image seems to be the last refuge of violated human dignity."[80]

In retrospect, this utopian statement smacks of desperation. Koch notes, "that the images themselves contain something which exudes some sort of holy awe to prevent their misuse is an assumption that unfortunately does not

---

78 Anger's remark on Hollywood's cannibalism stems from *Hollywood Babylon* and relates to the supposed exploitation of John Gilbert's fate for the plot of A STAR IS BORN (William Wellman, USA 1937). See Anger: Hollywood Babylon, p. 211.

79 Koch: Kracauer zur Einführung, p. 145.

80 Siegfried Kracauer: From Caligari to Hitler: A Psychological History of the German Film, edited by Leonardo Quaresima, Princeton 2004, pp. 304–305.

apply to the Nazis."[81] From the standpoint of our investigation, one could go even further and claim that there are few filmmakers since the Second World War who have revealed Kracauer's miscalculation in this matter as clearly as Kenneth Anger, with his consistent attacks on anything that could be understood as holy in the image. The irony, so characteristic of Anger's aesthetic approach, would thus be legible as a cynical commentary on the failure of a second cinematic utopia – a commentary that perhaps appears in most brutal form in SCORPIO RISING. In this sense, Kracauer's critique of the avant-garde, which draws on the experience of the Second World War and the Holocaust, is actually redirected at himself. Anger's mediated recourse to the poetics of the 1920s and 1930s, namely Eisenstein's, announces a further paradigm shift in the relation between film and spectator, set against Kracauer's "*material* aesthetics" – a shift that does not just revive these poetics and their utopian implications but also reveals the intentions behind their effect, visible, not least, in the treatment of Nazi symbolism in SCORPIO RISING. Anger formulates this idea in clear terms: "I've always considered movies evil; the day that cinema was invented was a black day for mankind."[82] If, for the two leading film theorists of the post-war era, namely Bazin and Kracauer, the Hollywood genre film is seen as the most promising model, then SCORPIO RISING reveals to what degree this model is animated by the far-reaching mechanisms of corruption – albeit without being able (or willing) to deprive it of its seductive power.[83]

Here, the melancholic ambivalence is entirely transferred into the relation between film and spectator. It is no coincidence that SCORPIO RISING has come to be regarded as one of the most important forerunners of New Hollywood. Certainly, the film itself cannot be termed melancholy in the narrow sense of the word, that is, in terms of its mood; its significance lies, rather, in the fact that, in all its destructive and self-destructive[84] violence or, more precisely, its radical cannibalism, the film paves the way for a new form of melancholy.[85] If, as Kra-

---

81 Koch: Kracauer zur Einführung, p. 146.

82 Anger, quoted by Rowe: Myth and Symbolism, p. 11.

83 If one wanted to put a film historical hypothesis in Anger's mouth, it might go along the lines of the idea that the actual role model for Nazi image politics was not the avant-garde, but rather classical Hollywood cinema.

84 See Rowe: Myth and Symbolism, p. 26.

85 See also Leslie A. Fiedler: The Rebirth of God and the Death of Man. In: Salmagundi 21 (Winter 1973), pp. 3 – 26. Fiedler describes the transition from the 1960s to the 1970s as a consequence of how socially institutionalized religions were overthrown by new, anti-humanist forms of spirituality linked to the New Age (an overthrow of the kind emphatically carried out by SCORPIO RISING). The image that Fiedler uses for this transition is the movement away from the destructive ecstasy of Euripides' *Bacchae* (taking Richard Schechner's staging of the play *Dionysus in*

cauer asserts, the shift towards photography is the "go-for-broke game of the historical process,"[86] then SCORPIO RISING represents the moment at which bankruptcy is declared: the film builds up a veritable mountain of debt, which New Hollywood will be left to pay off.

4.2 Analysis

ELECTRA GLIDE IN BLUE

When looking at the immediate aftereffects of SCORPIO RISING, along with the early films of Martin Scorsese, a whole series of biker films and road movies must be mentioned, which may serve as suitable objects for demonstrating an affect poetics of melancholy in New Hollywood. Indeed, the expressive form of the road movie cannot be properly understood without this affective mode, much like the police film genre that arose from the ruins of the Western.[87] ELECTRA GLIDE IN BLUE (James William Guercio 1973) is located at the point where these two quasi-genres meet, following the end of the classical genre system, and forms the basis of the following analysis. This work has been largely neglected by film historiography and is representative of an affect poetics of melancholy in New Hollywood for two main reasons. First of all, it demonstrates the principles of the melancholy style in unusually concentrated fashion, while, further, allowing the film historical entanglement of this style to be recognized with unusual clarity. As previously mentioned, particular attention will be given to the concepts of mood and reflection over the course of the following analysis.

The film begins with two interior sequences, separated by an emphatically outdoor shot of Monument Valley; the first sequence shows a murder, disguised as suicide, while the second introduces the film's protagonist, policeman John Wintergreen, and leads into the title sequence. At an initial level, this title sequence picks up on the themes of fetishism and ritual from SCORPIO RISING, in almost too obvious fashion. Wintergreen's act of getting dressed in the morn-

---

'69 as her example, which was also famously adapted by Brian De Palma as the film of the same title) towards the melancholy of the legend of the Holy Grail.

86 Kracauer: Photography, p. 435.

87 Mark Shiel deals with ELECTRA GLIDE IN BLUE within the context of the road movie as well as within that of the urbanized, revisionist Westerns of the late 1960s and early 1970s, see Shiel: Banal and Magnificent Space in ELECTRA GLIDE IN BLUE (1973), pp. 93–100. On the connection between the Western and the police film, see Sascha Keilholz: Verlustkino. Trauer im amerikanischen Polizeifilm seit 1968, Marburg 2015.

ing exhibits the same obsession with clothing and its texture[88] evident in Anger's film, extending even into the composition of individual shots – with the added irony that, rather than someone dressing up as or pretending to be a policeman, here we have the "real deal," whose virile heterosexuality was accentuated with relish just a moment ago (see figs. 1–4).

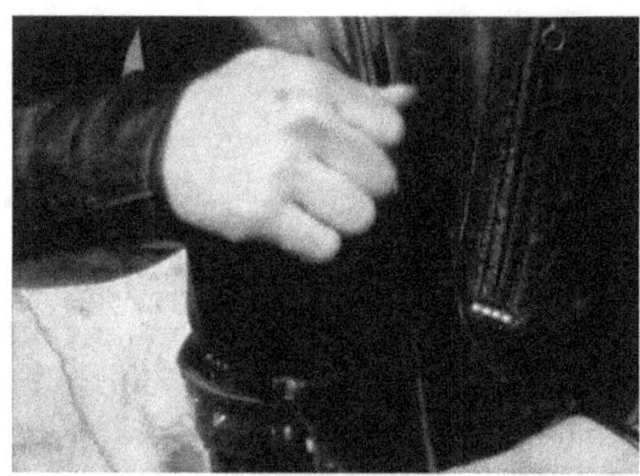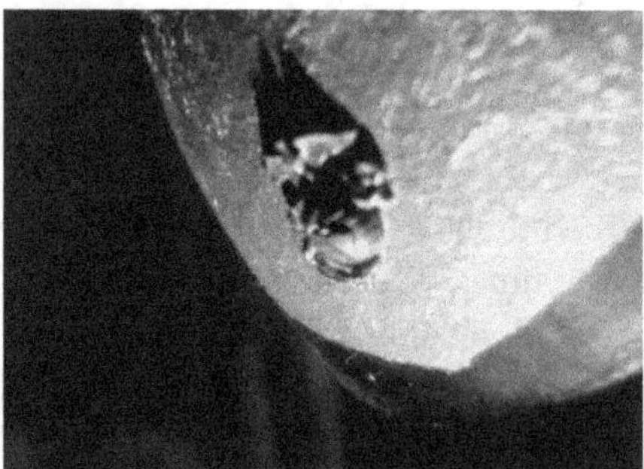

Figs. 1–4: SCORPIO RISING and ELECTRA GLIDE IN BLUE: Subversion and institution.

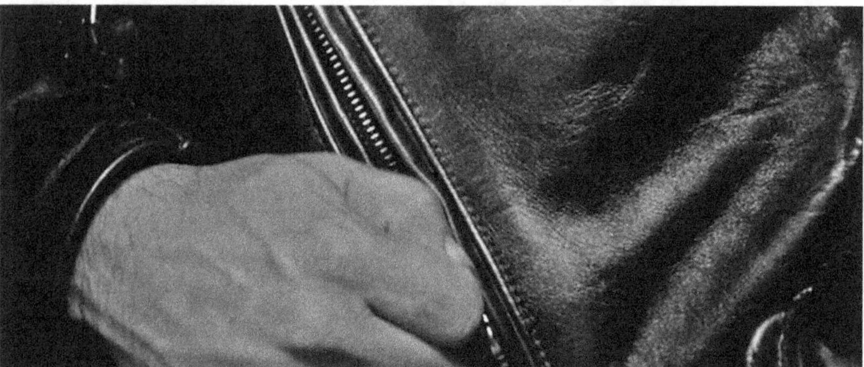

Fig. 3

---

88 The films of Kenneth Anger would form the perfect basis for an investigation of the theme of texture, a theme which the whole of the American post-war avant-garde explored intensively – the films of Marie Menken, Stan Brakhage, Jack Smith, Bruce Baillie, Carolee Schneemann, and Jonas Mekas all come to mind here.

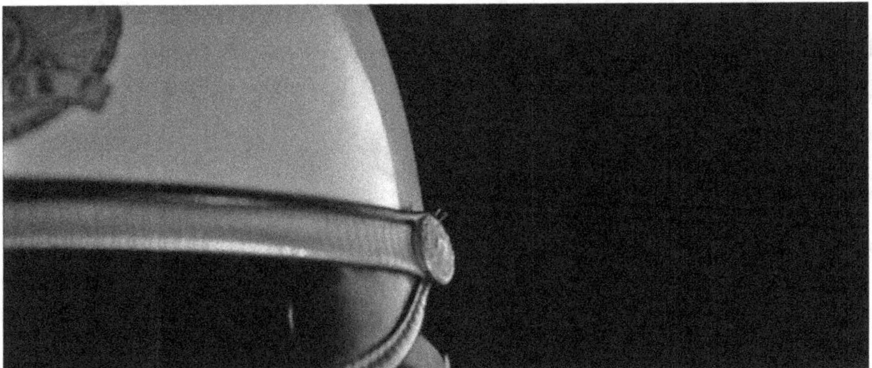

Fig. 4

The detail-obsessed gaze of the camera places a clear emphasis on Wintergreen's actions in its fixation; though, whether this emphasis is meant ironically or not can never be definitively ascertained. Thus, Wintergreen's small stature is repeatedly accentuated by the choice of framings, while the camera lingers again and again on the impressive play of his muscles and the insignias of state violence, which carry a quasi-fascist connotation: his revolver, police badge, and helmet. The stirring music reaches a level of exuberance, which similarly threatens to tip the scales and produce an ironic incongruence with what we see onscreen. From the very beginning, these techniques and others like them establish the relationship between film and spectator as one which perpetually alternates between devotion and distance. With this principle in mind, a statement from Hermann Kappelhoff about another film of the period can be equally applied to SCORPIO RISING and ELECTRA GLIDE IN BLUE: "The film depicts an aesthetic pleasure that isn't so much beyond good and evil but rather one that denies the spectator any opportunity to enjoy and take on a moral standpoint at the same time."[89]

Accordingly, the reference to SCORPIO RISING (and other such references made repeatedly at different points in the film[90]) is not simply an ironic gesture towards film history; to the contrary, ELECTRA GLIDE IN BLUE creates the exact same kind of cannibalistic temporal relationship which characterizes Anger's film in its relationship with classical Hollywood. The relationship between the two films, therefore, far outstrips a simple, implicit homage, as Mark Shiel be-

---

89 Kappelhoff: Realismus, p. 175. The film in question here is A CLOCKWORK ORANGE, which, from this perspective, may be regarded, in turn, as a reflection upon SCORPIO RISING.
90 Wintergreen's partner Zipper is, for example, introduced as a reader of comics in parody of the character of Scorpio.

lieves to recognize in this context:[91] SCORPIO RISING functions as a catalyst, as the disquieting, destructive force that sets the objects of film history in motion – in a word, the storm that we call progress, to use the words of Walter Benjamin.[92]

The End of the Film

This hypothesis is to be explicated by way of an analysis of the film's final scene. The ending of the film begins as an epilogue: Wintergreen has just been forced to discover that his partner benefitted financially from the murder that set the film's plot in motion. As a result, he was also forced to shoot his partner dead in self-defense; his hopes of rising through the ranks from the everyday banality of his job in the Highway Patrol, to one day work in the Department of Criminal Investigation, have now been dashed. At the end of the film, he seems to have arrived exactly where he was at its beginning, having merely suffered several disappointments and collected bitter memories along the way. The final scene shows him carrying out a routine inspection on a minibus, delivering hippie memorabilia and, as the film implies, probably also drugs, from Los Angeles to the various head shops in the area.[93] Wintergreen is connected to the bus driver by a sense of guilt regarding something that occurred at the beginning of the film: his partner had attempted to plant a small amount of drugs on him, so that he could be arrested. When Wintergreen now realizes it is the same man, he refrains from carrying out a further inspection of the vehicle, although the spectator receives several, obvious indications (like the passenger's nervous behavior) that an inspection may well be justified this time around. The policeman allows the two of them to continue on their way and only notices too late that he still has the driver's license in his hand.

Wintergreen thus attempts to catch up with the minibus in order to return the license. When he is about ten meters away, the back window of the bus is

---

91 See Shiel: Banal and Magnificent Space in ELECTRA GLIDE IN BLUE, p. 104.

92 See Walter Benjamin: Theses on the Philosophy of History. In: id.: Illuminations, edited by Hannah Arendt, London 1999, pp. 245–255, p. 249.

93 Shiel describes at length how ELECTRA GLIDE IN BLUE depicts the relationship of road and landscape as the idea of a rural space being corrupted by the road and the vehicles that travel on it to and from Los Angeles. See Shiel: Banal and Magnificent Space in ELECTRA GLIDE IN BLUE, pp. 98–99. In my view, however, the opposition constructed by Shiel is too smooth. I see the point of the film as stemming from the fact that it does not actually allow the spectator to side with either the city or the country or, rather, take on a politically liberal or conservative stance, as Shiel implies.

rolled down and the passenger aims a shotgun at him. A cut follows to Wintergreen, whose face is frozen in an expression of mindless horror, inscribing an interstitial space into the events. A cut back to the gun ensues and a flash zoom to its being fired, the cracking sound of the shot audible on the soundtrack, followed by brief shots of Wintergreen, shown from in front and behind, as he is hit and falls off his motorbike in slow motion (fig. 5), and as the camera subsequently follows the motorbike as it continues to roll forwards. Then comes the final shot of the film: it also begins in slow motion, with a symmetrically organized, frontal, American shot, showing the policeman falling onto the road, with the peaks of Monument Valley visible in the distance. Only the quiet sound of the wind blowing across the wilderness can be heard on the soundtrack, which serves to enhance the impression of total silence. The blood-spattered Wintergreen attempts to stand up, but only manages to reach a sitting position, before his strength finally leaves him and his head and torso tip forward, held up only by the stiff leather of his uniform (fig. 6). As if nudged to life by this movement of dying, the camera begins to slowly track backwards, while the first piano chords of the song *Tell Me* strike up on the soundtrack, replacing the sound of the wind. Over a period of four minutes, the camera moves further and further away from Wintergreen, until the image finally comes to a standstill in a freeze frame; over an additional two minutes, the color gradually leaches out of the image, growing progressively darker until it becomes a murky black-and-white, onto which the credits then roll. After another two minutes, the final fade to black coincides with the end of the song, which, with the exception of the first, few seconds, has been playing over the entire course of the shot.

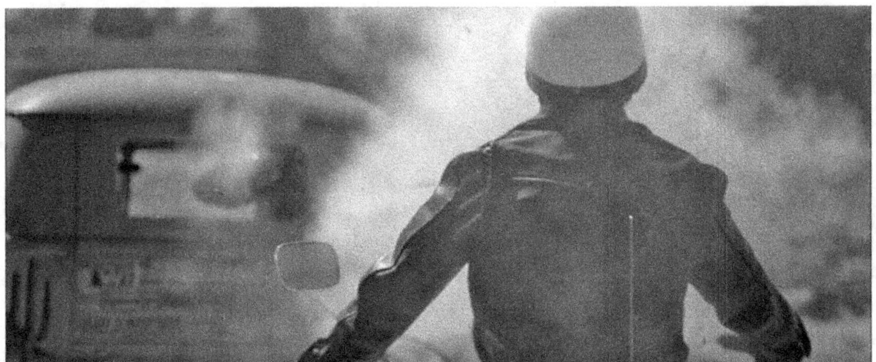

Figs. 5–6: The inversion of EASY RIDER.

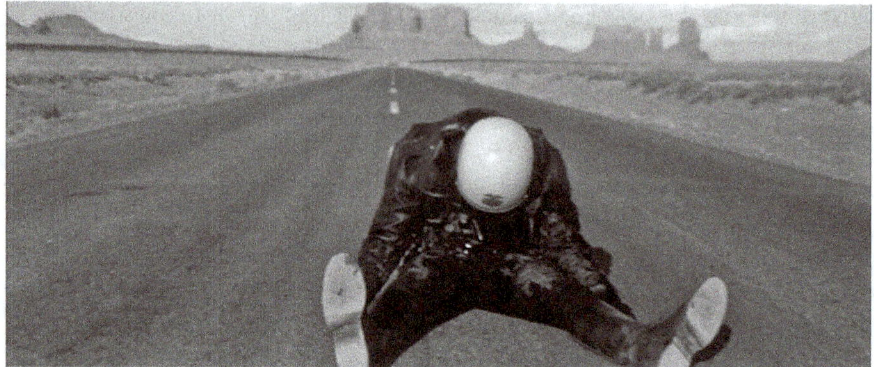

Fig. 6

Only over the course of this backwards tracking shot (figs. 7–9) does the actual drama unfold: in the eye of the beholder, the longer it lasts, the harder it becomes to decide whether the camera is moving away from Wintergreen or the road itself is carrying the dying man away, like some gigantic conveyor belt. The road's center line, at once never-ending and constantly interrupted, maintains a connection to the figure, stretching further and further without ever reaching a breaking point. This effect is amplified by the use of slow motion: each new marking appears with a sort of anaesthetized regularity. Finally, as a result of the extremely wide-angle lens, the panorama of Monument Valley remains largely unchanged, despite the camera's unceasing, backward movement, creating the impression that the backdrop is progressively ossifying behind the image rather than merely moving away (this is also linked to the fact that the road is only visible up to the table mountains).

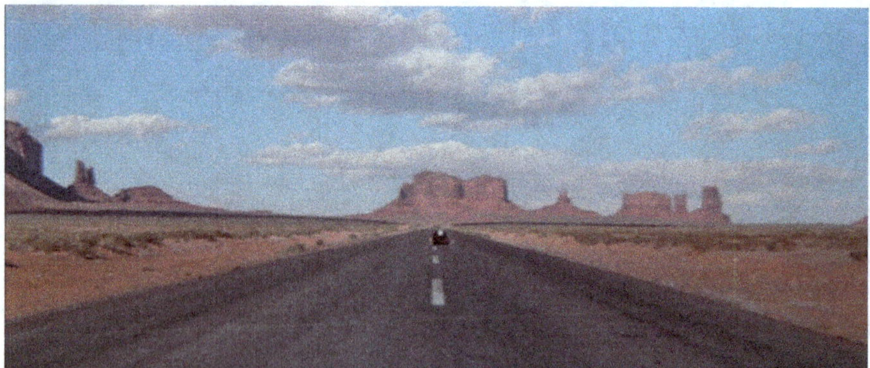

Figs. 7–9: An electric glide in blue: SHANE/THE SEARCHERS via SCORPIO RISING.

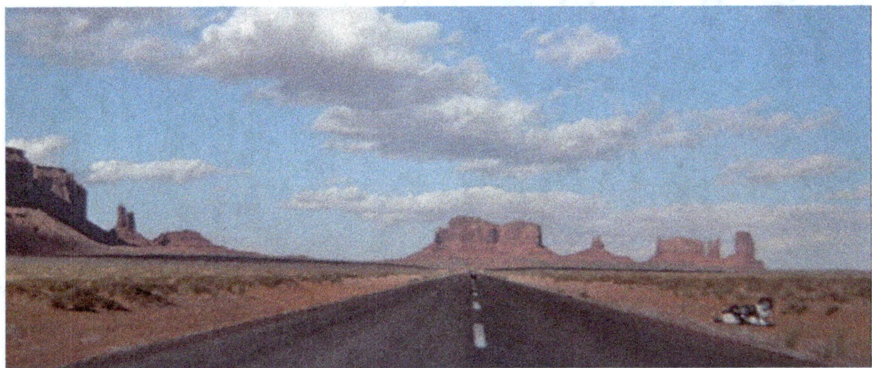

Fig. 8

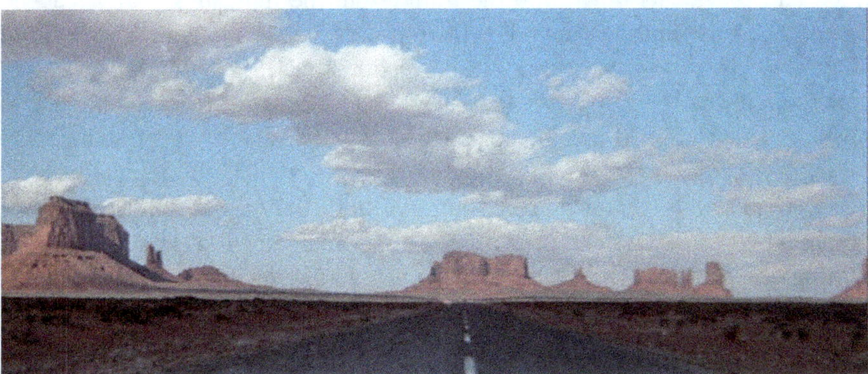

Fig. 9

Meanwhile, the song gradually builds intensity, moving from the first verse into the second. The rhythmic piano chords[94] are first joined by the voice of the singer ("Tell me about the sun, tell me about the rain"), drums and strings are added in the second line ("Tell me about the fields, tell me about the plains"), while a sense of pain begins to make itself felt as the voice cracks at certain points in the vocal track – a pain that will grow into desperation as the song reaches its climax.

---

94 The piano in question here is the characteristically off-tune Western piano familiar from countless saloons in classical Hollywood films. A connection to the Western is thus created on the soundtrack.

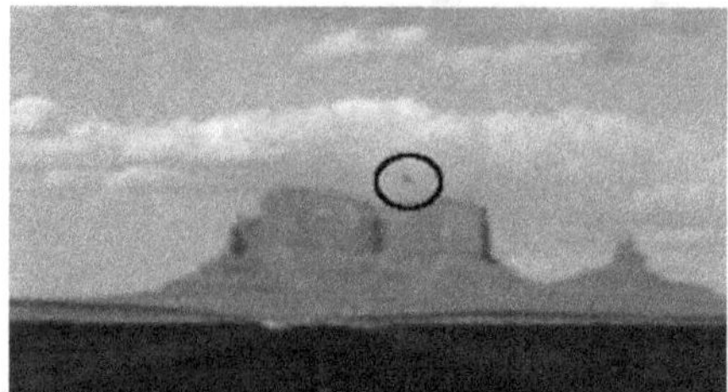

Fig. 9a: Zooming in on a section of the image – the eagle.

The next step building toward this climax is reached as the image freezes during the second verse, with the line "Tell me somebody, all about wars." At the precise moment of the freeze frame, a bird of prey (an eagle, according to Guercio), which had previously flown into the frame from the right, has nearly reached the middle of the image. The end of the formerly steady, ongoing movement of the backwards tracking shot generates a vection effect,[95] creating a momentary impression in the spectator that the road is actually coming towards them; as if some impulse were stirring in the image itself to prevent its sinking into the past. However, the freeze-frame does not actually stop the image from moving, as it grows progressively darker and de-saturated until the credits finally appear, a process which takes up nearly two minutes, by which time the classical, Western color palette of THE SEARCHERS has given way to gloomy black-and-white (figs. 10 – 11). This shift in the image's texture inclines it even more strongly towards two-dimensionality and plainly sets it apart from the outside world. The scene inverts the same movement from the initial exterior shot at the beginning of the film, which moves from motionless black-and-white to moving color – as if the chain of events depicted were just one chapter in a whole chronicle of misfortune, revived for a short time, exclusively for the purpose of this suffering's renewal, before congealing into an artefact, once again, to be filed back in the

---

95 Vection is a concept introduced by Ernst Mach, which refers to the illusion of bodily movement normally produced in the cinema – in this case, the illusion that the spectator is moving away from Wintergreen together with the camera. Due to the steady nature of the movement, the use of slow motion, the lengthy duration of the shot, and the very wide camera angle, however, the vection effect is significantly attenuated here, creating the impression that the road itself is moving away from the camera. Alain Berthoz lists the different factors that give rise to the vection effect or prevent it from occurring and traces the phenomenon back to the fact that the perception of movement is not a passive process, but rather a highly active one. When the image freezes, the compensatory activity of the now-idle brain creates a sort of surplus represented in the spectator's perception as an inversion of the previous movement. See Alain Berthoz: The Brain's Sense of Movement, Cambridge/London 2000, p. 52.

archive. This final movement thus inscribes a verdict of irrevocability onto the events of the film, without diminishing the presence of the image before the final fade-to-black.

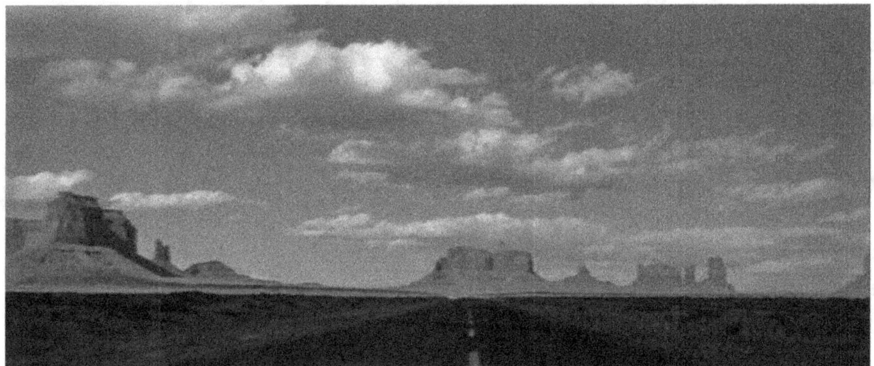

Figs. 10–11: Drifting into the perfect.

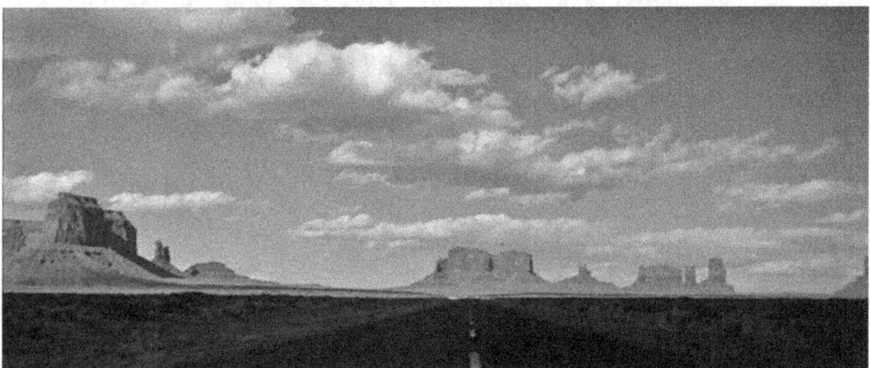

Fig. 11

Two aspects of the final shot have thus been identified: multilayered compression and petrification. The process of compression turns the frame itself into an all-consuming, cannibalistic maw, where Wintergreen joins all those who have perished there previously[96] – the Western heroes of classical cinema, but also the road movie hippies of New Hollywood. This act of devouring gets to the very heart of the difference between Kracauer and Anger's respective positions: on the one hand, the landscape exhibits the sort of assimilation or absorp-

---

96 My thanks to Sarah Greifenstein for this idea.

tion that Kracauer sees as representing redemption from forgetting.[97] Yet the focus here is equally and emphatically on pointing out to the spectator the world they inhabit, which forms the very essence of mood.[98] But, on the other hand, this world is not just made up of external reality, and this is where Anger's objection comes in: it is also, at the same time, always an image, a film image whose ambivalence cannot be resolved. To use the words of Gertrud Koch, what "is immune to being rescued"[99] does not vanish from this image, for the image does not provide any sort of refuge. This is precisely why the final shot, while remaining present all the while, nevertheless seems to elude the spectator's grasp, to turn to stone, to become inaccessible.

As the image petrifies, it is almost as if it is resisting the song in terms of both form and content: the singer's delivery intensifies as the first verse moves into the second, while the lyrics seem to look for some way out of the inevitable: "God above, is there not anything that we might do / To try and make this world of ours / A better place for me and you?" In the second verse, the cajoling lyrics directly relate to the problem of time: "Oh pray, it's not too late, oh no." This appeal to the higher power of fate finally brings the song to its climax: in the form of a painfully paradoxical chorus, sung in alto, reminiscent of a gospel hymn and supported by the *unisono* of the brass section, the female choir lifts their voices to sing "God bless America today" – a benediction desperate and affirmative in equal measure, intended to ward off the power of time, relentlessly repeated until the screen fades to black and the song and film end.

Accusation and Paradoxical Temporality

As already described, the final shot is constructed to establish oppositions on all levels, thus corresponding to the fundamental principle of melancholy, namely contradiction. In this film, this contradiction extends to the very name of the protagonist (Winter/Green) and takes as its starting point the irresolvable core of the misunderstanding that leads to his death. These oppositions are produced as an effect of the concrete experience of time during which this shot transpires. This begins at the level of perceptible movement and extends into higher semantic registers, which place the film in relation to contemporary history and genealogy.

---

97 See Kappelhoff: Realismus, p. 65.
98 See Kerstin Thomas: Bildstimmung als Bedeutung in der Malerei des 19. Jahrhunderts. In: Anna-Katharina Gisbertz (ed.): Stimmung. Zur Wiederkehr einer ästhetischen Kategorie, Munich 2011, pp. 211–229. This aspect of the concept of mood is discussed at length in the final chapter.
99 Koch: Kracauer zur Einführung, p. 145.

In this way, as previously described, the centrifugal impulse that seeks to exceed the boundaries of the frame is countered by the competing urge to keep things centered along the road's imaginary vanishing point. As a result of this conflict, over the course of the shot, the entire visual space is pulled into a sort of undirected forcefield. The above-mentioned vection is the most spectacular effect of this operation, which further continues in the process of the desaturation of color, involving the image as a whole. The tension spread out over the image pulls the spectator into its forceful grasp as well and remains in place, unabated, until the end of the film. The final fade to black thus does not alleviate the conflict but, to the contrary, asserts that there is no gesture of escape capable of resolving it.

The song proceeds in similar fashion: the recurring attitude of the first-person narrator is one of indecision, uncertainty, ambivalence. This position is most keenly expressed by the constant need to question; it is not for nothing that the song is called *Tell Me.* Will the great plains return one day; can the decimation of ecological resources be rectified? "I don't know." There is clearly no answer to rhetorical questions such as these. The only solution lies in invoking God, but the benediction, "God bless America today," hardly brings relief. Instead, in its conciliatory gesture of linear, fatal certainty, it operates as a counterbalance to the pleas and entreaties of the soloist, which it seems to support at the level of content. The same intractability of this conflict, which started the whole movement in the first place, can thus also be found at a metaphysical level. The impossibility of resolution is consistently made manifest in the fact that not only are oppositional dyads established but, rather, that a sort of oscillation between extremes is also initiated, which prevents the conflict from escalating. Ultimately, the antagonism must be endured and borne by the spectator themselves.

The contrast between these tendencies of movement is also echoed in the conflict between the events of the plot and the song's function as commentary: while the focus of the former is on an isolated, individual drama, with all the accompanying lack of meaning and consequences, the song's verses conjure up a universal perspective ("Oh, tell me all about man, tell me, so I can understand"), which links, among other things, the relationship between humans and the environment and the Vietnam War to the trivial misunderstanding that costs Wintergreen his life. It is not simply that these two divergent tendencies cannot be isolated from one another in the spectator's concrete experience but, rather, that here the operation of allegory is, in fact, realized in clearest fashion: precisely the abyss dividing corporeal reality and meaning becomes the subject of reflection or, rather, contemplation – a contemplation not of a calm nature but suffused with bittersweet pain.

Additional tension emerges directly from the contrast between the different processes at work within the dramatic structure: the camera's constant, backwards movement until the freeze-frame and the leaching away of color that follows can be interpreted as both a climax and an anticlimax, while the song, which clearly builds towards a highpoint, inscribes a different temporal pattern into this steady motion, a *deviating rhythm* produced, above all, by the verse structure and the principle of constant syncopation. This contradiction in time, which constitutes the essential core of melancholy, can be experienced here in concrete terms. This is due to the way in which, both in terms of form and content, passages of the song set themselves apart from the gesture of inevitability established by the visual movement. This principle is also expressed in the fact that the lyrics of the song respond to the unexpected brutality (both in the sense of the represented action and, in the formal sense, of an interrupted story arc) of the event that brings the film to a close, albeit with a call for reconciliation and redemption that is, in turn, undermined by doubt, an invocation of "It's not yet too late."

This idea of an *appeal* is by no means arbitrary but is, rather, essential for the affect poetics of melancholy. While SCORPIO RISING, as previously discussed, confers a sense of melancholic ambivalence onto the relationship between film and spectator, the function of the appeal here is to make the spectator comprehend just how untenable their position is in physical terms. Put more precisely, the spectator is not just addressed by the song but by the entire audiovisual configuration of the shot (which obviously also carries the weight of all the previous events in the film) and, in particular, its unresolved contradictions. This generates the scene's characteristic effect, combining pain and euphoria in the spectator, an effect that also does not seem to fade after repeat viewings.

In my view, the key to a theoretical understanding of this contradiction appears to lie less (or at least not primarily) in Freud's thoughts on ambivalent identification but, rather, in the question of temporality itself. Ludwig Binswanger places exactly this question at the center of attention by taking a closer look at the melancholic self-accusations, which Freud interprets as the expression of a "delusion of inferiority."[100] Binswanger sets his ideas clearly apart from psychological approaches and speaks, instead, of a "style [...] of a melancholy manner of experience."[101] By drawing on Edmund Husserl's transcendental phenomen-

---

100 Freud: Mourning and Melancholia, p. 246.
101 See Ludwig Binswanger: Melancholie und Manie, p. 44. Within the current context, this concept is to be understood as analogous to what has already been written above about style in general and paranoid style, in particular. According to these previous discussions, style describes a manner of perception as well as a manner of expression; that is, a way of being in the

ology, he recognizes "disorders in the intentional construction of temporal objectivity"[102] as holding decisive importance for the melancholy constitution of the world. These melancholic self-accusations concern the fabric of temporal objectivity in that they refer to the past in the *conditional* or *unreal* form: "If only I had..." According to Binswanger, this concerns "nothing but *empty possibilities.*"

> When one talks of possibilities, they are *protentive* acts, for the past contains no possibilities. But *what is free possibility here is pulled back into the past.* This means that the protentive constitutive acts are forced to become so-called empty intentions. As a result, the protentive becomes independent in the sense that it is no longer about anything, that nothing remains to "produce" it, except for the temporal objectivity of "future" emptiness or emptiness "as the future."[103]

Melancholy is thus characterized by a paradoxical reversal of the functions of protention and retention; that is, the "moments" that create the future and the past, respectively. The future can no longer be accessed as a space of possibility, while the past merely consists of an accumulation of opportunities wasted or not properly exploited. This ultimately affects the present, too, where nothing remains that might enable a "theme," as Binswanger refers to it, to be constituted. The melancholic's desperation is thus fueled by the futile attempt to find one's footing or rather the constant fear of losing it, all of which unfolds in a present that, in the absence of any connection to either past or future, simply "hangs in the air."[104]

Binswanger's idea of possibility's withdrawal into the past serves to reframe Freud's distinction between mourning and melancholia. He states that, unlike grief, in a state of melancholy, "the natural experience [...] is no longer regarded without thought or problem but is rather reflected upon and laden down with problems to the greatest possible degree."[105] It is thus melancholy, in particular, where the loss suffered enters the conscious mind with full force and, in so doing, represents a problem, meaning it is denied any sort of positive semantic attribution.[106]

---

world which forms the basis for subject positions to be created in the first place. See Merleau-Ponty: The Film and the New Psychology, p. 53.

102 Binswanger: Melancholie und Manie, p. 26.

103 Binswanger: Melancholie und Manie, p. 27.

104 Binswanger: Melancholie und Manie, p. 33.

105 Binswanger: Melancholie und Manie, p. 123.

106 It does not appear necessary to relate, like Freud, melancholia "to an object-loss which is *withdrawn from consciousness,* in contradistinction to mourning, where there is nothing about the loss that is unconscious", Freud: Mourning and Melancholia, p. 245, emphasis my own. It

The past's accusatory presentness gets to the very heart of the concept of paradoxical temporality. Japanese psychiatrist Bin Kimura writes on this idea as follows: "The past of the post festum (melancholia) is [...] not that which passes and never returns, but rather that which is constantly accumulated in the depths of the present. One cannot speak here of the simple past, but rather of the perfect."[107] Dutch psychiatrist Piet Kuiper also adds that, "I understand that time may have passed, but the past is still present as an accusation."[108] In the final shot, this contradiction can be grasped as an audiovisual strategy: as Wintergreen's body is taken into the landscape and retreats from sight, the song becomes ever more present via the appeal it makes.[109] The focus below will be on making this formulation comprehensible as the description of a specific type of image, characterized by the moment of accusation as a kind of address, which has yet to be discussed.

The Camera as Angel of (Film) History

In his ninth hypothesis on the concept of history, Walter Benjamin creates a sort of "time-image," which also incorporates a reluctant, backwards movement. He writes:

> A Klee painting named Angelus Novus shows an angel looking as though he is about to move away from something he is fixedly contemplating. His eyes are staring, his mouth is open, his wings are spread. This is how one pictures the angel of history. His face is turned toward the past. Where we perceive a chain of events, he sees one single catastrophe which keeps piling wreckage upon wreckage and hurls it in front of his feet. The angel would like to stay, awaken the dead, and make whole what has been smashed. But a storm is blowing from Paradise; it has got caught in his wings with such violence that the angel can no longer close them. The storm irresistibly propels him into the future to which his back is turned, while the pile of debris before him grows skyward. This storm is what we call progress.[110]

is not clear why it is not apparently possible to conceive of a mode of reflection which the consciousness can indeed access, if perhaps not in propositional form (this is where the concept of mood comes into play, to which I will soon be turning my attention in greater detail).

107 Bin Kimura: Zeit und Selbst, quoted in Toshiaki Kobayashi: Melancholie und Zeit, Basel/Frankfurt a.M. 1998, p. 167.

108 Piet C. Kuiper: Seelenfinsternis, quoted in Kobayashi, Melancholie und Zeit, p. 168.

109 My thanks to Sarah Greifenstein for pointing this out.

110 See Benjamin: Theses on the Philosophy of History, p. 249.

Benjamin's conception of history is formulated within this image as a relationship between opposing impulses of movement – it is notable how much this image resembles the construction at the end of ELECTRA GLIDE IN BLUE in formal terms (even if the character of the movement Benjamin draws upon comes across as far more dramatic and spectacular).[111] In both cases, time – the relationship between past, future, and present – becomes distance, a space that, instead of disappearing, is progressively condensed in the image's background. At the same time, this relationship is directed toward the viewer, who functions as an agent of reflection; that is, the place where all contradictions are grouped together. It should be pointed out within this context that the movement of the camera – if it is grasped as a movement in space – reproduces the exact path taken by the minibus in which the murderers are sitting; or, rather, to use Benjamin's words, the path that embodies progress: the zeitgeist to which ELECTRA GLIDE IN BLUE positions itself as a countermodel.

This countermodel is instituted, in part, with regard to the mode of historicity characterizing the American situation at the beginning of the 1970s, as described at the start of the chapter – the present as empty of possibility, as a historical opportunity that has already been missed. Further, understood in its visual figuration, the ending of ELECTRA GLIDE IN BLUE just as fundamentally positions itself in reference to film history. In addition to its strategic relationship to SCORPIO RISING, Guercio's film places itself within two film historical contexts: the various offshoots of the classical Western, namely THE SEARCHERS[112] (John Ford 1956) and SHANE[113] (George Stevens 1953), and the road movie of the time, specifically EASY RIDER (Dennis Hopper 1969).[114] The end of the film connects these references (see figs. 5 – 9) and can thus either by read as an inversion of Hopper's film (the hippies shoot the policeman) or as the end of SHANE by way of SCORPIO RISING (a departing protagonist who dies after falling from his motor-

---

111 My thanks to both Hye-Jeung Chung and Sarah Greifenstein for this idea.

112 In his DVD introduction to the film, Guercio names John Ford and this film in particular as an essential reference point. Just before the epilogue begins, John Wintergreen can be seen with his motorbike at a famous viewpoint named John Ford's Point.

113 In one conversation, John Wintergreen compares himself to Alan Ladd, the star of SHANE. In this sense, he resembles Scorpio, who also defines himself based on film history, even if in his case the points of comparison are such rebellious, anti-authority figures as James Dean or Marlon Brando. Ladd would also have likely fitted well into Anger's *Hollywood Babylon:* he was allegedly homosexual, tried to commit suicide in 1962, and died from a combination of alcohol and drugs in 1964 before the premiere of his last film.

114 Wintergreen uses the poster of the film as a target during shooting practice; in the DVD commentary for the film, Guercio at one point says that "we were doing the reverse of EASY RIDER [...]."

bike). Yet the references made here are in no way abstract, but illustrated in concrete terms by how the respective codas are interwoven (see figs. 12–15).

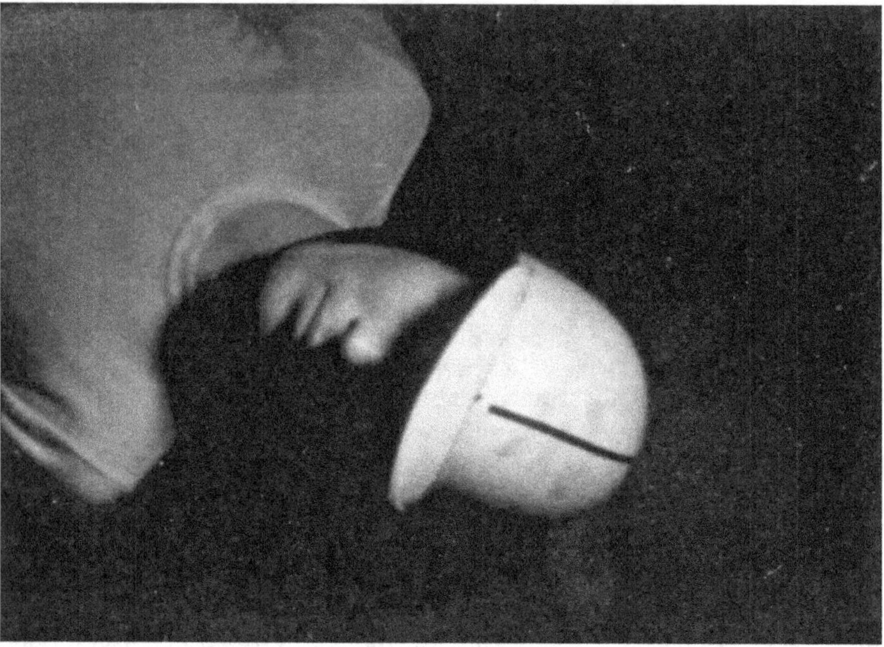

Figs. 12–15: The elements that make up the end of ELECTRA GLIDE IN BLUE: SCORPIO RISING, SHANE, THE SEARCHERS, EASY RIDER (from top to bottom).

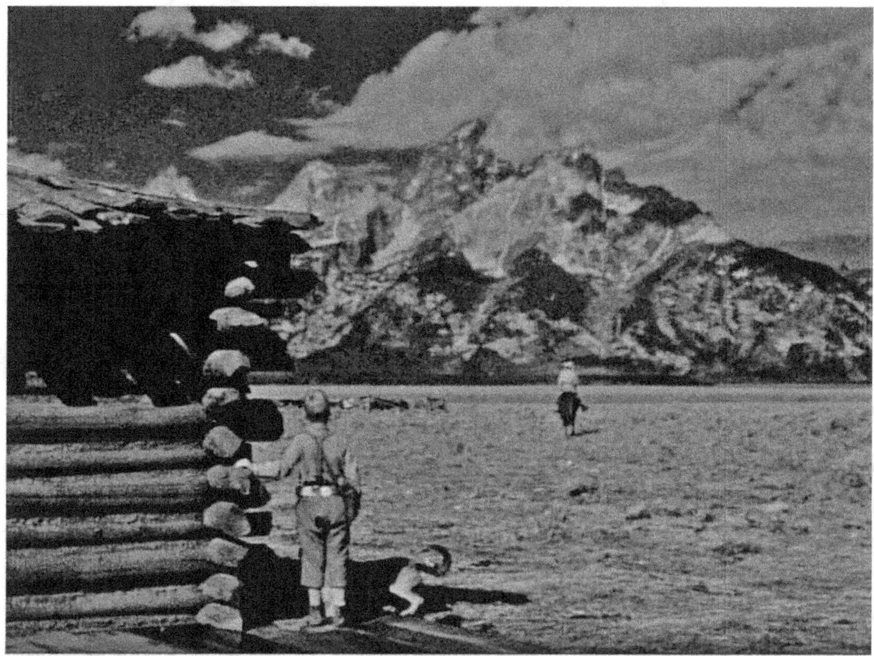

Fig. 13

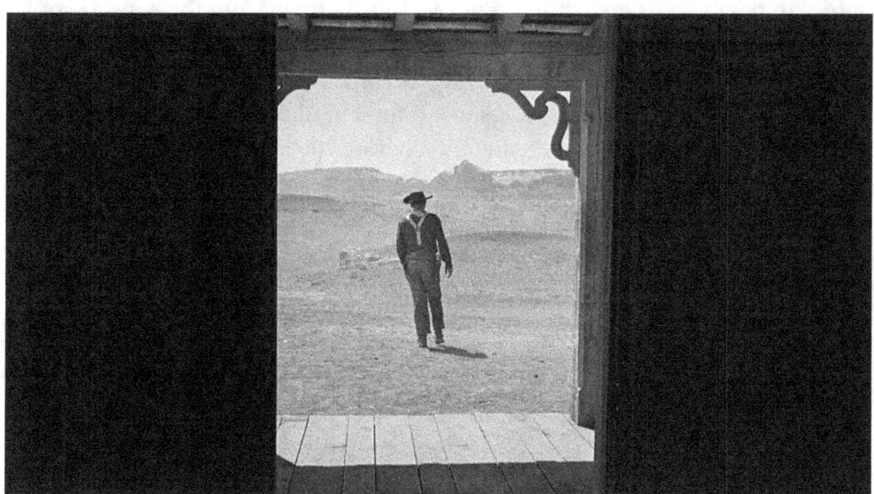

Fig. 14

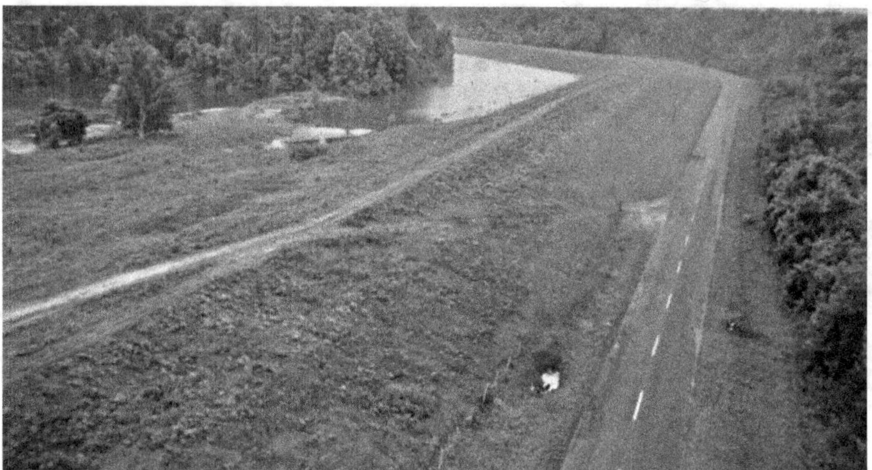

Fig. 15

The precise manner of these elements' interweaving is of secondary importance. What is significant is that the melancholy codas of both SHANE and THE SEARCHERS, themselves, which both represent farewell scenes of a contradictory nature,[115] make recourse to one of the enduring traditions of the classical Western, in order to heighten or take it to the next level: riding off into the sunset. For its part, Guercio's film works to rewrite film history as a history of decline, an idea palpable as the classical Western's destruction by countercultural cinema. From this perspective, the fields and plains mentioned in the lyrics of the song conjure up the broad planes, which had stretched before the movie-going-public in bygone eras, in front of the real landscape. This is naturally demonstrated in the choice of Monument Valley as a shooting location, a place not only inseparable from the films of John Ford but prominent also in EASY RIDER. Precisely these images of Monument Valley are the ones that have not just disappeared but remain under the banner of something that can never be redeemed.

---

115 See Benjamin, whose *One-Way Street* creates an image of farewell that is interesting in our context due to the roles played by texture: "How much more easily the leave-taker is loved! For the flame burns more purely for those vanishing in the distance, fueled by the fleeting scrap of material waving from the ship or railway window. Separation penetrates the disappearing person like a pigment and steeps him in gentle radiance." Walter Benjamin: One-Way Street. In: id.: Selected Writings. Vol. 1: 1913–26, edited by Marcus Bullock, and Michael W. Jennings, Cambridge, MA 2002, pp. 444–488, p. 450. What is also interesting here is the fact that the Freudian conflict of ambivalence also shines through in this description.

By the end of the film, the reference to SCORPIO RISING thus turns out to be not just an homage but, rather, constitutive of a poetic technique. It furthermore becomes clear why this reference appears in the title sequence at the very beginning of the film: Anger's film marks the "year zero" from which ELECTRA GLIDE IN BLUE constructs film history. Within this construction, macro- and micro-perspectives on (film) historical processes appear folded into one another in their respective, contradictory natures, as Benjamin remarks elsewhere on the structure of reflection: "Both these aspects of reflection are equally essential: the playful miniaturization of reality and the introduction of a reflective infinity of thought into the finite space of a profane fate."[116] In ELECTRA GLIDE IN BLUE, the real – that is, the event that closes the film at the level of the plot – is reduced, in a manner more painful than playful, to a film image folded in on itself and, ultimately, to a black-and-white freeze frame, a frozen cross-section of time, in which the world depicted is petrified: present but devoid of any possibility for change. As a direct consequence of melancholy ambivalence and the necessary process of its working through, *reflection as the opening up of a (film) historical space* forms the second characteristic of the affect poetics of melancholia in New Hollywood. This characteristic is of diacritic value in that reflection coagulates into a specific, melancholy image form – in short, into a film image *as* an image.

This image differs from the paranoid one in several respects. In its very nature of existence, having never possessed a present, the latter finds itself in a perpetual state of repetition. The melancholy image, on the other hand, takes the suffering of the present as its starting point, in order to circle it perpetually in repeated loops. The image-as-an-image in the melancholy mode thus always depicts a direct image of time, namely with respect to its transience. While the paranoia image-as-an-image is a surface that precludes any present, the melancholy image-as-an-image introduces a degree of depth into precisely this present moment. This has a direct effect on how the spectator experiences time.

Atomized Time

The tendency toward petrification, mentioned by Gertrud Koch, is already evident in the title sequence discussed above, when the various parts of Wintergreen's uniform and gear are framed in fragmentary fashion, frozen for a second and tinted, so as to provide the backdrop for a new title; a process that serves to accentuate the texture of each surface all the more (figs. 16 – 17). At first glance,

---

116 Benjamin: The Origin of German Tragic Drama, p. 83.

this procedure does not appear particularly unusual in the context of a title sequence – one may recall, for example, that a similar effect is used in THE WILD BUNCH (Sam Peckinpah 1969), whose own view of history is certainly, decidedly melancholy. Yet, if one also takes the reference to SCORPIO RISING and the ending of ELECTRA GLIDE into consideration, the technique gains a whole new significance in relation to the "style of a melancholy manner of experience" (Binswanger).

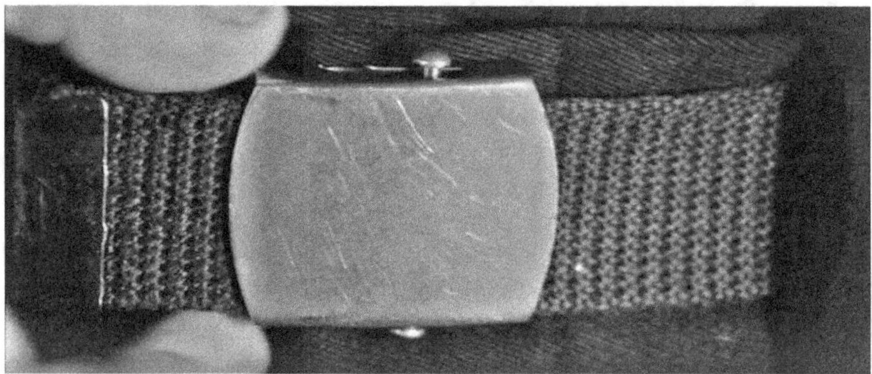

Figs. 16–17: The splitting off and freezing of things.

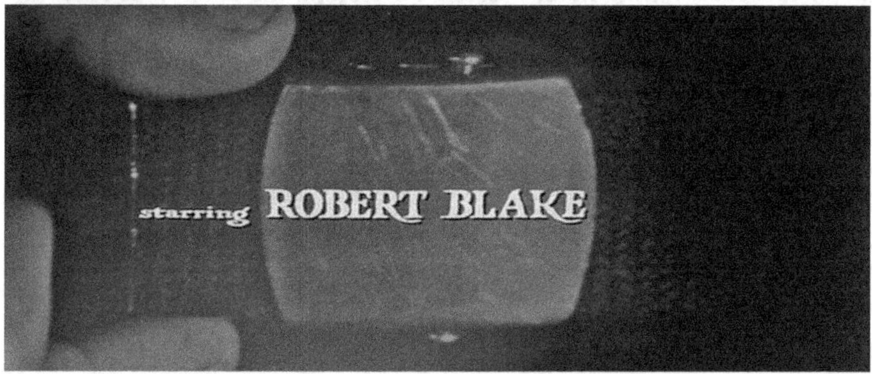

Fig. 17

The melancholic's affinity to the world of things, as opposed to the world of human sociality, is a well-established *topos* and for good reason. As Benjamin explains, when he identifies loyalty as one of the essential characteristics of the melancholic:

> All essential decisions in relation to men can offend against loyalty; they are subject to higher law. Loyalty is completely appropriate only to the relationship of man to the world of things. The latter knows no higher law, and loyalty knows no object to which it might belong more exclusively than the world of things. [...] Clumsily, indeed unjustifiably, loyalty expresses, in its own way, a truth for the sake of which it does, of course, betray the world. Melancholy betrays the world for the sake of knowledge. But in its tenacious self-absorption it embraces dead objects in its contemplation, in order to redeem them.[117]

Benjamin alludes to the fact that the relationship to the world of things is not a consequence of the melancholy grasp of time but, to the contrary, its cause: "The persistence which is expressed in the intention of mourning, is born of its loyalty to the world of things."[118] With this understanding of loyalty, it is now possible to grasp Freud's conflict of ambivalence as a form of temporality: the contradiction in the relationship to the "love object" and the inability to give it up (as an actual object in the literal sense).

This reveals the true scope of Bin Kimura's claim that the melancholy past is to be strictly understood as existing in perfect tense. When the past is codified in such a way (as a set of empty possibilities), both present and future are also robbed of any potential for "true" movement, which would form the very conditions of possibility for change. Toshiaki Kobayashi (whose work grapples with Kimura in detail) thus writes on how the melancholic experiences time:

> While the difference between past, present, and future remains, that which relates to movement in itself does not. Despite the expression "the passing of time", I am of the opinion that time no longer flows for these patients. A sort of ossified difference, as it were, lies before them instead, a sequence of events only static in nature, which now only conveys the appearance of time passing. [...] The difference produced in the melancholic is so rigidly fixed that he or she no longer has any room to move. This fixed difference without scope for movements is akin to something turned to stone or an object. In this sense, one can say that for the melancholic, time has become objectified.[119]

The emblems of this conception of time are the hourglass (such as in Dürer's *Melencolia I*) or the clock face (in the world of the baroque tragedy):[120] Cronos devouring his children.

As Kobayashi mentions, the key concept here is that of difference: time is not just transformed into space but, rather, divided up into infinite portions by

---

117 Benjamin: The Origin of German Tragic Drama, pp. 156–157.
118 Benjamin: The Origin of German Tragic Drama, p. 157. Benjamin does not distinguish in a strict sense between grief and melancholy.
119 Kobayashi: Melancholie und Zeit, pp. 164–165.
120 See Benjamin: The Origin of German Tragic Drama, p. 96.

equally infinite reflection. In this sense, the paradox of Zeno is also realized in the state of melancholy: "Without the category of movement, the infinite division causes a paradox. In the same way in which Achilles can never reach the tortoise, the melancholic – in the words of Tellenbach – always lags behind him or herself."[121] This sense of lagging behind one's self can be described as the spectator's affective-corporeal experience in the cinema, in which the fact of transience is inscribed onto consciousness, be it subtly or with full force. From the quality of contradiction at the heart of the melancholy style and the reflection that seeks to process this contradiction, the *objectification* or *atomization of time* consequently emerges as the third criterion of this style. Yet movement does not just disappear under the regime of atomized time, it is more that we encounter here a new form of movement, a movement burying itself in difference.[122] How can this form of movement be described more precisely in film theoretical terms?

Tonality and Pathos

Over the course of ELECTRA GLIDE IN BLUE's final shot, the movement of the camera comes to a standstill and the quasi-technicolor hues of sky and desert give way to black-and-white. Yet what happens here is not a transition between opposites but, rather, in both cases, a transition into a new quality. The tracking shot that moves backwards along the road is thus not just a movement in space that eventually halts: it is more a movement that stretches and contracts in relation to the space itself, taking on a different form as it contaminates the freeze-frame, before finally becoming sublimated in the movement of the music.[123]

---

121 Kobayashi: Melancholie und Zeit, p. 164. Kobayashi makes reference here to Hubertus Tellenbach's conception of remanence, which defines the melancholic's experience of time as lagging behind him or herself. See Hubertus Tellenbach: Melancholy. History of the Problem, Endogeneity, Typology, Pathogenesis, Clinical Considerations, Pittsburgh 1980, pp. 133 – 145.

122 It is no coincidence that Binswanger cites finding one's footing or the fear of losing it as a central characteristic of melancholy: faced with a mixture of protention and retention, the "presentatio" just hangs in the air, permanently suspended. See Binswanger: Melancholie und Manie, p. 33. The kinship between melancholy and suspense is alluded to here. The suspension created by melancholy differs from suspense in that, as Binswanger writes in the same passage, it cannot, on the one hand, be grasped as a continuation of a past only available in the conditional form, and lacks, on the other, any relation to the future, thus becoming less of a subject of speculation than an area of fatal certainty.

123 Steven Shaviro writes on the prologue of MELANCHOLIA (Lars von Trier, Denmark and others, 2011) correspondingly: "We no longer experience space as a container; instead, we feel it as

One possible way of describing this transformation is Eisenstein's category of tonality. Eisenstein famously separates it from the category of rhythm, which refers to movement as a change in location: "But here, in this instance, movement is understood in a wider sense. Here the concept of movement embraces all sorts of vibrations that derive from the shot."[124] Eisenstein thus initially separates the concept of movement from the idea of moving forward in space, which is at the heart of Zeno's paradox. In this way, movement becomes independent of any directionality within the narrative space and receives, instead, a character of intensity that unfolds in time. The "tonality" of a shot is not only to be understood here as the character to which all other elements are subject. Tonality refers to the category according to which the shot is presented to the spectator as a formal unit. In his book *Nonindifferent Nature*, Eisenstein goes into even greater detail on this subject, in reference to the idea of the "music of landscape."[125]

The starting point for Eisenstein's study is the emotional impact that films have on the spectator, a force he refers to as pathos. Pathos, as a principle of "being beside oneself,"[126] is to be understood in the sense of a psychophysical isomorphism, which constitutes the basis for the correspondence of cinematic form with the feelings of the spectator who reproduces it perceptually. This affective energy feeds on the principle of conflict, upon which form is constructed in the first place. The "*concrete trend* of emotions"[127] takes the place of a targeted movement. According to this assumption, as this conflict is resolved, the image's "being beside [itself]"[128] leads to a "being beside themselves" on the part of the audience:

> [...] *pathos* is what forces the viewer to jump out of his seat. It is what forces him to flee from his place. It is what forces him to clap, to cry out. It is what forces his eyes to gleam with ecstasy before tears of ecstasy appear in them. In a word, it is everything that forces the viewer to 'be beside himself.'[129]

---

something in ferment, its shape continually inflected by the camera that presents it, as well as by the bodies, forces, and events that unfold within it. There are no fixed points in this space, but only vectors: moving lines of ever-varying speeds and directions. Motionlessness is itself one of those speeds. [...] Stasis is thus not the opposite of movement. Rather, it is the degree zero, or the limit-form, of motion: a temporary congelation, or a quivering incipience." Shaviro: MELANCHOLIA, or: The Romantic Anti-Sublime. In: Sequence 1 (2012), p. 17.

124 Eisenstein: The Fourth Dimension in Film, p. 188.
125 See Eisenstein: Nonindifferent Nature. Cambridge 1987, pp. 216–383.
126 Eisenstein: Nonindifferent Nature, p. 216.
127 Eisenstein: Nonindifferent Nature, p. 218.
128 Eisenstein: Nonindifferent Nature, p. 216.
129 Eisenstein: Nonindifferent Nature, p. 27.

Based on this definition, we can connect pathos to that accusatory or beseeching aspect discerned in the final shot. This form of spectatorial address is manifested in dual, contradictory fashion: as an insistent accusation from the past, on the one hand, and in the entreaties of the lyrics, which run counter to this insistent demand ("pray it's not too late"), on the other. The spectator physically sitting in the cinema is not the one actually addressed here, in either the first or the second case: they are neither responsible for the events of the film, nor expected to say a prayer. The effect itself is produced only by the *friction* between these two forms of address; it cannot be conceived of outside the paradox of melancholy, which can always be traced back to a contradictory temporal experience.

In the same section of his book, Eisenstein discusses the pathos-generating possibilities for a specific *musicality* of film. For him, music marks a privileged expressive realm, in accordance with Modernism's more romantic traditions (he draws on Wagner, Schönberg and Saint-Saëns). When film makes recourse to musical principles, such as by the use of music on the soundtrack, it is "not so much a question of strengthening the effect (although to a great extent, it is), as in emotionally expressing what is inexpressible by other means."[130]

Landscape initially comes into play because, within the conditions of production for silent film, its function most closely resembles that of music, in terms of the "embodiment of this sphere of *pure emotionality*."[131] Eisenstein clearly distinguishes this from the narrative dimension of the progression of the plot: "For landscape is the freest element of film, the least burdened with servile, narrative tasks, and the most flexible in conveying moods, emotional states, and spiritual experiences. In a word, *all that*, in its exhaustive total, is accessible only to music, with its hazily perceptive, flowing imagery."[132]

For landscape to be able to perform this entire set of functions in film, it is insufficient for it to merely be employed as a picturesque backdrop. Landscape can only take on the function of music if it, itself, is treated musically; for Eisenstein, "the emotional effect is achieved not only by a set of *representational elements* of nature, but especially and mainly by the *musical development and composition* of what is being represented."[133] Eisenstein draws on the example of the mist "suite" from BRONENOSEC POTËMKIN (BATTLESHIP POTEMKIN, USSR 1925) to illustrate what he means:

---

130 Eisenstein: Nonindifferent Nature, p. 217.
131 Eisenstein: Nonindifferent Nature, p. 218.
132 Eisenstein: Nonindifferent Nature, p. 217.
133 Eisenstein: Nonindifferent Nature, pp. 225–226.

> The 'Odessa Mist' is like a connecting link between *pure painting* and the *music of audio-visual combinations* of the new cinematography.

> The suite of the mist is still painting, but a distinct type of painting that through montage already perceives the rhythm of the change of *real spans of time* and the tangible sequences of repetitions in time, that is, the elements of what in pure form is only accessible to music.[134]

At this point, it is worth mentioning that, with respect to the affinity between film and music, those filmmakers of the American avant-garde influenced by Eisenstein, such as Kenneth Anger and Stan Brakhage, work in similar fashion. Anger expresses this directly: "I'm working with visuals as a musician would work with symphonic material."[135] Eisenstein emphasizes the connecting factor that forms the basis of this dynamic: real expansion in time or, rather, duration. For our purposes, the way this duration is shaped in film is decisive. In this context, Eisenstein grasps this musical principle as the combination of *elementary forces*, like in the mist sequence, constituted by the coming together of mist (air), the reflective surface of the water, and the solid bodies of the ships anchored in the harbor (earth). He thus connects the idea of an emotional tone with an accentuation of *textures* that unfolds in time: "And it seems that the textures of the separate elements, just as the elements among themselves, form the same combination as an orchestra, unifying into the simultaneity and the sequence of the action – the wind and strings, wood and brass!"[136]

Mood and Dissonance:[137] Landscape and Texture

In Eisenstein's work, tonality or timbre – and the elementary forces that correspond to them – are thus grasped not in metaphorical terms but in highly con-

---

134 Eisenstein: Nonindifferent Nature, p. 220.

135 Kenneth Anger in the audio commentary on the Blu-Ray edition of his own *Magick Lantern Cycle*, British Film Institute 2009, in relationship to INAUGURATION OF THE PLEASURE DOME (1954). Stan Brakhage expresses himself about his work in similar fashion, as nearly all of his films do away with sound. See Scott MacDonald: The Filmmaker as Visionary. Excerpts from an Interview with Stan Brakhage. In: Film Quarterly, Vol. 56, No. 3 (2003), pp. 2–11, here p. 6.

136 Eisenstein: Nonindifferent Nature, p. 229.

137 The German original title of this section – "Stimmung und Ver-Stimmung" – is an allusion to the idea that the concept of mood is quite literally inherent to that of dissonance (or dejection). The English translation is unfortunately unable to capture this deliberate double meaning. In order to approximate its intention, as well as to allude to the concept of affective resonance, dissonance is preferred over dejection in the following. See Rainer Mühlhoff: Affective Reso-

crete fashion. With this in mind, the "music of landscape" refers to a specific mode of affective perception, not just closely related to Eisenstein's concept of expressive movement.[138] In addition, it approximates what is discussed under the banner of mood, for example, in the writings of Georg Simmel on the philosophy of landscape.[139] In analogous fashion to Eisenstein, Simmel recognizes the decisive criterion to be the perception of a landscape as a unified whole, and this perception as a whole is justified by the concept of mood:[140]

> The most important carrier of this unity may well be the 'mood', as we call it, of a landscape. When we refer to the mood of a person, we mean that coherent ensemble that either permanently or temporarily colors the entirety of his or her physical constituents. It is not itself something discrete, and often also not an attribute of any one individual trait. All the same, it is that commonality where all these individual traits interconnect. In the same way, the mood of a landscape permeates all its separate components, frequently without it being attributable to any one of them. In a way that is difficult to specify, each component partakes in it, but a mood prevails which is neither external to these constituents, nor is it composed of them.[141]

Simmel establishes that it is misleading to ask,

> [...] whether our unitary perception of an object or the feeling arising together with it comes first or second. There prevails, in fact, no cause-and-effect relationship between them [...]. Thus, both the unifying move which brings landscape as such into being, and the mood that a landscape projects at us and through which we comprehend it, are merely the result of a subsequent dismantling of one and the same psychic act.[142]

---

nance. In: Jan Slaby, and Christian von Scheve (eds.): Affective Societies. Key Concepts, London/ New York 2019, pp. 189 – 199.

138 "Strictly speaking, from the purely plastic aspect of a film, any *general surface of each shot* is a distinct tonal or color 'landscape' – not because of what it represents but because of the *emotional feeling* the shot must bear, which itself is perceived as a whole with the consecutive course of the montage pieces." Eisenstein: Nonindifferent Nature, p. 391.

139 Georg Simmel: The Philosophy of Landscape. In: Theory, Culture & Society 24 (2007), pp. 7–8, and pp. 20–29.

140 The theoretical problem of mood has been repeatedly discussed based on the *topos* of landscape, see David Wellbery: Stimmung. In: Karlheinz Barck et al. (eds.): Ästhetische Grundbegriffe. Historisches Wörterbuch in sieben Bänden. Vol. 5, Stuttgart 2003, pp. 703–733, here p. 718. On the film theoretical connection between the concept of mood developed here and the concept of expressive movement, see also Kappelhoff, Bakels: Das Zuschauergefühl, p. 83, in particular.

141 Simmel: The Philosophy of Landscape, p. 26.

142 Simmel: The Philosophy of Landscape, p. 27.

According to this understanding, it is not possible to regard landscape as an independent object. Landscape is at no point just a pure "intermingling of trees and hills, water-courses and stones" but, rather, "exists only through the unifying powers of the Soul [...]. Mood thus attains its whole objectivity as landscape within the scope of our formative acts. Since mood is a distinct expression, and specific dynamic within, these acts, it gains its full objectivity in and through landscape."[143]

Simmel draws a conclusion from this fact which also applies to the present investigation: as the product of the concrete combination of both spirit and material, mood cannot be represented as a collection of abstract categories and genres.

> Rather, the mood of a landscape pointed to here is one pertaining to *just this* particular landscape and never to any other, even though both may be possibly subsumed under a general concept, such as melancholic. Such a conceptually typical mood may, however, be attributed to a landscape already formed. But the mood immediately pertaining to it, which would be modified through the alternation of just one single line, this mood is innate to a landscape and is inseparably fused with the coming into being of its unitary form.[144]

By closely entangling the emergence of landscape with its correlating mood, Simmel's approach once again emphasizes the deeply historical dimension of melancholy pointed out at the beginning of this chapter: The cinematic mode of melancholy not only depends on spectators perceptually embodying the audiovisual composition of textures; it also, reflexively, enables these spectators to experience this embodiment as a historically situated event. If one grasps mood in this strict sense, then the methodological approach applied in this chapter requires that, instead of one film example, cited in abstract terms, representing all the others, diversity and mutability must be given their due as important, central dimensions of this phenomenon. In this way, it is possible to conceive of a spectrum of melancholy moods in New Hollywood cinema, whereby the despair of ELECTRA GLIDE IN BLUE lies close to one extreme and the gentle, irony-tinged comedy of the end of THE GRADUATE (Mike Nichols 1967) near the other, while MCCABE & MRS. MILLER (Robert Altman 1971) might occupy the midpoint between them. If, however, this individuality notwithstanding, something like a metric of comparison among them were to be established, then Simmel's

---

143 Simmel: The Philosophy of Landscape, p. 27. Simmel conceives of a relationship between nature and consciousness here that is similar to that which Kracauer describes as characteristic of the modern in his essay on photography. See Kracauer: Photography, p. 434.
144 Simmel: The Philosophy of Landscape, p. 28.

concept of mood can be honed slightly by drawing on Eisenstein. The difficulty of attributing mood, mentioned by Simmel, does not have to necessarily be grasped in negative terms. In *The Fourth Dimension in Cinema*, Eisenstein resists grasping the tonality of a shot as an "'impressionistic' measurement" and points out that the corresponding parameters can, indeed, be measured.[145] They fall into the category of what Eisenstein refers to as the *texture* of individual elements, a term which has been mentioned at various times over the course of this chapter.

Rudolf Arnheim understands texture "as the result of what happens when the level of perceptual comprehension shifts from the scrutiny of individual structural relationships within their total context to that of overall structural constants."[146] This, thus, addresses the effect on the perceptual disposition of the observer, arising from a certain structural quality of the art work (with painting serving as the example, just as it does for Eisenstein). Arnheim describes a Jackson Pollock painting as follows:

> Such a picture can be perceived only as texture – not because the number or size of the units of which it is made up go beyond the range of the human's eye capacity but because the units do not fit into more comprehensive shapes. The number of elements is large enough so that their variations as to color, shape, size, direction, relative position, etc., compensate each other, and a common denominator of textural qualities such as prickliness, softness, excitation, viscosity, mechanical hardness or organic flexibility emerges from an inspection of the whole. All movements, also, are compensated so that nothing "happens," except for a kind of molecular milling everywhere.[147]

We should, first of all, bracket Arnheim's obvious disdain for the artistic approach he describes. The decisive point for us, in this context (alongside the aspect of "the whole"), is the lack of focus in the spectator's attention; this is derived from two principles. First, the relationships between the elements are blurred; second, the field of perception resists objectification – Arnheim formulates the latter in the assertion that variations balance each other out, simply meaning that the eye is unable to find any fixed point to linger upon. Not without reason, Eisenstein remarks that it is "interesting that the most 'resonant' examples of landscape turn out to be landscapes connected to mist."[148] Mist func-

---

145 Eisenstein: The Fourth Dimension in Film, p. 188.

146 Rudolf Arnheim: Accident and the Necessity of Art. In: The Journal of Aesthetics and Art Criticism, Vol. 16, No. 1 (1957), pp. 18–31, here p. 25.

147 Arnheim: Accident and the Necessity of Art, p. 26. As a side comment here, Pollock is seen as one of the most important influences on Stan Brakhage. See MacDonald: The Filmmaker as Visionary, p. 5.

148 Eisenstein: Nonindifferent Nature, p. 237.

tions as a force of decentralization that blurs outlines and shrouds the entire field of perception, to point to its common denominators; mist thus operates as a 'landscape-like' force par excellence. Above, I described movement under the regime of atomized time as "burying itself in difference"; this form of movement can be defined as the most important characteristic of texture as it forms a perceptual relationship.

What Eisenstein refers to as a combination of elements is found in ELECTRA GLIDE IN BLUE as the contraction and expansion of space and the interplay between color and brightness, and both of these in connection with the music. The audiovisual composition aims at the creation of a unity under the banner of contradiction. Within these aspects, the level of "perceptual comprehension" (Arnheim) shifts onto the dynamics of oscillation, such that textural qualities emerge as dominants[149]. The result of this shift is not present beforehand, however, but, as a spectatorial experience, the subject of the drama itself: the gradual compression of space; the time it takes for Wintergreen to become one point among many before disappearing entirely;[150] the eagle that flies into the frame shortly before the image freezes, and remains motionless close to the center of the image, an additional point in an ocean of them; the momentary pulsations of the image due to the vection effect; the final draining away of color and light. The drama here is one of *textural becoming* – the time during which the film image recedes from perceptual accessibility. Although the backdrop of the rock formations of Monument Valley remains virtually unaltered, at the same time everything changes.

This conception of cinematic landscape does not bring any sort of psychological factor into play through the concept of mood; rather, as Simmel emphasizes, the act of grasping the whole of something and the mood that goes along with it coincide completely. This idea is formulated even more pointedly by Ludwig Binswangers's derivation of melancholy; indeed, once again, the problem of ambivalence raises the question of the unified whole. According to Binswanger, unity in the experience of a worldly context is exactly what is lacking in melancholy, due to the destruction of the necessary temporal framework, producing dissonance as a result.[151] This concept clearly differs from how Freud character-

---

149 See Eisenstein: The Fourth Dimension in Film, p. 189.

150 According to Hubertus Tellenbach, one characteristic of the spatiality of melancholy existence is the creation of individual points. See Hubertus Tellenbach: Die Räumlichkeit der Melancholischen. II. Mitteilung. Analyse der Räumlichkeit melancholischen Daseins. In: Der Nervenarzt, Vol. 27, No. 7 (1956), pp. 289–298, here p. 294.

151 Binswanger: Melancholie und Manie, p. 123.

izes melancholia, as "a profoundly painful dejection,"[152] since Binswanger does not establish this dissonance based on a psychological notion of mood, in the sense of a momentary, emotional state: "This injury to the existence – not of the (mundane) personality – does not *create* the dissonance of the melancholy, but rather *is* already the melancholy mood of loss."[153] Hubertus Tellenbach also articulates this sort of dissonance in pointed fashion, clarifying the opposition with grief, once again, with a pertinent delineation: "[...] the atmospheric can no longer permeate the individual in the sense of a mood. Here it becomes clear in sensory terms what W. Schulte is referring to when he says that the essence of depressive dissonance consists instead of an inability to be sad."[154]

In line with Binswanger, the becoming-texture of the image is exactly a melancholy dissonance, understood as an "expression of experience in the sense of loss,"[155] a mood under the banner of reflection. It is not that the gradual discoloring of the sky conjures up a melancholy feeling as if by magic; rather, as discussed at length above, the discoloration is the expression of a deeply conflicted experience of time that has been "reflected upon to the highest possible degree."[156] Dissonance thus does not mean the absence of mood but suggests, rather, that affective, corporeal experience, itself, has a dissonant quality. Mood and reflection are inseparable in melancholy and come together in this feeling of dissonance. Here, the paradox is taken to an extreme: the concept of mood addresses feeling as constituted of temporal unity, the melancholy dissonance shapes how this is paradoxically felt as a disunity – or at least not as a unity that integrates itself into a linear sequence of units.

Binswanger's argument is perfectly demonstrated by ELECTRA GLIDE IN BLUE. In this film, every image of the landscape, every tiny stone and single blade of grass, brings with it a film historical association. And not just any association but a deeply contradictory one: namely the setting of both the great, classical Westerns and the quasi- or anti-genre of the road movie. The movement that renders the image progressively inaccessible also makes the cannibalistic temporality of film history manifest in crystal clear fashion: the protagonist is not just consumed by the landscape, but this movement is itself staged as the devouring of the Western by the road movie. If, with this in mind, one returns to Benjamin's angel of history, then the pile of debris growing towards the sky does not only

---

152 Freud: Mourning and Melancholia, p. 244.
153 Binswanger: Melancholie und Manie, p. 47.
154 Hubertus Tellenbach: Geschmack und Atmosphäre. Medien menschlichen Elementarkontaktes, Salzburg 1965, p. 127.
155 Binswanger: Melancholie und Manie, p. 47.
156 Binswanger: Melancholie und Manie, p. 123.

function as a metaphor for blatant injustice. It describes a perceptual relationship devoid of and no longer dependent on any distance between subject and object: in other words, texture.

The Self-Alienation of Movement

We must take one, final step to further specify the connection between melancholy, dissonance, and texture, in relation to corporeal, affective experience, by focusing on the temporal dynamic inherent to texture as a perceptual relationship. Several of Maurice Merleau-Ponty's considerations proceed in this direction in *The Visible and the Invisible*. These are aimed at overcoming Merleau-Ponty's own understanding of intentionality, in favor of a conception of perception, not *a priori* contingent upon the dichotomy of subject and object but, rather, depicted as a reciprocal, reversible relationship. Texture plays an important role in such a conception, namely in how it connects to what is referred to as "flesh," a sort of "generality of the Sensible in itself,"[157] which precedes the establishment of a subject:

> The flesh is not matter, is not mind, is not substance. To designate it, we should need the old term "element," in the sense it was used to speak of water, air, earth, and fire, that is, in the sense of a general thing, midway between the spatio-temporal individual and the idea, a sort of incarnate principle that brings a style of being wherever there is a fragment of being.[158]

This concept of flesh clearly throws up the same problem of localization we have already encountered, in similar fashion, in Simmel's thoughts on mood. Merleau-Ponty situates flesh in an in-between space, "midway between the spatio-temporal individual and the idea." It asserts itself by introducing a "style," that is, a way of positioning perception and expression in relation to one another.[159]

When the flesh or "element" is thus newly realized in a specific style, this context is to be understood as a temporal dynamic related to the act of film perception. As Merleau-Ponty writes: "Perception is not first a perception of *things,*

---

157 Merleau-Ponty: The Visible and the Invisible, p. 139.
158 Merleau-Ponty: The Visible and the Invisible, p. 139.
159 This idea can be directly related to Binswanger's formulation of "style as a melancholy manner of experience." On style as the description of the relationship between perception and expression in film theory, see Sobchack: The Address of the Eye, in particular pp. 212–219.

but a perception of *elements [...]*, of *rays of the world,* of things which are dimensions, which are Worlds [...]."[160] One is reminded of Eisenstein's discussion of the mist, touched on above, and how the mobile figure of the seagull glides from one element into another, appearing in each case according to a specific "style of being": "The sea gull in the air – seems to be part of the mist and sky. The sea gull, alighting down like a black silhouette on the buoy – is an element of solid earth."[161] Clearly, we are beyond any conventional model of representation at this point. The status of the eagle in ELECTRA GLIDE IN BLUE changes in analogous fashion when it is caught in the freeze-frame: the dynamics of *film* mood, unfolding in time, can thus be derived from the clash of different, conflicting principles, different styles of being (Eisenstein speaks appropriately here of "a mutual play"). In Eisenstein's model, the realization of the difference between these styles issues from the transition from rhythmic to tonal montage: at the point where the movement of the seagull crystallizes into the sail.[162]

Inasmuch as flesh is located "midway" between the individual and the idea, we are not yet essentially any further than Simmel, who establishes, in largely negative fashion, that mood is only identical to itself. The decisive step towards concretization can be made based on the discovery that flesh (or the element) is made evident in the form of texture:

> This concentration of the visibles about one of them, or this bursting forth of the mass of the body toward the things, which makes a vibration of my skin become the sleek and the rough, makes me *follow with my eyes* the movements and the contours of the things themselves [...], this pact between them and me according to which I lend them my body in order that they inscribe upon it and give me their resemblance, this fold, this central cavity of the visible which is my vision, these two mirror arrangements of the seeing and the visible, the touching and the touched, form a closebound system that I count on, define a vision in general and a constant style of visibility [...]. The flesh [...] is not contingency, chaos, but a texture that returns to itself and conforms to itself.[163]

Merleau-Ponty is describing a mode of perception in which the hierarchical distinction between subject and object is nearly suspended, without, however, the two "mirror arrangements" ever becoming truly identical. From this perspective,

---

160 Merleau-Ponty: The Visible and the Invisible, p. 218.
161 Eisenstein: Nonindifferent Nature, p. 229.
162 "[...] a naked color, and in general a visible, is not a chunk of absolutely hard, indivisible being, offered all naked to a vision which could be only total or null, but is rather a sort of straits between exterior horizons and interior horizons ever gaping open, [...] less a color or a thing, therefore, than a difference between things and colors, a momentary crystallization of colored being or of visibility." Merleau-Ponty: The Visible and the Invisible, p. 132.
163 Merleau-Ponty: The Visible and the Invisible, p. 146.

the relationship between element and texture is represented as a perpetual dynamic, constantly oscillating between actuality and virtuality.[164] The characteristic elusiveness of mood is, to a large extent, traceable to this dynamic, which Arnheim locates at the "molecular" level.[165] An altered relationship between the artwork and those that observe it or, in our case, between film and spectator is expressed *ex negativo* in Arnheim's critique of allegedly formless art. Thomas Elsaesser, in writing about the New Hollywood road movie, has brought this altered relationship into connection with the concept of a "new" realism:

> [...] if one considers, as I have suggested, the pervasive pessimism of the American cinema in the 1970s less as a personal statement of their authors and more as the limiting constraint of a new, modern realism, the price this cinema pays for being exploratory and tentative, then the strength of a film like TWO-LANE BLACKTOP lies in the way that, sheltered by the structure of the journey motif, it quietly steers towards a level of abstraction, a documentary minimalism unknown in the Hollywood canon except perhaps in the work of Jacques Tourneur. Released from the strong fable and from the need to engineer the narrative into didactic shape, the images develop an energy that charges representation with something other than symbolic overtones or metaphoric substitutes.[166]

The energy that Elsaesser refers to here is precisely the same "molecular" dynamic of texture. On this basis, melancholy reflection, as the relationship between film and spectator unfolding in time, can be described as a movement burying itself in the in-between (explaining, thereby, talk of documentary minimalism). Elsaesser relates this observation to road movies, whose ostensible motto could be derived from the soundtrack of one biker film, namely HELL'S ANGELS ON WHEELS (Richard Rush 1967): "Moving But Going Nowhere."

This (stationary) movement has two aspects: first, it loses itself in the infinite contemplation of the visible and thus ends up "wholly out of itself,"[167] as Merleau-Ponty puts it in a (perhaps not entirely coincidental) paraphrase of Eisenstein. Further, it becomes entirely embroiled in difference as it congeals and remains inexorably behind itself. This divergence finds expression in the two main characteristics of melancholy spatial experience provided by Tellenbach: "an often huge distancing from things as well as from one's own self"; and, sec-

---

164 On the film theoretical significance of the connection between the actual and the virtual, see Deleuze: Cinema 2, pp. 66–85.

165 Arnheim: Accident and the Necessity of Art, p. 26. For the distinction between the molar and the molecular, see Deleuze, Guattari: Thousand Plateaus, pp. 45–67.

166 Thomas Elsaesser: The Pathos of Failure, p. 291.

167 Merleau-Ponty: The Visible and the Invisible, p. 136.

ond, "almost total isolation at certain points."[168] This contrast continually resurfaces in the temporal dynamic of the act of perception itself. The clearest example of this from the previous analysis is perhaps the strange pull that emanates from the final shot and allows the spectator's gaze to both sink into the image and be held in position in front of it. Tellenbach writes the following in relation to the experience of the mentally ill: "*In the depressive mode of lived space, movement becomes fundamentally alienated from itself.*"[169] Reflection is the explanation for this, as it makes movement fizzle out much like in Zeno's paradox of the tortoise and Achilles. It is for precisely this reason that an image of totality can no longer be attained during the perception of film. This self-alienation of movement forms the basis for the new relation between film and spectator. As an expression of this self-alienation, the *dissolving of spatial and temporal connections into textural becoming* is the melancholy mode's fourth and final characteristic.

4.3 Historical Outlook

Melancholy in New Hollywood

In reference to film, texture is always to be understood as an audiovisual principle, which, as we have seen, is expressed by Eisenstein's concept of the "music of landscape." Textural qualities already played a big role in the sound design of films of the American avant-garde – such as the use of the sound of the sea in Carolee Schneemann's FUSES (1967) or the industrial noises in Bruce Baillie's CASTRO STREET (1966), which seem to be taken up again at EASY RIDER's climax in the graveyard scene. In neither FUSES nor CASTRO STREET do these sounds perform the function of spatial localization; instead, their continuity creates a sort of spatiotemporal shroud in the face of the constant, visual discontinuity of FUSES, in particular. By comparison, the relationship between sound and image is inverted in the films of Jack Smith or Kenneth Anger: here, the music (or, in the case of Anger, motorbike noise) structures the sprawling visuals in rhythmic fashion (in the work of Jack Smith, in particular, it is the textural qualities of music that come to the fore: rustling, distortion, etc.).

---

168 Hubertus Tellenbach: Zum Verständnis von Bewegungsweisen Melancholischer. In: Der Nervenarzt, Vol. 28, No. 1 (1957), pp. 16–17, here p. 17.
169 Tellenbach: Zum Verständnis von Bewegungsweisen Melancholischer, p. 17.

If one understands texture as an audiovisual principle – as a combination of image and sound, which cannot automatically be utilized by the narrative economy – and applies this principle to the cinema of New Hollywood,[170] a broad field of different manifestations emerge. First and foremost, texture is obviously relevant for the road movie in general, especially in the form of engine noise. The sound of the motor does not just provide a jolt of initial energy in films like EASY RIDER, TWO-LANE BLACKTOP (Monte Hellman 1971), VANISHING POINT (Richard C. Sarafian 1971), THE SUGARLAND EXPRESS (Steven Spielberg 1974), or THUNDERBOLT AND LIGHTFOOT (Michael Cimino 1974); it also has a continuous, dynamic effect on the image, preventing the spectator from focusing their attention. This function of noise can also be attested to in scenes from other representatives of the melancholy mode in New Hollywood, such as THE WILD BUNCH, JUNIOR BONNER (Sam Peckinpah 1972), or THE DEER HUNTER (Michael Cimino 1978).

The principle of texture also asserts itself beyond the realm of noise, as in the depiction of landscape in the films of Terrence Malick – BADLANDS (1973) and DAYS OF HEAVEN (1978) – or the lighting and color design of several Woody Allen films – INTERIORS (1978) and MANHATTAN (1979). An emphasis on dirt, rain, and changing light is also typical for the depiction of landscape in many late-period Westerns like JEREMIAH JOHNSON (Sydney Pollack 1972), BAD COMPANY (Robert Benton 1972) or THE CULPEPPER CATTLE CO. (Dick Richards 1972). In JEREMIAH JOHNSON, for example, the assimilation of human figures into the landscape until they can hardly be distinguished from it forms a recurring theme. A particularly impressive example of this tendency is the final sequence of Robert Altman's MCCABE & MRS. MILLER, which gives the impression of a return to the end of TIREZ SUR LE PIANISTE (François Truffaut, France 1960) viewed through the prism of DOG STAR MAN (Stan Brakhage, 1962–1964).[171]

An interplay between interior and exterior textures, between fire and water, or rather snow, reaches its zenith in this final sequence. The snow, superimposed onto the image, falls with trance-like regularity; it soon appears as if the image itself is dissolving into patches of light, finally slipping away from the spectator.

---

170 See Michel Chion: Quiet Revolution... and Rigid Stagnation. In: October, Vol. 58 (1991), pp. 69–80, here p. 69.

171 "MCCABE AND MRS. MILLER [...] may be thought of as a film about snow, documented in a range of phases which filter the action, as the thaw-fed river mediates the image of a cowboy hovering eerily beneath its surface; one of the chief characters is a man frozen into an image, a 'rep' that precedes and outlives him, just as his contours are swept smooth in the final snowstorm; and its plot concerns his struggle for control with that matriarchy which usually prevails in Altman's films, and which here offers shelter from the frozen snowscape." MacLean: The Big-Bang Hypothesis, p. 2.

The emotional core of the scene is reached at the end, which draws parallels between McCabe (another protagonist who dies sitting down) outside, freezing and sinking into the snow, and the isolated Mrs. Miller inside, high on opium, followed by a cut to a detail shot of her eye (figs. 18–19). The desperate attempt to stop the progress of history is thus directly confronted with the infinitely distanced perspective of someone who has known the outcome of such efforts all along – a perspective that uses past tense to address what will happen in the future and which is already expressed by the Leonard Cohen song that plays over the title sequence at the beginning of the film: "It's true that all the men you knew were dealers / Who said they were through with dealing every time you gave them shelter." The final shot of the film shows a small opium jar in Mrs. Miller's hand, which turns into a revolving globe.[172]

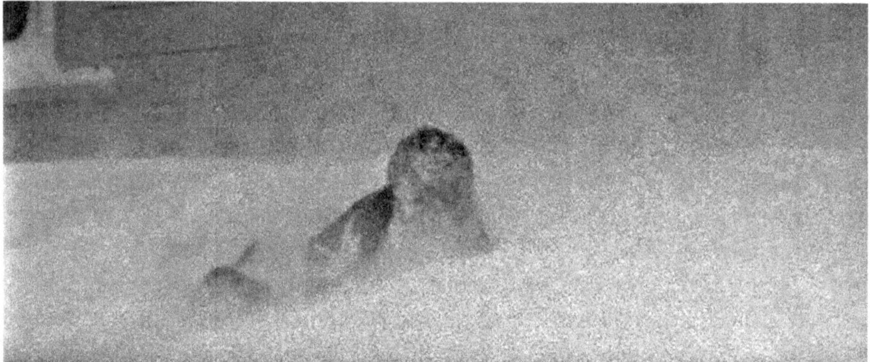

Figs. 18–19: MCCABE & MRS. MILLER: Becoming-texture and the depths of reflection.

---

172 For a thorough analysis of this sequence, see Hauke Lehmann: Becoming-Texture. New Hollywood Melancholy in MCCABE & MRS. MILLER. In: mediaesthetics, No. 1 (2016). doi: http://dx.doi.org/10.17169/mae.2016.43.

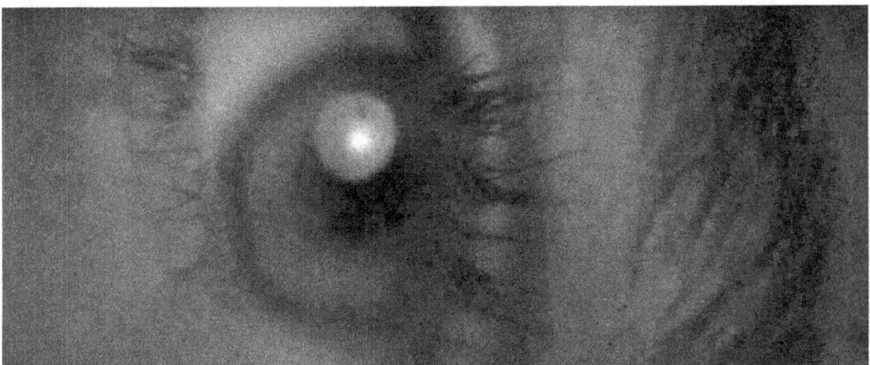

Fig. 19

Numerous examples of the next criterion, namely the atomization of time, can also be found in the cinema of New Hollywood; from a psychologically nuanced melodrama like A SAFE PLACE (Henry Jaglom 1971), with its fragmentary shots and endless repetitions, to a historical drama like BARRY LYNDON (Stanley Kubrick 1975), which captures its characters in painterly compositions, all the way to a quasi-gangster film like THE KILLING OF A CHINESE BOOKIE (John Cassavetes 1976/1978). Other examples might include the hippies stranded at the end of the 1960s in ALICE'S RESTAURANT (Arthur Penn 1969), the boxers that lack any prospects in FAT CITY (John Huston 1972), or a film like THE GREAT GATSBY (Jack Clayton 1974), where sheer heat condemns the characters to inaction. DUSTY AND SWEETS MCGEE (Floyd Mutrux 1971), a semi-documentary about the Los Angeles drug scene, extends this lounging around and state of inaction to the length of an entire film. The film constantly retains a slight, almost dazed distance to the events its shows, composed of fictional scenes acted out or re-enacted by 'real' heroin addicts; textures come to the fore here, mainly in extreme close ups or detail shots: the skin's penetration by the needle, bed sheets, sweat on faces. THE KILLING OF A CHINESE BOOKIE provides another good example of this principle. Philip Lopate writes that, "Cosmo's strip club, the Crazy Horse West, functions as a viscous flypaper to which the film keeps attaching itself, where time dawdles and dilates in a constant night."[173] Lopate mainly links this accumulation of dead time to the acting style, manifested in this film in a manner representative for Cassavetes' entire oeuvre: "In Cassavetes' cinema, these delays, these eruptions of the messy, frustrating, time-consuming and inconvenient

---

173 Philip Lopate: The Raw and the Cooked. In: Booklet for the DVD Release of John Cassavetes: Five Films, The Criterion Collection 2004, pp. 35–37, here p. 35.

ways that everyone, bit player to star, asserts his or her right to be taken seriously, are not impediments to the plot, but are the plot."[174] And at the film's climax, the actual killing of a Chinese bookmaker, Thierry Jousse recognizes a shift from suspense to suspension[175] – as if Achilles had suddenly stopped in his tracks while overtaking the tortoise.

Reflection now burrows into this dead, atomized time. Here too, a broad range of films present themselves: from PUZZLE OF A DOWNFALL CHILD (Jerry Schatzberg 1970) to FIDDLER ON THE ROOF (Norman Jewison 1971), CARNAL KNOWLEDGE (Mike Nichols 1971), THE KING OF MARVIN GARDENS (Bob Rafelson 1972) and CHINATOWN (Roman Polanski 1974), leading to HEAVEN'S GATE (Michael Cimino 1980) and including melodramas, musicals, neo-noirs, and westerns. Chronicles of individual fates, such as those foregrounded in films by Schatzberg, Rafelson, and Nichols, are constantly intertwined with overarching historical contexts, as articulated especially in FIDDLER ON THE ROOF and HEAVEN'S GATE. The significance of texture is to be emphasized in Jewison's film, in particular, which brings the musical into surprisingly close proximity with a late-period Western like HEAVEN'S GATE.

If we now, as discussed above, grasp melancholy reflection as a specific visual form, we also find numerous examples, whether the slideshow at the end of CARNAL KNOWLEDGE, the film sets in THE DAY OF THE LOCUST and THE LAST TYCOON, the photo shoots in PUZZLE OF A DOWNFALL CHILD or, as a particularly moving example, the home movie at the end of THE KING OF MARVIN GARDENS.

GREY GARDENS, a documentary by Albert und David Maysles from 1975, presents a veritable surfeit of dead time: a film that could be described as extending Anger's PUCE MOMENT to feature-length. The distinction being that here the fleeting film-star fantasy is embedded in the wreckage of reality, giving it the character of the absurd. The dilapidated house of the Bouvier Beales, the only location, is represented as the past made flesh – providing the basis for the rumination of the two protagonists, mother and daughter (the latter in particular), on all the promises that never amounted to anything, all the bygone relationships, and all the mistakes of the past, which can no longer be redeemed. While the house itself functions as a sort of rotting still life,[176] photos and other pictures, newspaper cuttings, and paintings are the focal point of reflection: both as material witnesses of an inaccessible past and as allegorical signs of the current

---

174 Lopate: The Raw and the Cooked, p. 37.
175 Thierry Jousse: John Cassavetes, quoted by Ivone Margulies: John Cassavetes. Amateur Director. In: Jon Lewis (ed.): The New American Cinema, Durham/London 1998, pp. 275 – 306, here p. 302.
176 Many thanks to Sarah Greifenstein for pointing this out.

contradictory state of affairs. The film's lengthy shots of clutter and faces activate an attempt by the spectator to locate the central core of the image, from where this present might be grasped. What Deleuze wrote about the films of Antonioni also applies here:

> If we are sick with Eros, Antonioni said, it is because Eros is himself sick; and he is sick not just because he is old and worn out in his content, but because he is caught in the pure form of a time which is torn between an already determined past and a dead-end future. For Antonioni, there is no other sickness than the chronic. Chronic is sickness itself. This is why chronosigns are inseparable from lectosigns, which force us to read so many symptoms in the image, that is, to treat the optical and sound image like something that is also readable.[177]

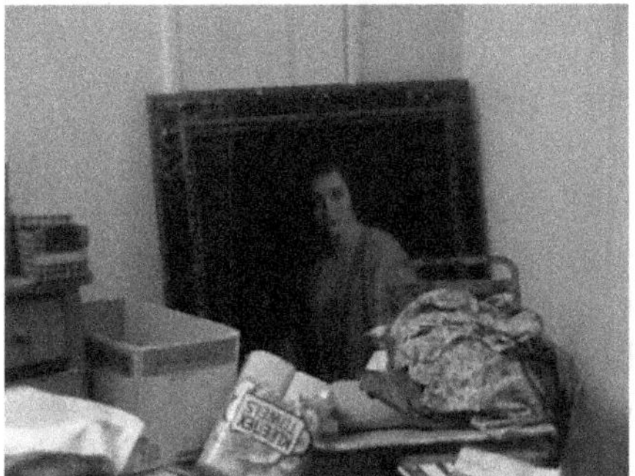

Fig. 20: GREY GARDENS: Faces and clutter.

New layers of discrepancy continually reveal themselves to the 'reading' spectator, like the portrait of Edith hidden behind a pile of trash (fig. 20): between "here" and an unreachable "there," but, above all, between a "now" and a foreclosed "back then" and equally unreachable "one day." The film thus ends with an image of Edie dancing, trapped between the poles of the banister (fig. 21).

---

177 Deleuze: Cinema 2, p. 23.

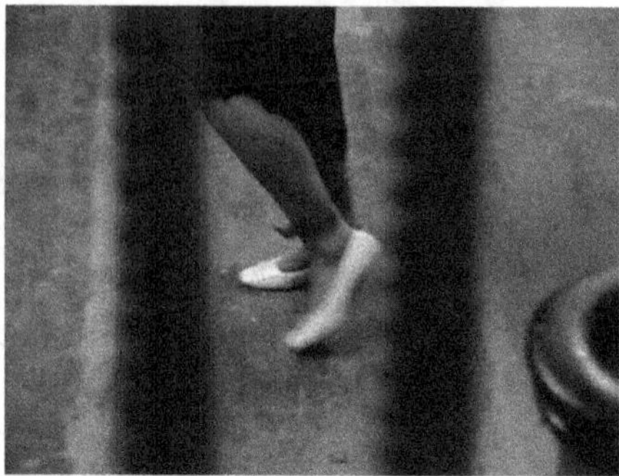

Fig. 21: GREY GARDENS: one leg standing, one leg free.

The Spectrum of Moods and the Search for Balance

It is this crystallization of contradiction that characterizes the affect poetics of melancholy. Examples of melancholy ambivalence can be found in droves in the cinema of New Hollywood, particularly in the relationship between the spectator and the characters. We could start with Benjamin Braddock from THE GRADUATE, distinctly lacking in motivation, followed by two similarly designed protagonists in GOODBYE, COLUMBUS (Larry Peerce 1969) and THE HEARTBREAK KID (Elaine May 1972), who unflinchingly reveal the earlier character's contradictory motives and thus truly put the spectator's loyalties to the test. The same extends to encompass the notoriously ambivalent bandits in THE WILD BUNCH, the suicidal protagonists of THE HOSPITAL (Arthur Hiller 1971), the characters of THE GODFATHER (Francis Ford Coppola 1972) and MEAN STREETS (Martin Scorsese 1973), who fall ever deeper into irresolvable conflicts, and the characters in MIKEY AND NICKY (Elaine May 1976), KILLER OF SHEEP (Charles Burnett 1977), and COMING HOME (Hal Ashby 1978), who continually betray and disappoint one another. The degree of ambivalence varies here, from mild to strong. In the same way one can attest to a broad spectrum of moods for the films of New Hollywood as a whole – compare the dry, flat intonation of the voiceovers in BADLANDS and DAYS OF HEAVEN to the emotional ardor of FIDDLER ON THE ROOF.

One possible way of systematically describing these differences emerges from the fact that nearly all of the films listed here strive for a state of balance, as it pertains to the dynamics of dramatic structure (the fiddler on the roof, for example, operates precisely as a metaphor for this). In this sense, different moods can be grasped in terms of a pendulum swinging with varied intensity, which nonetheless remains fixed to the same focal point. This desire for balance is often expressed most clearly towards the end of the films. The shot of Benjamin Braddock and Elaine Robinson, at the end of THE GRADUATE, lasts just long enough for doubt to creep in about the film's supposed happy ending. For two whole minutes, the final shot of ALICE'S RESTAURANT balances the relationship between camera and character through a backwards tracking shot and the use of zoom, only to end at the decisive moment with a hard cut. This sometimes subtle, sometimes brutal cut at the "right" moment, as opposed to a slow fade out, is used to maintain balance in a whole series of films; GREY GARDENS, THE GODFATHER and BADLANDS offer some prominent examples. If above we described the dynamics of texture as a permanent oscillation, then the cut at the "right" moment is an attempt to translate this instability into a temporal experience: a prompt for the spectator to maintain their own equilibrium, as if someone were to suddenly let go of you on a balance beam. A similar effect is created by a technique advanced almost to a cliché over the course of the 1970s – the final freeze-frame, found in such different films as WANDA (Barbara Loden 1970), THE DEER HUNTER, THE MACK (Michael Campus 1973), TWO-LANE BLACK-TOP, JEREMIAH JOHNSON, and BRING ME THE HEAD OF ALFREDO GARCIA (Sam Peckinpah 1974).

It is no coincidence that when the characters of the cinema of melancholia die, they tend to die sitting rather than lying down, as can be seen in ELECTRA GLIDE IN BLUE, MCCABE & MRS. MILLER, THUNDERBOLT AND LIGHTFOOT or THE NICKEL RIDE (Robert Mulligan 1974). The melancholy mood is characterized by the maintenance of tension: when balance is reached, stability has not been attained but, rather, a precarious state lasting only a certain duration. The length of time determined by the staging is closely linked to the emotional intensity of such codas. In this way, the melancholy mode is to be understood not least as a function of dramatic structure that "sneaks its way" into films operating according to other modalities – one thinks here of a concert film such as WOODSTOCK (Michael Wadleigh 1970), which ends on exactly such a note, and only finds a complement in an actual melancholy concert film at the end of the 1970s, namely THE LAST WALTZ (Martin Scorsese 1978). Other films with melancholy codas include STRAW DOGS, THE MACK, and DOG DAY AFTERNOON (Sidney Lumet 1975).

In BEING THERE (Hal Ashby 1979), on the other hand, the melancholy mode's attempt to maintain balance is shown in its purest form: the carefully contained, highly nuanced acting by Peter Sellers, the reserved camerawork, and the sparing use of music all work together to transform the energy of the other characters; the result is a very mild variant of melancholy that shows more obvious ruptures at certain moments, such as the end. The final scene and final shot, in particular, capture this precarious set-up in an image charged with irony: during the funeral of his rich mentor, Chance, the film's protagonist, wanders through the area around the grave – obviously impassive and isolated from his surroundings. He neither pays heed to the eulogy, which consists of quotes from the deceased, nor does he get wind of the plans forged by the pallbearers to make him the new presidential candidate, the highpoint of his absurd career. Piano music can be heard in addition to these two audio tracks, a piece by Satie. In the last shot of the film, Chance, who is now seemingly unstoppable, wanders out across the lake and actually walks on water (fig. 22). At the same time, the piano piece and the speech both come to their respective ends and one final quote can be heard accompanying the last notes: "Life is a state of mind." Following a brief moment of surprise, after which Chance accepts the strange situation, the shot ends abruptly and transitions into the credits, which appear over a backdrop of television disturbance.

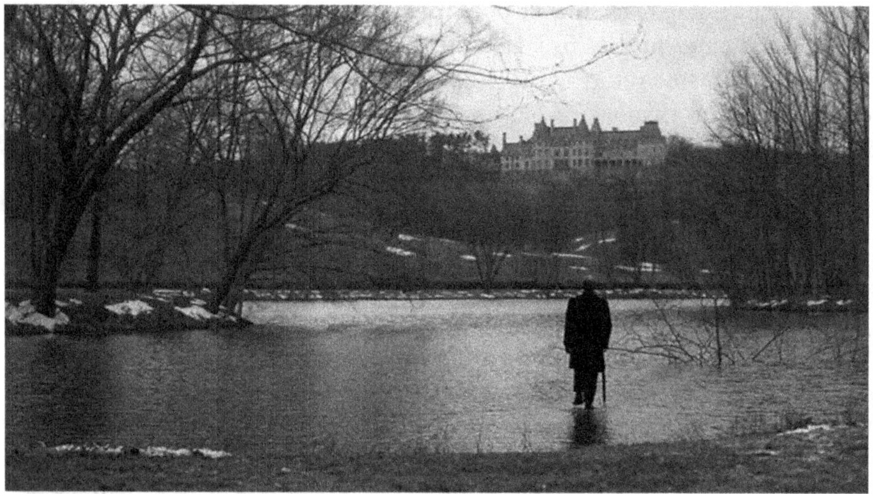

Fig. 22: BEING THERE: Life is a state of mind.

The melancholy nature of the scene is essentially derived from the way the various different levels it contains diverge, before culminating in a brief moment of harmony under the aegis of an overcast winter day: walking on water is both an ironic metaphor for the constant misunderstandings between Chance and his surroundings, as well as an expression of the emptiness of all those intrigues and vain hopes.

It seems notable that the melancholy mode comes to prominence towards the end of the 1970s. In this sense, films such as FOXES (Adrian Lyne 1979) or OUT OF THE BLUE (Dennis Hopper 1980) can be very much understood as providing a summary of New Hollywood and ushering in the 1980s, respectively. Some interesting film historical parentheses are created in the process, such as when FOXES ends at a graveyard that resembles the one from the beginning of NIGHT OF THE LIVING DEAD (George A. Romero 1968), or when Jim McBride directs BREATHLESS in 1983, a remake of the film, which, for many, represents the central inspiration for New Hollywood, namely À BOUT DE SOUFFLE (Jean-Luc Godard 1960). Aside from the quotes and allusions, more important is the creation of a sense of history, whose invocation of older films always includes an awareness of New Hollywood itself as a film historical period, manifested in an affective spectatorial experience – whether with parodic or more wistful inflection. One particularly appealing parenthesis (linked to Kubrick's 2001: A SPACE ODYSSEY) is also alluded to in BEING THERE, when Chance moves out of his old apartment to the funkily arranged sounds of *Also sprach Zarathustra*, before walking towards the Capitol in a deliberately symmetrical shot (reminiscent of the planetary constellation in Kubrick's film). In such parenthetical arrangements, the cinema of New Hollywood becomes the subject of its own cannibalism.

A film like DRIVE (Nicolas Winding Refn 2011), which for its part refers to SCORPIO RISING, proves that this cannibalistic dynamic is still effective and productive, on the one hand in the form of a resumption of New Hollywood films, such as BULLITT (Peter Yates 1968), TAXI DRIVER and THE DRIVER (Walter Hill 1978), and on the other hand through the lens of the very 1980s that followed New Hollywood cinema – with films like THIEF (Michael Mann 1981) and TO LIVE AND DIE IN L.A. (William Friedkin 1985). Another example are the films by Harmony Korine, which, from GUMMO (1997) through JULIEN DONKEY-BOY (1999), MISTER LONELY (2007) and TRASH HUMPERS (2009) to SPRING BREAKERS (2012), are composed of fragments, characters and pop songs, the waste products of Hollywood machinery. From these set pieces they build new devices for creating balance states – be it cycling in GUMMO, the flying nuns in MISTER LONELY, or loitering in parking lots in TRASH HUMPERS. Balance here has nothing of stability; rather it resembles a dance of fabulation in the Deleuzian sense, which, not unlike Edie in GREY GARDENS, carefully avoids any narratively concretizing fixation (SPRING BREAKERS deals in detail with this conflict with concretion).

From the point of view of the present study, it seems entirely clear that 1980 was not simply the beginning of a revision or denial of New Hollywood. The model of film-historical cannibalism contradicts such notions by the fact that the films that are located in film history are granted a role in the writing of this very history. Thus film history itself becomes a movement that progresses less linearly than it burrows into difference – accepting all the dangers and possibilities hidden in the abysses of this difference.

5 A History of Feeling

5.1 The Interplay of the Affective Modes and the Generation of New Forms

Classifying the Affective Modes

Having dealt with the individual modes at length in the previous chapters, the time has now come to evaluate their systematic significance for the cinema of New Hollywood as a whole. This evaluation is also intended to serve as a conclusion and summary of the present work. While the relationship between the modes has been addressed at different points, it is useful to start by schematically comparing them, to clarify their relationships in more systematic fashion.

Table 1: The affective modes of New Hollywood.

	Suspense	Paranoia	Melancholy
Paradigm	Hitchcock	JFK/the Zapruder film	Genre/ the avant-garde
Tense	Future perfect	Aeon	Perfect
Temporal Relationship to the Event	No longer – not yet: deferral	too early – too late: to predate/repetition	no longer – still: empty possibility
Dramatic Structure	Inversion	Cycle	Chronicle
Spatial Relationship	Attention	Mediality	Contemplation
Gestural Process	Focusing	Parallax	Petrification
Affective Relationship	Balance	(Lack of) agency	Mood

The very question of this relationship alludes already to what has been repeatedly emphasized over the present work: that these modes are by no means individual pigeonholes, according to which one can classify films. Instead, they become apparent, in each case, over the course of a film's concrete perception; which, further, means that they are combined, interfere with, or form transitions between one another. This dynamic combination of affective modes is a key prerequisite for what I have referred to as a *history of feeling* or *affective history* because it opens up possibilities for expressive forms to change and new ones to be formed. What interests me here, first and foremost, are the systemic conditions for such combinations as are listed in the table above.

https://doi.org/10.1515/9783110580761-006

The element of the table most in need of explanation is the parameters for distinguishing between modes. Several of these parameters have been established with theoretical rigor, while others are to be understood more as ciphers. This is the case for the first category, paradigms, which represents an attempt to identify a genealogical lineage for each mode, a sort of history of visual forms. It should be emphasized that the link to each of these paradigms is formed differently in each mode, as mentioned at the beginning of the chapter on suspense; suspense, for example, opens up a conceptual space for dialogue between different films. The focus here is less on the recognition of references to other images but, rather, on reengaging with specific visual forms, interrogated with respect to their stability or instability. The paranoid style, on the other hand, forges references to other images and their medial memory to obliterate the present in the film image. In this respect, the reenactment of certain poses and configurations within the image-space produces an affect-poetic sense, based on the interplay between the spectator's sense of power and powerlessness. Finally, the melancholy mode assembles a whole world of images within in the depths of the space of reflection, opened up within the film image. Surveying this space in all its contradictory nature motivates the contemplative state into which the spectator sinks through the film image.

The second parameter, temporal form or tense, has been explored in depth in the respective chapters and requires no comprehensive explanation here. It should merely be noted that each tense contains contradiction, to be developed in the next category: the temporal relationship. At the level of these respective temporal relationships, we can formulate an initial answer to the question of how the different modes are connected or how one moves from one mode to another. It is evident, for example, that suspense and paranoia deal with very similar temporal relationships and that only the standpoint changes from which they are experienced: in suspense, we find ourselves *in the very midst* of the paradoxical interweaving of past and future, whereas from the standpoint of paranoia, we are simultaneously *before* and *after*, but never *in* the "actual" moment. The feeling of being thrown into contradiction is shared by suspense and melancholy; the latter lacks any sort of alignment with the future since, within it, the present becomes a space filled with the past. The stagnation toward which it moves leads us back to paranoia once again – it is thus no coincidence that melancholy contemplation is not so very far from the cycle of paranoia. In paranoia, the empty possibility through which melancholy, in its suffering, relates to the past becomes the subject of endless, yet cold and distanced repetition.

The dramatic structure of the paranoid style is, accordingly, cyclical: THE PARALLAX VIEW comes to a close with a meeting of the same commission that started the film, THE CONVERSATION replaces the improvisation of the opening sequence with that of the ending, GIMME SHELTER begins and ends in the Maysles brothers' editing room. If, in the melancholy mode, there is always previous knowledge of the end, the path that leads there still must be endured first – the permanent catastrophe recorded in the chronicle – a path which paranoia has always already taken. For suspense on the other hand, the end offers no certainty other than the fact that nothing is certain – an attitude which requires no great mental leap to see how it can tip into the relativism of paranoia, exchanging one perspective for any other infinitely. This step from suspense to paranoia can be observed, for example, in De Palma's BLOW OUT, when the film shifts from the mode of the slasher horror to that of the conspiracy theory (to finally return to the subject of horror once again).

The next parameter, the spatial relationship, also permits movements between the individual modes. Here it can be seen that paranoia does not necessarily represent the end point; hence, the movement of attention inherent to suspense integrates and sets in motion all the visual worlds which spread out like a screen over paranoid consciousness. On the other hand, melancholy singles out an individual image and becomes engrossed in it, while paranoia strives to exchange it for the next image, the next surface. Focusing, parallax, and petrification are the gestural processes that correspond to the respective relationship in each case. They do not necessarily merge but optional connections are formed between them: the focusing of suspense can thus end in melancholy petrification, without the visual order crashing down ("shifting suspense into suspension"[1]).

The final and most important parameter, the affective reference in the strict sense, enables the complex relationships between the modes to adopt new form once again. In suspense, as previously discussed, this connection is created via the manipulation of balance, whereby balance refers to both spatial configuration and temporal composition, namely as the temporal form of expressive movement. Suspense therefore constantly poses the question whether the organization of sense itself is reliable or not – whether the rules of the world still apply, or if there might be a bomb under the table. The paranoid mode can likewise be determined as a reflexive relationship to a similar kind of expressive movement, the only difference being that, here, it is not a question of stability but, rather, that a virtual, expressive movement, an alternative description of reality, begins to compete with the current movement. Both the total power and the powerlessness of the paranoid consciousness is manifested in this alternative perspective; points of view are infinite, but none of them sufficient – the re-

---

1 Ivone Margulies: John Cassavetes, p. 302.

sult is agency panic, which can result in either a complete blockade or a paranoid cinema of action, which seeks to compensate through a sort of hyperactivity. The affective reference of the melancholic mode has been discussed the most thoroughly in theoretical terms. Any connection to plot is absent in this case; the reflexive relationship to expressive moment is represented not as pointed subversion but as infinite differentiation, which culminates in the characteristic of melancholy ambivalence – an entirely unique state of equilibrium.

It is far from my intention to use this table to explain the whole of New Hollywood cinema (as in, all the films in their entirety); that would be neither possible nor desirable. What the analysis of the affective modes does yield, however, is an explanation for the specific historical dynamic of American cinema of the late 1960s and the 1970s, in terms of how it grapples with the classical genre system – in a nutshell, the basis for an affective history. The concept of affective modes introduces a fundamentally critical element to film historiography: while it claims no universal validity regarding the essence of a given period, it holds the potential to trace the course of different aesthetic genealogies, which unfold in a by no means linear fashion. The model of affective modes not only enables a more precise description of the films in question, it further allows them to be situated poetically within the context of New Hollywood. In this way, the films go from singular events to elements of affect-poetic genealogies – of genealogies that sidestep the distinction between art house and commercial cinema and all the normative value judgements that go along with it. The story of the downfall of New Hollywood is replaced with a historiography in which the variations and transformations in affective modes are described far more precisely because they are viewed in their own right.

One last step is still missing before this goal can be reached: relating affective modes to the composition of new forms of expression characteristic of New Hollywood. I will restrict myself here to three of the most important: the modern horror film, the road movie, and the neo-noir. The implications of this are, however, related to the entire New Hollywood cinema – not least because these forms, too, are not to be understood as rigid containers but, rather, as complex modalities that circumvent old generic delineations and appear in hugely diverse contexts.[2]

---

2 Robin Wood indicated this principle for the horror film, see Wood: Hollywood from Vietnam to Reagan, p. 45, and p. 76.

Cannibalism: The End of the World in the Horror Film

Using cannibalism as a determinative figure of thought for the melancholy mode does not just enable the cinema of New Hollywood to be described in relation to its own history, but also in relationship to the cultural history of the same period – the opening of the corresponding chapter contains an overview of its melancholy state in the 1970s. The most prominent examples of the application of this figure of thought can obviously be found in the modern horror film, such as NIGHT OF THE LIVING DEAD, THE TEXAS CHAIN SAW MASSACRE, THE HILLS HAVE EYES (Wes Craven 1977), and DAWN OF THE DEAD (George A. Romero 1978). Craven's film, for example, quotes Goya's famous painting *Saturn Devouring His Son* (around 1821–1823) in one of its shots and the allegorical content of the cannibalism theme in Romero's films, most obviously in DAWN OF THE DEAD, has been the subject of extensive film and cultural historical investigation.[3] The end of the world has always been a privileged subject of melancholy imagination and the 1970s are no exception.[4] New Hollywood picks up on this preoccupation and views it through the prism of the Vietnam War, dwindling economic resources, and the failure of the utopian projects of the 1960s, albeit with a clear inversion: the mode of imagination is horror.

The first (proper) dialogue in THE TEXAS CHAIN SAW MASSACRE, for example, is about astrology. Pam, an obvious cliché of a new age hippie, quotes Llewellyn George's *A to Z Horoscope Maker and Delineator* during their journey in the minibus: "Okay, listen: 'The condition of retrogradation is contrary or inharmonious to the regular direction of actual movement in the Zodiac, and is, in that respect, evil. Hence, when malefic planets are in retrograde' – and Saturn's malefic, okay? – 'their maleficence is increased.'" Jerry, somewhat annoyed, makes fun of her: "Have you been doing those Reader's Digest Word Power columns again?" Pam insists: "Jerry, it just means Saturn's a bad influence. It's just particularly bad influence now, because it's in retrograde." Jerry gives up und turns in disbelief to Kirk, Pam's boyfriend: "Hey man, you believe all that stuff your old lady is hawking me?"

---

3 See Wood: Hollywood from Vietnam to Reagan, pp. 63–119; Linnie Blake: Another One for the Fire. George A. Romero's American Theology of the Flesh. In: Mendik (ed.): Shocking Cinema of the Seventies, pp. 151–165, here p. 160. On the melancholy ambivalence of NIGHT OF THE LIVING DEAD, THE LAST HOUSE ON THE LEFT and THE TEXAS CHAIN SAW MASSACRE see Matt Becker: A Point of Little Hope.

4 See Lois Parkinson Zamora (ed.): The Apocalyptic Vision in America. Interdisciplinary Essays on Myth and Culture, Ann Arbor 1982.

It is more than just an amusing aside when none other than Saturn, the child-eating God of time (in his form as a fate-affecting heavenly body), appears at such a prominent moment in a film about cannibalism – an aside easy to overhear at the same time. The determinism of astrological ideas can, in fact, be interpreted as a model for the dramatic structure of not just this horror film but the genre in general, in which the victims die one after another with cruel regularity. Christopher Sharrett has pointed out that the macrocosmic implications of the events are signaled from the very beginning in the pictures of planets, which also find their microcosmic echo in Sallie's wide-open eyes towards the end of the film.[5]

According to Sharrett, the film's model of history unites a primitive perspective with a modernist one:

> The 'primitive' aspect refers to the ritual atmosphere surrounding the film's horrors and the way characters interact in a situation of chaos; the 'modernist' aspect denies the primitive belief in a cyclical view of history and asserts instead an absolute dead end without the possibility of renewal or even resolution.[6]

The refusal to offer any resolution seems to me to be the decisive point, bringing Hooper's film into close proximity with the same line of melancholy heritage I mapped out in the corresponding chapter of the present book. This concept of time can be traced all the way up to the present day in films such as SOUTHLAND TALES (Richard Kelly, USA 2006), 4:44 LAST DAY ON EARTH (Abel Ferrara, USA 2011) and MELANCHOLIA (Lars von Trier, Denmark and others. 2011), all of which depict the end of the world in one form or another. When, for example, Rudolf Arnheim speaks in an essay about the lack of form in American *trompe l'oeil* painting and states that "the phenomenal chaos of accident from which man seeks refuge in art, has invaded art itself,"[7] he could just as easily be talking about THE TEXAS CHAIN SAW MASSACRE. (Furthermore, it is this tendency towards a lack of form which Arnheim criticizes in Kracauer's theoretical conception.[8]) The dissolution of form goes so far in this film that even physical violence is kept to a minimum:

---

5 See Christopher Sharrett: The Idea of Apocalypse in THE TEXAS CHAINSAW [sic] MASSACRE. In: Barry Keith Grant (ed.): Planks of Reason. Essays on the Horror Film, Metuchen/London 1984, pp. 255–276, here p. 261.

6 Sharrett: The Idea of Apocalypse in THE TEXAS CHAINSAW MASSACRE, p. 262.

7 Arnheim: Accident and the Necessity of Art, p. 24.

8 See Arnheim: Melancholy Unshaped, in particular p. 294. This once again reveals Kracauer's poetological proximity to the cinema of New Hollywood. On the differences with regard to genre cinema, see the discussion in the chapter on melancholy.

> Hooper focuses not so much on what the cannibals do to Sally (which is relatively little) as on the extremes of her terror and the way the cannibals project their hate and collective violence upon her. Sally is by turns honored and vilified, as in primitive ritual, to a point where she is literally driven insane. [...] The real ritual dimension may be Hooper's refusal to accede to the most important conventions of the genre and of drama itself; the catharsis meant to be reached by the work is denied, destroying a common code shared by the audience. Just as the blood Sally *might* shed has no role in 'replenishing' Hooper's horrific wasteland, the vacuousness of the horror film's language must be recognized.[9]

At a superordinate level, the aim of the ritual is the destruction of ritual, the denial of a cathartic effect (which recalls Anger's SCORPIO RISING and anticipates the end of MELANCHOLIA). We are already well-acquainted with this self-destruction mechanism under the watchword of cannibalism. Sharrett ultimately relates this mechanism to the image of society depicted in the film, which corresponds to the descriptions of American sociality at the beginning of the 1970s:

> I have spoken of the cannibalism of the film (which is never actually seen, pointing to the metaphoric value Hooper gives to the idea) as representative of a process of inverting all values, myths and symbols of culture. The cannibals' meal, rather than a communion, suggests the utter fragmentation and atomization of society.[10]

What is notable is that even in a horror film like this one, cannibalism primarily operates as a metaphor. This social and cultural historical reference contained within the film can be honed further by drawing on the concept of mood. The intertwining of subject and object performed in the process of perception in mood gives cultural and historical specificity to this reference. Kerstin Thomas thus writes as follows on the function of mood in the work of French post-impressionist Georges Seurat:

> The strength of mood-based art seems to me [...] to lie in particular in the specificity of its depiction of phenomenal qualities, which is closely linked to the historical discursive space. Mood as a modern artistic approach aims at the subjective by allowing the unified tinge of what is being depicted to be transferred to the state of heightened perception within this mood: the experience that particular events, meanings and thoughts, memories and feelings can be condensed into a unified tone.[11]

In this way, the concept of mood can be emphatically employed as a means of countering the ahistorical positing of basic emotions, whereby films merely

---

9 Sharrett: The Idea of Apocalypse in THE TEXAS CHAINSAW MASSACRE, p. 266.
10 Sharrett: The Idea of Apocalypse in THE TEXAS CHAINSAW MASSACRE, p. 270.
11 Thomas: Bildstimmung als Bedeutung in der Malerei des 19. Jahrhunderts, p. 218.

form stimulus material for the generation of such emotions, to portray the cognitivist position in somewhat exaggerated fashion. Thomas expands upon this idea as follows:

> Instead of the formulaic reproduction of the values sad, happy, and indifferent [...], far more differentiated moods are expressed in Seurat's work, which emerge from the special coloring applied to the individual subject. While in Carus's oeuvre, motifs and mood-related content are still seen as anthropologically fixed quantities – a view that is taken over by the aesthetics of empathy [Einfühlung] – it becomes clear in Seurat's work that the quality of the mood and content of the expression are determined in precise historical terms.[12]

What should be added here is that the quality of mood and the content of expression are not only determined in precise historical terms but the condition that makes them possible in the first place is justified within the film form. With regard to THE TEXAS CHAIN SAW MASSACRE, this can be seen in the film image itself – in particular in the combination of the materiality of the setting (dirt, sweat, heat, etc.) with the specific cinematic techniques of lighting, color, and framing, which produce these very characteristic textural qualities of decay and depravity. Further, the soundtrack is especially important in that it aims to create audiovisual textures, as Frank Hentschel remarks in his analysis of the film:

> What can be very clearly distinguished [from another group of sounds] are the flatter, noisier, more atmospheric ones, that are partially composed of higher frequencies and partially appear in the form of dronings and rumblings. They create an acoustic background layer that is mainly quiet, but always perceptible, which is essential for the mood of the film. Echo and vibration effects, which also set the metallic sounds in motion from time to time, are applied to these flatter sounds in particular, which begin to judder and thus amplify the disconcerting effect.[13]

He continues:

> The constant presence of noise prevents the audience from ever finding peace. Silence practically does not exist in THE TEXAS CHAIN SAW MASSACRE. Even nature is restless and uneasy. Already the sunrise [...] is accompanied by metallic sounds, becomes a disconcerting experience visually underlined by the black sky. The sounds wear you down; they announce the undefined presence of a threat approaching from all sides. Even the most trivial of scenes thus receive a veneer of the cold and the forbidding.[14]

---

12 Thomas: Bildstimmung als Bedeutung in der Malerei des 19. Jahrhunderts, p. 227.
13 Frank Hentschel: Töne der Angst. Die Musik im Horrorfilm. Berlin 2011, p. 67.
14 Hentschel: Töne der Angst, p. 68.

The decisive point here is that these noises are not just of any origin but, rather, generate a specific cultural and historical horizon for the events of the film, which accordingly correspond to the micro- and macro-cosmos:

> The total eschewal of conventional musical sounds plays a substantial role in conjuring up the atmosphere of the fundamentally perverse, dysfunctional, and morbid [...]. The extra-diegetic noises fall silent before the protagonists appear on screen for the first time to allow the reports of terror on the radio and the sound of passing trucks to continue. Normality is not just disturbed when a family of cannibals invade a healthy world at some point, as if to say that if they were removed it would be intact once again, but rather such a state never existed in the first place. The noises in THE TEXAS CHAIN SAW MASSACRE are the existential noises of Western culture.[15]

This negation of an assumed normality which might offset the dread precisely evokes Robin Wood's definition of the apocalyptic horror film.[16] The certainty of irredeemable disintegration is realized in the omnipresence of a world of depraved noise. Plot and film music "melt"[17] into one another completely in the sound of the titular chainsaw. The level of sound thus gains a reflexive dimension directly related to the dramatic structure of affect experienced by the spectator. This reflexive dimension is certainly not contemplative and can therefore hardly be related directly to a melancholy mood. It does, however, allow a fundamental dilemma of the melancholy style to play out – if at a different level of intensity, namely that of the grotesque. This dimension reenacts the sense of being stuck in the undergrowth with Sally (once again, a parallel to MELANCHOLIA, this time to the prologue), only to coalesce into pure motion in Leatherface's almost complete aimlessness, a motion that no longer leads anywhere.

Sudden shifts into the grotesque are very much inherent to the melancholy style; according to Friedrich Piel, the central characteristic of the grotesque is "dual determination,"[18] similar in nature to melancholy ambivalence. This dual determination results in a fundamental "instability,"[19] an unrelenting threat that things will fall apart. In terms of dramatic structure, it manifests in a hectic back-and-forth, a complete reversal from one moment to the next.[20] The movement annihilates itself in this upending – space and time are threatened with

---

15 Hentschel: Töne der Angst, pp. 68 – 69.
16 See Wood: Hollywood from Vietnam to Reagan, p. 170.
17 Hentschel: Töne der Angst, p. 70.
18 Friedrich Piel: Die Ornament-Grotteske in der italienischen Renaissance, Berlin 1962, p. 45.
19 Piel: Die Ornament-Grotteske in der italienischen Renaissance, p. 33.
20 Piel: Die Ornament-Grotteske in der italienischen Renaissance, p. 33.

disintegration (Piel talks here of "chronophagy," of time being consumed[21]). While melancholy movement digs itself into difference, the grotesque is suffused with the principle of inhibition, resulting from the contrast between its contradictory tendencies: "The 'movement of the grotesque' *is* in inhibition. In inhibition, neither present nor future is made manifest. In it, the past appears, dying."[22] All movement thus remains appearance and nothing more, quasi-movement. Precisely this idea of moving without ever getting anywhere connects the modern horror film to the road movie, structurally speaking, in what seems like a curious manner. We will soon see, however, that this connection is by no means a coincidence.

Suspended Suspense in the Road Movie

What the chainsaw is to the horror film, the engine sounds are to the road movie. Both organize the dramatic structure of affect on the basis of a specific attitude of movement, respectively, and in this regard, both tend towards self-reflexivity. As several remarks on the road movie have already been made in the chapter on melancholy, I would like to concentrate here on the systematic link between the road movie and horror film, as well as the question of the role played by the affective modes in this context.

The connection between the road movie and the horror film can be grasped most clearly by looking at the treatment of space or, to be more precise, the relationship between the road and the landscape.[23] At the outset, the relationship between the road movie and the road must be considered against the backdrop of the disappearance of the Western border, the frontier. EASY RIDER inverts the east-west movement of the settlers' treks and sends its protagonists on a trip from California to Alabama, while in BONNIE AND CLYDE, the gangster couple's movements as they attempt to flee and evade capture become increasingly directionless over the course of the film.

The disappearance of the Western frontier finds a clear echo in the "Limits to Growth," declared in 1972. America's previously endless plains were incorporated into a space made accessible and brought ever closer by the expansion of the road network. The frontier is thus replaced by the practically infinite reach of the road and thus transposed into the interior of a continually shrinking territory, the

---

21 Piel: Die Ornament-Grotteske in der italienischen Renaissance, p. 59.

22 Piel: Die Ornament-Grotteske in der italienischen Renaissance, p. 60.

23 See also Lehmann: Schrecken der Straße in relation to the following discussion.

imaginary space of possibility of a once "untouched" promised land now projected onto the optical vanishing point of the road. This vanishing point is, of course, movable, constantly subject to the shifts in the perspective that constitute it. Richard C. Sarafian's VANISHING POINT (1971) expresses this principle in the ambiguous nature of its title, an idea consistently implemented in the film's complex dramatic structure: vanishing point is meant both literally and figuratively, as both the point of something's disappearance and the disappearing point, itself. The road thus represents, at once, a means of making natural space accessible and the internalized margins of social space, providing both an opportunity to flee standardized social contexts while simultaneously cutting through the very idylls that were the original goal of this flight.

The ambivalence of the road thus fits seamlessly into the affective dynamics of the melancholy mode and could also be observed in the example of ELECTRA GLIDE IN BLUE. In this respect, the hippies' minibus in this film is a direct antecedent of the one that appears in THE TEXAS CHAIN SAW MASSACRE. And if the opening dialogue from the latter film demonstrates the utter commercialization of the countercultural lifestyle (to such an extent that it can already be found in Reader's Digest), then it also acts as a continuation of Guercio's film, in which the minibus is itself piled high with merchandise.

It is revealing to examine the dramatic function performed by the minibus in each of the films. In ELECTRA GLIDE IN BLUE, it functions as an inversion of the pick-up truck from EASY RIDER, with whom the protagonists have their fateful encounter at the end of the film. In THE TEXAS CHAIN SAW MASSACRE, the bus becomes stranded relatively early on in the white trash wilderness of Texas and then never moves again. Certain basic patterns relating to dramatic structure can be derived from this comparison; the determination of these respective patterns leads us back to the question of affective modes.

The road movie does not typically, as a matter of course, operate in such directionless fashion. Goals for movement do, indeed, exist and are traced out across such films, although they are often relativized to a greater or less extent over the course of the film. In reference to TWO-LANE BLACKTOP, Elsaesser thus writes:

> Taking to the road comes to stand for the very quality of contingency, and a film like TWO-LANE BLACKTOP is symptomatic in this respect: there is only the merest shadow of an intrigue, the action provocatively avoids the interpersonal conflicts potentially inherent both in the triangular relationship and in the challenge personified by the Warren Oates character,

and finally, the film toys with goals (the race to Washington) in an almost gratuitous, ostentatiously offhand way.[24]

TWO-LANE BLACKTOP is paradigmatic in this respect. The film introduces a "classically" oriented goal, yet loses sight of it after just a few minutes, in order to shift into a state that Elsaesser paraphrases by drawing on the concept of contingency, thus moving quickly from suspense to suspension. Another example is VANISHING POINT: here the purpose behind the protagonist's movements is undermined by a flashback structure, which makes his journey fizzle out in the middle of nowhere before culminating in his death at the end of the film. A third possibility plays out in BADLANDS (Terrence Malick 1973), where the couple's journey is purely a movement of flight and evasion that nearly inevitably comes to a standstill in the wasteland, as if a mathematical series were converging on its limit. WANDA (Barbara Loden 1970) offers an even more reserved variation on this principle, depicting a woman's constant search to find and evade stability, the drifting of a character who always moves behind the pace of her surroundings.

The shift from suspense to suspension as a dramatic principle is one of the mechanisms that enables the road movie to wander into seemingly foreign generic contexts; such films as THE GRADUATE, MIDNIGHT COWBOY (John Schlesinger 1969), STRAW DOGS, THE MACK, STRAIGHT TIME (Ulu Grosbard 1978), and DOG SOLDIERS/WHO'LL STOP THE RAIN (Karel Reisz 1978) all end like road movies, namely with the protagonists moving down the road. As Timothy Corrigan has also established, the progression of the journey and the progression of the film converge in the road movie until they are inseparable.[25] To the degree that driving is only aligned with a clear goal in the rarest of cases, the dramatic structure also tends towards a reflexive, self-referential state of pure motion – this is the precise meaning of the closing figures of these road movies. For this reason, most road movies are episodically constructed, without forming a strong causal relationship between any one episode and those preceding or following it. The state of contingency, however, does not completely merge into disinterested drifting but is, rather, revealed in this very juxtaposition of events to be susceptible to disturbance. The most obvious manifestation of this sort of disturbance is the accident.

---

24 Elsaesser: The Pathos of Failure, p. 281.

25 "If the thriller makes the camera a weapon and the melodrama makes it a family member, in the road movie the camera adopts the framed perspective of the vehicle itself. In this genre, the perspective of the camera comes closest of any genre to the mechanical unrolling of images that defines the movie camera." Corrigan: A Cinema without Walls, pp. 145–146.

While accidents in road movies can have fatal consequences, they can also merely mean the journey's interruption. Yet when a road trip is interrupted, that is precisely the moment when countless modern horror films begin or take the fatal turn that sets everything in motion – from PSYCHO to NIGHT OF THE LIVING DEAD, THE LAST HOUSE ON THE LEFT, THE TEXAS CHAIN SAW MASSACRE, THE HILLS HAVE EYES, THE CHANGELING (Peter Medak 1979), THE EVIL DEAD (Sam Raimi 1981), and THE HITCHER (Robert Harmon 1986), all the way to the remakes and variations of the 2000s: JEEPERS CREEPERS (Victor Salva 2001), JOY RIDE (John Dahl 2001), WRONG TURN (Rob Schmidt 2003), HOUSE OF 1000 CORPSES (Rob Zombie 2003), and VACANCY (Nimród Antal 2007). All these films can be seen as interrupted road movies.

As the road is left behind and the journey interrupted, a different dramatic logic begins in the horror film, wherein the episodic is replaced by the serial. The series of encounters becomes a series of acts of killing and torture, each inexorably following on the others. This difference can be illustrated by looking at a brief scene from THE TEXAS CHAIN SAW MASSACRE. In this scene, the young, prospective victims discover a fleet of cars behind the cannibals' house. The clear implication is that this is where all the vehicles of those already fallen victim to the cannibals have been collected. In this way, the film tips its hat to an almost obligatory motif of the road movie, namely the car wreck by the side of the road (an anecdotal appearance, a *memento mori*), and recreates it according to a serial logic. At this juncture, the combination of modes becomes even more complex, for the different units of the series in the horror film operate, in turn, within the suspense mode – in this sense, the spectator must constantly be prepared to be confronted with their own affect, as Bill Schaffer writes.[26] Unlike the slasher films of the 1980s, however, modeled on HALLOWEEN, the suspense in THE TEXAS CHAIN SAW MASSACRE ultimately peters out. The grand dinner scene does not treat the crumbling of the cinematic form as an event at a specific point in time (like the fall of the bucket in CARRIE) but, rather, as a state in its own right, which can primarily be attributed to the melancholy mode – the cool distance of the road movie gives way to the corporeal persistence of one's own abandonment and mortality. The horror film looks at the road from the position of the (automobile) graveyard.

When a film retains the suspense, the delicate balance between the two forms is maintained. The textbook example here is, of course, Spielberg's DUEL, located at the crossroads between the road movie and horror film. As such, the landscape in DUEL is not of particular interest; as one recognizes at

---

26 See Schaffer: Cutting the Flow.

the end of the film, it represents the road's exact inverse. When the road is left behind, it is in the form of an accident, the crash over the cliff: an irreversible movement that deforms into wrecks the car and truck that follow its trajectory. The plunge from the road is a plunge into the world of horror and thus coincides with the end of the film. For as long as it is still on the road, the truck itself is nothing other than the embodiment of this negative landscape, an undead, wandering wreck whose driver never becomes visible.

The suspense mode and its suspension within the road movie can thus be defined precisely as a precarious form, which reaches its melancholy balance via the creation of distance. Yet this rejection of engagement also means that the form is open to contingent, potentially catastrophic events. The windows onto the horror film are sometimes small and inconspicuous (the episode with the old woman and her granddaughter in TWO-LANE BLACKTOP) and sometimes transform the entire film, like in BRING ME THE HEAD OF ALFREDO GARCIA (Sam Peckinpah 1974), whose protagonist, after his figurative death, spends the second part of the film trying to erase its first half. In this film, the ambivalence of the landscape – somewhere between an idyll and a land of the dead – is particularly pronounced.

One permutation of the relationship between the road movie and the horror film is created when the landscape becomes an image in its entirety, like in WILD AT HEART (David Lynch 1990) or NATURAL BORN KILLERS (Oliver Stone 1994). The road movie and the horror film start to overlap in such cases, as is the case in KALIFORNIA (Dominic Sena 1993) and, with a degree of grotesque, amusing exaggeration, FREEWAY (Matthew Bright 1996). The other permutation consists of transposing the road movie *into* the horror film, like in DELIVERANCE (John Boorman 1972); here the car wreck appears at the end of the film and functions ironically as a welcome sign of civilization. Melancholy seems to have disappeared from this configuration, replaced entirely by paranoia. How paranoia and melancholy themselves work in tandem to create new forms of expression is now to be explored in the following section.

Paranoia and Melancholy in the Neo-Noir

The third major form in New Hollywood cinema, alongside the road movie and horror film, is the neo-noir. This term seems to have established itself in research literature,[27] even if its precise point of reference has yet to be clarified. In my opinion, it makes sense to use neo-noir to refer to a specific form that differs from noir for such New Hollywood films as THE LONG GOODBYE (Robert Altman 1973), CHINATOWN (Roman Polanski 1974), and NIGHT MOVES (Arthur Penn 1975), since their respective referencing of the films of the 1940s and 1950s takes place against the backdrop of the theoretical and/or film critical debate about the concept of film noir.[28]

Just like the horror film and road movie, it is hardly possible to delineate the neo-noir by way of the standard genre system (even if there is a notable tendency to retrospectively unite the disparate 'components' of the classical film noir into a set of family resemblances, in the notorious use of blinds, for example). Its influence can instead be found in the most diverse contexts – from psychological gangster films such as IN COLD BLOOD (Richard Brooks 1967) and THE HONEY-MOON KILLERS (Leonard Kastle 1970) to Blaxploitation movies like SHAFT (Gordon Parks 1971) and meta-Hollywood films like THE KILLING OF A CHINESE BOOK-IE, all the way to an erotic thriller like AMERICAN GIGOLO (Paul Schrader 1980). For this reason, I am more interested in those approaches that, instead of defining noir via genre, attempt to do so via a specific tone, a specific mode, and a particular *style*, much like André Bazin already did in relation to its French forerunners.[29] As James Naremore remarks, such attempts gain increasing relevance in view of the fact that poetologically, neo-noir films refer to a supposed essence, understood in popular discourse under the term noir – however problematic such a notion might be from a film historical perspective.[30] The question of how to define film noir is nearly as old as the term itself, although a growing consensus has formed in the meantime that casts fundamental doubt on whether it can actually be defined at all, even if one refrains from applying the supposedly more strict criteria of the concept of genre.[31] The problems begin when the concept of style is reduced to a series of visual motifs and compositional princi-

---

27 See Foster Hirsch: Detours and Lost Highways. A Map of Neo-Noir, New York 1999; Steve Neale: Genre and Hollywood, New York 2000, p. 165.

28 Two of the most influential essays in this respect have already been mentioned: Durgnat: Paint it Black, and Schrader: Notes on Film Noir.

29 See James Naremore: American Film Noir. The History of an Idea. In: Film Quarterly, Vol. 49, No. 2 (1995/1996), pp. 12–28, here p. 18.

30 See Naremore: More than Night. Film Noir in its Contexts, Berkeley/Los Angeles 1998, p. 167.

31 "As a single phenomenon, *noir*, in my view, never existed." Neale: Genre and Hollywood, p. 164. For a similarly radical perspective, see Marc Vernet: "As an object or corpus of films, *film noir* does not belong to the history of cinema; it belongs as a notion to the history of film criticism [...]." Marc Vernet: Film Noir on the Edge of Doom. In: Joan Copjec (ed.): Shades of Noir, London/New York 1993, pp. 1–31, here p. 26.

ples, as in the aftermath of an influential essay by Janey Place and Lowell Peterson.[32] Attempts at definition of this kind are clearly doomed to failure and have been rejected from several sides as, at once, too selective and too unspecific.[33]

By contrast, the concept of style developed over the course of the present study enables the actual, affect-poetic principles of these films to be taken into account, on the basis of which something like a repository of visual motifs could be constituted in the first place.[34] This makes it possible to find an answer to the question posed by Charles Scrugg: "The question is, what relationship does 'visual style' have to that 'harsh' worldview [...]?"[35] With this in mind, one quickly realizes that the criteria developed for the paranoid and melancholy modes, respectively, are very well suited to describing this corpus. What I would like to focus on is the depiction of relations, conflicts, and transitions between these modes.

Let us, for example, consider Arthur Penn's NIGHT MOVES. On one level, the film is about solving a crime, namely the murder of young runaway Delly and the conspiracy that goes along with it. Yet this detective plot unfolds in a panorama of private and societal contexts, pervaded by a feeling of significant disillusionment: the sense that the past represents a collection of false decisions, unable to be shaken off, weighs heavily on all the characters. In two key scenes, the intertwining of paranoia and melancholy is made evident in particularly striking fashion. The first of these takes place in a cinema: Delly has died on a film shoot and there is talk of an accident. The protagonist, private detective Harry Moseby, now watches the film footage shot shortly before the "accident." Initially, a configuration typical of the paranoid mode plays out: the detective tries to

---

32 See Lowell Peterson, Janey Place: Some Visual Motifs of Film Noir. In: Alain Silver, and James Ursini (eds.): Film Noir Reader, New York 1996, pp. 65–76.

33 "Place and Peterson base their analysis on a small sample of films, and several of their generalizations seem questionable – for instance, their claim that 'camera movements are used sparingly in most *noir* films.' All the stylistic features they describe can be found in pictures that have never been classified as noir. By the same token, relatively few can be found in a certifiable hard-boiled classic such as THE BIG SLEEP [...]." Naremore: More than Night, p. 167. For a summary of this discussion, see Neale: Genre and Hollywood, p. 160.

34 Note that this is not about film noir as such but, rather, its reincarnation as neo-noir. Only in reference to this reincarnation does a degree of agreement (in the sense of shared genealogical references) between the films emerge that justifies speaking about an expressive form in its own right.

35 Charles Scruggs: The Power of Blackness. Film Noir and Its Critics. In: American Literary History Vol. 16, No. 4 (2004), pp. 675–687, here p. 677. The second part of the question – "is film noir coherent enough to constitute a genre?"– which Scruggs (from a literary studies perspective) answers in astoundingly positive terms, I find on the other hand significantly less interesting.

find clues but the various different camera angles all leave out the moment of the actual accident; a series of insufficient perspectives are exchanged for one another. In addition, images shot on a 16 mm camera exist, which show the girl before and after the accident. Yet rather than superimposing the "too early" onto the "too late" in these images from a position of cold distance, as would correspond with paranoid logic, the staging marks the painful difference between these two states. The staging thus imbues these last images with the burden of missed opportunities – namely, but not only in view of Harry's failure to get in contact with Delly before she is murdered because of what she knows, as becomes clear at the end of the film. These brief shots thus depict an image of transience in very succinct form: one moment, the girl is cheerfully smiling on the passenger seat, while just a few seconds later she is covered in blood, upside down in the overturned car.

The combination of the two modes intensifies in the final scene of the film: Harry is now on a motor boat attempting to uncover the conspiracy – the activities of a smuggling ring. Suddenly an airplane appears, which opens fire on Harry in the boat. But the pilot miscalculates, the plane crashes into the boat, which subsequently begins to sink, initially without Harry being able to see who was firing at him. Through a window in the hull of the boat, however, he ultimately manages to catch sight of the attacker, sitting in the pilot's cabin of the airplane: his ostensible friend, the same stuntman who was sitting with Delly in the car before her accident. The web of the conspiracy thus draws together in these last moments, just as the plane slowly begins to slip into the depths of the sea. This moment of helpless recognition that arrives too late is staged as a series of shot/counter shots, which show the two men's gazes meeting through two panes of glass, the water in between, and a stream of air bubbles – a configuration paradigmatic of the film's paranoid logic, already knowingly, ironically anticipated by the name of the boat: *Point of View*. It is precisely this point of view that is now set in motion one, last time in the final shots that follow: the mortally wounded Harry starts the engine but is no longer able to properly take control of the steering, meaning that the boat merely begins to circle the site of the accident and, thereby, the omniscient perspective – presumably until it runs out of gas.

Through the identification of this point of view with the protagonist, this paranoid recognition simultaneously becomes melancholy, namely because it inexorably contains the sum of all things that the detective – and with him the spectator – overlooked in terms of clues, and all that went wrong in his life (a life that comes to stand in for American society as a whole with the stereotypical question posed to Moseby earlier, "Where were you when Kennedy died?"). It is precisely in this deeply melancholy sense that, as Michael Sellmann writes, present and past overlap in the shot/counter shot configuration, producing a "look into time itself."[36] We experience a similar intertwining of paranoia and melancholy at the end of CHINATOWN, where grand conspirator and manipulator Noah Cross's total triumph is sealed by the emblematic statement "Forget it, Jake, it's Chinatown" – a painfully contradictory beacon of ultimate futility (the ambiguous call to forget is, of course, impossible to carry out), its entire scope buried in a past that has filled up the present to the very last centimeter.

Vivian Sobchack has developed this sense of being stuck in time and space into a fundamental principle of film noir, which can also be established *mutatis mutandis* for the neo-noir.[37] The characters linger too long and find themselves trapped in the in-between spaces of apparently temporary stays – hotel rooms, bars, and lounges – places without almost any identity, as Sobchack refers to them: "quasi places that substitute perversely for the hospitable and felicitous places and domesticity of a 'proper' home."[38] Within these spaces, time comes down to little more than waiting for the arrival of death, as in MIKEY AND NICKY (Elaine May 1976), a more obscure neo-noir, in which paranoia and melancholy both feed on the same cause – namely the loss of the friendship between the two protagonists, two petty gangsters who now betray and disappoint one another. In view of the earlier films, the reflexive punchline consists of the fact that, after open season is declared on one of the gangsters, he is shot dead in the doorway of his friend's house, while the latter, together with his wife, barricades the door using the furniture from their middle-class suburban living room.

It thus seems that melancholy prevails wherever personal relationships between the characters form the focus of noir – even when these relationships are of a conspiratorial nature. Such as in THE LONG GOODBYE, whose character construction Robin Wood describes as follows: "Whatever we may deduce about Eileen Wade's motivation and guilt, there is no longer any coherent moral position established in the film from which she might be judged. If she and her husband remain the film's most moving characters, it is purely because they have

---

36 See Michael Sellmann: Hollywoods moderner Film Noir, Würzburg 2001, p. 173. This "time-image" can, however, hardly be traced back to the subjective consciousness of the protagonist, as Sellmann assumes – for this moment of recognition, as well as the image itself (we are talking about a shot/countershot construction here) is constantly bound to the perspective of the camera, which places the spectator in relation to this protagonist.
37 See Sobchack: Lounge Time. Postwar Crises and the Chronotope of Film Noir. In: Nick Browne (ed.): Refiguring American Film Genres. History and Theory, Berkeley 1998, pp. 129–170.
38 Sobchack: Lounge Time. Postwar Crises and the Chronotope of Film Noir, p. 138.

the greatest capacity for suffering."[39] This conceptualization of characters according to the degree of their suffering leads from paranoia to melancholy, and its profound ambivalence can also be seen as a characteristic unique to the neo-noir: "We may occasionally, in the 40s have remained in some uncertainty as to the chain of events [...], but never as to what to think of the characters [...]."[40]

As in the horror film and the road movie, the neo-noir connects the affective modes in a specific balance, which, in each case, determines the tone of the film. Seen in this way, the table introduced at the beginning of the chapter, which lists the three modes alongside one another, is to be thought of as a sort of three-part picture puzzle, which variously allows for the recognition of different aspects of New Hollywood, according to each respective point of view. While the different perspectives can never be shown at the same time in their "pure form," their dynamic combination in the corporeal presence of the spectator makes this cinema possible in all of its diversity.

5.2 Futures Past: Cinema after 9/11

So, what to make of this short history of affective experience? What do we gain if we understand the cinema of New Hollywood as a constellation of modes of affectivity? More concretely: what does it mean for the writing of film history to conceptualize the spectator's position in postclassical cinema as being split?

Fairly basically, the concept of affective modes and modalities introduces a critical element into the writing of film history: it does not claim total validity as the essence of a given period, but unfolds its potential, among other things, with regard to the concept of genre, as shown above. But the consequences of introducing this critical concept into the writing of film history go much further. I will briefly outline two possible perspectives: firstly, we gain the ability to write a kind of history that regards the films not as its mere objects, as set pieces to be sorted into categories and periods, but as *agents* of history:[41] films, from this perspective, are not passive documents that simply record or mirror the conditions of their historical emergence; rather, they enable us to conceive of these circumstances as a meaningful context in the first place. Without these films,

---

39 Wood: Hollywood from Vietnam to Reagan, p. 32.
40 Wood: Hollywood from Vietnam to Reagan, p. 32.
41 See Marc Ferro: Film as an Agent, Product and Source of History. In: Journal of Contemporary History, Vol. 18, No. 3 (1983), pp. 357–364.

there would be no New Hollywood, and there would exist a decidedly different idea of how the 1960s and 1970s are to be regarded as a historical phenomenon: as a historical "space of experience"[42] that relates in some way to the present day. This creative and critical dimension of aesthetic experience is the basic prerequisite for the films to still concern us at all today.

Secondly, writing film history as an affective history opens up the possibility of grasping the cultural and political relevance of cinema beyond models of reflection or representation, in which the films are always secondary to historical developments or social discourse. The dimension of affectivity can be understood as a medium through which the films communicate with and intervene into the very sensorium of a society – into its affective economy, if you will.[43] I would like to demonstrate this idea in a concluding example: two films representative of the American cinema after 9/11.

* * *

The plot of MINORITY REPORT (Steven Spielberg 2002) is quickly told: In the year 2054 there are no more murders in Washington. Psychically gifted telepathic seers, so-called pre-cogs, foresee in their visions every murder taking place in the future, so that the police can intervene in time and prevent the crime. When the head of the unit, John Anderton, sees himself in a vision, committing a murder on a man he does not know, he has to flee from his own colleagues and at the same time find out what fateful connections he has become entangled in.

From the very first sequence, MINORITY REPORT closely intertwines suspense and paranoia. The initial constellation on a first level can be described as a classic "race to the rescue" à la Griffith, a parallel montage based on the principle of continuous acceleration: a jealous husband catches his wife with her lover and is about to kill them both. At the same time, the police do everything they can to find him and prevent the crime. However, this constellation is framed twice from the outset: on the one hand by the vision of murder with which the film begins. This is a rough impressionistic sketch that not only introduces the basic plot of the event, but also a whole series of audiovisual motifs in which the plot condenses into a dramaturgy: the scissors serving as a murder weapon, distinct arrangements of the figures in space, various dialogue elements ("You know how blind I am without them"; "Howard, don't cry"). These motifs, which are brought together here in a confined space, reappear selectively in the subsequent course

---

42 See Reinhart Koselleck: Futures Past. On the Semantics of Historical Time, New York 2004, pp. 255–276.

43 See Hauke Lehmann, Hans Roth, Kerstin Schankweiler: Affective Economy. In: Slaby, and von Scheve (eds.) Affective Societies, pp. 140–151.

of action and constantly re-update what will have happened. Thus the temporality of suspense, the future perfect, crystallizes in them.

On the other hand, the course of events is fed into the police surveillance apparatus, the pre-crime unit, by means of this initiating vision. There it becomes manipulable and editable (like the shots of a film in postproduction) and can be evaluated according to the information it contains. In this strictly data-based, digital perspective, the murder has already happened, and everything that follows is nothing but a repetition. The theme of the whole film can be described as a paradoxical struggle between suspense and paranoia: is there room for maneuver in the future, or is it illusory? The answer to this question, how could it be otherwise, is ambivalent. It is seeing itself that introduces the paradox: the vision of the pre-cogs enables the police to intervene and refute the vision in the first place. The perpetrators are arrested and sentenced for acts they have not (yet) committed.

As already indicated at the end of the chapter on paranoia, the relation between suspense and paranoia is established via the third mode, melancholy. As remarked above with reference to the neo-noir, this is also introduced here through the theme of personal relationships: Anderton has lost his son, and his marriage has fallen apart. The space of the present literally becomes an image of the past when he watches holographic film footage of his lost family. In fact, the moment of loss is the paradigm of a guilt-ridden empty possibility in Binswanger's sense: the son was kidnapped in an outdoor pool while Anderton was submerged in water for a moment – a fatal moment of blindness.

From these paradigmatic constellations of seeing, overlooking and not seeing, the film develops an enormously dense network of ever new viewing conditions, which in its complexity far exceeds the framework of this brief discussion. A central node of the plot, however, fuses suspense, paranoia and melancholy and thus provides a first hint to the question of what is at stake when all three modes are related to each other. Anderton's escape inevitably leads him towards the moment in the future when he is supposed to commit the predicted murder – murder of a man completely unknown to him. And as at the beginning of the film, the motifs of the vision really do gradually condense until Anderton stands opposite this man in a hotel room and learns that it is this man who kidnapped and murdered his son at the time. Obviously we are dealing here with another irresolvable paradox: if Anderton had not seen the vision of his murder, there would have been no reason for him to flee to the very place where it would happen in the future. In the moment of confrontation, not only is the empty possibility of the melancholic perfect reanimated – in the guise of revenge – but the question of the *possibility of action* arises simultaneously from the present and the future, or from their relationship.

Unsurprisingly, the film is not meant to clarify all the contradictions that arise in its course. The solution it offers at its end has two faces: one unites the couple into a new small family (complete with a pregnant belly), the other isolates the pre-cogs now freed from their duties far away from any civilization in a lonely hut. This is a double temporal relationship of retreat and new beginning, which not only in its affective gesture has some similarities with the end of Zack Snyder's graphic novel adaptation WATCHMEN.

WATCHMEN adds another factor to the complexity of temporal relations that makes the film particularly interesting for the context of this work: it refers to the very historical period that coincides with the New Hollywood cinema as a critical intersection of US-American history. The film's plot is thus situated in an alternative historical reality: it takes place in the USA in 1985. With the help of a group of superheroes, the *Watchmen*, the USA have won the Vietnam War; Watergate never happened, and Richard Nixon is president in his fifth term. At the same time, the Cold War with the Soviet Union has escalated to such an extent that a nuclear strike is to be feared at any moment. In this situation, a stranger begins to put the group of superheroes out of action, although most of them have already retired. These attacks are part of a conspiracy to induce humanity to live together peacefully through fear of the most powerful of the superheroes, Dr. Manhattan. This is to be achieved by simultaneous attacks on the major cities of the world, for which Dr. Manhattan is blamed.

In this brief description of the plot, it already appears how deeply the film is entangled in the vicissitudes of American history. While for its source material, the graphic novel by Alan Moore and Dave Gibbons, the Cold War and the atomic bomb were the determining metaphors around which the dramaturgy was organized, the film – whether intentionally or not – short-circuits this constellation with the terrorist scenarios of the 21st century. Stuart Moulthrop attributes this impression chiefly to the end of the film, which represents a significant change from Moore's original:

> Yet for all its careful evasions of real, historical horror, the *Watchmen* film nonetheless proceeds from, and reproduces, a distinctly post-9/11 ideology. Moore insists on the implausibility of any utopia, while Snyder and company seem attuned to a different *Realpolitik*. [...] The film gives us terror absolute, terror metastatic, terror as inevitable condition of everyday life. The revelation-proof utopia of the *Watchmen* film thus offers a rather clear portrait of the current world order – a recognition that might wipe away our initial smile.[44]

---

44 Stuart Moulthrop: *Watchmen* Meets The Aristocrats. In: Postmodern Culture, Vol. 19, No. 1 (September 2009), URL: http://pmc.iath.virginia.edu/text-only/issue.908/19.1moulthrop.txt, accessed March 27th, 2019.

Even though the attacks of September 11 are more invoked in the form of a cipher, they almost inevitably inscribe themselves into the temporality of the film – which at first says more about this temporality than about the relationship of this film to reality. Bob Rehak, for example, notes that the New York Twin Towers are prominently featured in two scenes of the film, but sums it up with the following conclusion: "The tragically ineradicable stamp of September 11 on *Watchmen*'s cinematic incarnation may be less about what is absent or altered than about how difficult it has become to read the film otherwise."[45] In our context, this diagnosis can be understood to mean that it is the cinematic construction of temporal relations that establishes the reference to historical reality in the first place.

Because it is by no means a coincidence that the filming was done without shifting the plot to the present.[46] Rather, it is actually the New Hollywood period that reflects the critical potential that the concept of an alternative history is aimed at. Here, at this point, the decisive turn-off takes place. This becomes more than clear already in the title sequence, which functions as an audiovisual abbreviation of the concept of an alternative history: one after the other, the iconic stations of American history are recreated, each with small shifts, caused by the inscription of the *Watchmen* into this history: a different couple kisses on Times Square on V-Day, one of the *Watchmen* shoots John Kennedy, another films the moon landing, etc.

This does not simply refer to historical events, but rather to media events, and thus to precisely those affect-poetic paradigms on which the film WATCHMEN itself is based – by means of the affective modes established in New Hollywood. The *Watchmen* group embodies the paranoid dimension of history, or more precisely what was described above as the paranoid cinema of action: the *Watchmen* enter the mirror world of the image surfaces through action, in which the parallactic shift finds the desperately sought anchor. However, the line of flight of this shift is the implementation of the American Dream with all available means. The song that accompanies this enumeration of key events is Bob Dylan's *The Times They Are A-Changin'*, also an example of paradoxical temporality – on the one hand the song was granted prophetic power, while in the same breath it was attested that it had been overtaken by the very changes it itself announced.[47]

This paradoxical function is also shared by some of the other songs used in the film, notably *The Sound of Silence* by Simon and Garfunkel and *All Along the*

---

45 Bob Rehak: Adapting *Watchmen* after 9/11. In: Cinema Journal, Vol. 51, No. 1 (Fall 2011), pp. 154–159, here p. 159.
46 See Rehak: Adapting *Watchmen* after 9/11, p. 157.
47 See Michael Gray: Song and Dance Man III. The Art of Bob Dylan, London 2000, p. 131.

Watchtower in Jimi Hendrix's interpretation, both of which refer to the New Hollywood era – the former known as the title song for THE GRADUATE, one of the pioneer films of the period. If there it represents a beginning, it is here associated with an irretrievable loss, namely with the image of the Twin Towers, which rises in the background of a funeral scene. The Twin Towers' figurative burial introduces the temporal relationship of mourning, which runs through the film as a whole in order to occasionally surface here and there. The paradoxes thus arise from the double or triple reference to the various universes that collide in this film; the emphasis on the music of the 1960s can be read as a reference to the failed social utopias of the time, which find their belated redemption in the cynical utopia of a new equilibrium of terror – especially in view of the decidedly apocalyptic impact of this music (the credits are accompanied by another Dylan song from this period: a cover version of *Desolation Row*). Thus utopia and dystopia coincide in what Moulthrop aptly calls *Realpolitik*. The affective surplus of this coincidence is realized in the viewer's feelings (and only there) as grief, that is: as farewell and as an orientation towards the present.

If among the affect-poetic paradigms the film is concerned with at first that of paranoia dominates, then this is fanned out over the course of the film by a complex interplay of affective modes. This also has to do with the fact that the 1960s and 1970s in this setting are the subject of a recollection from the perspective of the 1980s. A central sentiment associated with this is that of nostalgia – not as a poetics of the film, however, but as an attitude that determines almost all of its characters in one way or another: a longing for a time in which action was still possible, a longing for a time of ignorance, for a state of being desired. This nostalgia is opposed by the form of the chronicle, which records in detail all the cruelties of which people are capable, and which in doing so intoxicates itself with its own lacony. The other resistance to nostalgia is irony, which presents itself as an act of dissociation in the face of increasing hopelessness. Both the impulse of the chronicler and that of the parodist are deeply melancholic; both find their own embodiment in one of the *Watchmen*, the vigilante Rorschach, and the paramilitary Comedian, respectively. Dr. Manhattan, however, embodies the highest degree of complexity with regard to the embodiment of temporal relations and becomes the central figure for the film even more than for the graphic novel.

With this figure, Moore creates something like a metaphor for the temporality of graphic novels themselves: Dr. Manhattan, named in obvious reference to the Manhattan Project and associated with the symbol of the hydrogen atom, perceives the past, present and future simultaneously. Time thus becomes a collection of static frames in a 'movement' of incessant self-fulfillment in absolute predetermination. This is a paradoxical attempt to think of time without a perspective on time, or to understand time as a self-transparent subject, as a total (i.e. perspectiveless) consciousness of time. Conceived of in this way, time freezes. For the film WATCHMEN, however, another dimension of this temporality gains more importance, which at the same time represents a constellation to which the fabric of affective modes could possibly be pinpointed: if the future is apparently fixed and predestined, the past remains highly present and effective – and this also applies to every moment of the present, which radiates infinitely like the light of distant stars, which only reaches the earth when they have long since extinguished. The supposed stillness thus transforms into a picture of fascinating and restless vitality. And in this very sense, the *pen*ultimate scene of WATCHMEN states: "Nothing ends. Nothing ever ends." This corresponds to what Merleau-Ponty writes: "In short, since in time being and passing are synonymous, by becoming past, the event does not cease to be."[48]

The grief and farewell that become so important for WATCHMEN are based on this very realization; only this makes it possible to understand the present as a critical moment of decision, introducing a perspective based on subjectivity. To quote, one last time, Merleau-Ponty: "The past, therefore, *is* not past, nor the future future. It exists only when a subjectivity is there to disrupt the plenitude of being in itself, to adumbrate a perspective, and introduce non-being into it. A past and a future spring forth when I reach out towards them."[49] These sentences, so the conclusion of my considerations, could be applied with full justification not only to history in general, but also to the history of cinema in particular and finally also to the cinema of New Hollywood, insofar as it still means something today and in this (highly real) way is again entangled with life and history. The present work was an attempt to get an idea of this paradoxical interplay of cinematic time with cinematic affectivity and, if the undertaking was successful, to understand it a little better.

---

48 Merleau-Ponty: Phenomenology of Perception, p. 488.
49 Merleau-Ponty: Phenomenology of Perception, p. 489.

List of figures

(According to the numbering of the figures in the text, sorted by chapter.)

2 Suspense: Forms of Cinematic Thinking

3 Paranoia: Forms of Mediatization

4 Melancholy: Ways of Perceiving History

https://doi.org/10.1515/9783110580761-007

Bibliography

Altman, Rick: Moving Lips. Cinema as Ventriloquism. In: Yale French Studies, No. 60 (1980), pp. 67–79.

Andrew, Geoff: The Director's Vision. A Concise Guide to the Art of 250 Great Filmmakers. Chicago 1999.

Anger, Kenneth: Hollywood Babylon [1975]. New York 1981.

Anger, Kenneth: Modesty and the Art of Film. In: The cover booklet of the Blu-Ray edition of Kenneth Anger: Magick Lantern Cycle, British Film Institute 2009, pp. 1–8.

Arnheim, Rudolf: Accident and the Necessity of Art. In: The Journal of Aesthetics and Art Criticism, Vol. 16, No. 1 (1957), pp. 18–31.

Arnheim, Rudolf: Film as Art. Berkeley/Los Angeles/London 1957.

Arnheim, Rudolf: Melancholy Unshaped. In: The Journal of Aesthetics and Art Criticism Vol. 21, No. 3 (Spring 1963), pp. 291–297.

Assassination Research, URL: http://www.assassinationresearch.com/v2n2/zfilm/ zframe001.html, last accessed March 13th, 2019.

Babington, Bruce: Twice a Victim. Carrie meets the BFI. In: Screen, Vol. 24, No. 3 (1983), pp. 4–18.

Balázs, Béla: Early Film Theory. Visible Man and The Spirit of Film, New York/Oxford 2010.

Barker, Adam: Cries and Whispers. In: Sight and Sound, Vol. 1, No. 10 (February 1992), pp. 24–25.

Barthes, Roland: An Introduction to the Structural Analysis of Narrative [1966]. In: New Literary History, Vol. 6, No. 2 (Winter 1975), pp. 237–272.

Bartsch, Anne, Jens Eder, and Kathrin Fahlenbrach (eds.): Audiovisuelle Emotionen. Emotionsdarstellung und Emotionsvermittlung durch audiovisuelle Medienangebote. Cologne 2007.

Bazin, André: A Bergsonian Film: THE PICASSO MYSTERY. In: Bazin at Work: Major Essays & Reviews from the Forties & Fifties, edited by Bert Cardullo. New York/London 1997, pp. 211–219.

Bazin, André: Vittorio De Sica, Metteur-en-Scene. In: id.: What is Film?, pp. 61–78.

Becker, Matt: A Point of Little Hope. Hippie Horror Films and the Politics of Ambivalence. In: The Velvet Light Trap, No. 57 (2006), pp. 42–59.

Bellour, Raymond: Le Dépli des Émotions. In: Trafic 43 (September 2002), pp. 93–128.

Benjamin, Walter: One-Way Street. In: id.: Selected Writings. Vol. 1: 1913–26, edited by Marcus Bullock and Michael W. Jennings, Cambridge, MA 2002, pp. 444–488.

Benjamin, Walter: The Origin of German Tragic Drama, Brooklyn/London 2009.

Benjamin, Walter: Theses on the Philosophy of History. In: id.: Illuminations, edited by Hannah Arendt, London 1999, pp. 245–255.

Benjamin, Walter, Lloyd Spencer, and Mark Harrington: Central Park. In: New German Critique, No. 34 (Winter, 1985), pp. 32–58.

Bergson, Henri: The Possible and the Real. In: id.: The Creative Mind. New York 1968, pp. 107–125.

Berliner, Todd: The Genre Film as Booby Trap. 1970s Genre Bending and THE FRENCH CONNECTION. In: Cinema Journal, Vol. 40, No. 3 (Spring 2001), pp. 25–46.

Berliner, Todd: Hollywood Incoherent. Narration in Seventies Cinema. Austin 2010.

https://doi.org/10.1515/9783110580761-008

Bernardoni, James: The New Hollywood. What the Movies Did with the New Freedoms of the
Seventies. Jefferson, NC/London 1991.

Berthoz, Alain: The Brain's Sense of Movement. Cambridge/London 2000.

Binswanger, Ludwig: Melancholie und Manie. Phänomenologische Studien. Pfullingen 1960.

Blake, Linnie: Another One for the Fire. George A. Romero's American Theology of the Flesh.
In: Xavier Mendik (ed.): Shocking Cinema of the Seventies, Hereford 2002, pp. 151–165.

Blumenberg, Hans (ed.): New Hollywood. Munich/Vienna 1976.

Blumler, Jay G., and Dennis Kavanagh: The Third Age of Political Communication. Influences
and Features. In: Political Communication, Vol. 16, No. 3 (1999), pp. 209–230.

Bonitzer, Pascal: Deframings. In: Cahiers Du Cinéma, Vol. 4, 1973–1978, pp. 197–203.

Bonitzer, Pascal: Hitchcockian Suspense. In: Slavoj Žižek (ed.): Everything You Always Wanted
to Know About Lacan (But Were Afraid to Ask Hitchcock), London/New York 1992,
pp. 15–30.

Bonitzer, Pascal: Système des émotions [1982]. In: id.: Le champ aveugle. Essais sur le
réalisme au cinéma, Paris 1999, pp. 95–102.

Bordwell, David: On the History of Film Style. Cambridge 1997.

Bordwell, David, Janet Staiger, and Kristin Thompson: Classical Hollywood Cinema. Film Style
and Mode of Production to 1960. London 1988.

Boulding, Kenneth: The Shadow of the Stationary State. In: Daedalus, Vol. 102, No. 4
(Fall 1973), pp. 89–101.

Brakhage, Stan: In Defense of Amateur. In: id.: Essential Brakhage. Selected Writings on
Filmmaking, edited by Bruce McPherson, Kingston 2001, pp. 142–150.

Braudy, Leo: The Sacraments of Genre. Coppola, De Palma, Scorsese. In: Film Quarterly,
Vol. 39, No. 3 (Spring 1986), pp. 17–28.

Brenez, Nicole: De la figure en général et du corps en particulier. L'invention figurative au
cinéma. Paris/Brüssel 1998.

Brewer, William F.: The Nature of Narrative Suspense and the Problem of Rereading. In: Peter
Vorderer, Hans J. Wulff, and Mike Friedrichsen (eds.): Suspense, pp. 107–127.

Brottman, Mikita: Introduction. Force and Fire. In: Jack Hunter (ed.): Moonchild. The Films of
Kenneth Anger, London 2002, pp. 5–10.

Brown, Royal S.: Considering De Palma. In: American Film, Vol. 3, No. 4 (July/August 1977),
pp. 54–61.

Brunner, Philipp, Jörg Schweinitz, and Margrit Tröhler (eds.): Filmische Atmosphären.
Marburg 2012.

Brütsch, Matthias, Vinzenz Hediger, Ursula von Keitz, Alexandra Schneider, and Margrit
Tröhler: Kinogefühle. Emotionalität und Film. Marburg 2005.

Burton, Robert: The Anatomy of Melancholy. New York 2001.

Calabresi, Guido, and Philip Bobbitt: Tragic Choices. New York 1978.

Cameron, Ian, Victor F. Perkins, Michael Walker, Jim Hillier, and Robin Wood: The Return of
Movie. In: Movie, No. 20 (1975), pp. 1–25.

Carroll, John: Puritan, Paranoid, Remissive. A Sociology of Modern Culture. London 1977.

Carroll, Noël: Embodied Visions. Evolution, Emotion, Culture, and Film, Oxford 2009.

Carroll, Noël: The Future of Allusion. Hollywood in the Seventies (and Beyond). In: October,
Vol. 20 (Spring 1982), pp. 51–81.

Carroll, Noël: The Paradox of Suspense. In: Peter Vorderer, Hans J. Wulff, and Mike
Friedrichsen (eds.): Suspense, pp. 71–91.

Carroll, Noël: The Philosophy of Motion Pictures. Malden 2008.

Carroll, Noël: Toward a Theory of Film Suspense. In: Persistence of Vision, No. 1 (Summer 1984), pp. 65–89.

Carroll, Peter N.: It Seemed Like Nothing Happened. America in the 1970s. New Brunswick/New Jersey/London 2000.

Casetti, Francesco: Eye of the Century. Film, Experience, Modernity, New York/Chichester 2008.

Cataldi, Sue: Emotion, Depth, and Flesh. A Study of Sensitive Space. Reflections on Merleau-Ponty's Philosophy of Embodiment. New York 1993.

Caughie, John (ed.): Theories of Authorship [1981]. London/New York 2001.

Childs, Mike, and Alan Jones: De Palma has the Power! [1977]. In: Brian De Palma. Interviews, edited by Laurence F. Knapp, Jackson 2003, pp. 37–45.

Chion, Michel, and Ben Brewster: Quiet Revolution... and Rigid Stagnation. In: October, Vol. 58 (1991), pp. 69–80.

Cobley, Paul: "Justifiable Paranoia". The Politics of Conspiracy in 1970s American Film. In: Xavier Mendik (ed.): Shocking Cinema of the Seventies, Hereford 2002.

Conard, Mark T. (ed.): The Philosophy of Neo-Noir. Lexington 2007.

Cook, David: Lost Illusions. American Cinema in the Shadow of Watergate and Vietnam, 1970–1979, Berkeley 2000.

Copjec, Joan: Imagine There's No Woman. Ethics and Sublimation. Cambridge 2004.

Corrigan, Timothy: A Cinema Without Walls. Movies and Culture after Vietnam. New Brunswick, NJ 1991.

Curtis, Robin: Narration versus Immersion. Die Falschen Fährten der Analyse. In: Maske und Kothurn Vol. 53, No. 2 (2007), pp. 341–352.

Dammann, Lars: Kino im Aufbruch. New Hollywood 1967–1976. Marburg 2007.

Dayan, Daniel: The Tutor-Code of Classical Cinema. In: Film Quarterly, Vol. 28, No. 1 (1974), pp. 22–31.

Deleuze, Gilles: The Brain is the Screen, [1986]. In id.: The Brain is the Screen: Deleuze and the Philosophy of Cinema, edited by Gregory Flaxman, Minneapolis 1986, pp. 365–374.

Deleuze, Gilles: Cinema 1. The Movement-Image. Minneapolis 1997.

Deleuze, Gilles: Cinema 2. The Time-Image. Minneapolis 1989.

Deleuze, Gilles: Letter to Serge Daney. Optimism, Pessimism, and Travel [1986]. In: id.: Negotiations, pp. 68–79.

Deleuze, Gilles: On the Movement-Image. In: id.: Negotiations 1972–1990, New York 1995, pp. 46–56.

Deleuze, Gilles, and Félix Guattari: Anti-Oedipus. Capitalism and Schizophrenia. Minneapolis 2000.

Deleuze, Gilles, and Félix Guattari: A Thousand Plateaus. Capitalism and Schizophrenia. New York 2004.

Deren, Maya: Amateur Versus Professional. In: Film Culture 39 (1965), pp. 45–46.

Didion, Joan: Slouching Towards Bethlehem [1967]. In: id.: Slouching Towards Bethlehem. New York 1981, pp. 94–132.

Didion, Joan: The White Album. In: id.: The White Album. Essays [1979], New York 2009, pp. 11–48.

Dilling, Horst, W. Mombour, and M.H. Schmidt (eds.): Internationale Klassifikation psychischer Störungen. ICD-10, Chapter V (F) [5th Edition]. Bern 2005.

Dixon, Wheeler Winston: Film Noir and the Cinema of Paranoia. New Brunswick 2009.

Dumas, Chris: Un-American Psycho. Brian De Palma and the Political Invisible. Chicago 2012.

Durgnat, Raymond: Paint it Black. The Family Tree of the Film Noir. In: Cinema, No. 6/7 (August 1970), pp. 49–56.

Elsaesser, Thomas: American Auteur Cinema. The Last – or First – Picture Show? In: id., Alexander Horwath, and Noel King (eds.): The Last Great American Picture Show. New Hollywood Cinema in the 1970s, Amsterdam 2004, pp. 37–69.

Elsaesser, Thomas: The Pathos of Failure. American Films in the 1970s. Notes on the Unmotivated Hero [1975]. In: id., Alenxander Horwath, and Noel King (eds.): The Last Great American Picture Show, pp. 279–292.

Eisenstein, Sergei: Beyond the Shot. In: id.: Selected Works. Volume 1. Writings 1922–34, edited by Richard Taylor, London 1988, pp. 138–150.

Eisenstein, Sergei: The Fourth Dimension in Cinema. In: id.: Selected Works Vol. 1 Writings 1922–34, edited by Richard Taylor, London 1988, pp. 181–194.

Eisenstein, Sergei: Laocoön. In: id.: Selected Works. Volume 2: Towards a Theory of Montage, edited by Michael Glenny, and Richard Taylor, London 1991, pp. 109–202.

Eisenstein, Sergei: Montage in 1938. In: id.: Problems of Film Direction, Honolulu 2004, pp. 10–45.

Eisenstein, Sergei: Nonindifferent Nature. Cambridge 1987.

Eisenstein, Sergei: The Problem of the Materialist Approach to Form. In: id.: Selected Works. Vol. 1, pp. 59–64.

Eng, David L.: Melancholia/Postcoloniality. Loss in THE FLOATING LIFE. In: Qui Parle 11, No. 2 (Fall/Winter 1999), pp. 137–150.

Epstein, Jean: Magnification [1921]. In: October, Vol. 3 (Spring 1977), pp. 9–25.

Farber, Stephen: End of the Road? In: Film Quarterly, Vol. 23, No. 2 (Winter 1969/1970), pp. 3–16.

Farber, Stephen: Movies That Reflect Our Obsession With Conspiracy and Assassination. In: The New York Times, August 11th, 1974.

Ferro, Marc: Film as an Agent, Product and Source of History. In: Journal of Contemporary History, Vol. 18, No. 3 (1983), pp. 357–364.

Fiedler, Leslie A.: The Rebirth of God and the Death of Man. In: Salmagundi 21 (Winter 1973), pp. 3–26.

Flatley, Jonathan: Affective Mapping. Melancholia and the Politics of Modernism. Cambridge/ London 2008.

Foucault, Michel: Nietzsche, Genealogy, History. In: The Foucault Reader, edited by Paul Rabinow, New York 1984, pp. 76–100.

Freedman, Carl: Towards a Theory of Paranoia. The Science Fiction of Philip K. Dick. In: Science Fiction Studies, Vol. 11, No. 1 (March 1984), pp. 15–24.

Friedman, Lester D. (ed.): American Cinema of the 1970s. Themes and Variations. Oxford 2007.

Freud, Sigmund: Group Psychology and the Analysis of the Ego. In: id.: The Standard Edition of the Complete Psychological Works of Sigmund Freud: Volume XVIII (1920–1922): Beyond the Pleasure Principle, Group Psychology and Other Works, edited by James Strachey, pp. 65–144.

Freud, Sigmund: Mourning and Melancholia. In: id.: The Standard Edition of the Complete Psychological Works of Sigmund Freud. Volume 14: On the History of the Post

Psychoanalytic Movement, Papers on Metapsychology and Other Works, edited by James Strachey. London 2001, pp. 243–259.

Freud, Sigmund: On Narcissism [1914]. In: id.: The Standard Edition of the Complete Psychological Works of Sigmund Freud, Volume XIV (1914–1916): On the History of the Psycho-Analytic Movement, Papers on Metapsychology and Other Works, pp. 67–102.

Freud, Sigmund: Psycho-Analytical Notes on an Autobiographical Account of a Case of Paranoia (Dementia paranoides) [1911]. In: id.: Collected Papers, Vol. 3, New York 1959, pp. 387–470.

Freud, Sigmund: Some Neurotic Mechanisms in Jealousy, Paranoia and Homosexuality. In: id.: The Complete Psychological Works of Sigmund Freud, Volume 18: Beyond the Pleasure Principle, Group Psychology and Other Works, edited by James Strachey, London 1955, pp. 221–234.

Frölich, Margrit, Klaus Gronenborn, and Karsten Visarius (eds.): Kunst der Schatten. Zur melancholischen Grundstimmung des Kinos. Marburg 2006.

Gerrig, Richard J.: Is there a Paradox of Suspense? A Reply to Yanal. In: The British Journal of Aesthetics, Vol. 37, No. 2 (April 1997), pp. 168–174.

Goldberg, Robert Alan: Enemies Within. The Culture of Conspiracy in Modern America. New Haven/London 2001.

Gray, Michael: Song and Dance Man III. The Art of Bob Dylan. London 2000.

Greenspun, Roger: Carrie, and Sally and Leatherface Among the Film Buffs. In: Film Comment, Vol. 13, No. 1 (January/February 1977), pp. 14–17.

Greifenstein, Sarah, and Hauke Lehmann: Manipulation der Sinne im Modus des Suspense. In: Cinema, Vol. 58 (2013), pp. 102–112.

Greven, David: Representations of Femininity in American Genre Cinema. The Woman's Film, Film Noir, and Modern Horror. New York 2011, pp. 91–115.

Grodal, Torben: Moving Pictures. A New Theory of Film Genres, Feelings, and Cognition, Oxford 1997.

Groß, Bernhard: Pier Paolo Pasolini. Figurationen des Sprechens. Berlin 2008.

Guattari, Félix: The Poor Man's Couch. In: id.: Chaosophy. Texts and Interviews 1972–1977, pp. 257–267.

Gunning, Tom: Moving Away from the Index. Cinema and the Impression of Reality. In: Gertrud Koch, Volker Pantenburg, and Simon Rothöhler (eds.): Screen Dynamics. Mapping the Borders of Cinema, Vienna 2012, pp. 42–60.

Hampton, Howard: Everybody Knows This Is Nowhere. The Uneasy Ride of Hollywood and Rock. In: Thomas Elsaesser, Alexander Horwath, and Noel King (eds.): The Last Great American Picture Show, pp. 249–266.

Hanich, Julian: Cinematic Emotion in Horror Films and Thrillers. The Aesthetic Paradox of Pleasurable Fear. New York/London 2010.

Hansen, Miriam: With Skin and Hair. Kracauer's Theory of Film, Marseille 1940. In: Critical Inquiry, Vol. 19, No. 3 (Spring 1993), pp. 437–469.

Harris, Mark: Pictures at a Revolution. Five Movies and the Birth of the New Hollywood. New York 2008.

Heller-Nicholas, Alexandra: Life in the Old Girl Yet. CARRIE (1976) and the Unbearable Lightness of De Palma Bashing [September 5th, 2008], URL: http://filmbunnies.wordpress.com/category/alex/depalmas-carrie/, last accessed March 27th, 2019.

Hendershot, Cyndy: Paranoia, the Bomb, and 1950s Science Fiction Films. Bowling Green 1999.

Hendriks, Leah: Beyond the Infinite. In: Offscreen Vol. 6, No. 9 (2002), URL: http://www.horschamp.qc.ca/new_offscreen/kubrick.html last accessed March 13th, 2019.

Hentschel, Frank: Töne der Angst. Die Musik im Horrorfilm. Berlin 2011.

Hertzberg, Hendrik, David C.K. McClelland: Paranoia. An Idée Fixe Whose Time Has Come. In: Harper's Magazine, June 1974.

Hirsch, Foster: Detours and Lost Highways. A Map of Neo-Noir. New York 1999.

Hoberman, James: The Dream Life. Movies, Media and the Mythology of the Sixties. New York/London 2003.

Hofstadter, Richard: The Paranoid Style in American Politics. In: id.: The Paranoid Style in American Politics and other Essays, New York 1965, pp. 3–40.

Holland, Max, and Johann Rush: J.F.K.'s Death, Re-Framed. In: New York Times, November 22nd, 2007, URL: http://www.nytimes.com/2007/11/22/opinion/22holland.html?ref=abrahamzapruder, last accessed March 13th, 2019.

Horton, Andrew: Political Assassination and Cinema. Alan J. Pakula's THE PARALLAX VIEW. In: Persistence of Vision 3/4 (1986), pp. 61–70

Horwath, Alexander: A Walking Contradiction (Partly Truth and Partly Fiction). In: id., Thomas Elsaesser, and Noel King (eds.): The Last Great American Picture Show, pp. 83–105.

Hughes, Matthew: The Films of Kenneth Anger and the Sixties Politics of Consciousness. University Dissertation at the University of Westminster 2011. URL: http://westminsterresearch.wmin.ac.uk/10179/1/Matthew_HUGHES.pdf, last accessed March 13th, 2019.

Hutchison, Alice L.: Kenneth Anger. A Demonic Visionary. London 2004.

Kobayashi, Toshiaki: Melancholie und Zeit. Basel/Frankfurt a.M. 1998.

Illger, Daniel: Heim-Suchungen. Stadt und Geschichtlichkeit im italienischen Nachkriegskino. Berlin 2009.

Internet Movie Database, URL: imdb.com, last accessed June 1st, 2013.

Jacobs, Diane: Hollywood Renaissance. Cranbury 1977.

James, David E.: Amateurs in the Industry Town. Stan Brakhage and Andy Warhol in Los Angeles. In: Grey Room 12 (Summer 2003), pp. 80–93.

James, William: What is an Emotion?. In: Mind, Vol. 9, No. 34 (April 1884), pp. 188–205.

Jameson, Fredric: The Geopolitical Aesthetic. Cinema and Space in the World System, Bloomington/Indianapolis/London 1992.

Jameson, Fredric: Postmodernism, or, The Cultural Logic of Late Capitalism. Durham 1991.

Jensen, Paul: The Return of Dr. Caligari. Paranoia in Hollywood. In: Film Comment, Vol. 7, No. 4 (Winter 1971), pp. 36–45.

Jones, Kent: "The Cylinders Were Whispering My Name." The Films of Monte Hellman. In: Thomas Elsaesser, Alexander Horwath, and Noel King (eds.): The Last Great American Picture Show, pp. 165–194.

Jutkewitsch, Sergej: Der große Nigromant. In: Hartmut Albrecht, Christiane Mückenberger (eds.): Lew Kuleschow, Berlin 1977, pp. 112–137.

Kael, Pauline: The Curse. In: The New Yorker, November 22nd, 1976, pp. 177–183.

Kakmi, Dmetri: Myth and Magic in De Palma's CARRIE. In: Senses of Cinema, February 2000, URL: http://sensesofcinema.com/2000/cteq/carrie/, last accessed March 27th, 2019.

Kanfer, Stefan: Hollywood: The Shock of Freedom in Films. In: Time Magazine, December 8th, 1967, URL: http://www.time.com/time/printout/0,8816,844256,00.html, last accessed June 5th, 2010.

Kappelhoff, Hermann: Der Bildraum des Kinos. Modulationen einer ästhetischen Erfahrungsform. In: Gertrud Koch (ed.): Umwidmungen. Architektonische und kinematographische Räume, Berlin 2005, pp. 138–149.

Kappelhoff, Hermann: Matrix der Gefühle. Das Kino, das Melodrama und das Theater der Empfindsamkeit. Berlin 2004.

Kappelhoff, Hermann: Realismus. Das Kino und die Politik des Ästhetischen. Berlin 2008.

Kappelhoff, Hermann: Die vierte Dimension des Bewegungsbildes. Das filmische Bild im Übergang zwischen individueller Leiblichkeit und kultureller Fantasie. In: Anne Bartsch, Jens Eder, and Kathrin Fahlenbrach (eds.): Audiovisuelle Emotionen. Emotionsdarstellung und Emotionsvermittlung durch audiovisuelle Medienangebote, Cologne 2007, pp. 297–311.

Kappelhoff, Hermann, and Jan-Hendrik Bakels: Das Zuschauergefühl. Möglichkeiten qualitativer Medienanalyse. In: Zeitschrift für Medienwissenschaft, No. 5 (2011), pp. 78–95.

Kappelhoff, Hermann, Bernhard Groß, and Daniel Illger: Einleitung. In: id. (eds.): Demokratisierung der Wahrnehmung? Das westeuropäische Nachkriegskino, Berlin 2010, pp. 9–21.

Keathley, Christian: Trapped in the Affection Image. Hollywood's post-traumatic Cycle (1970–1976). In: Thomas Elsaesser, Alexander Horwath, and Noel King (eds.): The Last Great American Picture Show, pp. 293–308.

Keilholz, Sascha: Verlustkino. Trauer im amerikanischen Polizeifilm seit 1968. Marburg 2015.

Kent Bathrick, Serafina: CARRIE Ragtime. The Horror of Growing up Female. In: Jump Cut, No. 14 (1977), pp. 9–10.

Killen, Andreas: 1973 Nervous Breakdown. Watergate, Warhol, and the Birth of Post-Sixties America. New York/London 2006.

King, Geoff: New Hollywood Cinema. An Introduction, London 2002.

King, Stephen: The Dead Zone, New York 1979.

Kirshner, Jonathan: Hollywood's Last Golden Age. Politics, Society, and the Seventies Film in America. New York 2013.

Klibansky, Raymond, Erwin Panofsky, and Fritz Saxl: Saturn and Melancholy: Studies in the History of Natural Philosophy, Religion, and Art. London 1964.

Knight, Peter: Introduction. A Nation of Conspiracy Theorists. In: id. (ed.): Conspiracy Nation. The Politics of Paranoia in Postwar America, New York/London 2002, pp. 1–17.

Knight, Peter: Conspiracy Culture. From Kennedy to the X Files. London/New York 2000.

Koch, Gertrud: Kracauer zur Einführung. Hamburg 1996.

Koch, Gertrud: A lecture series at the Freie Universität Berlin during the winter semester 2004/2005 entitled "Movement," held together with Gabriele Brandstetter and Gunter Gebauer.

Kolker, Robert Phillip: A Cinema of Loneliness. Penn, Kubrick, Scorsese, Spielberg, Altman (2nd Edition). New York/Oxford 1988.

Koselleck, Reinhart: Futures Past. On the Semantics of Historical Time. New York 2004.

Kracauer, Siegfried: From Caligari to Hitler: A Psychological History of the German Film, edited by Leonardo Quaresima, Princeton 2004.

Kracauer, Siegfried: Photography. In: Critical Inquiry, Vol. 19, No. 3 (Spring 1993), pp. 421–436.

Kracauer, Siegfried: Theory of Film. The Redemption of Physical Reality. New York 1960.

Krämer, Peter: The New Hollywood. From BONNIE AND CLYDE to STAR WARS. London 2005.

Krämer, Peter: Post-classical Hollywood. In: John Hill, and Pamela Church Gibson (eds.): The Oxford Guide to Film Studies, Oxford 1998, pp. 289–309.

Krämer, Peter, and Yannis Tzioumakis (eds.): The Hollywood Renaissance. Revisiting American Cinema's Most Celebrated Era. New York 2018.

Krause, Marcus, Arno Meteling, and Markus Stauff (eds.): The Parallax View. Zur Mediologie der Verschwörung, München 2011.

Lacan, Jacques: De la psychose paranoïaque dans ses rapports avec la personalité, Paris 1975.

Lacan, Jacques: The Problem of Style and the Psychiatric Conception of Paranoiac Forms of Experience, trans. Jon Anderson. In: Critical Texts, Vol. 5, No. 3 (1988), pp. 4–6.

Lacan, Jacques: The Psychoses: The Seminar of Jacques Lacan, Book III, Trans. Russell Grigg. New York 1993.

Laderman, David: Driving Visions. Exploring the Road Movie. Austin 2002.

Lagier, Luc: Les mille yeux de Brian De Palma. Paris 2008.

Lasch, Christopher: The Culture of Narcissism. American Life in an Age of Diminishing Expectations. New York 1979.

Lawrence, Novotny: Blaxploitation Films of the 1970s. Blackness and Genre. New York 2008.

Lehmann, Hauke: Becoming-Texture: New Hollywood Melancholy in MCCABE & MRS. MILLER. In: mediaesthetics No. 1 (2016), URL: https://www.mediaesthetics.org/index.php/mae/article/view/43/144, last accessed March 7th, 2019.

Lehmann, Hauke: Schrecken der Straße. Steven Spielbergs DUEL als Road Movie-Horrorfilm. In: Uta Felten, and Kerstin Küchler (eds.): Kino und Automobil, Tübingen 2013, pp. 159–185.

Lehmann, Hauke: Shock and Choreography. Dying and Identity in GIMME SHELTER. In: Snodi 6 (2010), pp. 144–154.

Lehmann, Hauke, Hans Roth, and Kerstin Schankweiler: Affective Economy. In: Jan Slaby, and Christian von Scheve (eds.): Affective Societies. Key Concepts, London/New York 2019, pp. 140–151.

Leitch, Thomas M.: How to Steal from Hitchcock. In: David Boyd: After Hitchcock. Influence, Imitation, and Intertextuality, Austin 2006, pp. 251–270.

Lessing, Gotthold Ephraim: Laocoon: An Essay on the Limits of Painting and Poetry. Baltimore 1984.

Lepenies, Wolf: Das Ende der Utopie und die Wiederkehr der Melancholie. In: id.: Melancholie und Gesellschaft. Mit einer neuen Einleitung: Das Ende der Utopie und die Wiederkehr der Melancholie, Frankfurt am Main 1998, pp. vii–xxviii.

Lepenies, Wolf: Melancholy and Society. Cambridge 1992.

Lev, Peter: American Films of the 70s. Conflicting Visions. Austin 2000.

Leys, Ruth: The Turn to Affect. A Critique. In: Critical Inquiry, Vol. 37, No. 3 (Spring 2011), pp. 434–472.

Liptay, Fabienne, and Susanne Marschall (eds.): Mit allen Sinnen. Gefühl und Empfindung im Kino. Marburg 2006.

Lopate, Philip: The Raw and the Cooked. In: Booklet for the DVD Release of John Cassavetes: Five Films, The Criterion Collection 2004, pp. 35–37.

Lowry, Ed: The Appropriation of Signs in SCORPIO RISING. In: The Velvet Light Trap, No. 20 (Summer 1983), pp. 41–46.

MacDonald, Scott: The Filmmaker as Visionary. Excerpts from an Interview with Stan Brakhage. In: Film Quarterly, Vol. 56, No. 3 (2003), pp. 2–11.

MacKinnon, Kenneth: Misogyny in the Movies. The De Palma Question. Newark 1990.

MacLean, Robert: The Big-Bang Hypothesis. Blowing Up the Image. In: Film Quarterly, Vol. 32, No. 2 (Winter 1978/1979), pp. 2–7.

Madsen, Axel: The New Hollywood. American Movies in the '70s. New York 1975.

Man, Glenn: Radical Visions. American Film Renaissance 1967–1976, Westport 1994.

Margulies, Ivone: John Cassavetes. Amateur Director. In: Jon Lewis (ed.): The New American Cinema, Durham/London 1998, pp. 275–306.

Marks, Laura U.: Touch. Sensuous Theory and Multisensory Media. Minneapolis/London 2002.

Martin, Adrian: To Wax Zizekian. On *Un-American Psycho: Brian De Palma and the Political Invisible*. In: Screening the Past, July 2012, URL: http://www.screeningthepast.com/2012/07/to-wax-zizekian/, last accessed April 30th, 2019.

Massumi, Brian: Parables for the Virtual. Movement, Affect, Sensation. Durham/London 2002.

Matusa, Paula: Corruption and Catastrophe. Brian De Palma's CARRIE. In: Film Quarterly, Vol. 31, No. 1 (Fall 1977), pp. 32–38.

Meadows, Donella H., Dennis L. Meadows, Jørgen Randers, and William W. Behrens III: The Limits to Growth. A Report for the Club of Rome's Project on the Predicament of Mankind. New York 1972.

Medovoi, Leerom: The Cold War and SF [Review]. In: Science Fiction Studies, Vol. 27, No. 82 (November 2000), pp. 514–517.

Melley, Timothy: Empire of Conspiracy. The Culture of Paranoia in Postwar America. Ithaca/London 2000.

Merleau-Ponty, Maurice: Phenomenology of Perception [1945]. London/New York 2002.

Merleau-Ponty, Maurice: The Film and the New Psychology. In: id.: Sense and Non-Sense, trans. H. Dreyfus, and P. Dreyfus, Evanston 1964, pp. 48–59.

Merleau-Ponty, Maurice: The Primacy of Perception. And Other Essays on Phenomenological Psychology, edited by James M. Edie. Evanston 1964.

Merleau-Ponty, Maurice: The Visible and the Invisible. Followed by Working Notes, edited by Claude Lefort. Evanston 1968.

Michotte van den Berck, Albert: The Character of "Reality" of Cinematographic Projections. In: Michotte's Experimental Phenomenology of Perception, edited by Georges Thinés, Alan Costall, and George Butterworth, pp. 197–209.

Michotte van den Berck, Albert: The Emotional Involvement of the Spectator in the Action Represented in a Film. Toward a Theory. In: Michotte's Experimental Phenomenology of Perception, edited by Georges Thinés, Alan Costall, and George Butterworth, pp. 209–218.

Miller, Stephen Paul: The Seventies Now. Culture as Surveillance. Durham/London 1999.

Modleski, Tania: Clint Eastwood and Male Weepies. In: American Literary History Vol. 22, No. 1 (Spring 2010), pp. 136–158.

Mühlhoff, Rainer: Affective Resonance. In: Jan Slaby, and Christian von Scheve (eds.): Affective Societies. Key Concepts, London/New York 2019, pp. 189–199.

Musgrove, Frank: Ecstasy and Holiness. Counter Culture and the Open Society, London 1974.

Moulthrop, Stuart: *Watchmen* Meets The Aristocrats. In: Postmodern Culture, Vol. 19, No. 1 (September 2009), URL: http://pmc.iath.virginia.edu/text-only/issue.908/19.1moulthrop.txt, accessed March 27th, 2019.

Nancy, Jean-Luc: Abbas Kiarostami. The Evidence of Film. Paris 2001.

Naremore, James: American Film Noir. The History of an Idea. In: Film Quarterly, Vol. 49, No. 2 (1995/1996), pp. 12–28.

Naremore, James: More than Night. Film Noir in its Contexts. Berkeley/Los Angeles 1998.

Naziri, Gérard: Paranoia im amerikanischen Kino. Die 70er Jahre und die Folgen. Sankt Augustin 2003.

Neale, Steve: New Hollywood Cinema. In: Screen, Vol. 17, No. 2 (1976), pp. 117–122.

Nicholls, Mark: Male Melancholia and Martin Scorsese's THE AGE OF INNOCENCE. In: Film Quarterly, Vol. 58, No. 1 (Fall 2004), pp. 25–35.

O'Donnell, Patrick: Latent Destinies. Cultural Paranoia and Contemporary U.S. Narrative. Durham 2000.

Paech, Joachim: Der Bewegung einer Linie folgen... Notizen zum Bewegungsbild. In: id.: Der Bewegung einer Linie folgen... Schriften zum Film, Berlin 2002, pp. 133–161.

Panofsky, Erwin: Style and Medium in the Motion Pictures [1947]. In: id.: Three Essays on Style, edited by Irving Lavin, Cambridge 1997, pp. 91–128.

Parkinson Zamora, Lois (ed.): The Apocalyptic Vision in America. Interdisciplinary Essays on Myth and Culture. Ann Arbor 1982.

Pasolini, Pier Paolo: Observations on the Long Take [1967]. In: October Vol. 13 (1980), pp. 3–6.

Paul, William: Laughing Screaming. Modern Hollywood Horror & Comedy. New York 1994.

Peckinpah, Sam, Michael Pye, and Lynda Myles: The Movie Brats. How the Film Generation took over Hollywood, London/Boston 1979.

Peterson, Lowell, and Janey Place: Some Visual Motifs of Film Noir. In: Alain Silver, and James Ursini (eds.): Film Noir Reader, New York 1996, pp. 65–76.

Peretz, Eyal: Becoming Visionary. Brian De Palma's Cinematic Education of the Senses. Stanford 2008.

Piel, Friedrich: Die Ornament-Grotteske in der italienischen Renaissance. Berlin 1962.

Plantinga, Carl: Moving Viewers. American Film and the Spectator's Experience. Berkeley 2009.

Plantinga, Carl, and Greg M. Smith (eds.): Passionate Views. Film, Cognition and Emotion. Baltimore 1999.

Plessner, Helmuth: Die Deutung des mimischen Ausdrucks. Ein Beitrag zur Lehre vom Bewußtsein des anderen Ichs [1925]. In: id.: Gesammelte Schriften VII. Ausdruck und menschliche Natur, edited by Günter Dux, Frankfurt 2003, pp. 67–130.

Polan, Dana: Power and Paranoia. History, Narrative, and the American Cinema, 1940–1950. New York 1986.

Pratt, Ray: Projecting Paranoia. Conspiratorial Visions in American Film. Lawrence 2001

Prince, Stephen: Savage Cinema. Sam Peckinpah and the Rise of Ultraviolent Movies. Austin 1998.

Rancière, Jacques: Film Fables [2001]. Oxford/New York 2006.

Randl, Chad: Revolving Architecture. A History of Buildings that Rotate, Swivel, and Pivot. New York 2008.

Ray, Robert B.: A Certain Tendency of the Hollywood Cinema, 1930–1980. New Jersey 1985.

Rehak, Bob: Adapting *Watchmen* after 9/11. In: Cinema Journal, Vol. 51, No. 1 (Fall 2011), pp. 154–159.

Ribot, Théodule: The Psychology of the Emotions. London 1898.

Robins, Robert S., Jerrold M. Post: Political Paranoia. The Psychopolitics of Hatred. New Haven/London 1997.

Robnik, Drehli: Körper-Erfahrung und Film-Phänomenologie. In: Jürgen Felix (ed.): Moderne Film Theorie, Mainz 2002, pp. 246–280.

Rose, Jacqueline: Paranoia and the Film System. In: Screen, Vol. 17, No. 4 (1976), pp. 85–104.

Rosenbaum, Jonathan: Dead Man. London 2000.

Routt, William D.: [Review] De la figure en général et du corps en particulier: l'invention figurative au cinéma. In: Screening the Past, No. 9 (2000), URL: http://www.screeningthepast.com/2014/12/de-la-figure-en-general-et-du-corps-en-particulier-linvention-figurative-au-cinema/, last accessed March 11th, 2019.

Rowe, Carel: Illuminating Lucifer. In: Film Quarterly, Vol. 27, No. 4 (Summer 1974), pp. 24–33.

Rowe, Carel: Myth and Symbolism. Blue Velvet. In: Jack Hunter (ed.): Moonchild. The Films of Kenneth Anger, London 2002, pp. 11–46.

Sargeant, Amy: Vsevolod Pudovkin: Classic Films of the Soviet Avant-garde. London/New York 2000.

Sass, Louis A.: Affectivity in Schizophrenia. A Phenomenological View. In: Journal of Consciousness Studies, Vol. 11, No. 10–11 (2004), pp. 127–147.

Sass, Louis A.: Madness and Modernism. Insanity in the Light of Modern Art, Literature, and Thought. New York 1992.

Sass, Louis A.: The Paradoxes of Delusion. Wittgenstein, Schreber, and the Schizophrenic Mind. Ithaca/London 1994.

Schaffer, Bill: Cutting the Flow: Thinking PSYCHO. In: Senses of Cinema, No. 6 (2000), URL: http://www.sensesofcinema.com/2000/6/psycho/, last accessed March 12th, 2019.

Schatz, Thomas: Old Hollywood/New Hollywood. Ritual, Art, and Industry. Ann Arbor 1983.

Schneider, Manfred: Das Attentat. Kritik der paranoischen Vernunft. Berlin 2010.

Schrader, Paul: Notes on Film Noir. In: Film Comment, Vol. 8, No. 1 (Spring 1972), pp. 8–13.

Schrag, Peter: The End of the American Future. New York 1973.

Schumacher, Ernst Friedrich: Small is Beautiful. Economics as if People Mattered. London 1973.

Schwarz, Eva: Visual Paranoia in REAR WINDOW, BLOW-UP and THE TRUMAN SHOW, Stuttgart 2011.

Scruggs, Charles: The Power of Blackness. Film Noir and Its Critics. In: American Literary History Vol. 16, No. 4 (2004), pp. 675–687.

Sellmann, Michael: Hollywoods moderner Film Noir. Würzburg 2001.

Sharrett, Christopher: The Idea of Apocalypse in THE TEXAS CHAINSAW MASSACRE. In: Barry Keith Grant (ed.): Planks of Reason. Essays on the Horror Film, Metuchen/London 1984, pp. 255–276.

Shaviro, Steven: MELANCHOLIA, or: The Romantic Anti-Sublime. In: Sequence 1 (2012) 1.

Shiel, Mark: Banal and Magnificent Space in ELECTRA GLIDE IN BLUE (1973), or An Allegory of the Nixon Era. In: Cinema Journal, Vol. 46, No. 2 (2007), pp. 91–116.

Sierek, Karl: Spannung und Körperbild. In: montage/av, Vol. 3, No. 1 (1994), pp. 115–121.

Simmel, Georg: The Philosophy of Landscape. In: Theory, Culture & Society 24 (2007), pp. 7–8, and pp. 20–29.

Simon, Art: Dangerous Knowledge. The JFK Assassination in Art and Film. Philadelphia 1996.

Sinnerbrink, Robert: Stimmung. Exploring the Aesthetics of Mood. In: Screen, Vol. 53, No. 2 (Summer 2012), pp. 148–163.

Sobchack, Vivian: The Address of the Eye. A Phenomenology of Film Experience. Princeton 1992.

Sobchack, Vivian: Lounge Time. Postwar Crises and the Chronotope of Film Noir. In: Nick Browne (ed.): Refiguring American Film Genres. History and Theory, Berkeley 1998, pp. 129–170.

Sobchack, Vivian: Toward Inhabited Space. The Semiotic Structure of Camera Movement in the Cinema. In: Semiotica, Vol. 41, No. 1/4 (1982), pp. 317–335.

Smith, Greg M.: Film Structure and the Emotion System. Cambridge 2003.

Smith, Murray: Altered States. Character and Emotional Response in the Cinema. In: Cinema Journal, Vol. 33, No. 4 (Summer 1994), pp. 34–56.

Smith, Murray: Engaging Characters. Fiction, Emotion, and the Cinema. Oxford 1995.

Smith, Murray: Theses on the Philosophy of Hollywood History. In: id., Steve Neale (eds.): Contemporary Hollywood Cinema, London/New York 1998, pp. 3–20.

Smuts, Aaron: The Desire-Frustration Theory of Suspense. In: The Journal of Aesthetics and Art Criticism, Vol. 66, No. 3 (Summer 2008), pp. 281–290.

Stamp Lindsey, Shelley: Horror, Femininity, and Carrie's Monstrous Puberty. In: Journal of Film and Video, Vol. 43, No. 4 (Winter 1991), pp. 33–44.

Stern, Daniel N.: The Interpersonal World of the Infant: A View from Psychoanalysis and Developmental Psychology. New York 1985.

Stern, Daniel N.: The Present Moment in Psychotherapy and Everyday Life. New York 2004.

Stewart, Garrett: THE LONG GOODBYE from CHINATOWN. In: Film Quarterly, Vol. 28, No. 2 (Winter 1974/1975), pp. 25–32.

Tan, Ed: *Emotion and the Structure of Narrative Film. Film as an Emotion Machine,* Mahwah 1996.

Taylor, Henry M.: Bilder des Konspirativen. Alan J. Pakulas THE PARALLAX VIEW und die Ästhetik der Verschwörung. In: Krause, Meteling, Stauff (eds.): The Parallax View, pp. 217–234.

Taylor, Henry M.: Conspiracy! Theorie und Geschichte des Paranoiafilms. Marburg 2017.

Tellenbach, Hubertus: Die Räumlichkeit der Melancholischen. II. Mitteilung. Analyse der Räumlichkeit melancholischen Daseins. In: Der Nervenarzt, Vol. 27, No. 7 (1956), pp. 289–298.

Tellenbach, Hubertus: Geschmack und Atmosphäre. Medien menschlichen Elementarkontaktes. Salzburg 1965.

Tellenbach, Hubertus: Melancholy. History of the Problem, Endogeneity, Typology, Pathogenesis, Clinical Considerations. Pittsburgh 1980.

Tellenbach, Hubertus: Zum Verständnis von Bewegungsweisen Melancholischer. In: Der Nervenarzt, Vol. 28, No. 1 (1957), pp. 16–17.

Thomas, Kerstin: Bildstimmung als Bedeutung in der Malerei des 19. Jahrhunderts. In: Anna-Katharina Gisbertz (ed.): Stimmung. Zur Wiederkehr einer ästhetischen Kategorie, Munich 2011, pp. 211–229.

Thompson, Hunter S.: Fear and Loathing in Las Vegas. London 2005.

Thompson, Kristin: Storytelling in the New Hollywood. Understanding Classical Narrative Technique. Cambridge 1999.

Thoret, Jean-Baptiste: 26 Secondes. L'Amérique Éclaboussée. L'assassinat de JFK et le Cinéma Américain. Pertuis 2003.

Tröhler, Margrit: Einleitung. Filmische Atmosphären – eine Annäherung. In: id., Philipp Brunner, and Jörg Schweinitz, (eds.): Filmische Atmosphären, pp. 11–23.

Truffaut, François: Hitchcock (Revised Edition), New York 1985.

Uidhir, Christy Mag: An Eliminativist Theory of Suspense. In: Philosophy and Literature, No. 35 (2011), pp. 121–133.

Vernet, Mark: Film Noir on the Edge of Doom. In: Joan Copjec (ed.): Shades of Noir, London/New York 1993, pp. 1–31.

Vorderer, Peter, Hans J. Wulff, and Mike Friedrichen (eds.): Suspense. Conceptualizations, Theoretical Analyses, and Empirical Explorations. Mahwah 1996.

Warshow, Robert: Re-Viewing the Russian Movies [1955]. In: id.: The Immediate Experience. Movies, Comics, Theatre & Other Aspects of Popular Culture, Cambridge/London 2001, pp. 239–252.

Wead, George: Toward a Definition of Filmnoia. In: The Velvet Light Trap, No. 13 (Fall 1974), pp. 2–6.

Wedel, Michael: Filmgeschichte als Krisengeschichte. Schnitte und Spuren durch den deutschen Film. Bielefeld 2011.

Wellbery, David: Stimmung. In: Karlheinz Barck et al. (eds.): Ästhetische Grundbegriffe. Historisches Wörterbuch in sieben Bänden. Vol. 5, Stuttgart 2003, pp. 703–733.

Westphal, Uwe: Werbung im Dritten Reich. Berlin 1989.

Wheen, Francis: Strange Days Indeed. The 1970s: The Golden Age of Paranoia [2009]. New York 2010.

de Wied, Marie Annette: The Role of Time-Structures in the Experience of Film Suspense and Duration. A Study on the Effects of Anticipation Time upon Suspense and temporal Variations on Duration Experience and Suspense, university dissertation at the University of Amsterdam, 1991.

Wiesen, S. Jonathan: Creating the Nazi Marketplace. Commerce and Consumption in the Third Reich. Cambridge 2011.

Williams, Linda: Film Bodies. Genre, Gender, and Excess. In: Film Quarterly, Vol. 44, No. 4 (Summer 1991), pp. 2–13.

Williams, Raymond: Marxism and Literature. Oxford/New York 1977.

Willman, Skip: Spinning Paranoia. The Ideologies of Conspiracy and Contingency in Postmodern Culture. In: Knight (ed.): Conspiracy Nation, pp. 21–39.

Wittgenstein, Ludwig: Philosophical Investigations. Oxford 1986.

Wolfe, Tom: The Me Decade and the Third Great Awakening. In: id.: The Purple Decades, London 1984, pp. 265–293.

Wood, Robin: Hollywood from Vietnam to Reagan… and Beyond [1986]. New York 2003.

Wulff, Hans J.: Empathie als Dimension des Filmverstehens. Ein Thesenpapier. In: montage/av, Vol. 12, No. 1 (2003), pp. 136–161.

Wulff, Hans J.: Spannungsanalyse. Thesen zu einem Forschungsfeld. In: montage/av, Vol. 2, No. 2 (1993), pp. 97–100.

Wulff, Hans J.: Suspense and the Influence of Cataphora on Viewers' Expectations. In: id., Peter Vorderer, and Mike Friedrichsen (eds.): Suspense, pp. 1–17.

Wuss, Peter: Grundformen filmischer Spannung. In: montage/av, Vol. 2, No. 2 (1993), pp. 101–116.

Wyatt, Justin: High Concept. Movies and Marketing in Hollywood. Austin 1994.

Yanal, Robert J.: The Paradox of Suspense. In: The British Journal of Aesthetics, Vol. 36, No. 2 (April 1996), pp. 146–158.

Zillmann, Dolf: The Psychology of Suspense in Dramatic Exposition. In: Peter Vorderer, Hans J. Wulff, and Mike Friedrichsen (eds.): Suspense, pp. 199–231.

Subject index

https://doi.org/10.1515/9783110580761-009

Name index

Altman, Robert   32, 44, 97, 112, 213, 221, 244
Anger, Kenneth   163, 168, 169, 170, 171, 172, 173, 174, 175, 176, 178, 179, 180, 181, 182, 184, 185, 186, 188, 189, 195, 196, 201, 205, 211, 220, 224, 236
Arnheim, Rudolf   23, 120, 180, 214, 215, 219, 235

Balázs, Béla   179, 181, 182
Barthes, Roland   83
Bazin, André   27, 96, 110, 186, 244
Bellour, Raymond   18, 24, 25, 26, 57, 93, 121, 136
Benjamin, Walter   34, 164, 167, 172, 176, 177, 178, 181, 190, 200, 201, 204, 205, 207, 216
Bergson, Henri   2, 10, 11, 18, 20, 41, 71, 83, 96
Binswanger, Ludwig   90, 198, 199, 206, 208, 215, 216, 217, 250
Bonitzer, Pascal   54, 55, 57, 58, 80, 81, 83, 92
Bordwell, David   31
Brakhage, Stan   168, 170, 188, 211, 214, 221
Brenez, Nicole   89

Carroll, Noël   13, 14, 15, 31, 32, 48, 50, 51, 52, 113, 168
Cassavetes, John   223
Chion, Michel   221
Cimino, Michael   44, 221
Copjec, Joan   131, 132, 133, 141, 153
Coppola, Francis Ford   11, 30, 151, 226
Craven, Wes   99, 234

Deleuze, Gilles 18, 19, 20, 24, 25, 40, 45, 53, 54, 55, 56, 69, 71, 75, 76, 79, 90, 94, 97, 106, 108, 109, 110, 111, 112, 124, 136, 144, 150, 152, 158, 161, 169, 219, 225

De Palma, Brian   24, 42, 46, 47, 57, 58, 59, 60, 72, 83, 84, 89, 90, 93, 94, 97, 98, 99, 159, 160, 187, 232
Deren, Maya   168, 170
Didion, Joan   101, 110, 156, 164

Eisenstein, Sergei   24, 25, 79, 111, 116, 135, 146, 147, 179, 180, 181, 182, 186, 209, 210, 211, 212, 214, 215, 218, 219, 220
Elsaesser, Thomas   29, 32, 36, 42, 133, 165, 219, 240, 241
Epstein, Jean   57

Foucault, Michel   45
Freud, Sigmund   38, 104, 108, 145, 146, 147, 148, 160, 164, 166, 174, 175, 198, 199, 204, 207, 215, 216
Friedkin, William   38, 98, 160, 229

Guattari, Félix   39, 40, 97, 106, 108, 109, 124, 136, 158, 219, 259
Guercio, James William   187, 194, 201, 204, 240

Hellman, Monte   32, 155, 221
Hitchcock, Alfred   45, 46, 47, 49, 53, 54, 55, 56, 57, 59, 61, 71, 83, 94, 95, 99, 144, 230
Hofstadter, Richard   102, 104, 107
Hooper, Tobe   235, 236

Kael, Pauline   46, 84
Kappelhoff, Hermann   5, 813, 14, 15, 16, 17, 22, 24, 25, 26, 39, 45, 56, 60, 71, 73, 80, 94, 110, 116, 135, 169, 182, 183, 184, 189, 196, 212
Kracauer, Siegfried   163, 168, 169, 170, 171, 172, 179, 180, 181, 182, 183, 184, 185, 186, 187, 195, 196, 213, 235
Kubrick, Stanley   11, 30, 160, 168, 184, 223, 229

https://doi.org/10.1515/9783110580761-010

www.ingramcontent.com/pod-product-compliance
Lightning Source LLC
Chambersburg PA
CBHW061622250726
48659CB00004B/1049